Express Delivery

Also by this author:

They came from Burgundy

Express Delivery

The men brought back by the Shelburn escape line, and the people who made it possible

Keith Janes

Cover design by Helen Duffee

Matador
9 Priory Business Park,
Wistow Road, Kibworth Beauchamp,
Leicestershire. LE8 0RX
Tel: 0116 279 2299
Email: books@troubador.co.uk
Web: www.troubador.co.uk/matador
Twitter: @matadorbooks

ISBN 978 1838590 741

British Library Cataloguing in Publication Data.
A catalogue record for this book is available from the British Library.

Printed and bound in the UK by TJ International, Padstow, Cornwall
Typeset in 11pt Aldine401 BT by Troubador Publishing Ltd, Leicester, UK

Matador is an imprint of Troubador Publishing Ltd

MIX
Paper from responsible sources
FSC® C013056

For the Helpers.

Contents

The Gunboats from Dartmouth

Early on the morning of Sunday 30 January 1944, a dark grey gunboat made her way slowly up the river Dart to her depot ship, where a group of nineteen men in civilian clothing disembarked. Any witnesses, and there were very few, might have noticed that they looked a little odd, somehow foreign in their mix of ill-fitting sweaters, jackets and trousers, perhaps partly covered by a borrowed duffle coat or oilskin. They also looked tired, even exhausted, and seemed particularly relieved to finally step onto something more substantial than the dangerous little warship.

The gunboat was HMMGB 503, skippered by 26-year-old Lt Robert Michael Marshall RNVR. She had a crew of four officers and twenty-six ratings, and was heavily armed but crucially, she also had the range and speed to cross the English Channel to Brittany and back in a single night.

MGB 503 and her sister boat, MGB 502, were two of five "Vosper" boats built by Camper Nicholson in Southampton. They were originally destined for a foreign government but with the outbreak of war, the contract was never completed. Two more boats were built to the same specification and all but 502 and 503 taken into the merchant service where they served as blockade runners to Sweden. In late 1943, MGBs 502 and 503 were assigned to 15 MGB Flotilla, tasked with taking agents to, and bringing agents and evaders back, from enemy-occupied France. The wooden-hulled gunboats were 120 feet long, armed with cannon and machine-guns, and with their three diesel engines, had a top speed of up to 35 knots and a theoretical range of 2,000 nautical miles.

Sixteen of the men who stepped off MGB 503 on that unusually mild January morning were Allied aircrew – two British, one Rhodesian and thirteen Americans – who had been shot down over France the previous year and evaded, some for several months. They had just completed the final stage of their journey back to England via the escape line known as Shelburn.

15 MGB Flotilla

The key to the success, and in fact the creation, of Shelburn was the availability of suitable Royal Navy gunboats and their experienced crews from the 15 MGB Flotilla, based at Dartmouth in Devon. Actually, their headquarters (HMS Cicala) was in the Royal Dart Hotel, just across the river at Kingswear, and the Flotilla's depot-ship, the converted paddle-steamer Westward Ho! was moored midstream, about 100 metres from Kingswear railway station.

> *"Westward Ho! provided a large wardroom and cabins for the use of the base staff of the 15 MGB Flotilla as well as for agents in transit. Its closeness to Kingswear railway terminus meant that passengers and their baggage could be ferried between her and the station without attracting much attention." (Secret Flotillas)*

Built on the Clyde in 1894 as a passenger excursion steamer, the 225 foot long Westward Ho! had been requisitioned as a minesweeper in 1939, served in the evacuation from Dunkirk in 1940, and as an anti-aircraft ship in 1942 before being converted to an accommodation vessel to be used by 8 MTB and 15 MGB Flotillas as their depot-ship.

A little further upstream was HMS Belfort, the converted 1919 French naval vessel which served as the depot-ship for the Free French 23 MTB Flotilla which had been based at Kingswear since their advance party had arrived in January 1943.

Although RN gunboats, MTBs and launches had been crossing the English Channel to France on various missions throughout the war, in the autumn of 1943, 15 MGB Flotilla was officially formed with the specific role of delivering and collecting agents, and generally supporting the various resistance and intelligence gathering groups in France. They were later given the additional task of bringing back stranded evaders.

Sir Brooks Richards, in his brilliantly researched 1996 book "Secret Flotillas" (HMSO), describes the procedures used by the gunboats for leaving harbour and then finding their anchorage pin-points off the French coast.

"An accurate compass fix of the departure point was vital and by no means easy when the weather was poor and the visibility bad. In winter, mist and salt-laden spray often obscured Start Point and on those occasions, they got as close to the headland as possible and prayed for a break in the low scudding clouds. Usually the dim gaunt shape of the lighthouse was visible for long enough to get a quick bearing and to judge its distance. Then, on to the pre-calculated course.

The ideal weather conditions were a slightly choppy sea (to reduce the chances of detection by enemy radar) and an overcast sky but they seldom prevailed. Usually it was either too smooth and starlit, or too rough for personal comfort or boatwork (launching and retrieving the surfboats), and there was the occasional unexpected south-westerly gale for good measure.

After a six-hour passage, during which the QH position-finding system might or might not be working, an approximate position check could also be derived from the echo-sounder when crossing the Hurd Deep, a depression 86 miles long, stretching from off Alderney to a point 32 miles north of the Ile-de-Batz. At their usual point of crossing from Dartmouth, it was about two and a half miles wide and gave a dramatic increase of soundings on entering, and an equally sudden decrease on leaving. One could also make an inspired guess at one's position from the time it took to cross.

Lighthouses on the Breton coast were usually extinguished but occasionally might be working at about half or quarter strength. This provided a useful compass bearing but it meant that a German coastal convoy was moving along the convoy route about 10 miles offshore and parallel to it. So at about 15 miles off the coast, engines were silenced and all eyes strained for signs of ships moving across their approach course.

At 10 miles from the coast they would alter course to counter the fierce tidal stream, which at spring tide reaches over 5 knots, and all available binoculars would be trained on the darkness ahead for the first indication of the denser darkness that represented the Breton coast, or for surf breaking on outlying rocks. All the time, the echo-sounder would be at work to indicate any dramatic changes of depth.

Anchorage positions might be anything between 150 and 800 yards from the pinpoint. Then the long wait began, sometimes as little as an hour and a half, with an absolute maximum of four hours. Walkie-talkie contact was maintained between the ship and the surf-boats at infrequent intervals, as the danger of transmissions being picked up by the Germans was always present.

The pinpoint and anchorage were almost always in the field of fire of German artillery or machine-guns and it was difficult to believe at a 110-

foot ship so close to a hostile shore could not be seen, especially on a starry night when every splash or ripple glowed with phosphorescence. They could occasionally see the enemy lighting cigarettes on the cliff top, and their vehicles with dimmed headlights crawling along the coast roads.

When the surf-boats returned, an engine had to be started up, which though silenced, sounded to the crew's over-sensitive ears like a lion's roar. It was considered wise to be at least 30 miles offshore on the way back to England before dawn."

Most of MGB 502's operations were carried out for SIS and SOE, with MGB 503 primarily responsible for bringing out evaders, although both gunboats engaged in both activities at various times. The main difference from an operational point of view was that when the objective was to collect evaders, the gunboat would be less likely to be carrying passengers (aka Joes) on the outward journey.

"Moonless nights were always chosen, and sailings so timed that the craft would not be within 30 miles of any enemy-held coast until two hours after sunset. Getting closer to the shore, speed was always cut to reduce the sound and the wash and the phosphorescence. Close inshore, S-phone contact was usually made; failing that, the beach party would flash an agreed Morse letter from a hand-torch. The MGB anchored offshore to a grass rope – a rating standing by with a hatchet to cut it in an emergency. The landing party was rowed in with muffled oars in a surf-boat which had been newly designed for the purpose." (Lloyd Bott, First Lieutenant, HMMGB 502)

The S-phone system used a pair of directional UHF radiotelephones for secure voice transmissions. Originally designed for use by agents on the ground to communicate with low-flying aircraft, their limited range minimised the risk of enemy interception. Other navigation aids included QH gear (to home on RAF beacons), especially placed sonar buoys, and hydrophones in the surf-boats to hear the gunboat's sonar for the return trip, and MAB walkie-talkie radios.

Described as PD surf-boats, Richards explains that the PD1 praam dinghies used on these operations were designed by Lt Whalley (member of DDOD(I) staff) on the basis of a Dutch prototype that had turned up at Felixstowe. Modified to give additional stability and carrying power, they rode light in the water, being specifically built to carry a heavy load with enough buoyancy to get through broken surf when landing. Normally crewed by two oarsmen plus a sweep oar/steering sweep, they could also be rowed by four men as in the case where a second "pram" was towed. PD1s were carried on the deck of the gunboats and put into the water, and later reboarded, by hand.

Although the surf-boats were double-ended and probably didn't require turning around on the beach, that is precisely what they did in practice as described by one of the men who rowed the PD1s ashore:

> *"The procedure as we closed on the beaches was that whoever was on the sweep oar, usually a leading seaman or sub-lieutenant, gave the order "Oars – out boat" whereupon I would jump out to port and Pusser (George Hill) to starboard, run the pram up the beach and turn her bow for the return trip. The advantage of the sweep oar steering as against a normal tiller was never more apparent than when Pusser and I, with 502's cox'n Fred Smith, were at practice at Helford, Cornwall when Smith gave a demonstration of sweep oar capability in and out of rocks with a skill that had to be seen to be appreciated." (Alf Harris, seaman gunner HMMGB 502)*

> *"The drill followed by those on board the MGB had by now (Feb 44) been carefully standardised: no talking or smoking on deck; S-phone contact would be established with the beach wherever possible, failing which the reception party would be flashing the agreed light signal to seaward. The first surf-boat carried an armed look-out in its bows. Any agents to be landed would be in a second boat. They would be wearing gas-capes over their clothes to avoid tell-tale salt-water stains and would be carried the last metre or so to ensure they landed dry-shod. They were on no account to contact people waiting to embark or indeed talk at all. No-one involved was to wear headgear in case it should fall, or be blown off. Passengers should be "briefed to behave as much like luggage as possible". The actual time spent by seamen on the beach was supposed to be only three or four minutes. Usually the MGB was at anchor for about an hour and a half although Peter Harratt (SOE conducting officer) recorded 35 minutes as the shortest time. Landings were made on a rising tide to minimise footprint traces and someone from the shore party would visit the beach again at first light to ensure that there was nothing suspicious to be seen." (Secret Flotillas)*

My grateful thanks to David Lingard and Mike Bradbury at the Dartmouth History Museum who helped me so much when I visited them in January

2017, on the seventy-third anniversary of the first Shelburn Operation Bonaparte.

For more information about war-time operations from Dartmouth, see "The Free French in Kingswear" by Tony Higgins, published in 1994 by the Dartmouth History Research Group, "The Secret War from the River Dart" by Lt Lloyd Bott RANVR, published in 1997 by the Dartmouth History Research Group, and "Kingswear at War" by David Williams, published in 2011 by Kingswear Historians.

Author's Note

I don't think it's possible to write a book like this in isolation, so although I had spent some seventeen years researching escape lines in western Europe before even starting on this project, that alone would never have been enough. However, over those seventeen years, I have made numerous contacts with like-minded researchers, many of them real experts in their particular areas, and consider myself very fortunate in being able to go to any of them for help in filling out details. There have also been significant contributions from families and friends of some of the evaders and helpers, so although it's my name on the front of this book, it has been very much a collaborative effort.

Extra special thanks for their particular contributions to this work to (in alphabetical order) Daniel Droniou, Michael Moores LeBlanc, Dominique Lecomte, Dave and Gisele Minett, and Franck Signorile .. all of whom not only shared their expertise but also spent considerable amounts of time answering my many, many questions.

Also to Claude Benec'h, Patrick Chatelin, Oliver Clutton-Brock, Douglas Doig, John Howes, Mme Jeanne Huot, Jean-François Le Bihan, Patti Marcellus, Roger McKeon, Yvonne Millar, Rodney Seddon, Mary Shier, Heather Steele, Jean-Pierre and Michèle Thuillier, Beverly Patton Wand – and Warren Carah (son of B-17 co-pilot evader John Carah) for answering my technical queries about American aircraft.

Although one of the the main purposes of telling this story is to include as many of the helpers (the totally inadequate term used for these extraordinary people) as possible, the following accounts are based around the evaders' escape reports. There are variations in the quality and accuracy of the reports and some of those differences are hard to reconcile. Some helper names and addresses have been corrected from additional sources but there are others mentioned whose identities I have not been able to confirm. I have also used some of the many Helper files held in the US National Archives and Records Administration (NARA) in Maryland – which also vary in accuracy and levels of detail.

Evaders stories and comments are mostly taken from their escape reports, which are held in The National Archives (TNA) at Kew in the

WO208 series of folders (for British and Commonwealth servicemen), or from NARA – figures in brackets after a man's name refer to his report number. Details of helpers, including their comments and opinions, are mostly taken either from the Helper files at NARA, or from IS9 documentation (including post-war recommendations for awards) held at Kew. Other sources, such as personal memoires, other publications, and contributions from other researchers, are noted in the text.

I was hoping to be able to claim this as being the complete story of the men brought back by Shelburn but despite my best efforts, there are still some gaps. This is partly due to my inability to decipher the finer details in some of the hand-written notes of the (sometimes very detailed) American escape reports, and where in too many cases, I've not found any other sources. There are also numerous cases where sources fail to agree with one another.

In cases where I have not been able to confirm the name of a helper from other sources, I have used the notation (nf) for not found. I have also used the term (sic) where I have quoted from a source but been unable to verify the accuracy of that particular point.

Even with those limitations, may I respectively suggest to anyone who thinks they already know about Shelburn, that they reconsider their position. Despite my many years' experience, during the research for this book I was regularly finding new and sometimes surprising information that, so far as I know, has not appeared elsewhere. Evaders brought back from Plage Bonaparte came from as far afield as Germany and Holland, and the number of other organisations and groups of people involved in helping them is amazingly varied – ranging from SIS and SOE networks to Princess Charlotte of Monaco – and so to borrow the words used by Edward Stourton in his endorsement my previous publication, let me introduce you to a (another) new set of heroes and heroines to admire from that extraordinary period.

Introduction

Between July 1940 and August 1944, some 1,500 Allied military evaders (including almost exactly 500 American aircrew), crossed the Pyrenees to Spain.[1] Some of these crossings, especially in the early days of the war, were comparatively easy treks that could be completed in a single day or night but following the German takeover of southern France in November 1942, border security was increased and it often became necessary to use much tougher trails. Even in good weather, some of these high mountain routes took several days and nights, and in the winter months, many were impassable. There had to be a better way.

The Shelburn escape line only existed for a few months but in that short time, was remarkably successful – 119 military personnel (including 94 American airmen) were brought safely back to the UK with only two men lost to the enemy. Although some of the evaders spent many months in enemy-occupied territory, once in the hands of Shelburn, they were generally back in England within days.

The name Shelburn (or Shelburne) was, I am sure, chosen from a random list of names generated by Britain's Secret Intelligence Service (SIS) – other SIS/MI9 missions of the period included Oaktree, Possum and Marathon. The MGB operations for Shelburn were called Bonaparte, and other operations for SIS included Jealous, Envious, Felicitate, Flannelfoot (for BCRA) and Glover – with operations for SOE having a similar selection of unrelated names, such as Mirfield, Easement, Septimus and Scarf.

The Shelburn escape line can trace its origins back to the Pat O'Leary escape line, the first of the major escape lines running through France, and originally known simply as "the organisation" – in the summer of 1942, they organised two evacuations from the beach at Canet Plage when the Polish-crewed felucca Seawolf collected a total of forty-three evading servicemen for delivery to Gibraltar – and to the MI9 Oaktree mission of Val Williams and Ray Labrosse in 1943. Oaktree was originally intended

1 These (often disputed) figures are taken from the individual MI9 and MIS-X reports available from the two National Archives.

to build on work done by Louis Nouveau for the Pat line in Brittany but many of his contacts had been arrested after the organisation was infiltrated by the French traitor and German agent Roger Leneveu.[2]

Some evaders were brought back to England by French fishing vessels, notably the Suzanne-Renée, which left Camaret-sur-Mer on 23 October 1943 with nineteen airmen on board, and the fourteen aircrew who returned on the Briez-Izel, which sailed from Treboul harbour (Douarnenez) on 22 January 1944. Both these operations were aided by BCRA agent Georges Broussine and his Bourgogne escape line but Broussine was as aware as those in London that while sea evacuations direct to England were preferable to sending evaders on the long trek across the Pyrenees, the use of French fishing boats was never going to be enough. On his visit to London in November 1943, Broussine had discussed the problem with MI9, where he found Airey Neave particularly enthusiastic about the idea of using MGBs but it seems that Neave (understandably) omitted to mention to him that MI9 were about to launch a second such mission of their own.

British gunboats and launches had been visiting the Aber-Benoit estuary area (about 60 kms west of Roscoff) to service various SOE and intelligence networks since October 1941, and in November 1943, they were further tasked with evacuating a group of downed aircrew who had been collected in the Brest area, including four who couldn't be accommodated on board the Suzanne-Renée. However, after the near disastrous Operation Envious IIb of 1 December, together with increased German activity following the extraordinary Operation Felicitate II on Christmas Day, those pick-up points had to be abandoned.

It may be worth noting that although ever increasing numbers of Allied aircrew were landing in Brittany in late 1943, all but two of the airmen picked up from the islands off Aber-Benoit came from other areas and were brought to Brittany specifically for evacuation by sea. The two exceptions were Sgt Joseph Quirk (#247) and 2/Lt Herman Schafer (#291) whose unarmed Liberator was on a flight from Marrakesh to England when it was shot down north of Brest on 19 November.

Lucien Adelard Dumais (born Montreal in June 1905, married and with two teenage children) was a Platoon Sergeant Major in 1 Bn Les Fusiliers Mont-Royal when he landed at Dieppe on 19 August 1942.

2 Roger Eugène Victor Leneveu (aka Roger le legionnaire) (Feb 1919 – May 1944).

He was captured that afternoon but escaped from the train taking him to Germany and made his way to Marseille where he was helped by the Pat O'Leary organisation – he was evacuated from Canet Plage on board the felucca Seawolf on Operation Rosalind the night of 11-12 October 1942.

Dumais was recruited by MI9 the following year to head the Shelburn mission, given the agent name Yukon, and landed back in France by 161 SD Squadron Lysander on the night of 16-17 November 1943, along with his radio operator Ray Labrosse. For the Shelburn operations, Dumais carried a carte d'identité in the name of Lucien Desbois although the French in Brittany knew him as Leon. To the evaders, Dumais generally presented himself as Captain Hamilton, or sometimes Harrison.

Raymond Joseph Marcel Labrosse (born Ottawa in November 1920) was a signalman in the Royal Canadian Corps of Signals when he was recruited by MI9 as radio operator for Val Williams and they were parachuted into France on 20 March 1943 to set up the Oaktree mission. Following the arrest of Williams in June, Labrosse joined a group of five airmen who were helped by the Bourgogne organisation and taken across the Pyrenees to Andorra in August, and Labrosse returned to England the following month. After a period of re-training, Labrosse was assigned as radio operator to Lucien Dumais. The French in Brittany knew Labrosse as Claude – although his carte d'identité was in the name of Marcel Desjardins.

The two agents first priority was to establish a secure base in Paris where they could live, and from where Labrosse could operate his radio to stay in touch with London. They also had to find suitable logeurs to shelter the evaders, provide them with food, identity cards – and so much more – until it was time to send them to Brittany. In other words, they had to find someone who knew the city and its inhabitants well enough to establish a series of safe houses, reliable guides and all the other things that a clandestine organisation needed in order to survive and operate.

The only contact provided by MI9 was a hairdressing salon (which I've always thought appropriate as Dumais gives his civilian profession as coiffeur) at 6 rue des Capucines, Paris II where they were to ask for a "Mme Georges". This was Mme Lucienne Christiane Bodin (aka Marie Christine) and her friend Suzanne Bosnier. On their arrival in the capital, Dumais and Labrosse went to Mme Bodin's salon, and were staying in her apartment at

38 rue des Petit Champs when just days later, both women were arrested.[3] This left the two Shelburn agents homeless and at something of a loss.

The answer to their problems was Labrosse's original Oaktree contact, a man named Paul Campinchi.

3 Mme Bodin (born November 1908) and Mme Bosnier (born October 1905) both survived deportation and were each recommended for the King's Medal for Courage.

Reseau François

Visitors to Plage Bonaparte near Plouha in Brittany may notice that the French memorials refer to "Reseau François-Shelburn" but few people will know who or what the name François refers to.

Many readers will be familiar with the MI9 Shelburn escape line using Royal Navy Motor Gunboats to bring evaders from Plage Bonaparte in Brittany to Dartmouth in Devon but what you may be less familiar with is the French organisation in Paris which brought so many of these men together, and fed and sheltered them until it was time to send them to Brittany.

The reseau of logeurs and guides in Paris was organised by a man whose name doesn't appear in any of the Shelburn evaders' escape reports – he was Paul Campinchi – aka François. For the majority of Parisian logeurs and guides, their chef de reseau was François – few of them ever met Lucien Dumais or Ray Labrosse, and they only heard the name Shelburn long after the war was over.

Paul François Campinchi was born in Saint-Georges-sur-Cher (Loir-et-Cher) on 10 October 1903. Married to Thérèse (born July 1899 – she spoke much better English than Paul, having studied as a nurse in England) and with a young daughter Jeanne (born 1935), they lived at 19 rue des Ursins, on the Île de la Cité, Paris IV, about a 100 metres from Notre-Dame cathedral. Paul and Thérèse both worked at the Prefecture de Police where Paul was responsible for issuing identity cards, and Thérèse in the anti-venereal dispensary at 3 Quai de l'Horloge.

On 11 January 1943, RAF evader Sgt Reginald Smith (1074) was brought to the Campinchi apartment. Mlle Marguerite Larue (born Apr 1906), one of Campinchi's colleagues at the Prefecture, had been visiting Smith in Livry-Gargan, where he had been sheltered since the previous November, until Smith asked her to help him get back to England. Eight-year-old Jeanne Campinchi was sent to stay with friends in La Pin-la-Garenne in Normandy, and Smith took over her bedroom until 2 February, when Thérèse Campinchi (dressed as a nurse and armed with a medical certificate from Dr Yves Porc'her saying that Smith was a patient from a psychiatric hospital) took him to Quimper (Finistere), and then Carantec. On 5 February, Smith left for England from the north-coast port of Carantec on board the French fishing vessel Yvonne – they were intercepted off the English coast by a British patrol boat two days later and towed into Salcombe, Devon.

Because Campinchi had asked Smith to give his name and details to MI9 in London, Val Williams and Ray Labrosse contacted Campinchi when they arrived in Paris a few weeks later to set up the Oaktree escape line. Following the collapse of Oaktree in June, and a visit by German police to their apartment in September, Campinchi and his wife (along with Genevieve de Poulpiquet who had been lodging with the Campinchis since the arrest of her husband Cesaire in March 1943) left their apartment at rue des Ursins and moved to stay with Genevieve's friend, Mme Olga L'Hoir Sivry (aka Guette) at 6 rue Nicolet.

Campinchi had a long-held ambition of sending groups of evaders direct to England by sea. His first-hand experience with Reginald Smith, and then with Oaktree – which basically failed because various delays meant the shortening nights made it impossible for an MGB to make a successful crossing under cover of darkness – had not dampened his enthusiasm, so when Labrosse returned to Paris in November with Lucien Dumais, Campinchi saw it as an opportunity to finally realise his dream.

To read any of the accounts of Shelburn available elsewhere, one might think that Dumais appointed Paul Campinchi to work for him. Campinchi, and everyone else involved with reseau François, saw things differently – Dumais was simply their contact with London, the man who could call in the gunboats. To reseau François, Dumais was the last link in a long chain that began where airmen landed in the French countryside, and then centred on Paris where they were sheltered and cared for until word came from Dumais that they could be sent to Brittany. For his work with Shelburn and reseau François, Paul Campinchi was awarded the OBE.

Genevieve de Poulpiquet was Mme Vve la comtesse Genevieve de Poulpiquet de Brescanvel (aka Gilberte) (born Feb 1905). She and her husband, le comte Césaire, had sheltered six evaders in their home at the Chateau de Trefy near Quéménéven, Finistere before Cesaire's arrest on 29 March 1943 – he was deported to Germany where he died. Genevieve, who was fortunate to avoid the same fate, contacted Georges Jouanjean (to whom she had passed the five American airmen mentioned below) and Job le Bec of the Breton "Pen Called" group. She later acquired the address of Paul Campinchi in Paris (given to her, along with the password, by Val Williams), and later moved to the capital where she stayed with the Campinchis at rue des Ursins and continued her escape line work with Oaktree.

The six men sheltered at the Chateau de Trefy were F/Sgt Albert Wright (895) (who stayed for 65 days, February-April 1943), and five evaders from the B-17 41-24584 SUSFU, which was shot down over Brittany on 23 January 1943. The five Americans were captured at Tours with Louis Nouveau and Suzanne Gerard of the Pat line in early February. The other two evaders from SUSFU – 2/Lt Mark McDermott (#12) and S/Sgt Sebastian Vogel (#13) – were evacuated on board the fishing vessel Yvonne with Sgt Reginald Smith, the first evader to be helped by Paul and Thérèse Campinchi.

One day in September 1943, when Mme de Poulpiquet returned to rue des Ursins for lunch, she found the concierge in a panic because there were German police in the Campinchi apartment. Mme de Poulpiquet set off immediately to the Porte Maillot restaurant where the Campinchis were celebrating a friend's wedding. They arranged a rendezvous that evening at the brasserie la Closerie des Lilas on boulevard du Montparnasse, where Mme de Poulpiquet told Paul Campinchi she had been offered the services of "une femme de monde". Not quite getting the joke, Campinchi was finally persuaded to go with her to meet Olga L'Hoir-Sivry, widow of an artist, and the lady who sheltered Genevieve and the Campinchis in her apartment at 6 rue Nicolet, "un hôtel particulier", until the liberation of the city, and where Lucien Dumais and Ray Labrosse stayed when they came to Paris in November to set up the Shelburn line.

Her recommendations for an American Medal of Freedom with Bronze Palm, and the British King's Medal for Courage, credit Mme de Poulpiquet with helping more than thirty Allied servicemen, sheltering some (as mentioned above), and for Oaktree and reseau François, bringing groups of evaders to Paris, and taking groups to Brittany.

Jeanne Huot (née Campinchi) remembers Gilberte from her childhood as being rather small, with blazing blonde hair, clear skin and freckles.

Dr Yves Jean Marie Porc'her (born June 1887) of 1 rue Cabanis, Paris XIV was a pre-war friend of Paul Campinchi. He was a pathologist, and head of a section in a large psychiatric establishment in Paris, who took on the task of printing false papers for the evaders. He was arrested on 7 February 1944 following the capture and torture of Mary-Rose Zerling. Dr Porc'her was one of the very few reseau François helpers who knew where Campinchi was living but his training and experience enabled him to convincingly feign madness during his own interrogation by the Masuy gang, and he was transferred to Fresnes.[4] *Dr Porc'her was handed over to the French Red Cross just before the liberation of Paris, and after the war, recommended for a KMC.*

Following Dr Porc'her's arrest, the equipe Porc'her group of logeurs was taken on by Mme Suzanne Guelat (aka Aline) of 68 boulevard Auguste Blanqui, Paris XIII. Born November 1912, and a supervisor at l'Hopital Sainte Anne, she and her husband Olivier had sheltered numerous evaders for Bourgogne before joining reseau François.

Dr Jean Albert Peiffert (born Nov 1914) was a small, quiet man of deceptively weak appearance who also happened to be an excellent racing driver of both cars and self-prepared motorcycles. A friend of Paul Campinchi since his student days, in addition to offering medical assistance, Dr Peiffert put his physics laboratory, securely located behind iron gates in the basement of the Faculty of Medicine, at the reseau's disposal. He became responsible for photographing many of the François-Shelburn evaders and providing them with identity cards – and I am guessing that he was the unnamed photographer who so often accompanied Marcel Cola – see later.

Dr André Le Balc'h lived at 1 Quai aux Fleurs, about 200 metres from the Campinchi home. He was a doctor at Saint-Denis hospital who (according to Roger Huguen) was introduced to Paul Campinchi by his colleague Dr Peiffert. In early 1943, Dr Le Balc'h let Ray Labrosse (as radio operator for Oaktree) use the balcony of his sixth-floor apartment to try and contact London. With the demise of Oaktree, Campinchi suggested that Dr Le Balc'h return to his native Plouezec (just north of Plouha) and take over from former Oaktree contact, Dr Meynard, who had had to leave his surgery in Paimpol following a similar local threat of arrest. When Lucien Dumais arrived in Paris and told Campinchi he was looking for a base in northern Brittany, Campinchi suggested he contact Dr Le Balc'h, and gave him a

4 Christian Masuy was the pseudonym used by Belgian collaborator Georges Delfanne, who specialised in the infiltration of resistance groups, and was infamous for his interrogation techniques.

letter of introduction. It was then Dr Le Balc'h who recommended Henri Le Blais at Saint-Brieuc as local chief, and François Le Cornec at Plouha as "beach-master" to Dumais.[5]

Mary-Rose Zerling (aka Claudette) (born Feb 1908) had been living in Paris with her parents Armand and Helene at 12 rue Saint-Ferdinand, Paris XVII at weekends, and teaching biology at Valenciennes during the week – where she also worked for the local organisation. When her chief was arrested, Claudette took three months sick-leave from the school and moved back to Paris where she shared with her aunt, Marcelle Hiaux, at 87 boulevard de Courcelles.

Claudette says she first became involved with helping evaders in May 1942 when Madeleine Michelis asked her to find a refuge (asile) for two British airmen who had been shot down on a raid to Cologne – lodging were quickly found but Claudette was not directly involved, and it is not clear who they were or what happened to them. A year later, in May 1943, a friend in the resistance, Jean Texcier, introduced her to Doctor Porc'her.

Campinchi says that he was was introduced to Claudette by Dr Porc'her, although Mary-Rose Zerling says (in her 1946 report) that she first met Campinchi in July 1943 when her friend Marie Betbeder-Matibet was sheltering American evader S/Sgt Allen Robinson (#103) – Claudette also brought Ray Labrosse to the apartment shortly before he left for England himself. Either way, with her excellent English, having spent a year at Wellesley College in Boston, she became Campinchi's 'principale collaboratrice' and 'responsable du logement' for reseau François in Paris. Mary-Rose Zerling was recommended for an MBE.[6]

Henri Gabriel Emile Bois (born Oct 1901) was a schoolteacher, divorced and with one son, Jean Baptiste Henri Bois of Drucat, Somme. Recruited into the group SR Region Nord by Mary-Rose Zerling in June 1943, Henri resigned his teaching job on 20 October 1943 to work full-time in the north until Claudette introduced him to Paul Campinchi in December. He joined reseau François as "chef d'equipe Henri", taking parties of evaders himself and recruiting numerous other convoyeurs until the Liberation. He was diagnosed with glaucoma by Doctor Peiffert, who examined him in February

5 Roger Huguen (1976) "Par les nuits les plus longues" Les Presses Bretonnes Saint-Brieuc.

6 All the above paragraphs include information from Campinchi family files courtesy of Daniel Droniou and Mme Jeanne Huot (née Campinchi).

1944, but refused to take time off in order to be operated on, consequently losing all sight in his right eye. Note that few evaders name (or even describe) their guides to Brittany so it is hard to identify which parties Henri Bois may have taken himself.

Named convoyeurs recruited by Henri Bois include Raymond Mauret and his fiancée Jacqueline, Charles Rouet, Jean Kocera-Massenet, Jean Vaina (who had the added responsibility of bringing supplies (including radios) back to Paris), Georges Schmalzer, Julien Dreyfus and Georges Fromageot – others are given as first names only – Paul, Francis, Yolande, Yvonne, René and Robert ..

Gabrielle Wiame (aka Mme Marie), who worked so diligently with Comète, Oaktree and Bourgogne, is included on Campinchi's list of helpers, and on the post-war diagrammatic representation of the original structure of reseau François but I have not found any mention of her in any of the Shelburn evaders' reports, nor (apart from Suzanne Guelat) of any of the numerous helpers that she lists in her NARA file.

Paul Campinchi organised reseau François into specialist equipes (groups). Henri Bois (equipe Henri) organised the guides and Marie-Rose Zerling (equipe Claudette) organised the safe houses, and there were others responsible for security, making false papers (Dr Peiffert) and providing food and clothing for the evaders. Not mentioned (or known) by any of the Shelburn evaders were Mme Olga L'Hoir-Sivry who provided Campinchi with his headquarters at her home at 6 rue Nicolet, nor any of the various addresses that Ray Labrosse used to send his radio messages to London, including 1 rue Dante where Marguerite Larue, who had worked with Campinchi at the Prefecture de Police, regularly allowed Labrosse to use her fifth-floor apartment.

The story of reseau François in Paris is far from simple, and many of the people who worked with François are also associated with other organisations but trying to compartmentalise them into discrete groups is pointless. Evaders were collected from several different organisations and areas and the only thing they have in common (for this story) is their being in Paris prior to being taken to Brittany for evacuation by sea. It should also be remembered that Campinchi's escape line work didn't end with the Bonaparte operations – many evaders handled later by François in Paris were either taken across the Pyrenees to Spain or to the MI9 Mission Marathon camp at Freteval.

Fortunately for the convenience of this story, the one hundred evaders brought back from the beach at l'Anse-Cochat in the first two months can be grouped into each of the five Bonaparte operations (and similarly, the nineteen men brought out on the first two Crozier operations) – there being little interaction between the groups – and so that's how the story will be told.

Various publications state that Dumais and Shelburn were responsible for returning upwards of 300 airmen (sic) and agents, although none of the publications making such claims include further details, and I can only speculate on who some of the remaining 175 or so people might have been. However, I believe that Shelburn should more properly be defined by the men brought back on the gunboats.

Lucien Dumais and Ray Labrosse arrived in Paris on 19 November 1943. They made their planned contact with Lucienne Bodin and Suzanne Bosniere at rue des Capucines but tragically both women were arrested two days later. The only option left for Dumais was to ignore the instructions they had received in London and find Ray Labrosse's friend from the Oaktree mission, Paul Campinchi. This wasn't quite as easy as they hoped as Campinchi had moved house since Labrosse had last been in Paris but through an intermediary they were able to meet and convince him that their security would be a lot better than that of his previous British contact. Once that was agreed, Campinchi took charge everything in Paris, including temporary accommodation for the two Canadians at his new home on rue Nicolet.

Evaders had obviously been passing through Paris long before the Shelburn operations began but from December 1943 onwards, some of them were taken on by the François network. It should also be noted that not all the men brought back by Shelburn went through Paris and reseau François – as will be seen later in the text, some had landed and been helped in Brittany, not visiting the French capital at all.

SIS/MI9 Operation Bonaparte 1 (28-29 Jan 1944) MGB 503 (Mike Marshall)

Some of the men evacuated on this first Bonaparte operation were brought into the François network by Marie-Rose Zerling either through her contacts with Bordeaux-Loupiac in the Pas-de-Calais (King and Sentkoski) or with the remnants of the John Carter organisation in Paris (Cufley, Harvey, Hathaway, Casden and Dickerman), which dead-ended in Paris with Jeanne Huet and Marguerite Schmitz following Carter's arrest in January 1944. Others were helped by various people and organisations in northern France before being taken to Paris where, I suspect, it was simply a question of who knew who that determined which escape line the evaders were passed on to.

The Evaders

Sgt Norman B Cufley (1728) was the wireless operator, and **Sgt John Harvey** (1729) the flight engineer of 77 Sqn Halifax JD247 (Charlesworth) which was returning from Ludwigshafen on the evening of 18 November 1943. One engine had failed on the outward journey, forcing them to jettison their bomb load but for safety reasons, they had stayed in formation. However on the return leg, two more engines failed and the aircraft was abandoned to crash near Moÿ-de-l'Aisne (Picardy). Two of the crew were killed and three captured – Cufley and Harvey were the only successful evaders.

Norman Cufley was seventeen days past his twenty-second birthday when he landed in a tree just as a clock in the nearby village struck ten o'clock. The ex-accountant from Putney Hill, London says it was too dark to see if it was safe for him to drop and so remained hanging in the tree until daylight. Fortunately some locals spotted his parachute and did their best to help him down. Apparently one elderly man felt it was his duty to notify the gendarmes but another man took Cufley and hid him in the loft of a barn. Cufley believes that a gendarme did respond (and may have actually seen Cufley) but took no action. Later that evening, the man who had hidden Cufley returned and took him into an empty house, returning half an hour later with some food, a young girl and a woman. The woman was Margarite Miller, an American (married to a Frenchman) and she explained that Cufley would be moved to another house the following morning. On 20 November, Cufley's original helper visited several times with cigarettes and food, telling him that his flight engineer Harvey was being sheltered nearby and explaining that Margarite would not be able to come until that evening. He also brought civilian clothes and moved Cufley to another house where a young couple gave him a meal, before Margarite Miller arrived to take him to yet another another house for night. Next day, a man came with a bicycle and took Cufley to a house in nearby Berthenicourt (passing the two flower-covered graves of his pilot W/O Alan Charlesworth and bomb-aimer Sgt Frederick B Wise on the way) where he joined Harvey.

John Harvey, a 23-year-old tailor from Dalston, East London, had landed in a field, hidden his parachute and Mae West and set off walking. He passed through the village of Alaincourt, over a canal bridge and across some fields to spend the rest of the night in a wood. Early next morning, he returned to the village, and seeing no-one about, hid himself in a barn. When he saw the farmer who owned the barn, Harvey approached him and was soon surrounded by people. A woman brought him some bread before leading him into her garden and indicating that he should climb over the fence into her neighbour's garden and enter the house. He was then taken to a café and given some food before a lady (Margarite Miller) arrived and told him that Norman Cufley was being sheltered nearby. Harvey spent the night in the café and next morning, the café proprietor took him by bicycle to a railway station where he spent the night in the station-master's house. Next morning (21 November) two men took Harvey by bicycle to Berthenicourt where he joined Cufley.

That same afternoon, Cufley and Harvey were taken to the village of Flavy-le-Martel (Aisne) where they were sheltered by a man named Jean Bruxelles, his wife and three children at 40 rue Maurice Moreau. They stayed with the Bruxelles family until 29 November when an unnamed man took them by car to a garage in Chauny (Alfred Logeon at 24 rue du Brouage) and they spent the night next door with butcher René Felix. Next day, the same man who had driven them to Chauny, took them and S/Sgt John Lowther (#2335) by train to Creil where they stayed in separate houses (addresses not known) – Lowther being handed over to dentist

Georges Budin who took him to 15 rue Charles Somasco where he was sheltered with a short, red-haired, middle-aged Scottish lady, married to a Frenchman – this was Marguerite Toussaint, married to Paul Toussaint (born Feb 1873), he worked in the office of a chemical factory.

On 3 (query) December, the three evaders were taken by train to Beauvais, where Lowther says they spent the day with a man, wife and son. That evening, they were collected by Gilbert Thibault who drove them to his home on rue de Saint-Léger in Auneuil where they joined Sgt Robert Griffith (1744), and Thibault took all four airmen to be sheltered by retired schoolteachers Raphael and Hélène Lefevre.

Gilbert Jean Joseph Thibault (born July 1912) was the Huissier (Courts Service official, bailiff or legal officer, there doesn't seem to be an English equivalent) at Auneuil. He was mobilised as sous-lieutenant in the French army in August 1939, captured, and escaped from Bagnoles-de-l'Orne in June 1940. He made his way to Morocco in February 1941 where he was transferred to the cavalry in September and promoted to lieutenant. He returned to France as Agent A-6 (aka Zephyrin) under Colonels Stephens and Malaize (in Madrid) in October 1942. He first became involved with helping evaders on 27 September 1943 when B-26 gunner S/Sgt Lloyd Frazer (#265) landed in a wood near Auneuil. Thibault and his mother Yvonne sheltered Frazer for three days before Thibault drove him to an organisation in Beauvais, which took him to Paris, and Yvonne Deplanche of Comète.

In addition to his resistance activities with OCM (Organisation Civile et Militaire), Thibault established reseau Alsace. Originally intended to help fellow French soldiers escape to North Africa (via Ruffino Jaureguy at Cambo-les-Bains), reseau Alsace evolved to sheltering Allied evaders until they could be passed to other organisations (Comète, John Carter, Shelburn) to be taken back to the UK. On 16 February 1944, Thibault was almost caught in a German trap at Evelyn Vassius home on rue de Clichy following the arrest of Mme Schmitz (see later) – his cousin André Bureau being amongst those captured that day – and Thibault was wounded during his escape. Thibault also continued his evasion work after Shelburn, helping literally scores of evaders until the Liberation – his contributions being widely recognised by IS9 who recommended him for an MBE.

On 15 (query) December, Gilbert Thibault drove the four airmen to Paris where Griffith says they met Thibault's cousin André (André Bureau) and were taken to a church where they were handed over to a Mme Colette. This was Madeleine Grador, and she took them to an apartment at 87 rue Rochechouart, Paris IX where they were sheltered by Mme Marguerite Schmitz. Cufley and Harvey stayed overnight at rue Rochechouart, joining American airmen Jean Pitner (#375), Arno Plischke (#376) and Delton King (#2217), while Griffith and Lowther were taken to stay with a young law student named Jean Jacques Piot (of 2 Square Alboni). Next day, Cufley and Harvey were taken to stay overnight with Robert Roques at 7 rue Chaligny, Paris XII before returning to Mme Schmitz for another night – Pitner, Plischke, Lowther and King having left for Lyon. On 18 December, Cufley and Harvey were moved to 48 avenue du President Wilson, Paris XVI where they were sheltered by Mme Jeanne Huet.

At this point, the airmen were being helped by the John Carter organisation. John Carter (aka Jules/Julien) was born 1891 in Gouvieux near Chantilly (Oise) of English parents, and had dual nationality. Carter was put in contact with the Pat O'Leary line in August 1942 when George Whittinghill at the American Consulate in Lyon asked him to deliver the five-man crew from 138 SD Whitley Z9232 (Outram) which had crashed near Vierzon, to Dr Georges Rodocanachi in Marseille. Following O'Leary's arrest in February 1943, Carter went to Switzerland where he contacted Victor Farrell (SIS station chief) who asked him to start taking evaders along the SOE Vic line route to Spain through Perpignan, or via Lavelanet to Andorra. Carter, who soon based himself in Lyon (where I believe he had an apartment on rue Vendome) says he made many useful contacts through his assistant, Annie Sabourault. He also had good contacts in Paris where he says that Madeleine Grador represented him, while Jean Calmet, of 12 rue de Marseille in Lyon, helped as his "conductor". Carter continued passing on evaders (including Operation Frankton survivors Herbert Hasler and William Sparks) until his arrest with three American airmen at the hôtel de France in Pamiers on 6 January 1944. John Carter was deported to Germany and survived Mauthausen.

Marguerite Schmitz (born July 1888) was widowed from her first husband and divorced from her second, Marcel Schnerb. She first became involved with helping evaders on 13 September 1943, when W/O George F Thomas (LIB/1580), the navigator of 103 Sqn Lancaster ED751 (Cant), was brought to her apartment by Maurice Fort. She sheltered Thomas until 18

October when he left for the Pyrenees with the Wyssogotha organisation that her god-son, Robert Burba, had found. Thomas was captured (with others) near Bagneres on 29 October by a German border patrol.

It was while looking for an escape line to take George Thomas that Mme Schmitz was first put into contact with, amongst others, Gilbert Thibault and John Carter – and most of the evaders she subsequently sheltered were brought to her by Thibault to be passed to the John Carter organisation. Mme Schmitz says that she introduced Thibault to Mary-Rose Zerling.

Mme Schmitz also sheltered P/O Henry B Hall (1747), air bomber of 35 Sqn Halifax HR798 (piloted by William Dallin – mentioned later) for a few days in December 43 and again at the beginning of January until he left for Bordeaux with Evelyn Vassius of the Wyssogotha-Lorraine escape line – Hall crossed the border into Spain during the night of 10-11 January.[7]

Madeleine Grador (born Jan 1914 in Paris) was married to fellow veterinarian Pierre Grador, who had a practice in Brittany. She was arrested in June 1944. Jeanne Marie Huet (born June 1899 in Belgium) was arrested on 7 February 1944, along with her husband, daughter and housekeeper Irma Manteau, and F/Lt Hugh L Parry (LIB/1057), pilot of 41 Sqn Spitfire MB802, who had been shot down the previous September and brought to the Huet apartment on 24 January by Paule Vastel. Mlle Paule France Vastel (born Sept 1922 in Bawako, French Sudan) was also arrested in February. All three women were liberated from Fresnes prison in August.

Lowther and King left Paris for Lyon on 16 December, and Pitner and Plishcke the following day – Lowther and King being taken to Switzerland at the end of February. Cufley and Harvey would presumably have followed them had it not been for John Carter's arrest at Pamiers on 6 January, news of which soon reached the organisation in Paris. On 10 January, Madeleine Grador took Robert Griffith to Lavelanet, along with S/Sgt Clifford Hammock (#391) (who had been sheltered by Jeanne Huet, sharing with Cufley and Harvey since 31 December), where they joined Pitner and Plischke, and three days later, left with two Spanish guides to cross the Pyrenees to Andorra. This just left the two Halifax crewmen in Paris, who stayed on with Mme Huet until contact was made with reseau François.

---

7 Mme Evelyn Vassius (née De Graaf January 1897) was arrested on 16 February in her home at 26 rue de Clichy, Paris IX and deported – she died at Ravensbruck.

Cufley and Harvey say they enjoyed complete freedom in Mme Huet's seventh-floor, eight-room apartment on avenue du President Wilson for the month they were there, and often went out. They also say that Mme Huet's husband was an American who apparently didn't know that she helped evaders, and that their son was serving in Algeria.

On 19 January, they report being visited by a Captain Hamilton (Lucien Dumais) of the British Intelligence Services who passed them over to guides who took them that evening by overnight train to Saint-Brieuc, arriving at 0600 hrs the following morning. After staying briefly in a house (no details), they were taken on to Plouha where they say that thirteen Americans were waiting.

> *"A boating operation which had been planned was postponed from day to day whilst we stayed on a farm. On 24 January, F/O Blackwell (1727) arrived, and the remainder of our narrative is the same as his." (WO208/5582-1728/1729)*

T/Sgt Andrew F Hathaway (#346) was the engineer/top-turret gunner of 100BG/349BS B-17 42-31215 (Ford) which was on the way to Paris on 26 November 1943 when they were hit by flak. As they fell out of formation somewhere south of Beauvais, they were attacked by fighters and the aircraft abandoned to crash near La Neuville-Garnier (Oise). Hathaway was one of four men from this aircraft to evade successfully, the others being co-pilot 2/Lt Jean B Pitner (#375), navigator 2/Lt Arno E Plischke (#376) and waist-gunner S/Sgt Delton L King (#2217) who, as already mentioned, were helped by the John Carter organisation.

23-year-old Hathaway, an apprentice tool and die maker from Hillside, New Jersey, reports them being hit by flak on the way to their target which stopped the #2 engine. As they fell out of formation, they were attacked by fighters which hit his turret and damaged their tail – causing the aircraft to "mush" – and set fire to the bomb-bay. He heard the bail-out order but because of the fire, exited through the front escape hatch, following his pilot (2/Lt George W Ford), co-pilot and navigator.[8]

Hathaway says he jumped from about 6,000 feet but delayed pulling his rip-cord until about 1,000 feet, and then landed in a field about thirty yards

8 On an American heavy bomber, the engines are numbered 1 to 4, counting from left to right (port to starboard), so the #2 engine is nearest the fuselage on the left-hand side and #4 engine is the starboard-outer.

from a house. He gathered up his parachute and starting running down a country lane, only pausing to stuff his parachute into a hedge and cover it with leaves. He didn't see anyone around as he ran to some trees, at which point he slowed to a fast walk, carrying on through the trees, avoiding a wood-cutter he heard working, until finding some thick bushes to hide in. He was still wearing his uniform and flying gear, including both heated and flying boots, but unfortunately he'd left his GI shoes in the aircraft.

GI shoes were US Army issue, ankle-high, brown leather boots which proved to be near ideal for crossing the mountains, and were highly recommended by escape and evasion lecturers. Unfortunately, with decent leather footwear almost unobtainable in war-time France, the wearing of early version GI shoes in public could be a giveaway. Later issue boots however, made with the leather rough side out, had the additional advantage of looking (according to at least one evader) or could be made to look, just like French peasant shoes – another evader also recommended dying them black at the first opportunity. One sergeant, who wore GI shoes under his flying boots, described them as being a curse in the city (where the rubber soles and heels were easily recognisable) but a blessing when travelling cross-country. Because it got so cold, especially in the rear of their aircraft, American bomber crews wore electrically heated suits, often including footwear – some of the more experienced (or perhaps better advised) attaching GI shoes to their parachute harness ready for use in the event of bailing out.

On which subject, there is some debate about the way to spell bail or bale, as in where a man bales out. Americans tend to use bail – as in sounding the bail-out (alarm) bell – so I have used that spelling for them, only retaining bale for the RAF airmen.

Hathaway set off running (as best he could in his heavy footwear) until he came to a wooded hillside where he hid for the rest of the day. He could see people working in the fields but no single person that he thought it safe to approach. He could also hear cars on a nearby road, and there was a small village about a mile away. That evening, he followed the edge of the wood, not heading in any particular direction and simply hoping to find someone who could help him. He finally stopped a farmer who was driving a horse and cart, and used his cigarette lighter to illuminate his French phrase-card. Communication was obviously difficult but Hathaway understood that there were Germans in a nearby house, and so headed off in the opposite direction. He carried on walking across fields, making little progress because of the many fences and hedges, until daybreak, when he stopped to eat one of the candy bars (chocolate or peanut were the standard issue) from his escape kit. After a short rest he carried on until about mid-morning when he decided to hide himself on the outskirts of a small village, where he stayed for the rest of the morning. Sometime that afternoon, he managed to attract the attention of an elderly woman, and used his phrase-card to ask her for help. It seems she had no idea what he was trying to say and so went and fetched another woman, who did. Hathaway was taken into their house, given some food and allowed to rest there until late evening when a man came to see him. The man was friendly enough but not very helpful although Hathaway was given more food and allowed to stay for the rest the night. Next morning, Hathaway was woken early, given breakfast, a package of food and some odd pieces of clothing before being sent on his way.

After getting himself lost in a large village, Hathaway decided to stay on the main road for a while, passing through several smaller villages before stopping another man with a horse and a cart. After using his phrase-card once more to explain that he was an American parachutist in need of help, the man took Hathaway back to a house where he was the caretaker of a large estate, and gave him coffee and bread. For some unstated reason, Hathaway soon moved on, and by the time it began to get dark, had reached the outskirts of a large town. After an unfortunate encounter with a woman and her husband, Hathaway stopped a passing cyclist who directed him to a church. The priest declined to help beyond giving Hathaway some food, and Hathaway spent an uncomfortable few hours sleeping in a field before continuing his walk. At about midnight, he reached another town (Méru, Oise) where he went to the railway station to see if he could sleep there, and the ticket-seller let him stay in a back room. After another early morning start, Hathaway spotted a signpost for Paris and decided to head that way using his compass. However, he wound up using numerous secondary roads and wasn't making much progress when he met a local man. Using his phrase card once more, Hathaway asked him for help and was taken to a house where he met two more men, and his journey was arranged.

After some discussion amongst themselves, one of the men directed Hathaway up a dirt path away from the main road and towards some houses. On the road he was followed by a man on a bicycle who then led Hathaway into the courtyard of Fermes de Mezieres at Vallangoujard where Hathaway was taken in by the man of the house, Emile Vaillant. M. Vaillant had two teenage daughters, one of whom could write enough English to tell Hathaway there was a German airfield about 20 kms away.

After four days with the Vaillants, a man and woman from Pontoise came to see him. They took Hathaway by bicycle to an English-speaking woman, after which he was driven by truck to a two-room house on the edge of the little village of Pouilly (Oise), home of a mechanic who worked in Paris. Hathaway spent the night in a tavern (sic) before returning to the house next day, escorted by the man's brother. Later that morning, he was taken by bicycle to the outskirts of Pontoise and the home of the couple who had visited him at M. Vaillant's house. He stayed in Pontoise for the next eight days until the woman took him to a café in Pontoise and asked him where he would like to go from there. Hathaway told her he wanted to go to Spain, and after a night at the café, a man from the organisation took him to Franconville (Val d'Oise).

Hathaway was sheltered in Franconville for 16 days with a M. Cogez at 139 rue de Paris. M. Cogez was in the black market, had a 14-year-old daughter, and a son who was in prison in Spain. They received regular visits from the organisation man – no name is given but Hathaway describes him as being a small man with black hair and moustache – and a woman who had worked in NYC and been an interpreter in the last war. On about 20 December, Mme Julie Cogez took Hathaway to a café where they met the organisation man, and he took Hathaway to Paris.

In Paris, Hathaway was handed over to Marie Therese Labadie, and a doctor who had previously visited him at Franconville with the English-speaking woman. Hathaway stayed at Mlle Labadie's apartment until the afternoon when he was taken to Miss MacCarthy (an Irish woman who taught English at a university) on rue Sainte-Anne, and she and Mlle Labadie took him to stay with an English woman (she had a 12-year-old daughter but her Greek husband had died in prison) – this was Mme Vve Lily Asselanidis at 75 rue Fondary. Hathaway stayed with Lily Asselanidis for three days until Marie Therese Labadie took him and Sidney Casden (#355) to her home in Ecouen (Val d'Oise) – and Hathaway travelled with Casden from that point on.

Marie Therese Labadie was an apparently wealthy lady of about thirty-one. Helene Gill (see later) gives the address where she lived with her mother as 8 rue de Paris, Ecouen although the (post-war) IS9 Helper List has her and her brother Pierre living at 12 rue du Pontcel, Luzarches.

Elsa Janie MacCarthy (aka Jeanne Rose) (born Jan 1885) was an Irish-born English professor from Killarney (Kerry) who lived at 64 rue Sainte-Anne, Paris II. Janie MacCarthy had moved to Brittany in 1910 before studying at the Sorbonne in Paris where she obtained advanced degrees in English and French. In 1939, with the outbreak of war, and to avoid being interned, she obtained an Irish passport (to replace her British one), and continued giving language classes. She also became involved with helping evaders, working with Robert Aylé of Comète, Lucienne Bodin (mentioned earlier) and Elisabeth Barbier's groupe Vaneau – the organisation in Paris centered around the Barbier apartment at 72 rue Vaneau that sheltered so many men for Comète and Oaktree until Elisabeth's arrest on 19 June 1943.

2/Lt Sidney Casden (#355) was the 22-year-old bombardier of 384BG/546BS B-17 42-30058 (Rosio) which was hit by flak and fighters on 26 June 1943 near their target of Villacoublay aerodrome, and at about 10,000 feet, abandoned to crash near Dourdan (Essonne).

All ten crew landed safely and eight of them evaded successfully, the other seven – pilot 1/Lt Joseph Rosio (#54), co-pilot 1/Lt George W Evans (#55), navigator 2/Lt Leonard J Fink (#180), radio operator S/Sgt Lester Brown (#52), ball-turret gunner S/Sgt John H Houghton (#53), and waist-gunners S/Sgt John H Kuberski (#56) and S/Sgt Anthony F Cucinotta (#71) – were all helped by the Bourgogne organisation and crossed the Pyrenees the following month – apart from Fink, who was sheltered in Ymonville for eleven weeks before being taken to Paris and on to cross the Pyrenees to Andorra in October 1943.[9]

Casden spent seven months in France, helped initially by people not connected with any organisation, and then with a group of helpers in Juvisy-sur-Orge linked to the Bourgogne escape line but who (temporarily) lost that contact in November with the arrest of Madeleine Melot. It wasn't until January 1944, when he was passed to the remnants of the John Carter organisation in Paris, that Casden finally met Mary-Rose Zerling of reseau François.

Casden says that he baled out on hearing the order and then on looking up and seeing eight parachutes above him (and despite the advice he should have been given in his E&E lectures), figured it was time to open his. Unfortunately he still had a walk-around oxygen bottle with him and

9 For details of all the men helped by Bourgogne, see "They came from Burgundy".

when his chute opened, the bottle smacked him in the face. After that, and having nothing much to do while he drifted down, Casden lit a cigarette. When he did finally land, he landed hard and although wearing GI shoes under his flying boots, still turned his ankle – he blames the flying boots for that mishap – and so was unable to run from the five men working in the field who came to check him out. Casden spoke enough French to ask if there were any Germans in the area and on misunderstanding the hand-gestures this question provoked, asked if they would help him. They reluctantly showed Casden on his escape map that he was somewhere north of Chartres (he says between Saint Germain and Versailles, and 19 kms from Paris so perhaps near Plaisir, Yvelines) and pointed the way south for Spain. They also pointed to a town where they thought Casden could get help but as he was still in uniform, Casden was understandably reluctant to approach any built-up areas. The men took Casden's flying jacket and coveralls, swapping them for a beret and an old jacket for him to put on over his OD (oliver drab) uniform shirt, and he started walking towards the nearest road.

He was soon spotted by two men on bicycles who took him to hide in a wheat field, saying they would come back later, and leaving Casden to examine the contents of his aids box. When the two men did eventually return, they seem to have changed their minds about helping him so Casden continued along the road until he was stopped by a peasant family who wanted to know where he was going. When he told them he was heading south for Spain, the family advised him to get off the road at once as it was heavily travelled by the Germans, and suggested he go back to his wheat field and wait for them. It wasn't until the afternoon of the following day that the family finally came back, bringing another man with them. The new man had brought a rhubarb tart and a bottle of wine – for which he charged Casden 130 francs – and insisted on exchanging clothes with him, including his shoes, which Casden readily accepts was a mistake. The man then led Casden through the town to a café where Casden was shown off and given a meal of lamb chops before heading for the railway station and being taken by local train to Paris.

Casden thought the man was called Champignon – he was about 40 years old, a heavy-set, balding man of medium height. He sheltered Casden for the night but it was clear that he wanted Casden to move on and after consulting a map, Casden decided he would like to go to Bayonne. Next day, Champignon took Casden to the gare d'Austerlitz, bought a third-class ticket (which cost Casden 400 francs) and put him on the train but there were no available seats and Casden, who had no experience of French trains, was unsure if he would be allowed to travel standing up. Seeing a young girl sitting alone in a compartment, Casden asked if he could share with her. She immediately realised he wasn't French and leaned out of the window to consult with her young man who was on the platform. Champignon was also there and Casden decided to take the chance and tell the young man who he was. The young man asked if Casden had any papers and when told that he did not, offered to get him some and so Casden got off the train. Casden didn't have photographs either so he and Champignon went to a department store to get pictures taken (six for twelve francs) and then spent the rest of the day sight-seeing until it was time to go to the café where they were due to meet the young man. At the café they met Auguste Valentin Brila (who worked on the wagon-lits) and his friend Paul (a short, blond, married man who worked as an agent with the Police Bureau) who told Casden that he would be leaving by aircraft within the next two weeks. M. Brila took Casden to Le Perreux-sur-Marne (east of the city) and his home at 99 rue du Maréchal Joffre, where Brila suggested that Casden could pose as his deaf and dumb son. Three days later, he presented Casden with a new identity card, courtesy of Paul.

Unfortunately, when M. Brila took Casden back into Paris, the man they were hoping to meet failed to arrive and on telephoning Paul, learned that he had been arrested with 50,000 bread tokens in his possession – which cancelled the aircraft idea. Paul then suggested that Casden wait a few days after which he would be taken to Marseille to board a submarine but apparently the Allied landings of 12 July on Sicily put a stop to that plan and contact with Paul was lost soon afterwards.

Casden spent the next four months living in some squalor at Le Perreux-sur-Marne, Auguste Brila apparently being unwilling to let Casden go for fear he might "fall into the wrong hands" but towards the end of September, a neighbour's child realised that Casden was an American airman and word quickly spread. Casden was taken to stay with an old man named Cartalade (at 17 rue Denfert Rochereau – query) for a few days before returning to the Brila household where, despite staying in his room, word soon spread again, this time as far as the local resistance chief, who said he had to be moved.

"One night they came for me with Alfred and Emile Courtet of 6 rue Nouvelle Monceau. They had pistols, slouch hats, horn-rimmed glasses and false moustaches. There were look-outs on every corner. It was all very Hollywood, and all very bad. I went to the home of Alfred and Emile where I was given new civilian clothes and a really good identity card." (Casden MIS-X #355)

It was not until about 28 November (five months after he bailed out) that Casden seems to have been taken on by anyone associated with an escape network when Marie Therese Labadie (31 years old, about five feet tall with jet black hair) and Elsa Janine MacCarthy (Irish, about 45 years old, plump with greying hair) took him to the gare d'Austerlitz. They handed Casden over to a blonde-haired nurse (about 19 or 20 years old, about 5 foot 6 inches tall, nicely dressed, with a floating eye over which she had no control) who took him to an apartment at 74 rue du Moulin Vert, Paris XIV where he stayed overnight with Mme Vve Cecile Maynial (about 45 to 50 years old with henna dyed hair), and next day Maurice Bidaud took Casden to his Garage du Parc in Juvisy-sur-Orge.

Casden slept in a hotel next door to the garage for three nights, along with an escaped POW called Edmond, during which time Maurice's wife Marie went into Paris and returned to tell Casden that the organisation (sic) had been caught and that Marie Christine had been arrested (this was Madeleine Melot, arrested 19 November). Maurice Bidaud took him to visit wine merchant André Lefevre at 29 rue Hoche where three other American airmen – T/Sgt Otto Bruzewski (#320), Sgt William Howell (#328) and 1/Lt Norman Schroeder (#329) – were just leaving for the Pyrenees with the Bourgogne escape line.

Albert and Emile Courtet stayed in touch with Casden and he returned to Le Perreux to spend Christmas with them but on 26 December, Marie Therese Labadie took Casden to the home of an English woman (Lily Asselanidis) where he met Andrew Hathaway (#346), and Mlle Labadie took them both her house in Ecouen where they stayed with her and her mother for the next three weeks. Casden says that while they were at Ecouen, Marie Therese contacted Miss MacCarthy who got in touch with another organisation, and on about 6 January, a striking blonde woman called Nell came to see them.

Mme Helene Gill (aka Nell aka Mme Antoine) (née Feodossief 12 May 1917 in Petrograd) of 12 rue Le Sueur, Paris XVI, was naturalised as a

French citizen in 1936 but then became a British subject by marriage to Englishman James Charles William Gill (who was interned at La Grande Caserne, Saint Denis) and had a young son named Daniel. Like Marguerite Schmitz, Nell worked with the John Carter organisation until Carter was captured in early January 1944.

Mme Gill says in her diaries that it was her John Carter contact, Jean-Pierre de la Hutiere, who sent her to collect Casden and Hathaway from Ecouen on 13 January, and Jacques Dupuis who gave her Mme Schmitz address to deliver them to that same evening.

Nell took Casden and Hathaway to stay with Marguerite Schmitz at 87 rue Rochechouart, where they joined S/Sgt Walter Dickerman (#354), F/O Norman Maybee RCAF and S/Sgt Paul Saunders. There was also a suspicious character staying there (variously named as Olaf/Olafson/Alfred/Fred) who claimed to be Norwegian. On 17 January they were visited by Madeleine Dupre (this was Madeleine Grador) and others, and by Mary-Rose Zerling (aka Claudette) who worked for Captain Hamilton. Casden says that Claudette's organisation was prepared to take them on and next day (18 January) she took Casden, Hathaway, Maybee and Saunders to "another house". That evening, they were questioned by Captain Hamilton (a short dark man with a moustache) who asked them about the Flatiron building (in New York) and theatres in Times Square, before Claudette took them to the station. They were joined by a girl, a young man and an elderly man who took them by overnight train to Saint-Brieuc – where Maybee and Saunders were arrested by a French gendarme. Casden and Hathaway were taken to a room above a bar while they waited for the train for Plouha.

F/O Norman W Maybee RCAF baled out of 401 Sqn Spitfire MH845 near Gravelines on 20 December 1943 following a collision with another aircraft from his own squadron. S/Sgt Paul R Saunders was one of the waist-gunners of 384BG/547BS B-17 42-30033 Little America (Goulder) which was abandoned over Belgium on 1 December 1943 after the loss of three engines. The two men were brought to Paris by Mary-Rose Zerling and lodged initially with Mme Mansienne at 10 rue de Geoffroy Marie.

Saunders says (in a letter dated 22 May 1946 to Major John F White Jnr of MIS-X) that they were arrested by the Chief of Gendarmes at Saint-Brieuc, and that after holding them for 36 hours, and being fully aware they were evading Allied airmen, he handed them over to the Gestapo. Saunders describes the man as being a "definite collaborator".

"They arranged to arrive at Saint-Brieuc at about four o'clock in the afternoon, when inspections were likely to be the most relaxed. Apart from the first two airmen, none of the evaders were questioned about their papers. It was the responsibility of the Saint-Brieuc crew to look after the evaders for an hour or so until the connection to the local train arrived. Sometimes they went to Mme Boschat, who had a café-tabac, and sometimes to M. Le Ster, who lived nearby, to wait for the local train to take them to Plouha. At Saint-Brieuc, the new guides were often young girls from the local youth hostel – Henri Le Blais and Adolphe Le Troquer thought they would attract less suspicion.

The evaders were then dropped off in small groups at Kertugal, Plouha-Ville, Plouha-Embranchement, Keregal, Dernier-Sou and Lanloup. At each stop, a member of the Plouha group, Marie-Thérèse Le Calvez, Pierre Huet, Job Mainguy or Jean Tréhiou, waited to take the men to their new hosts scattered amongst the community – Mme Léonie Le Calvez at Kerlérot, Mlle Françoise Monjaret at Ville-Dé, Mme Marie Tréhiou at Lizandré, famille Couffon at Kérizago, famille Lesné at Kerverzio, famille Ropers at Camblac'h, and Jean and Marie Gicquel at Saint-Samson." (my translation from Huguen 1976)

The train which took the evaders from Saint-Brieuc to Plouha was the one metre gauge Chemin de Fer des Côtes-du-Nord (CdN) – aka "Le Petit Train" or "Le Tortillard". There were numerous CdN routes but this particular line ran to Paimpol from Saint-Brieuc gare Centrale (which is now a university building at boulevard Waldeck Rousseau) and just a few hundred metres from the main-line Saint-Brieuc Ouest station.

Note that it was only the men taken out on this first Bonaparte operation who travelled on the CdN Saint-Brieuc to Paimpol line, and they probably got off at either Plouha-Embranchement (which was south of the town, near the first roundabout of the present-day D786) or Plouha-Ville, on the western edge of the town, near the mairie and behind the present-day Collège Jean-Louis Hamon, or perhaps the unmanned "halte" at Keregal.[10]

10 My thanks to Daniel Droniou, Roland Savidan and l'Association des Chemins de Fer des Côtes-du-Nord for the locations.

S/Sgt James A King (#343) was the tail-gunner of 305BG/365BS B-17 42-29530 (Moore) which was shot down by flak near Saint-Martin-au-Laert (Nord-Pas-de-Calais) on the afternoon of 27 August 1943 during an operation against a rocket site near Saint Omer. The only other successful evader was Combat Photographer S/Sgt William S Wood (#252) who had joined the aircraft shortly before take-off. He was helped soon after landing and sheltered with Marguerite Fillerin and her children at Renty before being passed to the Bordeaux-Loupiac organisation at Auxi-le-Chateau, and taken across the Pyrenees to Spain in November.

James King, from Morton, Mississippi, was 27 years old and had already served eight years in the army when he bailed out. He landed in the backyard of a farm near Watton and as he was discarding his parachute harness, a woman at the farm pointed to a haystack where she helped him hide just moments before a group of German soldiers arrived. While the woman directed the soldiers one way, King ran off in the other direction to hide in a ditch until dark before making his way south across the fields. Early the following morning, King approached a farmer who invited King into his house where he was given breakfast and a packet of food before being sent on his way again. The following day, King was intercepted by another farmer who pointed towards two women in the fields. They already had a bundle of civilian clothes for him and after King had changed, he was taken to a house where his journey was arranged.

That afternoon, three men came with bicycles and took King to the home of a railway station-master in Cassel. He asked King for some identification and when he saw the photographs King was carrying, tore them up (they were too small) and took new ones. The next morning, King was told that he would leave by aircraft within the next ten days and the day after that, King was taken to a chemists shop in Armentieres where he was given new clothes and shoes before going on to stay with Raoul Demagt and his wife at 41 rue Paul Bert where he met 2/Lt Francis Harkins (#115). Harkins left on about 4 September when the chemist's wife (Mme van Kemmel) took him to Amiens and the Joe Balfe organisation, which passed him on to Comète, and Harkins crossed the Pyrenees to Spain later that month.

On 10 September, King was moved about four kilometres to the village of Frelinghien to stay with Raoul's nephew, Robert Demagt (Robert's father Paul was Raoul's brother) and his wife Cecile at 15 rue d'Armentieres, where he met S/Sgt Walter Sentkoski (#348) and 2/Lt Joseph Birdwell

(#471). On 28 October, Sentkoski and Birdwell left for Villereau (see later) and on 26 November, Marie-Rose Zerling (Claudette) took all three of them to Paris. They stayed overnight with her parents at 12 rue Saint-Ferdinand and next day, King was taken to stay with Bertranne d'Hespel at 7 rue Maspero. A Gestapo scare soon had King moved again, this time to stay with Mme Lucienne Mansienne (born Sept 1893) at 10 rue Geoffoy Marie, Paris IX, where he joined Sentkoski for five days before Mme d'Hespel took him back to rue Maspero – where he was later rejoined by Sentkoski. On 19 January, King and Sentkoski left for Saint-Brieuc and Plouha with 1/Lt Richard Smith (#349) and 2/Lt Morton Shapiro (#353).

Robert and Cecile Demagt of 15 rue d'Armentieres, Frelinghien were arrested on 29 November 1943 – betrayed (with many others, including Marie Boidin) by Pte Robert Norgan, a British soldier they had sheltered earlier who was captured that month – and deported. Cecile (born April 1907) returned but Robert (born August 1905) died in Germany. Robert's father, Paul Demagt (married to Elvire) was also arrested and deported – he died in Germany on 7 April 1945.

Comtesse Mme Vve Bertranne Marie d'Hespel (née de la Bourdonnais Sept 1919 – her husband was killed in 1939) was a 24-year-old medical student who lived at 7 rue Maspero, Paris XVI. She was recruited in November 1943 (query) by Bernard d'Havrincourt (who she sheltered while he was being hunted by the Germans) and Marie-Rose Zerling. Mme d'Hespel is credited with sheltering nineteen airmen (giving some of them much needed medical attention) and on 21 March 44 convoyed six men from Paris to Guingamp (see later). Mme d'Hespel also sheltered several evaders for reseau François after the Bonaparte operations, at least some of whom were sent to the MI9 camp at Chateaudun (Freteval). Mme d'Hespel was arrested on 15 June 1944 when her apartment was raided by the Gestapo looking for Bernard d'Havrincourt – taken to rue des Saussaies, she denied all knowledge of him and was released three hours later. Mme Vve d'Hespel was recommended for a KMC.

S/Sgt Walter J Sentkoski (#348) was the engineer/TTG of 390BG/569BS B-17 42-3306 Phoenix (Lawrence) which was abandoned to crash near Sainte-Marie-Kerque (Nord-Pas-de-Calais) on 15 August 1943 following a mid-air collision with another B-17 which cut off their tail.

Three other crew from the Phoenix also evaded successfully: bombardier 2/Lt Francis Harkins (#115) (mentioned above), co-pilot 2/Lt William F Middledorf (#114), who evaded for a while with Harkins before crossing the Pyrenees to Spain with Comète on 29 August 1943 – and 2/Lt Joseph Birdwell (#471).

Sentkoski was just four days short of his twenty-second birthday when he jumped, delaying opening his parachute until about 5,000 feet, and then landing close to a farmhouse. While he was removing his parachute harness, a number of people watched but only a young girl offered him any help. Sentkoski was using his phrase-card to ask where the Germans were when an elderly man came over, took his parachute and flying gear and led him to a barn. At about midnight, the farmer and a girl who spoke English suggested that Sentkoski go to the nearby town and sit near the doorway of a large factory. As he was still in his uniform, Sentkoski didn't think much of that idea and so set off walking through the night, accidently straying into the field where the remains of his crashed aircraft were being guarded by two German soldiers. He walked until daylight when he found a haystack to sleep in for the rest of the day. That evening, he approached a farmhouse, and after using sign language and his phrase-card to explain that he needed food and clothing, acquired an old coat and cap (for which he paid 30 francs) before heading off once more. After another day of walking and a night in a field, Sentkoski approached another farmhouse where he explained that he was an American airman. The farmer promptly invited Sentkoski into the house where he was given breakfast with the family. The farmer was on his way to work and so Sentkoski was told to spend the day in a nearby field (where he was supplied with food by the farmer's family) and that evening, the farmer brought a man who could help him.

Sentkoski was sheltered in Frelinghien with Robert and Cecile Demagt at 15 rue d'Armentieres where he was soon joined by his navigator Joseph Birdwell, and then on 10 September by S/Sgt James King (#343). On 28 October, Sentkoski and Birdwell met Marie-Rose Zerling (Claudette) in Armentieres and she took them to Villereau where they stayed for four weeks with Emile Ducarne and his wife.

"On the 20th of November 1943, I heard about some so-called Gestapo investigations which were likely to endanger Mr Ducarne, and I decided to evacuate Birdwell, Sentkoski and King. I took them to Valenciennes, where I managed to lodge them with Mrs. Dietz. They spent about 48 hours in her

house, without her husband, her six children, or her maid knowing, taking their meals at Mr Singier's restaurant, 10 place d'Armes, which served us with perfect discretion. I then took them to Paris." (my translation from Rapport par Marie-Rose Zerling, 28 Fev 1946)

On 26 November, Claudette took Sentkoski, Birdwell and King to Paris where they stayed overnight with Claudette's parents at 12 rue Saint-Ferdinand. Next day, Sentkoski was taken to the 5th floor apartment of Lucienne Mansienne at 10 rue de Geoffroy Marie where he stayed for three weeks before being taken to stay overnight at 7 rue Maspero, where King was being sheltered by Bertranne d'Hespel – Sentkowski noting that Count Bernard d'Havrincourt was also living there. Next day, Sentkoski was moved again, this time to stay for twelve days with Mlle Genevieve Robin at 3 rue de la Cité Universitaire until Claudette returned him to rue Maspero, where he again rejoined James King. On 19 January, Sentkoski and King left for Saint-Brieuc and Plouha with 1/Lt Richard Smith (#349) and 2/Lt Morton Shapiro (#353).

The B-17s 42-30674 Destiny's Tot (Smith), 42-29963 Judy (Camp), 42-5997 Heaven Can Wait (Smith) and 42-31173 Maid to Please (Schrero), and the B-24s 42-7548 Bull O' The Woods (Heskett), 42-63973 (Schafer) and 42-7588 (Sibley) were among the many USAAF aircraft lost on a morning raid to Ludwigshafen on 30 December 1943. Their planned route took the bombers south to Fecamp before they headed east over Belgium to their target. The return route was further south, touching Luxembourg and passing north of Paris, and back to the coast.[11]

1/Lt Richard M Smith (#349), **2/Lt William H Booher** (#350), **T/Sgt Alphonse M Mele** (#351) and **S/Sgt Jerry Eshuis** (#352) were the pilot, co-pilot, radio operator and ball-turret gunner of 95BG/336BS B-17 42-30674 Destiny's Tot which lost one engine and was attacked by fighters before being abandoned to crash near Campremy (Oise), north-east of Beauvais.

Three other crew from Destiny's Tot also evaded successfully: navigator 2/Lt Louis Feingold (#419) and bombardier 2/Lt Warren Tarkington (#420) (see both later), and TTG/engineer T/Sgt Kenneth A Morrison

11 Brian D O'Neill "Half a Wing, Three Engines and a Prayer" Special Revised Version (1998) McGraw-Hill.

(#690) who was helped by Bourgogne and crossed the Pyrenees to Spain in April 1944.

22-year-old Richard Smith jumped from about 12,000 feet but delayed opening his parachute until about 2,500 feet. He says that he saw farmers in the fields below staring up at the chutes of his crew and that some were running towards the burning aircraft. He landed in a ploughed field, and after rolling his parachute into a ball and leaving it in a furrow, ran towards a farmer who was ploughing at the other end of the field. The farmer pointed to where other parachutes had landed and Smith set off in that direction. He was soon intercepted by three men who told him the Germans had already reached his aircraft and confirmed that some of his crew had landed in the direction he was headed. Smith swapped a Mars bar for some apples and carried on running but soon encountered more local men, one of whom directed him a clump of trees where he wanted Smith to hide and wait for him. At about six o'clock, Smith's helper returned with another man, who took charge of the American. Smith was given civilian clothes in exchange for his uniform and flying gear (keeping only his dog-tags), and taken back to his new helper's house, from where his journey was arranged.

Smith was taken across the fields to a railway line, which they followed to the village of Wavignies. He says that he was taken in the back way to a school which turned out to be a jail, and that his new helper, who was known as August but went under another name, was apparently sheriff of three counties. There was another man there, and Smith was taken by truck on a fifteen-minute ride to a farm where he met his co-pilot, William Booher.

William Booher was 23 years old when he made his delayed drop (as per the advice given in his E&E lectures), not pulling his ripcord until entering a small cloud at about 4,000 feet. He saw several people watching him soon after landing, as well as another parachute in a field nearby, and he was heading towards the second parachute when he was intercepted by a woman speaking English. Having confirmed that he was an American, a crowd soon gathered and Booher was led to the nearby village where three women took him into a house. They stayed while he changed into civilian clothes (keeping only his beige sweater) and a few minutes later, a man referred to as August arrived. August took him through some back alleys to a house where a doctor told him that two men from his crew (waist-gunners S/Sgt Robert F Adams and S/Sgt Anthony Onesi) had been found badly injured and sent to hospital. That evening, August brought his pilot, Richard Smith.

After being given some food, Smith and Booher were questioned by August and three other men about their target, who was their pilot, were they shot at by Germans. They were visited by a doctor (Edmond Caillard) who told them that two badly wounded airmen had been found (he thought they would both die) and had been trying to help a third man, a radio operator, but the Germans had stopped his car and he had had to turn him over to them. He also told them that he knew about another airman who they would meet next day. After the doctor left, Smith and Booher were put into a back bedroom, and at about midnight, August brought their radio operator, Alphonse Mele, to join them.

Alphonse Mele also delayed his jump, the 36–year-old ex-contractor from the Bronx finally pulling his rip-cord at about 3,000 feet and then watching as his aircraft crashed and burned. He remembered the advice given to him by a paratrooper and made a good rolling landing but before he could stand up, was surrounded by a group of Frenchmen, which included Georges Desfosse (nf), Gilbert Santune and his brothers, Germain and Gaston. One asked if he were Polish and when Mele replied that he was American, they gathered up his flying gear and took him to a barn near Wavignies, belonging to a M. Desesquelle. Gilbert Santune, brought Mele civilian clothing and told him (mostly by sign-language) that he would return at about eight o'clock and that meanwhile, Mele was to hide himself in the hay. M. Santune duly returned that evening and took Mele for a ten-minute walk to his house on rue du Tour du Pré in Wavignies, where Mele met his wife and two children, and the wife washed some of the blood off his face. Mele was given a meal, and a few hours later, was taken on foot about three kilometres to a farmhouse. He was put into a bedroom where he slept until midnight when a man referred to as August arrived and took Mele to another house, where he joined his pilot Richard Smith.

Dr Edmond Jean Baptiste Caillard (born April 1912 in Noumea, New Caledonia) of 6 boulevard Valentin-Hauy, Saint-Just-en-Chaussée, was married to Suzanne Marguerite (née Mangeol) with three young children. Dr Caillard began helping evaders in January 1943 when evasion activities in the Oise district, and especially around Saint-Just, were exceptionally active. He is credited by IS9 with helping between 20 and 30 Allied personnel, convoying, sheltering and giving them medical assistance where necessary, and was recommended for a King's Medal for Courage. MIS-X say that as a medical man he had the use of his car which he used to transport evaders from one point to another to avoid their capture – and credit him with helping as many as 87 Allied evaders, including sending some of the more seriously wounded to hospital. Dr Caillard names numerous other helpers, most of whom are included in this story.

Gilbert Santune (born Aug 1917) macon (bricklayer) of rue du Tour du Pré (now rue du Jeu de Paume), Wavignies (married with two young children) says he passed Mele on to Henri Vincenot (aka Gustave), chef de groupe, shot by the Germans on 3 July 1944 for helping Allied airmen. He also lists Doctor Caillard of Saint-Just-en-Chaussée, Marcel Bertin (chef de gare) and Mme Marie Reant of rue Gorelier (whose husband Henri died at Buchenwald) of Wavignies as the people he knew who were involved with helping Allied evaders.

Henri Vincenot (born April 1907) (aka Gustave) of Chateau de Wavignies (where he and his wife were caretakers), was married (on 30 Nov 1935) to Yvonne Jeanne Marie (née Lesné June 1912 in Saint-Brieuc) and they had two small children, Yves and Bernard. The chateau was raided on 3 July 1944 while a meeting of resistance people was in progress – betrayed by a man known as Raoul (Anicet Deilhes) – and Henri was killed in the subsequent gun-fire. Two RAF evaders – Sgt William C Brown (2196) and F/O Lou Greenburgh (2/149/321) – were helped to escape but two others – Sgt F J Carey and F/Sgt Richard Jack Woosnam (LIB/773) – were captured. Other evaders helped by the Vincenots include James Bormuth (#311), 2/ Lt Wendell McConnaha, Jerry Eshuis (#352) and Eldo Weseloh (#1001). In July 2010, a new road in Wavignies was named as rue Henri Vincenot.

It's not clear exactly where the three Americans were first brought together but they were soon taken by truck to Saint-Just-en-Chaussée and a house at 61 rue de Paris, home of Paul Begue and Yvonne Fossier, where they stayed until 10 January.

Paul Begue (born April 1918) (celibataire with an 18-month-old child) of 61 rue de Paris, Saint-Just-en-Chaussée, claims to have sheltered Smith and Mele (passed to him by Georges Jauneau) and Booher and the injured Jerry Eshuis (passed to him by Dr Caillard) for 6 days, although I don't think that Eshuis actually stayed there.

Only Richard Smith's file contains any detailed notes on the four men's evasions and they are hand-written, so extracting some of the finer details is sometimes difficult. However, research by Dominique Lecomte suggests that in Saint-Just-en-Chaussée, Smith, Booher and Mele were helped by Georges Jauneau – aka Capitaine Jacques (born Nov 1906), organiser of the Francs Tireurs Partisans (FTP) group "Jacques Bonhomme" – who lived with his wife Paulette of 58 (or 57) rue de Paris.[12]

Smith reports that at the house in Saint-Just-en-Chaussée, they met a man called Pierre, apparently brother-in-law of the woman who lived there, and Jacques – a tall, thin, tough looking man who spoke English (assume Georges Jauneau). The three Americans lived alone in the house with their food brought by Paulette Jeaneau. They received visits from August, and Jacques, who told them he had seen two of their officers (Feingold and Tarkington) and that they had been taken to Clermont (see later).

A week later, the activities around the usually empty house raised suspicions in the neighbourhood, and Georges Jauneau moved the three Americans to 61 rue de Paris where they were sheltered with Paul Begue and Yvonne Fossier, who had just become parents to a baby girl they named Paulette.

21-year-old Jerry Eshuis says that he saw waist-gunner S/Sgt Robert F Adams sitting by the escape hatch which was jammed until Mele got it open. Mele then pushed both Adams and Eshuis out before following them, and because he had been wounded in the leg and shoulder and was feeling dizzy, Eshuis opened his parachute almost immediately. By the time he got close to the ground he was drifting towards a village (Fumechon) where most of the population were watching him. He saw Adams land and then hit the ground about 100 yards from him. Eshuis was soon surrounded by local people, including a young boy named Gervais Gorge, who helped him with his parachute before taking him back to his house in the village, not even letting him stop to talk to Adams.

Eshuis had to be kissed by every member of the Gorge family – the father (a large man with just one arm), mother and brother – before his clothes were taken away, his various injuries treated and civilian clothing provided. Gervais went to fetch the local doctor (Dr Edmond Caillard of Saint-Just-en-Chaussée) and when he arrived, Eshuis learned that he had

12 As well as being a friend for many years, Dominique Lecomte is chairman of the ASAA (Association des Sauveteurs d'Aviateurs Allies), and an expert on researching evader stories in his local area of l'Oise.

already seen Adams and sent him to a hospital. Once Eshuis was dressed, he was fed and put into a bed but two and a half hours later, his helpers moved him to a barn because of German searches. He was carefully hidden in the hay but the Germans did no more than drive up and down the road, enquiring at houses whether anyone had seen any parachutists. After spending the rest of the night and all next day in the barn, only visiting the house at meal times, at midnight of the second day, the doctor returned. He drove Eshuis to Saint-Just-en-Chaussée, where he saw his pilot Richard Smith and co-pilot William Booher, and then on to Sains-Morainvillers, about 8 kms north-east of Saint-Just, where Eshuis was sheltered by Jacques and Colette de Baynast at their Chateau de la Borde until 10 January.

Jacques Georges Henri de Baynast (born Oct 1902) was married to Colette (née de Hauteclocque in 1906, sister of General Leclerc) – they had 8 children, aged between 3 and 14. Jacques was a farmer at Sains-Morainvillers, and he and his wife are credited with helping 15 Allied evaders, many of whom were then passed to Dr Caillard.

After being helped by the organisation in Saint-Just-en-Chaussée, all four men were taken to Paris on 10 January. Smith says they were taken by car, that he (at least) was given a hand-gun and told they would not be stopping for any German check-points and that they would shoot it out if necessary. In the capital, they were met by a young man called Pierre (about 21 years old, he was studying to be a history teacher), and the Americans were sheltered with English-born widow Rose Coulon at 204 boulevard Pereire, Paris XVII. Two days later, they were moved to 24 boulevard des Capucines, Paris IX where they stayed with the concierge, Albert Poncelet, and his step-son Pierre. They were also visited by Jacky du Pac and 2/Lt Joe Birdwell (#471) (who had delayed his own departure from Paris to work with the organisation, helping to check the identities of US airmen) who wanted their names, ranks and ASNs that they said would be sent to London. Birdwell returned later with Marie-Rose Zerling (Claudette), who gave Smith a "fairly thorough" briefing on his upcoming trip, and just before he left, Smith also received a visit from a dapper, hook-nosed Englishman (sic) known as Hamilton, who was head of the organisation, and later took them to the beach.

Jacky du Pac was Jacques Henri du Pac de Marsoulies. Born 1915 in Saigon, Jacky was multi-lingual and often interrogated evaders to confirm their identities. He had helped Val Williams of Oaktree (see later), and his main responsibility with reseau François was as the link between Paris and l'Oise. Always well dressed, Jacky would sometimes present himself as English, and is often referred to by American evaders as being a British Intelligence Officer (IO).

On Wednesday 19 January, Claudette arrived at rue Capucines to take Richard Smith to Montparnasse station, collecting Morton Shapiro (#353) (see below) from avenue Mozart along the way, where she pointed out a little Frenchman who was their guide (Adolphe Le Trocquer of Gommenec'h – query) and put them on an overnight train to Saint-Brieuc.

At Saint-Brieuc station next morning, their guide from Paris took Smith and Shapiro to another station and pointed out another man who bought their tickets before passing them to a new guide who took them to Plouha. Smith says that while they were in Saint-Brieuc, he met the head of the local organisation, a middle-aged man with blue eyes, a square flat nose and curly hair that he combed straight back. He was about 5 feet 8 inches tall, with a light complexion, and spoke very little English – presumably Henri Le Blais. Smith also noticed Walter Sentkoski and James King at the station, recognising Sentkoski as an American but thinking that King was his guide. At Plouha, the four Americans were passed on to a young girl, Marie-Thérèse Le Calvez, who took them to her mother's house.

Booher, Mele and Eshuis stayed on another night with Albert Poncelet and Pierre at rue Capucines, until the morning of Thursday 20 January when they travelled to Plouha with S/Sgt Walter Dickerman (#354). Eshuis says their guide to Plouha was a woman – I think he means from Paris but perhaps just from Saint-Brieuc.

2/Lt Morton B Shapiro (#353) was the navigator of 389BG/564BS B-24 42-63973 (Schafer) which was returning from Ludwigshafen on 30 December 1943 when they were attacked by fighters, and with one engine on fire, the aircraft went into a steep dive. It was brought under control again at about 12,000 feet and the pilot held it in level flight while the crew abandoned the aircraft, which finally crashed near Cambronne-les-Ribecourt, Oise.

Four other crew also evaded successfully: pilot 2/Lt Richard Schafer (#499) and waist-gunner S/Sgt Paul Dicken Snr (#500) (see both later), radio operator T/Sgt Felton R Luke (#618) who was helped by the John Carter organisation until the arrest of Jeanne Huet on 7 February when he was passed to Claude Charmet and taken across the Pyrenees in early March, and bombardier 1/Lt Robert V Krengle (#646) who made his way to Toulouse where he was helped by the Françoise Dissard organisation, and also crossed the Pyrenees in March.

Shapiro landed near the village of Berneuil-sur-Aisne (Oise) in the Foret de Compiegne and was still burying his parachute when a man ran up and asked (in good English) whether he was an American. He also asked if Shapiro could ride a bicycle and on learning that the 22-year-old American could not, led Shapiro to a cave in the nearby woods. The man's wife brought food and ration tickets that afternoon and the man himself came back later with some civilian clothes but no shoes, which meant that Shapiro had just his electrically heated boots. Once Shapiro had changed clothes, the man gave him directions to a sugar manufacturing plant in Berneuil-sur-Aisne where he was to ask for a M. Rinn. Shapiro followed the directions to the village (with some help from an elderly woman he met on the way) and on arrival, his first helper's wife met him in the street and took him to meet Marcel Rinn. M. Rinn kept Shapiro at the sugar plant until nightfall before driving him to his home near the railway station, where he lived with his wife Simone. Next morning, Shapiro's first helper and his wife took him to Paris and their apartment where he stayed with the wife while her husband went to find someone who could help Shapiro.

Arrangements were made for Shapiro to stay with a friend of the young couple, Jacques Aude (a French artillery lieutenant who spoke some English) at 28 rue George Sand, Paris XVI who seemed quite happy to keep Shapiro while the young couple looked for an organisation. A few days later, Shapiro received a visit from Claudette (Marie-Rose Zerling) and a young man who questioned Shapiro about his identity – Shapiro later learned that this was 2/Lt Joe Birdwell, an American evader who was working with the organisation helping to identify other American airmen. Shapiro was also visited by another girl who brought 2/Lt George Padgett who told Shapiro that he was staying in an apartment with 2/Lt Joe Burkowski. After five days with Jacques Aude, Claudette took Shapiro to stay with Mme Gabriele Maron and her daughter Suzanne at nearby 121 avenue Mozart, where he was visited by Captain Hamilton (Dumais). He also received another visit from Birdwell who told him that Claudette had gone to collect five airmen and that although they had already been caught, she did bring one American (S/Sgt Paul R Saunders) and one Canadian (F/O Norman W Maybee) back with her. On 19 January, Claudette arrived with 1/Lt Richard Smith (#349) to take Shapiro to the station where they were put on a train for Saint-Brieuc.[13]

2/Lt George C Padgett was the bombardier of 379BG/525BS B-17 42-29937 (Breidenthal) which was shot down near Rennes on 23 September 1943, and 2/Lt Joseph Burkowski was the bombardier of 379BG/524BS B-17 42-9893 El Diablo (Jamerson) which shot down south of Rennes on 16 September 1943 – both men were helped by Bourgogne before being captured at Toulouse railway station on 3 February 1944.

Gabrielle Maron and her daughter Suzanne (born Aug 1914) of 121 avenue Mozart, Paris XVI were arrested on 17 February 1944 and deported to Germany on 7 August. Suzanne Maron was repatriated to France in May 1945 but her mother Gabrielle died at Ravensbruck.

S/Sgt Walter E Dickerman (#354) was the tail-gunner of 447BG/711BS B-17 42-31173 Maid to Please (Schrero) which was returning from Ludwigshafen on 30 December 1943 when they were attacked by fighters and shot down near Henonville (Oise). Dickerman was only one of the ten-man crew to evade successfully.

20-year-old Dickerman followed the two waist-gunners (S/Sgt John C Bitzer and S/Sgt Herman F Holland) out of their doomed bomber, pulling his rip-cord as soon as he cleared the aircraft. He was helped on landing in a field just north of Beauvais by four men who cut him out of his parachute. They also supplied a bag into which Dickerman's parachute and flying gear were stuffed before taking him to a small house on a hill where he was hidden in the attic – and from where he was able to watch as one of his injured crewmates was captured by German soldiers. Dickerman was later given civilian clothes and moved into a hayloft where he stayed for four days, only coming down for meals, before being taken to a village, interrogated and turned over to a man who arranged his journey.

13 I have not been able to identify Shapiro's first helpers. The wife told Shapiro that her husband was 26 years old and had spent two years in a German prison camp, that she was 25 years old and they two children. They were apparently quite wealthy because in addition to the Paris apartment, the husband told Shapiro that he owned a large part of the woods where Shapiro was first hidden.

Dickerman was taken to a road where he was collected by car and driven to a village where he stayed with a man (not named) who ran a garage. Dickerman's helpers were unsure of his identity (he was not wearing his dog tags and had not been issued with an escape kit) until he was questioned by an unidentified Englishman who accepted his story. Dickerman was then moved to another village (probably Auneuil) where he was visited by an English-speaking Frenchman (5 ft 9 inches, dark hair, brown eyes, pale complexion – understood to be a solicitor) apparently the local organisation chief. This was Gilbert Thibault who passed Dickerman on to another man who drove him to Beauvais, where he was given identity papers, before a new guide took him by train to Paris. He was sheltered by Marguerite Schmitz at 87 rue Rochechourt for eleven days during which time he was visited by Claudette (Marie-Rose Zerling) who had a suspicious Norwegian known as Fred staying with her.

Fred, who could speak German, Dutch, French, Norwegian and English, claimed to have links to the BBC. He said that as a seventeen-year-old at the beginning of the war, he had left Norway and escaped to England. He claimed to have joined the British Army and been making a recording for the BBC when the B-17 he was flying in was shot down over Germany. He said that he was captured by the Germans but had escaped two days later with a Dutchman and returned to Norway before coming to France via Denmark.

On (about) 16 January, Dickerman met Sgt Saunders USAAF, P/O Maybee and 2/Lt Sidney Casden (#355), and on 19 January, Claudette took him to the apartment of a woman (described as old) where Casden and Andrew Hathaway (#346) had stayed previously. Next morning, the elderly woman took him to a Metro station where he met William Booher (see earlier) and they, Alphonse Mele and Jerry Eshuis, were taken by train to Saint-Brieuc and Plouha.

Sgt Fred T Schmitt (#344) and **Sgt John L Sullivan Jnr** (#345) were the tail-gunner and ball-turret gunner of 392BG/578BS B-24 42-7588 (Sibley) which was hit by flak over Ludwigshafen on 30 December which damaged at least two engines. They slowly lost touch with their formation and the aircraft was finally abandoned to crash near Montaure in Upper Normandy.

All ten crew landed safely but the only other successful evaders were top-turret gunner Sgt Nicholas M Carusone (#415) and navigator 2/

Lt William L Olsen (#448) who were both helped by Robert Thiriet in Paris and crossed the Pyrenees together two weeks later. Bombardier 2/Lt Edward M Boyle and radio operator S/Sgt Peter Garris were following the same route as Olsen and Carusone but Olsen was told in Spain that they were captured at Peyrehorade.

21-year-old Fred Schmitt says that the aircraft was in a slow spin when he pushed Sgt Everett F Satterley, who was manning a waist-gun, out of the waist-hatch just before Sullivan pushed him out at about 10,000 feet. He delayed pulling his rip-cord until going through some clouds and then landed in a ploughed field. He went to help another man, waist-gunner S/Sgt Frederick M Wald, who was injured but then left him because he thought the approaching Frenchmen were Germans. He then saw two other men land and ran towards them, finding Satterly in a tree and spotting Sullivan in the next field.

20-year-old John Sullivan says that after he pushed Schmitt out of the aircraft, he tried to help Sgt Wald but he had passed out at altitude and was still rather dazed. In the end Sullivan and Wald left the aircraft together, Sullivan blacking out when he pulled his rip-cord. The next thing he remembered was being on the ground (probably near La Saussaye, Eure) and some Frenchmen taking off his parachute. Sullivan started running and then saw Schmitt and Satterley running towards him and all three then ran to hide in a haystack while they regained their breath. They were soon surrounded by local men, and the Americans decided they should head for some nearby woods. On the way, two men with bicycles directed them to a hiding place and said they would return that evening. However, rather than wait near where their aircraft had crashed, the Americans decided to use their compasses to head south. That evening they tried to communicate with a man they found ploughing but they didn't have any common language and the airmen had not been issued with phrase-cards. Eventually the man pointed to a house where a man and woman took them in and provided bread, butter, cider and wine but were unwilling to let them stay the night. Finally, the couple took the three evaders to a barn where later they heard voices speaking English and found that two more of their crew, TTG Sgt Nicholas Carusone (#415) and radio operator S/Sgt Peter Garris, had come to the same barn.

The five Americans set off together early the next morning but soon decided they should split into smaller groups – Schmitt, Sullivan and Satterley staying together. At one stage they found themselves on a main road and suddenly saw a German army truck full of soldiers approaching but they remembered an E&E lecture given by Capt Robert Nelson (#170) and Sgt Raymond Genz (#171) describing a similar situation, and simply ignored it – the truck driving past despite them still being dressed in their flying covers and boots. Later that same day, as they approached the outskirts of a village, a French boy approached them and the Americans tried out their newly acquired French word for food. After bringing some bread and butter, the boy led them to a house where they met several people who donated civilian clothes – one of men even handed over his shoes – and from there, their journey was arranged.

> *On their return to the UK, American evaders were interviewed by MIS-X, and in many cases, their interviewer was 1/Lt Donald Emerson. Whilst I have no reason to doubt that Emerson was an efficient officer (he also went on to become a highly respected history lecturer), one of the great challenges of writing this story has been deciphering his hand-written, almost short-hand, notes – which can be close to illegible. Just to make it more interesting, Lt Emerson often wrote French names phonetically, as in the cases of "Elf Boules" and "Caré", which had me guessing for a while, and "Odeon" – which I thought was hilarious.*

Schmitt and Sullivan's combined report is in Donald Emerson's trademark style, and very hard to read from this point but they met a priest who supplied them with trousers, shirts and jackets, before taking them back his house (at Pinterville – query), where he had dog-tags from WG Frederick Wald and their pilot, 2/Lt James H Sibley. A couple of days later, three men came in a truck, Roger Mesle (about 26 years old and described by Schmitt as being about 5 ft 7 inches tall, 135 lbs, with dark wavy hair and a bad complexion – Schmitt thought that he had been in French army, possibly the motorcycle corps) – Jacques Saillard (about 22 years old, 5 ft 9 inches tall, 155 lbs, with long, light-coloured wavy hair, good looking, dressed very well, like a sportsman), and the driver, a M. Gagoin (nf), garagiste of Beaumont-le-Roger. They were driven for about an hour and half to a house in Beaumontel where they found their pilot (Sibley), co-pilot (2/Lt Leonard Volet) and waist-gunner (Wald). They also met a Spitfire pilot called Tony – P/O Anthony Bradshaw (see below) – and a B-17 radio operator called Paul – he was from NY, had broken hips, and been shot down seven months earlier – this was T/Sgt Paul J Ruska from B-17 42-30105 Slightly Dangerous (Sarchet), which was shot down on 10 July 1943.

Roger Mesle (born 6 Jan 1917) of Beaumontel, says he first became involved with helping Allied evaders when he heard that 2/Lt Norman Toft, S/Sgt Robert A Vandergriff and Sgt Delbert W Klump from B-17 42-3300, and F/O John W Brace (LIB/1264) bomb-aimer of Halifax DK240, were being sheltered in the town with Mme Trumelet. A man called Antoine (Brace says Antoine worked closely with their hostess) had taken them to Le Mans at the beginning of September but failed to find a contact there and so brought them back to Beaumontel, where they were returned to Mme Trumelet. While looking for a network for the repatriation of the aviators, Mesle says he came into contact with M. Valon (aka Amede), and through an intermediary of the Liberation group, Therese. Mesle also knew a man named Bouchard (nf) at Sucy-en-Brie, whose niece was in contact with Mme de Milleville (Mary Lindell) and Mesle says that he and Bouchard took the four airmen to Mme de Milleville at Ruffec.

John Brace says in his Liberation report that it was their hostess (assume Mme Trumelet) who took them as far as Paris on 5 November, along with a female representative of the organisation in Ruffec, who took them on to Ruffec next day by herself. All four airmen, and the French girl (Genevieve Favre) who was their guide from Ruffec, were captured on 20 November 1943 on a train from Limoges to Pau.

Later that year, Mesle learned that Mme Trumelet was sheltering F/Lt William C Dallin (pilot of 35 Sqn Halifax HR798, which was shot down the night of 11-12 Nov 1943). Mesle took Dallin to Paris, intending to take him on to Ruffec but on telephoning M. Bouchard, discovered that Mme de Milleville and several members of her organisation had been arrested. Mesle brought Dallin back to Beaumontel and placed him with M. Bouchard. It was at about this time that Mesle heard about the injured Paul Ruska, and placed him with blanket salesman Georges Ecalard and his wife Jeanne at Serquigny.

James Sibley told Schmitt and Sullivan that he had seen Olsen and Boyle's parachutes open, and that their aircraft had hit hard and gone up in flames. That night, Roger Mesle and Jacques Saillard took Everett Satterley and Spitfire pilot Anthony Bradshaw to another house. The following night, Roger took Schmitt and Sullivan to stay with an English couple – he had fought with the British in the first war and was a nationalised Frenchman, and they had son called Jacques in the French army who had been working in Germany. Schmitt and Sullivan stayed with the "English family" for about a week (5-12 January) until a friend came to ask if they would like to go to Paris with him.

Jacques was Jacques Lenferna de la Motte, and his parents were Paul Lenferna de la Motte (born 1891) and Ellen (née Singery). One of eleven children, Jacques was born in June 1911 on Mauritius. The island was a French colony (Ile de France) from 1710 until the British took it over in 1810, and although French continues to be the dominant language, it remained under British rule until the island's independence in 1968 – hence the "English family".

Jacques was a radio mechanic who lived with his parents in Beaumont-le-Roger. Schmitt and Sullivan describe him as being about 34 years old, 5 ft 9 inches tall, with a thick beard, thin lips, deep-set bulging eyes, a high forehead and thinning hair – he was round-shouldered and had stubbed hands that had been hurt in a weather-balloon incident.

Jacques says that on 3 Jan 44, Roger Mesle asked him to take charge of two American airmen from a B-17 (sic) that had been shot down near Saint-Didier, near Louviers. On 12 Jan, he asked a friend from Paris, Karel Wybrands (who was in the resistance) to come to Beaumont to discuss the possibility of repatriating the two Americans. On 14 January, 6 Gestapo men came to his parents' house with their chief Otto Meyer .. Denounced and arrested in early 1944, Jacques was sent to Auschwitz in April, transferred to Buchenwald the following month. When the Americans started advancing, Lenferna de la Motte was among 5,000 inmates who were sent to Flossenburg. He was liberated in May 1945, returning to France with dysentery, tuberculosis in both lungs and a double hernia.

P/O Anthony Bradshaw (LIB/884) was escorting Mosquito bombers in 129 Sqn Spitfire MH425 on 23 December 1943 when he was shot down by flak north of Rouen. After baling out safely, Bradshaw made his way south and was being sheltered by Henri Le Monnier at La Haye-Malherbe when he saw the Liberator brought down and was told that some of the crew were sheltered nearby. He had been introduced to a young Frenchman named Jacques Saillard (who apparently worked for a Captain Georges – Georges Trumelet of Beaumontel) and on the night of 1 January, Jacques took Bradshaw and three of the Americans – pilot (Sibley), co-pilot (Volet) and a gunner/engineer (Satterley) – to Beaumontel. They stayed overnight with Jacques' aunt where they met two more of the Liberator crew, Schmitt and Sullivan, and next day, Bradshaw and Satterley moved to stay with a young Frenchman named Charles Gougeon (born Mar 1911) and his wife Gilberte at another house in the village. On 13 January 1944, Bradshaw and Satterley were captured, along with their hosts, and put in a truck where they joined Jacques' aunt and four of the Americans (Sibley, Volet, Wald and Ruska). As they were being driven to a prison at Evreux, the truck stopped to pick up another prisoner, a man the Germans referred to as Captain Georges.

Paul Ruska says (in a telephone conversation with James Crabtree on 18 May 2009 for a Texas Veterans Land Board "Voices of Veterans" interview posted on the internet), that no bones were actually broken but severe bruising stopped him from moving about. He was sheltered by retired butcher Georges Jenisse (nf)[14] *for five months until someone asked if he would like to go back to England, at which point he "got into the underground" and was moved to a house in another town on the railway line to the coast (Georges Ecalard at Serquigny, Eure). After about a month, one of the young men on the underground was caught, and he "squealed".*

The friend, who was known to Schmitt and Sullivan as Carlos, was apparently god-father to the English couple's daughter's child. Schmitt describes Carlos was coming from Java, a slender man, about 5 feet 7 inches tall, aged about 34 but looked about 24, with straight black hair and a ruddy complexion. His real name was Karel Wybrands.

*Karel Wybrands (born Batavia, Sept 1907) of 4 rue Greneta, Paris III. He says he was a radio technician with the **** group Bearn, and not usually involved with helping evaders. In addition to Schmitt and Sullivan (and Heskett – see below) – to whom he says he was known as either Cacao or Max – he also helped Sqn/Ldr Jack Brandt (7/91/1261). Brandt, who was shot down on 23 May 1944, was brought to Paris from Roye (Somme) on 30 May and sheltered with Mme Marie Louise Parant at 22 rue Saint Sauveur for a week before she passed him on to another organisation.*

This is same Karel R Wybrands who gained a French pilot's licence in 1949, and is commemorated on the Smithsonian NASM Wall of Honor.

14 Ruska's RAMP file says Georges Dienis (nf) of Sait-Didier-des-Bois par La Haye-Malherbe, Eure.

Sometime after lunch on 13 January, Jacque's sister arrived to tell them that Bradshaw and Satterley had been captured and that the Germans knew everything. That evening, Jacques, Roger Mesle and Karel Wybrands went with Schmitt and Sullivan to the station, and Wybrands took the two Americans on the eight o'clock (2000 hrs) evening train to Paris. Wybrands led them to a lady's third-floor apartment (Mme Parant at 22 rue Saint Sauveur) where they had supper, and then to another house (Mme Tarin at nearby 144 rue Saint-Denis) where they met 1/Lt Donald Heskett (#347).

Karel Wybrands says that he took Schmitt and Sullivan from Mr and Mme Lenferna de la Motte (in Beaumont-le-Roger) and convoyed them to Mme Parant (her husband was in hiding) at 22 rue Saint Sauveur, Paris. Mme Parant sheltered them, together with Heskett, until an empty apartment at 23 boulevard Barbes (belonging to a Mr Soulier) was found – the three airmen frequently visiting Mme Parant. After about two weeks, Mme Parant and a young man named Jacques Tarin "discovered a way to send the airmen back to England and they left us on the 28th of January".

Roger Mesle confirms Wybrands taking the two Americans to Paris while he went to the capital separately. He says that Schmitt and Sullivan were sheltered with Mme Darin (sic Tarin) at rue Saint-Denis, and that due to his efforts, they were then passed them on to Mme Therese (actuellement Capitaine Vallier au ministere de la Guerre) who passed them on to a Belgian lady named Helene before he returned to Serquigny with his friend Antoine. Note that this last part does not agree with the evaders reports.

Meanwhile, M. Bouchard had passed Halifax pilot William Dallin on to a man called Simon at 59 bis rue Olivier Métra, Paris XX (IS9 has Louis Ginoux at this address). Simon was primarily involved in helping refracteurs, and was persuaded to hand Dallin over to man named Gilbert Asselin (IS9 has him at 8 rue du Jour, Paris 1) who claimed he was in the business of helping Allied airmen. However, when Roger Mesle approached Asselin so he could pass William Dallin on to Helene, Asselin refused, asked for money and tried to blackmail Mesle.

Roger Mesle was arrested at the home of fellow Marie-Claire member Bouchard in Sucy-en-Brie on 12 February 1944, following a visit the previous day by a man claiming to have come from Simon. He says that both Simon and Gilbert Asselin had been arrested in Paris (and William Dallin captured) and that one of them had given up Bouchard. Roger Mesle was deported to Dachau in July 1944 but survived to be repatriated to France in June 1945.

On the morning of 19 January, Jacques Tarin took Schmitt and Sullivan to a doctor's house near the Seine where there were what Schmitt describes as "German military evaders" – by which I assume he means young Frenchmen (*réfractaires*) avoiding STO (*Service du travail obligatoire* – compulsory labour service in Germany). Schmitt says that the doctor, who was just over six feet tall, thin, with heavy wavy hair and a long straight nose, was a good sculptor. His wife was about 5 feet 4 inches tall, with a medium build, square face, small knobbly chin and light brown hair – this was Doctor André Michel Lwoff (born May 1902), the multi-award winning microbiologist who was Head of Department at the Pasteur Institute, and his wife Marguerite, of 69 avenue de Suffren, Paris VII. They also met Madeleine, a medical student (sic), with a pale complexion and straggly light brown hair, who spoke English.

Next day, they were interrogated by a stocky man with a little moustache who they refer to as an English Captain – this was obviously Lucien Dumais. He told them to stay where they were, and that night got them train tickets and identity papers.

1/Lt Donald J Heskett (#347) was the 21-year-old pilot of 44BG/66BS B-24 42-7548 Bull O' The Woods which was on the way to Ludwigshafen on 30 December 1943 and still over France when they were attacked by fighters. Heskett reports that they were struggling to keep up with the formation and the first indication he had of an attack was when two of their engines stopped. The aircraft immediately went into a spin, and being unable to recover it, Heskett ordered the crew to bail-out and rang the alarm bell. Fighters continued to attack as Heskett sent co-pilot (1/Lt James R Billings) to check that everyone had left before kicking Billings out and leaving the aircraft to crash between Compiègne (Oise) and Soissons (Aisne).

Six other crew also evaded successfully: waist-gunner Sgt Charles W Cregger (#470) and TTG/engineer T/Sgt Elmer D Risch (#498) (see both later), bombardier 1/Lt Adolph Zielenkiewicz (#552) who was helped by the Marie-Odile organisation and crossed the Pyrenees to Spain in March 1944, radio operator T/Sgt Eugene Symons (#725) who crossed the Pyrenees in April, and ball-turret gunner S/Sgt Stanley G Langcaskey

(#691) and tail-gunner S/Sgt George R Miller (#847) who were both helped by Bourgogne and crossed the Pyrenees, Langcaskey in April and Miller in June 1944.

Heskett delayed pulling his rip-cord until he entered some clouds and then landed backwards in a big ditch, somewhere near Soissons. He was unhurt from the landing and quickly gathered up his parachute which he then stuck into a hole and covered with leaves. He saw some people running towards him but not knowing who they were, ran the other way to some woods where he took off his electrically heated suit and gloves (making a point of keeping his GI shoes) and hid them as best he could. He hid himself in a hole not far from a road that ran through the woods to a village, distributed the contents of his aids-box into various pockets and tried to locate himself on his silk escape-map. It seems that he didn't hide himself very well as he soon noticed a man watching him from the road. They didn't have much language in common but Heskett got the impression that the man wanted to know whether or not he wanted to be taken prisoner. On convincing the man that he did not, Heskett was taken to another place to hide until the man returned that evening to lead him to his house, from where Heskett's journey was arranged.

Like most American E&E reports, Heskett's basic report, from which the above is taken, is clearly typed but details of the rest of his journey are contained in the more interesting Appendix C – which is often hand-written, and like so many others in this story (including Schmitt and Sullivan above), his interviewer was 1/Lt Donald Emerson.

Heskett was taken to a small town that he was told was 15 kms north-east of Soissons. Next morning (query) he was taken by bicycle into Soissons where he seems to have been sheltered briefly with a man named Robert, brother-in-law of Parisian policeman, Marius Vaillant (of 6 rue de Maubeuge, Paris IX). On 3 January, a man called Jacques Karel (described by Heskett as being from Java – his father was part Dutch – about 37 years old, 5 foot 6 inches tall, with tortoise-shell glasses) took Heskett by truck to Paris, and an apartment at 144 rue Saint-Denis, and just around the corner from Mme Parant at 22 rue Saint-Sauveur.

Jacques Karel was another alias of Karel Wybrands. He says he collected an American flyer from Mr Chambrey at rue Maubeuge, Paris (this was

Etienne Cambrelin at 22 rue de Maubeuge – Cdt Cambrelin (aka Lionnel) of Liberation Nord) – in January and delivered him to Mme Parant.

Heskett says that he divided his time between staying at what he calls "Jacque's place" (at 144 rue Saint-Denis) (which I think was actually Jacques Tarin's mother's apartment) and another place, a block away from Chateau Rouge Metro station (at 23 boulevard Barbes), where he met an escaped French POW called Georges – aged about 24, he was about 6 feet tall, weighed 190 lbs, with a dark complexion and dark brown hair. On 12 January, Fred Schmitt (#344) and John Sullivan (#345) were brought to Jacque's place.

On 19 January, Heskett went to "the other house" (23 boulevard Barbes) where he was told about another five Americans being in Paris. He also met Madeleine – 35 years old, with regular features and light brown hair, she was about 5 foot 4 inches tall, "an ordinary person in appearance" – who had been to college in Boston. Madeleine told Heskett that he would not be going over Pyrenees (which must have confused him as he hadn't known there was an alternate route out of France), and she took him to a place in the Metro to get his photograph taken.

Madeleine was obviously Marie-Rose Zerling – who names all three Americans in her file. See also Casden and Hathaway earlier who say that Claudette (Zerling) took them, Norman Maybee and Paul Saunders to "another house" on 18 January, where they were questioned by Captain Hamilton (Dumais) before Claudette took them to the station that evening.

The following evening (20 January), Madeleine collected Heskett, Schmitt and Sullivan from "Jacque's place" (on rue Saint-Denis) and took them to the station. There was a man at the station who gave them their tickets, and Madeleine led them onto the train where she handed them over to two guides, a man (described by Schmitt and Sullivan as being small, about 5 ft 5 inches tall, with wavy hair and a boyish look) and a woman (about 5 ft 6 inches tall, heavily built, about 150 lbs, with reddish blond hair), who took them to Saint-Brieuc.

They arrived at Saint-Brieuc the following morning, where their papers were checked at the station by a gendarme, and their guides took them to a house a couple of blocks away. Heskett was surprised to learn there had been a Russian on the train with them – he is referred to as Ivan B and he remained with Heskett from that point. They also seem to have been joined by a man that Schmitt and Sullivan refer to as John Morgan, and who they describe as being a French aviator connected to the French army, about 5 foot 4 inches tall, about 135 lbs with black hair and a beard.

They stayed in Saint-Brieuc until about four-thirty that afternoon when Heskett says they met an English-speaking man called Jacky, a girl (who Heskett seems to say was a sister of the French aviator) and another man, and it was the girl and the second man who took them by train to Plouha while Jacky followed in a car.

Heskett describes Jacky as being aged 28, about 5 foot 9 inches tall, heavily bearded, a sergeant in the French infantry who had been on law course in England. Roger Huguen (who wouldn't have been aware of Heskett's description) says that Jacky was Jacky du Pac. I am guessing there is some confusion here and that, although no mention is made, Val Williams was also on the train to Saint-Brieuc (with Jacky Du Pac), from where, Henri Le Blais took them by car to Plouha – see later.

The Organisation in Plouha

While Shelburn was built on ideas pioneered by Oaktree, in Brittany that mission was mostly centred around logeurs at Etables-sur-Mer and Saint-Quay-Portrieux and didn't really involve the people of Plouha, so while some of them certainly knew about Val Williams, when Dumais went to Plouha, he was more or less able to make a fresh start.

"Campinchi suggested they contact Doctor André Le Balc'h at Plouézec. Le Balc'h, who had sheltered Labrosse in his Paris apartment earlier in the year, had replaced his friend Doctor Meynard, who had left Brittany following the arrests at Saint-Quay-Portrieux. Le Balc'h suggested they stay at the hôtel du Commerce where he introduced them as two visiting doctors. One of the regular visitors to the hotel was Henri Le Blais, a man that Dr Le Balc'h believed to be a patriot. Henri Le Blais had a Renault car and a German ausweis that allowed him to drive day or night on business. Le Blais thought his friend Adolphe Le Trocquer, a teacher at Pludual and fellow member of the Front National, would know of any local resistance members who could help. The local head of the FN was François Le Puluard – he was too old to take an active part but another FN member, François Le Cornec was head

of the local resistance cell. Le Cornec ran a café in Plouha that would be an ideal meeting place, as well as a large house that could be used for lodging. Following a visit by Trocquer and Le Puluard, François Le Cornéc was persuaded to join the group.

Le Cornec and Joseph Mainguy (alias Job), a merchant marine captain, inspected the originally suggested landing beach but queried it because of the deep water, the close rocks and lack of beach. There was also a German guard-post nearby. It was Pierre Huet (alias Tarzan) who first suggested the northern end of l'Anse-Cochat, known as Sous-Keruzeau, where there was access from a crumbling, sixty foot cliff.

Dumais (aka Leon in Brittany) appointed François Le Cornec as 'chef de plage' and 'responsable' for the evacuations in Dumais' absence. Henri Le Blais became 'responsable' of the reception centre to be established at Saint-Brieuc for evaders arriving from Paris. Dumais was able to send a message to London that preparations for Bonaparte were complete and requested that a more powerful radio be sent for Labrosse together with money, weapons and ammunition, food etc. Dumais gave Henri Le Blais a complicated procedure for contacting Paris in case of emergency. On 15 January, Dumais sent a message to London asking for the first MGB pick-up to take place during the next moonless period." (my simplified translation from Huguen 1976)

François Alfred Marie Le Cornec (born Plouha June 1905) is described as being a shop-keeper (IS9 says livestock negotiator) of place Marechal Foch, in the very centre of Plouha – he also owned the Café de la Mairie. He was married to Juliette with a young daughter Marie-Françoise. His parents François and Marie lived at Lezandré-en-Plouha, as did his brother Emmanuel (who was a POW in Germany at that time), and sisters Aline and Marie (Ropers) – his eldest sister Josephine (Geffroy) lived in New York and his youngest sister Madeleine (Le Frocquer) lived at Pléguien.

François Le Cornec had been involved with resistance activities, distributing de Gaullist propaganda, since being repatriated (fraudulently) as an "ancien combattant" from Compiègne in November 1941. Originally recruited by Joseph Darcel of Lanvollon, he says that he first became involved with Allied evaders in the spring of 1943 when he helped three (query) downed airmen, sheltering one called Martin for 2 days in June before taking him to Claude (Ray Labrosse) at Saint-Quay-Portrieux – this was S/Sgt Roy A Martin (#77) from the B-17 Boot Hill, who had escaped from the Chateau du Bourblanc after Betty de Mauduit was arrested. Le Cornec then worked directly with Labrosse, and helped him move the airmen to Paris after Williams' arrest earlier that same month.

"His services were of the very highest order, his courage and devotion to duty unsurpassed, and he can be considered one of the most outstanding personalities in the annals of evasion work." (extract from the IS9 recommendation of an MBE (Civil) for François Le Cornec)

Joseph Marie Mainguy (born Plouha Aug 1903) of rue du Port-Moguer, Plouha was a captain in the Marine Marchande, and a reserve lieutenant in the French Navy. Married to Jeanne (née Fichou) with two young children, he was also a nephew of retired seaman Georges Ropers, and cousin to Anne Ropers. François Le Cornec says that Mainguy was the first man he recruited – they had been friends for many years.

Mainguy says that he was responsible for organising transport to bring the evaders to Plouha from Saint-Brieuc, Guingamp and Châtelaudren. He could not shelter evaders at his own house because he lived on the main road but arranged to have them sheltered with his comrades. Mainguy took part in all eight operations, bringing groups of evaders to the Maison d'Alphonse before going down to the coast – the fact that, unlike Le Cornec, he spoke English must have helped. He was the one who signaled with a torch from the cliff-top to guide the surf-boats into the beach.

"It would be superfluous here to stress the salient qualities of tenacity and courage which enabled Monsieur Mainguy and his fellow helpers to carry such difficult and dangerous operations to such a successful conclusion. It can but be said that these outstanding Resistance and Evasion workers gained the admiration of all who knew them; their exploits constitute one of the most brilliant episodes in the annals of escape activity." (extract from the IS9 recommendation of an MBE (Civil) for Joseph Marie Mainguy)

Clément Pierre Marie Huet (born July 1907) (aka Tarzan) of Keruzeau (which is just north of Saint-Samson), Plouha had been a pilot with the Marine Militaire until demobilised and put on armistice leave in January 1943. He was married to Marcelle Louise Maria Françoise (née Michel Mar 1911) and had two daughters, Michèle (born Nov 1931) and Christiane (born Aug 1936). He was recruited into the local resistance group by François Le Cornec in June 1943, and they became involved with Dumais, helping evaders, that December. Like Job Mainguy, Pierre Huet took part in all eight operations, where he was in charge of taking the evaders from the Maison d'Alphonse and down to the beach – and it was he and Mainguy who later took on the dangerous task of locating and marking the mines that were laid across the route to the beach prior to the Crozier operations.

"Throughout the course of all these (Shelburn) operations, Monsieur Huet was constantly active and vigilant. His duties were often the most difficult and dangerous, but he managed to effect them with remarkable success. His courage and constant devotion to duty were beyond praise, and due to his undaunted efforts, a very large numbers were enabled to regain their own lines in safety." (extract from the IS9 recommendation of a BEM for Clément Huet)

Mme Vve Leonie Le Calvez (née Le Bitter April 1882) of Kerlerot, Plouha was the widow of Pierre, and mother of Marie-Thérèse Le Calvez. She was recruited by François Le Cornec to shelter evaders, her home being used on numerous occasions.

Pierre Le Calvez died in March 1940, his death almost certainly hastened by the loss of three of their five sons – Yves, Pierre and Henri – shortly before the war began. A fourth son, Victor had been denounced and was in hiding. Their other son Georges had been serving in the French air force, and escaped from France at the beginning of the war. He sailed from Sète in June 1940 disguised as a Polish officer, and arrived in Liverpool on 7 December. Unknown to the family at the time, Sgt Le Calvez was posted to North Africa, and died after his Free French GRB1 (Groupe Réservé de Bombardement) Blenheim T1867 was lost on a mission to Koufra on 4 February 1941.

Marie-Thérèse Le Calvez (born Aug 1924) of Kerlerot, Plouha was first recruited into the resistance by Yves Le Touzé (of avenue Clemenceau, Plouha) and Jean Trehiou in August 1942 to help make false identity cards for refracteurs, and then in January 1944, François Le Cornec asked her if she would work with an organisation involved with repatriating Allied airmen. She took part in all eight operations, guiding the men and sheltering many of them in her mother's house before taking them to the Maison d'Alphonse, and then down to the beach.

There is a book about Marie-Thérèse Le Calvez called "Une héroïne de la Resistance", written by Dominique-Martin Le Trividic and published in 2002 by Ouest-France. It is based on her own 1979 account, and comments in the text attributed to Marie-Thérèse are taken from a translated version of that book.

Mlle Françoise Maria Monjaret (born April 1899) spinster and cultivatrice of Ville Dé in Plouha, was the daughter of Victor Constant Monjaret (born 1867) and Maria Anna (née Noel 1875). Françoise had five sisters and three brothers, including Constant and Joseph (born Aug 1920) who escaped to England by fishing boat from Paimpol in June 1940. Constant joined the Free French Forces and was sent to Chad while Joseph became radio operator for Jean Moulin and parachuted into France with him and Raymond Fassin on 1 January 1942. Joseph (aka Hervé) Monjaret was captured in April 1943 and deported – he was repatriated back to France in May 1945.

Mlle Germaine Couffon (born April 1904) (couturiere) lived with her mother Mme Anne Marie Couffon at Kerisago/Kerizago – "une demeure isolée à Kerlerot" – "trois cent metres plus loin de Chênes-Verts" – on Route de Paimpol, Plouha. She sheltered numerous evaders, all received from Joseph Mainguy and passed to Pierre Huet. She is also said to have taken a group of evaders from Mme Lesné's home to the Maison d'Alphonse, and would have helped more but apparently the guides thought she talked too much.

Mme Vve Marie Le Saux (née Blanville Sept 1883) was the widow of Yves-Marie Le Saux, and they had three children, including daughter Marguerite (aka Guiguite) (born Feb 1925). She lived at Saint-Barthélémy (south of Plouha on the road to Plourhan), and sheltered evaders brought to her by Francis Baudet and then passed back to him (see later). She also sheltered Dumais and Labrosse for "all but first operation" – and they once stayed with her for a month – Labrosse often transmitting from her home "three times a day".

Francis Baudet (born Dec 1900), who gives his occupation as professional soldier (captured 21 July 1940, repatriated through illness 17 Oct 42 and released on 7 Jan 1943, says he joined the resistance group at Plouha on 2 July 43), also lived at Saint-Barthélémy. He was married (in Sept 1925) to the eldest Le Saux daughter, Anne-Marie (born 1906), and they had a teenage daughter of their own. Note that Baudet was highly praised in hand-written letter (dated 17 Jan 47) by Dumais who says he was Le Cornec's "right-hand man" and "very glad to have him".

Marie Tréhiou (born Jan 1919) (cultivatrice) and her brother Jean François Tréhiou (born April 1920) lived at Kergeffroy en Plouha, which is a few kilometres south of the town. They were two of four orphaned children, their mother, Marie Anne (née Hery Sept 1888) died in 1932, and their father, Jean Francois Adrien Tréhiou (born May 1895) died of malaria (in about 1936). It seems likely from their Helper file that Marie was the main beneficiary from their late parents as she is credited with owning three properties.

Augustin Lesné (born Aug 1895) and his wife Julie lived at Kerverzio (just NE of Plouha centre). Their daughter Jeanne Marie Lesné was engaged to Jean Tréhiou – they married in October 1944.

Georges Ropers (born July 1890) of Camblac'h en Plouha, was a retired sailor, married to Marie (née Guillou) and with four children. Ten airmen ate and spent the evening of 17 March at his house (see later), and on 24 March, four Americans and one Englishman were sheltered for 2 days and one night (see later). It was also the Ropers family who sheltered Guy Hamilton, Alfred Dellow and Hayward Rockwood for 17 days while they waited to be collected by MGB 503 in July – see later.

René Dagorne (born Paris Sept 1910) and Joseph Marie Garion (born Morlaix May 1898) were local gendarmes.

Jean Alexis Gicquel (born Sept 1911) and his wife Marie Therese Gicquel lived in a small two-part family house (the aunt was absent) at Saint-Samson en Plouha. They were recruited by François Le Cornec because their home was quite isolated but near enough to the beach at l'Anse-Cochat that it could be used as a final meeting place, and all the Shelburn evaders are said to have passed through what became known as "La Maison d'Alphonse".

Jean Francois Gouarin (born Aug 1883) was a farmer at Pléguien (about 3 kms east of Lanvollen). His IS9 recommendation for an award says that he worked with the organisation between January and June 1944, using his own transport to collect evaders from the surrounding area before guiding them to the beach. He also sheltered Dumais and Labrosse in two houses that he owned when they arrived from Paris in July – see later.

Although I am fairly confident that Sidney Casden and Andrew Hathaway left Paris with Norman Maybee and Paul Saunders on Tuesday 18 January by overnight train for Saint-Brieuc – where Maybee and Saunders were arrested – arriving in Plouha next morning, and that Fred Schmitt, John Sullivan and Donald Heskett arrived with Ivan on the evening of Friday 21 January, it's not certain from their (sometimes conflicting) reports exactly when the other ten airmen travelled from the capital in their various groups, nor where they all stayed (for up to 10 days) in and around Plouha while they waited to be taken down to the beach at l'Anse-Cochat, so the paragraphs below are my best guess.

Note that some groups seem to have travelled from Paris on the same day, and may even have travelled on the same trains without recognising one another, possibly leaving the CdN Petit Train at different stations around Plouha, as mentioned earlier – those staying with Françoise Monjaret for example, probably getting off before the town at Plouha-Embranchement.

Sidney Casden and Andrew Hathaway arrived at Plouha on the morning of Wednesday 19 January, where Casden says they stayed with a woman with sixteen children – I'm not sure about the sixteen children but am confident that they were sheltered by Françoise Monjaret at Ville-Dé. Casden reports that he met Val Williams, that there were eleven of them (including Williams), and they stayed indoors the whole time listening to the radio.[15]

Casden says that Val Williams told him he had been in prison for seven months at Rennes, and that after he had been "thoroughly gone over" by the Gestapo, was due to be shot. He also says that Williams explained the radio codes to them: "Yvonne pense souvent à l'heureuse recontre" would mean a twenty-four hour delay, and "Bonjour tout le monde à la Maison d'Alphonse" that the gunboat was on its way that night – details that were only supposed to have been known by Dumais and Labrosse.

Casden and Hathaway were joined at Ville-Dé the following morning (Thursday 20 January) by RAF evaders Norman Cufley and John Harvey, and that evening by Walter Dickerman, William Booher, Alphonse Mele and Jerry Eshuis. At about ten o'clock on the evening of Friday 28 January, Joseph Mainguy arrived to take the group to a farmhouse about a kilometre

15 I think there were actually seven other airmen sheltered with Casden and Hathaway – Cufley, Harvey, Booher, Mele, Eshuis, Dickerman – and later, Blackwell.

from the beach where they were joined by some Frenchmen, eight (sic) more evaders and Captain Hamilton, a very short, dark man with a moustache, who gave them their instructions.

Richard Smith, Morton Shapiro, James King and Walter Sentkoski also arrived in Plouha on the morning of Thursday 20 January. They were met at Plouha-Ville station by Marie-Thérèse Le Calvez who took them to stay with her mother Leonie at Kerlerot. Smith says that the four Americans lived in one room at the Le Calvez home while they waited for "the rest of the crowd" to arrive, and were visited there at some time by a "little Englishman" (Dumais). He says they arrived on Thursday, the others arrived on Friday (sic) and that they were due to leave that Saturday – but it wasn't until the evening of the following Friday, that Marie-Therese took the four airmen to another house, some miles away, where they joined the "rest of the crowd" and met Captain Hamilton again. Smith also comments on Captain Val Williams being in the party when a new guide led them in single-file across some "rugged country" and down to the beach.

When Fred Schmitt, John Sullivan, Donald Heskett and Ivan arrived at Plouha on the evening of Friday 21 January, Heskett and Ivan were taken to be sheltered with a farming brother and sister about three kilometres from the town – this was Jean and Marie Tréhiou at Lizandré – where they stayed until the night of their departure. On the evening of 28 January, Heskett and Ivan were taken back to Plouha and the house of a woman that Heskett says was engaged to the man who had met them at the station – this was Jean Tréhiou's fiancée, Jeanne Lesné, who lived with her parents Augustin and Julie at Kervizio, just NE of central Plouha.

Schmitt and Sullivan went with the short, bearded French aviator they name as John Morgan, first to "Yves' house" (presumably in Plouha) and then across the road to the building where they were sheltered. They seem to have been staying with John Morgan as they say that the same English Captain they saw in Paris (Dumais) visited them twice "at Morgan's".

I suspect that Yves was the Yves Touze (sic) that Marie-Therese Le Calvez says in her NARA file left for England in January 1944. Huguen says Yves Le Touzé was the son of the station master at Plouha – presumably Mons A. Le Touze of avenue (Georges) Clemenceau, Plouha as per IS9, which also lists Auguste Le Touze of 6 rue Alsace Lorraine, Saint-Brieuc.

Schmitt and Sullivan say that the aviator came back to England with them, and there are similar comments (and perhaps some clues) from Heskett. Richard Smith also mentions a French aviator, Blackwell (1727) (see below) includes an otherwise unidentified Frenchman on his list of "passengers" taken on board the MGB, and Joseph Mainguy says that a French agent was included in the party.

The sixteenth airman collected on this first Bonaparte operation was already in Brittany – he'd been sheltered in the little town of Guingamp, twenty-four kilometres south-west of Plouha, since Christmas.

F/O Samuel Peter J Blackwell (1727) was the 21-year-old Rhodesian pilot of 266 Sqn Typhoon JP906, escorting Mosquitoes attacking enemy shipping off Lorient on the morning of 1 December 1943 when he was shot down about 20 miles off the French coast by a Ju88. It's not clear whether he baled out or ditched but either way, Blackwell spent the rest of the day in his dinghy until being picked-up that afternoon by a Dornier 24 seaplane. Blackwell was flown to the seaplane base in the Bay of Poulmic and put into the local hospital. Next day, a Luftwaffe officer and a soldier escorted Blackwell by boat to Brest where they left him at the railway station. Blackwell was told that he would be going to Frankfurt and the officer and soldier returned that afternoon and all three boarded a train. Blackwell says that once the train started, he made three unsuccessful attempts to escape by pretending to be ill, going to the lavatory and trying to jump off before his fourth attempt finally succeeded somewhere near Lamballe (Côtes-du-Nord).

Blackwell left the train sometime between seven and eight o'clock in the evening and headed across country until three in the morning when he reached the village of Saint-Aaron. He knocked on the door of a farmhouse and explained to the farmer in his meagre French who he was. The man was obviously nervous but did agree to let Blackwell spend the rest of the night in his loft. After having some breakfast, Blackwell left early the next morning, still in uniform, and walked eastwards through the fields until evening when he reached the village of Pléven where he found help, was put in touch with an organisation and the rest of his journey arranged.

The place where Blackwood got help was the home of Charles Rohan, a blacksmith at La Forge, Pléven. When Blackwood told him who he was, M. Rohan immediately gave him a meal. M. Rohan was not a member of an organisation but he sent Blackwood to stay overnight with a young man called Le Feuvre who was evading German labour service (STO) and living alone in a room in Pléven, and next day, Blackwood was moved to a chateau (no name given) outside the village. Apparently Le Feuvre contacted a woman in Dinan who was supposed to be in touch with England but Blackwood felt that she seemed rather vague. Meanwhile, M. Rohan contacted a resistance group in Saint-Brieuc.

On 24 December, Blackwell had to be moved because the Germans had requisitioned the chateau, and he was taken to Lamballe where he met a man from Saint-Brieuc who belonged to a small resistance movement. Unfortunately neither this man nor his organisation had any experience of helping evaders but he did take Blackwell to Rennes where he met several more people. However, they all told him it was too dangerous to help evaders after a recent wave of arrests in the town. Blackwell's guide then took him back to Saint-Brieuc where they met a friend who was going to Guingamp for Christmas and so they all went there.

This was a particularly fortunate event as it was through some of the young men that Blackwell met at Guingamp, that Mathurin Branchoux heard about him. He arranged for Blackwell to stay with friends in Guingamp (Desire and Francine Laurent of 1 rue de l'Etang du Prieuré, on the corner with the main rue de la Trinité in Guingamp) until 4 January when he was taken a few miles south-west of the town to stay with René Rannou and his wife Helene, owners of the café at Pont-Melvez railway station. Meanwhile, Mathurin Branchoux contacted a man in Brest (Colonel Scheidhauer) who was supposed to come and see Blackwell, and on 14 January, Blackwell was taken back to Guingamp to meet him but he never arrived. Blackwell stayed on in Guingamp, sheltered by Mme Denise Le Cun (whose son Georges was a member of Branchoux's organisation) at place du Centre. Blackwell says that "On 22 Jan news had been received from the man in Brest that he was coming for me on 25 Jan, having been in Paris on business. After Hamilton's arrival on 23 Jan, Branchoux thought it advisable to take advantage of his offer."

"Yves Hugues, of Loudéac, commanded the rue Notre Dame Resistance group in Guingamp, and he knew Mathurin Branchoux and also, through Mme Laurent, Georges Le Cun. When Mme Laurent had sheltered Rhodesian pilot Peter Blackwell after he had escaped a train taking him to Germany, both Yves Hugues and Georges Le Cun had come to meet him.

After discussion with Mathurin Branchoux they decided to move Blackwell to stay with the Rannou family, near the [Pont-Melvez] station. Le Cun then told everyone that he had put Blackwell on the train to Paris, whereas he had in fact hidden the airman at his mother's house. Fortunately for Blackwell, Mme Le Cun spoke good English and had a collection of English books that he could read whilst waiting to join the the group taken out on the first Bonaparte operation." (my translation from Huguen 1976)

On 23 January, Captain Hamilton (Dumais) came to Guingamp to meet Blackwell but he was away that day (he doesn't say where) and Branchoux wasn't able to contact him in time for the operation that Hamilton apparently had planned for that night. However the operation was delayed by a storm and next day, Hamilton telephoned M. Branchoux and asked him to bring "the sack of potatoes" (Branchoux was a potato merchant) and so Georges Le Cun took Blackwood to Plouha in his car. M. Le Cun gave Blackwell half of a 10 franc note for anyone wishing to make contact with him – the note was passed on to James Langley at MI9.

In Plouha, Blackwell finally met "Captain Hamilton" who cross-examined him about England and the RAF and Blackwell learned from Hamilton that the man in Brest worked on similar lines to Hamilton but that his latest operation had failed after the Germans had fortified one of the off-shore islands. The Plouha operation was delayed until the night of 28-29 January and while he was waiting, Blackwell joined nine other British and American airmen at a house in Plouha which he says had been rented from a doctor, who visited occasionally.

Departure

On the evening of Friday 28 January, Donald Heskett and Ivan were taken from Lizandré to a house in Plouha (the Lesné home at Kerverzio) where they waited to hear a message on the radio, and at about ten o'clock, Jean Tréhiou, the same man who had met them at the station on their arrival at Plouha, took them to the coast. Heskett met the "English captain" – who he describes as being short, about 5 ft 5 inches tall, heavy-set, about 150 lbs, with broad shoulders, moustache and dark brown hair, he was probably 30 years old – who told Heskett (in case he hadn't already guessed) that he would be leaving by boat. He also met Val Williams, "a Captain in the British Army who had been with the Russian", who was on a stretcher.

Heskett was one of the men who tried to take Williams down to the beach on the stretcher but they soon found that didn't work and so he and another man carried him.

> *Heskett mentions the French pilot (referred to by Schmitt and Sullivan as John Morgan) apparently leaving for England with them, saying that they had stayed at his mother's house in Paris, and that his sister (Hélène Le Touzé – query) had been one of their guides, presumably on the train from Paris but perhaps just from Saint-Brieuc. However, the only places they seem to have stayed in Paris with anyone who could have been the aviator's mother were 144 rue Saint-Denis with Mme Tarin, and 22 rue Saint-Sauvier with Marie Parant – neither listed by IS9.*

The message broadcast by the BBC in London to confirm the first Bonaparte operation would take place that night was "Bonjour tout le monde à la maison d'Alphonse" – an otherwise meaningless phrase agreed in advance but probably chosen more or less at random. The message was only sent on that one particular evening (each operation had its own message) but it resulted in Jean and Marie Gicquel's little house at Saint-Samson forever being known as "La Maison d'Alphonse". Such "messages personnels" were transmitted each evening at seven-thirty (French time) and repeated at nine-thirty.[16]

> *"I was to take my group to the house of Jean and Marie Gicquel, who lived in a little isolated cottage, fairly near the Bonaparte beach and christened by the Shelburn network as "La Maison d'Alphonse". We were more than three kilometres away. These had to be covered as quickly as possible. German cars passed unceasingly on the main road where we hurried along, sometimes jumping into the ditches to avoid the vehicle headlights.*
>
> *At last we reached the little house (whose door was ajar) inside which, around Jean and Marie Gicquel, François Le Cornec, Chief of the Plouha Resistance, and the Canadian Leon Dumais, chief of the Shelburn network, were waiting for us. Then in turn came Joseph Mainguy, with his group of airmen, and Jean Tréhiou with his, followed by Pierre Huet, nicknamed Tarzan, who was to take us to Bonaparte Beach. The gendarmes Dagorne*

16 Subsequent messages included: "Yvonne attend toujours l'heureuse occasion", "Les vieux vins sont les meilleurs", "Louis-Philippe est un bon roi", "La classe salue bien les amis" and "L'abeille est un insecte laborieux".

and Garion, from the Plouha Brigade (thanks to whom we learned the habits of the Germans and in particular the times of the patrols), Le Blais and Le Trocquer, came to join us. We were all present." (Marie-Thérèse Le Calvez)

"The MGB's anchorage for the operations in this series was between 1,500 and 1,800 metres from the German bunker on Pointe-de-la-Tour, which was armed with cannon, heavy machine-guns and searchlights. Sixteen kilometres north, on Pointe-de-Guilben was an enemy coast-watching radar station and a battery of medium artillery.

From a navigational point of view, this was a fairly straightforward pinpoint. The gunboat needed to make a first landfall on a group of rocks surmounted by a tower, Le-Grand-Léjon, which lies in the middle of the Baie-de-Saint-Brieuc. This involved steering a south-easterly course from their departure point off Dartmouth. At Grand-Léjon, a change of course of at least 90 degrees was necessary and the ship headed in towards the Pointe-de-Plouha on one of her three engines at a reduced speed of 800 rpm. At the appropriate point, the engine was stopped and three (on subsequent operations, four) 14 foot surf-boats were hoisted out by hand – a job that required a dozen men. Once they were in the water, the silenced centre engine was restarted and course resumed until the Le-Taureau rock, which was crowned with another tower, came in sight, fine on the starboard bow. As soon as the agreed light signal was picked up, Mike Marshall, captain of MGB 503, would give the order to anchor, as always with a grass warp. Then the boats would be manned – two oarsmen to each boat, each with a pair of muffled oars and a coxswain to steer the boat with a long sweep. A fourth man, MI9's conducting officer, would take position in the bows of the leading boat, armed no doubt, with a sub machine-gun. On this first Bonaparte operation no radio-telephone was used because Dumais had not yet been equipped with the required sister set. Subsequently, this secure speech link was used.[17]

The first operation involved a long wait. The ebb had finished and the tide was coming in when, just as they were beginning to despair, they saw three dark specks to seaward. As they watched, they became more substantial, moving steadily in towards the shore in line abreast …

… In 12 minutes the transfer was complete and the three boats were on their way back to the anchored gunboat. Once they were alongside and passengers and crews had scaled the waiting scrambling-nets and reached the

17 The navigator for this operation was probably Lt Michael P Salmond RNR – Lt-Cdr David L Birkin RNVR was with 502 that night for the SOE Var Line Operation Easement to Beg-an-Fry.

MGB's deck, the anchor was weighed and the homeward passage began on a silenced centre engine, towing the surf-boats. When Marshall judged they were sufficiently far off-shore, the engine was stopped and the boats hauled back on board, stowed and secured, scrambling nets picked up and course resumed for Grand-Léjon. Only when they had closed into it and turned north-west for Dartmouth did they attain full speed, 1,800 rpm on all three main engines." (Secret Flotillas)

Richard Smith says they left the Brittany coast at about 0300, and on board the gunboat, he reports meeting Lt-Cdr Ray Guest, an American naval officer (Commander Raymond R Guest had previously been on board MGB 318 to observe the Felicitate operations off Aber-Benoit). Smith also reports that on their arrival at Dartmouth, army Captain Windham-Wright gave them a security talk and took good care of them. Smith counted 13 Americans, a Russian, Val Williams, a Typhoon pilot named Peter (Blackwell's second name), two Halifax crewmen, and a Frenchman aviator as being the passengers brought back from France that night.

Note that various publications (including Neave's own) say that Airey Neave's assistant at MI9, Patrick Windham-Wright, was on board the first surf-boat, exchanging passwords with Dumais each time they landed at Plage Bonaparte. I think the security implications make this unlikely, and none of evaders report meeting Windham-Wright until after they had disembarked at Dartmouth.

"Captain Hamilton, who was in charge of the operation, received a message by wireless on the night of 28 Jan that the operation was on. We left the house in small parties about 2200 hrs and were taken to the coast to a point near Sheet 7, S1525. We waited on the beach from about midnight till 0130 hrs (29 Jan) when four (sic) small rowing-boats appeared and took us out to an M.G.B. Captain Hamilton entrusted me with secret papers which I handed to Captain Wyndham Wright (sic) on arrival in the U.K.

The M.G.B. arrived at Dartmouth about 0900 hrs on 29 Jan, the "passengers" on board consisted of Cufley, Harvey, myself, 13 Americans, one Russian, one Frenchman and a British Intelligence Officer [Val Williams]." (Blackwell WO208/5582-1727)

Donald Heskett confirms their arrival Dartmouth at about 0930 hrs where they were transferred to another boat to eat. In addition to Williams, there were 13 Americans, 3 British, 1 Russian and a Frenchman pilot. A one-armed English captain (Patrick Windham-Wright) took delivery of papers brought from France, and lectured them on security – he warned them against saying anything to anyone about the operation. They were kept on the boat until dark, and at about ten o'clock were taken ashore by motorboat and put on a train for London, where all sixteen evaders were interviewed by the Intelligence Services next day.

On the successful conclusion of this first Bonaparte operation, Marie-Thérèse Le Calvez recalls that they returned to François Le Cornec's house in Plouha, where Ray Labrosse was waiting for them.

Val Williams

> *"It was Françoise Monjaret who later contacted Le Cornec to say she had two men hiding with her, one of whom claimed to be Val Williams, from Oaktree. The mystery was solved when Henri le Blais explained he had brought Williams and his companion (both escaped from Rennes) to Plouha in his car. During his interrogation, Williams had been able to deduce that Campinchi, Labrosse, Le Bec and Ricou (la «boîte aux lettres») had not been arrested." (my translation from Huguen 1976)*

François Le Cornec says (in his NARA file) that he thought Henri Le Blais brought Dumais, Labrosse and Williams together in his car from Saint-Brieuc. "Pour l'aide-memoire, je lui rapelle qu'il est arrivé a Plouha dans la voiture de Le Blais de Plouezec, en compagnie du Lieutenant Claude (Labrosse) at de Vale, ancien chef de l'organisation." However, Le Cornec seems to have got that second-hand and I think the bit about Dumais and Labrosse can be discounted.

According to Williams own rather vague report, after his escape from Rennes on 20 December 1943, he and Ivan went to Paris where Jacky du Pac put him in touch with Béatrice Bréauté who contacted Paul Campinchi, and it was Campinchi who arranged his journey to Brittany – probably travelling on the same train from Paris as Schmitt, Sullivan, Heskett and Ivan – see earlier.

René Loiseau says (in correspondance with Dominique Lecomte) that Williams and Ivan stayed with Marguerite Di Giacomo (which she confirms) at rue Baudin, Levallois-Perret until they were taken to Brittany on about 20 January. For more information about Val Williams, see Appendix A.

SIS/MI9 Operation Bonaparte 2 (26-27 Feb 1944) MGB 503 (Mike Marshall)

Soon after the departure of the first group of François-Shelburn evaders for England, the little Chemin de Fer des Côtes-du-Nord (CdN) railway line from Saint-Brieuc to Paimpol was taken over by the German Organisation Todt and closed to public traffic, so the six airmen that reseau François sent from Paris in February were taken further west to Guingamp, where Samuel Blackwell had been sheltered the previous month.

All of the men on this second Bonaparte operation, except Leon Harmel, Mike Olynik, Louis Feingold and Warren Tarkington, evaded in Brittany at some time and so in addition to the evader's reports, I have used Colonel Rémy's 1968 *"La Maison d'Alphonse"*, Roger Huguen's classic 1976 *"Par les nuits les plus longues"*, and his 2003 book *"La Bretagne dans la Bataille de l'Atlantique"*, to try and fill in some of the finer details. I have tended to assume that while the evaders may not have known the names of their helpers, they would remember the servicemen they travelled with. The two French historians don't mention many evaders by name (and did not have access to their evasion reports at the time), and so sometimes confuse the numbers and order of events, but they have a far more detailed knowledge of the helpers, many of whom they interviewed personally. Combining the various sources into a meaningful storyline has sometimes been a struggle.

The Organisation in Guingamp

The helpers in Guingamp were every bit as important to the success of Shelburn as those in Plouha, their town having been a centre for resistance throughout the war, with links to groups all over Brittany. Because Plouha was comparatively small, and in the militarised coastal zone, hiding airmen there for any length of time was obviously very dangerous, and with the closure of the CdN railway to public traffic making sheltering them in Saint-Brieuc pointless, Guingamp became the most logical place for evaders to be gathered before they were taken to the beach.

Mathurin Branchoux (born May 1896), potato merchant of 63 rue de la Trinité, was married to Marie (née Le Henaff 1884). He joined the army in April 1915, serving in the infantry until demobilised with the rank of sous-lieutenant in September 1919, and was head of the Guingamp Armée Secrète resistance group. In his work with Shelburn, he co-ordinated between Guingamp and other towns (Plouha, Pommerit-le-Vicomte, Châtelaudren etc), met evaders on their arrival at Guingamp station, arranged lodgings and food for them, and liaised with Dumais – when necessary, travelling to Paris to meet with him.

Branchoux had earlier worked with Louis Nouveau of the Pat Line, Henri Loch at Pontivy, Georges Jouanjean and (briefly) with Val Williams and Ray Labrosse of Oaktree – he also knew Colonel Scheidhauer in Brest (see later).

"Monsieur Branchoux stands out as a great patriotic and gallant Frenchman. His exceptional organising ability, great courage and untiring devotion made his services invaluable to the Allied cause. He can be considered one of the most outstanding personalities in the annals of evasion work." (extract from the IS9 recommendation of an MBE (Civil) for Mathurin Branchoux)

Georges Le Cun (born Oct 1897) (married, no children) radio-electrician of 50 rue de la Trinité, Guingamp, was the eldest son of Joseph (deceased) and Denise Le Cun (see below). He worked under Mathurin Branchoux, and says that in December 1943, having temporarily lost touch with Paul Le Baron, his link to Bourgogne, he contacted François le Cornec in Plouha in order to pass on the airman (Blackwell) that the organisation in Guingamp was sheltering. Le Cornec was by then working with Leon (Captain Harrison) and Claude (Labrosse) who asked the group in Guingamp to collect together as many airmen in the area as possible. Le Cun says that when they re-established contact with Bourgogne, they also sent airmen (from Brest) who were lodged and cared for in Guingamp until there was a departure scheduled, when François Kerambrun would arrange to have them taken by truck to Plouha. In March, at which time they had no more airmen in the region, Harrison (Dumais) sent some from Paris – Le Cun would meet them at the station ("toujours accompagné de son énorme chien" – a German Shepherd bitch, probably not called Fifi) and organise their lodging until the next departure.

The three departures in March were supposed to be the last but in April, Le Cun was involved in helping another six airmen – see Brennan (2025) and his crew later.

Mme Vve Denise Le Cun (born Oct 1869) lived above her Magasin d'Optique at 4-6 place du Centre in Guingamp. She sheltered one Englishman (Blackwell) for 16 days, and later, six Americans that her son Georges brought in at various times to spend the evening.

Desire Laurent (born Nov 1889) was a retired policeman, and his wife Francine (born Aug 1889) a retired nurse, of 1 rue de l'Etang du Prieuré, Guingamp. They first because involved with resistance activities in October 1943 when they sheltered Marcel Jaffrot (who was being hunted after helping T/Sgt John Scott (#70) from the B-17 Lady Godiva which crashed off Saint-Quai-Portrieux on 29 May 1943) and it was through Mathurin Branchoux that Jaffrot was evacuated by MGB 318 from Ile Guennoc on Operation Felicitate II. They were then recruited by Branchoux as logeurs for reseau Shelburn, and (uniquely) sheltered evaders for all five of the Bonaparte operations – Desire adding that extra food for the evaders was supplied by Le Guillou (assume farmer Jean Baptiste Guillou of Bulat Pestivien).

Mme Vve Louise Chareton (born Jan 1893) and her son André Georges Chareton (born Jan 1922) of 54 rue du Grand Trotrieux, Guingamp. According to their NARA file, André had two older sisters, aged 29 and 30 but no other details are given.

François Kerambrun of 2 et 6 rue du Vally, Guingamp was the mechanic-garagiste of "Etablissements F Kerambrun – Agences Citroën et Panhard". Born in November 1900, François was married to Aline (née Boussougant Sept 1907) and they had six children. He was recruited by Mathurin Branchoux and Georges Le Cun who wanted the use of his truck – "une pauvre vieille camionette à gazogène, just un engin capable de rouler à toute petite allure" – which was often driven by his mechanic, Jean Trifol, to take groups of evaders from Guingamp and Châtelaudren to Plouha where he says that François Cornec and his group were responsible for receiving them.

"Mathurin Branchoux had a friend named Jean Devienne (alias François) who was the responsable of another Front National group, and through fellow FN member Pierre Cottin, he met Adolphe Le Trocquer who told him there were half a dozen evaders hidden in the Gourin (western Brittany) area. Branchoux suggested that the airmen be transferred from Gourin to Plouha, and Le Cornec and Dumais agreed to take them on the next operation. Le

Trocquer went to Guingamp where Branchoux advised him to see François Kerambrun about transport. Kerambrun was away at the time but M. Trifol, one of his employees, agreed to take them in his employer's gazogène Citroën. He collected the six airmen and took them to Pommerit-le-Vicomte (north-east of Guingamp) where they were interrogated by the multi-lingual Jacky du Pac to ensure they were genuine. Le Trocquer and Joseph Mainguy persuaded M. Trifol to carry on collecting airmen from their various refuges and he finally delivered fifteen evaders safely to Plouha. Adolphe Le Trocquer then walked the men through the night, along the railway line, until they could be distributed amongst the various safe houses around the town.

In Guingamp, the usual first stop for evaders was M. and Mme Laurent at rue de l'Etang du Prieur, not far from Mathurin Branchoux. Others went to the flour mill of M. Lanoë on rue Chateaubriand near la place Saint-Sauveur. Another contact was M. De Sonis [Souis – query], a member of the A.S. who contacted Branchoux and, after consulting his mother, offered their home for sheltering evaders. Other occasional lodgers included Mme Rannou at Pont-Melvez, Mme Le Cun, and part-time teacher Mme Lefeuvre, whose daughter was married to an Englishman." (my translation from Huguen 1976)

In between the various Bonaparte operations, Dumais and Labrosse returned to Paris and the next mention I have of Dumais is when he was called to Levallois-Perret on 11 February to interrogate Belgian fighter pilot Leon Harmel.

Very few of the evaders met Ray Labrosse, who may have travelled to Brittany with Dumais but on the first operation as least, stayed away from the embarkation beach so as to able to report direct to London on the outcome. Labrosse spent much of his time in the capital sheltered by Charles Jean Marie Dorré (station master at gare de La Chapelle) and his family, and operated his radio from their home at 22 rue Pajol, Paris XVIII.[18]

The Evaders

F/Sgt Leon J G Harmel (1807) was the 22-year-old Belgian pilot of 350 Sqn Spitfire AD314. He was escorting B-26 Marauder bombers to Amiens on 20 December 1943 when he was hit by flak and crash-landed in a field near Vironchaux (Somme), about 20 kms north of Abbeville.

18 Labrosse later married Monsieur Dorré's daughter, Ginette.

Harmel threw his parachute and Mae West into the burning aircraft and ran to hide in some woods where he stayed until nightfall. That evening he set off walking southwards and after swimming across a river, came across a farm. Harmel declared himself to the farmer, who gave him some food, civilian clothes and shelter, and the farmer's son donated his identity card, to which Harmel attached one of his escape-kit photographs. It would seem that the family were (understandably) nervous of keeping an Allied airman in their house because Harmel was woken at three o'clock the following morning and sent on his way. Harmel walked into the southern part of Foret de Crécy (the farmer had warned him there were Germans in the western and eastern parts of the forest) where he hid for the rest of the day.

That evening, Harmel left the forest but as it was so cold, he soon approached another farm at Nouvion. Like the first family, the farmer was obviously nervous about sheltering an evader but he let Harmel sleep overnight in his barn. Next morning, Harmel made another early start, walking all that day (22 December) towards Abbeville, which he avoided, and on to Villers-sous-Ailly. He went to the village church and approached the curé who was preparing a Christmas tree but he was too afraid to help at all so Harmel went into a café and ordered a meal. Whilst paying his bill, Harmel confided in the woman at the café and produced the RAF wings from his uniform. She agreed to shelter him overnight and told him that he would be able to take a train to Paris "without any difficulty". Next day, an elderly lady friend of his hostess took Harmel to the village of Long where they crossed the Canal de la Somme to the station at Longpré-les-Corps-Saints and she bought him a ticket for Paris.

Harmel reached Paris at about nine o'clock in the evening, decided it was too late to contact his hostess' son and so took a room at a small hotel on Impasse de Budapest. Early next morning, Harmel set off to 8 rue de Londres, and on finding it to be an office for the SNCF, asked to speak to M. Ple. Harmel told M. Ple that he had been sent by his mother and Ple telephoned a M. Gauchet at the hôtel de Ville in Levallois-Perret. Harmel stayed at Ple's office for the rest of the day, taking lunch at his house and being given a better suit of clothes. That evening, Mme Henriette Gauchet took him back to her house at 57 rue Danton, Levallois-Perret, and then to the hôtel Beausejour on rue Jules-Guesde, where Harmel stayed, apart from two nights spent at the Gauchet house when Germans came to arrest young Frenchmen at the hotel.

While Harmel was at the hotel, M. Ple had sent a letter to Harmel's father in Izel (Belgium) and he came to Paris see his son on 7 January. Harmel's father then arranged for Leon to stay with his cousin, M. Mardon, a jeweller at nearby rue Aristide Briand, and Leon moved there that same day.

Harmel says that he continued to worry the Gauchets to help him get back to England, and Mme Gauchet made contact with a racing cyclist named René Loiseau, who had been connected with getting people out of France. M. Loiseau came to visit Harmel at Mme Gaugher's house and on about 24 January, took him to meet Margot (Marguerite Di Giacomo) at 5 rue Baudin, Levallois-Perret. Margot told Harmel that she had previously sheltered two other airmen (sic), one an American (sic), Captain Williams, and a Russian who had escaped from Rennes, and she showed Harmel their photographs. While he was at Margot's, Jacky du Pac came to see Harmel, told him not to go out and that another man would visit him shortly – and on 11 February, a man with a hooked nose (Lucien Dumais) arrived to interview him. On 13 February, Jacky du Pac took Harmel to stay with Albert Poncelet, the concierge at 24 boulevard des Capucines, Paris IX and again Harmel was told not to go out, and then on 20 February, two Americans (William Campbell (#473) and Frank Moast (#474) – see later) joined him. On 23 February, a man with a moustache (Marcel Cola) who had visited previously to make Harmel an identity card, took Harmel to gare Montparnasse where he was handed over to a guide who took Harmel and American escaper Lee Gordon (#434) to Guingamp.

René Alfred Loiseau (born May 1922) was about 5 ft 7 inches tall, with light coloured hair and blue eyes. He had served briefly with the French navy (and because his mother had given away many of his clothes, leaving just his uniform, he is described by some evaders as being a sailor) but been demoted after refusing to fire on the Allies in North Africa. His mother Suzanne had been helping evading Frenchmen since 1940 – her husband Alfred was blinded in the First War – and René had helped by taking some of them across the demarcation line to southern France. One of Mme Loiseau's lodgers at 4 rue Baudin, Levallois-Perret was Jacky du Pac and in November 1943 he recruited René to help him convoying military evaders. René's activities were already known to the authorities and so he had moved across the road from his parents' apartment to live with Marguerite Di Giacomo, who he subsequently recruited into the François organisation, along with her next-door neighbour Yvonne Latrace.[19]

Marguerite Di Giacomo (aka Margot) was 38 years old (born Jan 1906), about 5 ft 4 inches tall, with dark hair. In addition to sheltering evaders in her apartment, she also collected some of them from l'Oise. Margot lived next door to Yvonne Latrace, 34 years old, about 5 ft 3 inches tall with blonde hair and blue eyes. Both women's husbands were POWs in Germany. Evaders often stayed in Yvonne's apartment during the day while she was working at the Philippe restaurant on rue Daunou but spent the night in Margot's apartment. NARA lists 35 evaders (not all Shelburn) who were housed by Marguerite Di Giacomo.

Marcel Gustave Leonce Cola (aka Yvon) (born May 1907) was a widower who lived at 12 rue Piccini (or 74 avenue d'Argenteuil, Asnieres) and worked as chief of personnel at the Ford Motor Company. Cola was brought up in Canada and the US and is often described by evaders as French-Canadian. He was recruited by his friend Henri Bois in November 1943 and joined reseau François to work as a guide, taking evaders to Brittany. However, following the arrest of Marie-Rose Zerling on 5 February 1944, Cola resigned his position at Ford to work full-time with reseau François organising lodgings, and became "chef d'equipe Yvon" under Paul Campinchi. With his fluent English and knowledge of North America, he also took on the job of interrogator. Always well-dressed and with a superficially similar physical description to Jacky du Pac, it is possible to confuse the two men from some of the evader reports.

Marcel Cola had told Harmel and Gordon there would be a man at Guingamp station to meet them who would pass his hand over his head as a recognition sign but no such man appeared. After waiting for two or three hours, it was decided that their French guide should return to Paris while Harmel and Gordon waited in Guingamp. They went to "one or two cafés and had several drinks" and Harmel admits to getting very drunk. He asked at the cafés for the local cure's address but he declined to help them and so they went to find a hotel room before returning to one of the cafés and having more drinks.

---

19 Information from Dominique Lecomte, who knew René Loiseau for several years before his death in December 2016.

After a while, they noticed three men sitting at another table, and Lee Gordon said that one of them was wearing an American flying jacket under his civilian clothes. Harmel says that they "raised their voices, speaking English", at first with no effect but later the man with the American jacket came over and asked if they had been expecting to meet someone at the station that morning. On hearing the affirmative, he went and fetched a man wearing glasses who led the two airmen to the house of an elderly couple where they stayed overnight. That evening, Jacky du Pac arrived from Paris, very angry that Harmel had got so drunk, and they decided the rendezvous at the station had probably gone wrong because their contact had failed to make the recognition signal.

In the afternoon of 25 February, the man with the glasses took Harmel and Lee Gordon to another house where several Americans were waiting in a poultry house. An hour or so later, they were all loaded into a van and driven to Plouha where Harmel and three of the Americans were sheltered overnight with a woman who sold silks. Next day (26 February), they were told to be ready and that evening, the man with the hooked nose (Dumais) and three others came to fetch them. Dumais aimed an automatic pistol at Harmel while his hands were tied behind his back, and later attached him by rope to American 2/Lt Milton Church (#423) who was told that Harmel was his prisoner. They were all led to a hut where Dumais told them that they were leaving, and would be in England for breakfast.

That's Harmel's version of the story, taken mostly from his MI9 report. Roger Huguen also describes Harmel's arrival at Guingamp with Lee Gordon – and see Gordon's more detailed version later.

> *"Georges Le Cun had gone to Guingamp station to meet two airmen. Although he used all the usual recognition signs, he did not spot any guides or parcels. He assumed that the trip had failed and, after warning Branchoux, he returned home. At that time the interrogations were entrusted to Jacky du Pac, who spoke several languages and was staying with Mme Laurent. Then Fernand Trochel came to tell Le Cun that two unknown men, in a state of advanced intoxication, were making a scene at the Café du Cycle. One of them spoke in French but not the other. The owner, Ernest Josselin, who was also a resistant, had called Trochel thinking they might be airmen. Georges Le Cun went to the Laurent house to consult Jacky and ask him to come to the Josselin café. He refused to go there in case they were Gestapo agents, but agreed that Le Cun could check on their identities and then bring them to him.*

Georges Le Cun and Fernand Trochel, each armed with a revolver, went to the Café du Cycle and found the two men in question. One was completely drunk, leaned against the table, in a deep sleep. The other, more awake, said immediately to Le Cun.

Hey, here is a man that I know! I saw you at the station. You were leaning by the library and seemed to be waiting. – You did not have a convoyeur with you? – Yes, but as the train back to Paris was already in the station, I told him to take it and that I would manage. My friend here is an American airman who has escaped from Germany.

What did you do when you left the station? – As I did not know where to go, I went a bar to ask for the cleaner. At home in Belgium, he is always the one who knows these things. They told us he wasn't there, they didn't know where he was, but they gave me five hundred francs! – But did you have to get drunk? – Oh we only had a couple of glasses, but my friend was so happy to be free that it went to his head.

Georges Le Cun continued to question the French-speaking airman. He said he was fighter pilot in the R.A.F. who had been shot down over northern France. Le Cun told him follow ten metres behind while his American colleague, supported by the Guingampais, took the opposite pavement. Fernand Trochel, ten metres further back, was ready to draw his gun if the Belgian made the least attempt to escape. They crossed the town without incident to Laurent's house where the pilot was locked in the cellar. A little later Jacky du Pac arrived and he recognised the Belgian from having met him before in Paris. Then some questions were put to the American. It was very difficult to understand his answers, not only was he still very drunk but he also had a shocking (épouvantable) Californian accent. The following day, he managed to tell the story of his extraordinary escape – it was nearly a year since he had bailed out into the North Sea. Léo Harmel was forgiven for his behaviour of the previous day, which fortunately hadn't compromised the organisation. He had the time to thank heaven that it was Jacky he met, otherwise he might have found himself buried in the back of the Mme Laurent's garden, as there was no question of risking bringing an enemy agent into the network." (my translation from Huguen 1976)

S/Sgt Lee C Gordon (#434) was the ball-turret gunner of 305BG/365BS B-17 41-24623 (Stallman) which was shot down off Wilhelmshaven on 26 February 1943. At least two crew were killed and Gordon and the rest captured but Gordon, having spent his twenty-first birthday in captivity, escaped from Stalag VIIA (Moosburg) on 13 October 1943.

Lee Gordon's story is one of the most complex of all the men brought out by Shelburn (he really deserves a book of his own) but unfortunately, while a typed copy of his time in German hands is included in his MIS-X report, some of the finer details of his adventures in France are concealed by Lt Emerson's trade-mark style – although I think he may be forgiven on this occasion as Gordon's mammoth 348-page report includes 130 pages of Emerson's hand-written notes.

Briefly, having finally escaped from Germany (the second, and possibly only other, American airman to do so) and making his way to Lorraine, Gordon was picked up by an organisation which sent him and evader Mike Olynik to a woman in Paris who worked for SOE agent Henri Frager. She sheltered the two airmen in her apartment for three weeks but then had to flee Paris herself, leaving them with one of her friends. They were put in contact with SIS agent Pierre Hentic's Jade-Fitzroy intelligence network, and there was talk of them leaving by air but that possibility faded with Hentic's arrest in January. Gordon was then passed to Yves Le Hénaff's Dahlia organisation to be evacuated by sea from Finistere but that attempt ended in shipwreck. Having survived one maritime adventure relatively unscathed, and evading capture once more, Gordon then met a man who, after some persuasion, took him back to Paris where he rejoined Olynik, and the two Americans were finally taken on by reseau François.

Some parts of Gordon's report are particularly intriguing as he seems to have had an excellent memory, along with a great eye for detail, sometimes including names and incidents not found elsewhere.

The first American airman that I know to have escaped from a German camp is Sgt Charles E McDonald (1316) of Shreveport, Louisiana. McDonald had joined the RCAFVR as a 21-year-old in September 1940, and was shot down near Saint-Omer in 403 Sqn Spitfire R7279 on 21 August 1941. McDonald escaped from a work party near Gleiwitz (now Gliwice, Poland) on 11 August 1942, and was sheltered by the Polish resistance until being sent to Paris in March 1943. He was passed to the Oaktree escape line in April, and crossed the Pyrenees to Spain on 3 June 1943.

Cpl Raymond Sarant (#451) 168 Infantry, USA is the only other American I know to have successfully escaped from a POW camp in Germany. 29-year-

old Sarant was captured with his anti-tank company near Kassarine, Tunisia in February 1943, escaped from Stalag IIIB (Furstenburg) on about 22 October 1943, and crossed the Pyrenees to Spain in January 1944.

In contrast to one of his earlier attempts, when Gordon rode a bicycle bought from a German guard, and wore especially commissioned lederhosen to disguise himself as a member of the Hitler Youth, this time he simply changed into French civilian clothing and walked out of the camp, along with French-speaking LRDG Captain Richard Carr (of the water-biscuit family) as though on a work party. They made their way on foot to Munich – where Carr joined Captains George Tsoucas SBS (1886) and Ralph Palm SAAF (1628), who had escaped from Moosburg two weeks earlier (on 29 September) – and Gordon contacted a French arbeitskommando. He was then passed him on to other groups of French workers until he finally reached the relative safety of Strasbourg on 30 October. From there he went to Saint-Nicolas-de-Port (Lorraine) where, after asking numerous people for assistance, he finally found help in a café. He was taken to an organisation in Nancy that sent him and Mike Olynik (#431) to Paris in November.

According to Huguen, Gordon was sheltered by some people in a café near Luneville who, after verifying his identity with London, took him by bicycle to Nancy. I have not been able to identify the organisation at Nancy but Gordon says in his report that they asked if he knew about machine-guns, and showed him Sten guns, grenades, explosives and a brand new RCA radio, which I'm guessing were supplied by SOE.

S/Sgt Mike Olynik (#431) was the 29-year-old right waist-gunner of 96BG/337BS B-17 42-3348 Dottie J III (Bye) which was returning from Schweinfurt on 14 October 1943. The aircraft was damaged by flak over the target and attacked by fighters on the return. Down to two engines, losing altitude rapidly and with the pilot unable to warn his crew because the interphone was shot out, the aircraft, which the navigator described as a sieve, was crash-landed in flames near Thiaucourt-Regnieville (Meurthe-et-Moselle) at about four o'clock in the afternoon.

Three other crew from Dottie J III also evaded successfully: navigator 2/Lt Merle Woodside (#244) and pilot 2/Lt Raymond F Bye (#287) were evacuated by MGB, Woodside from Ile Tariec (near L'Aber Wrac'h) at the beginning of December (Op Envious IIb) and Bye from the neighbouring Ile Guennoc on Christmas Day (Op Felicitate II), and radio operator T/Sgt Kenneth H Nice (#772) who was helped by Bourgogne and crossed the Pyrenees to Spain in June 1944.

Despite the extensive damage to their aircraft, all ten crew were more or less safe on the ground although tail-gunner (S/Sgt Alton Baer Jnr) had been shot in the foot and was left with a farmer working in a nearby field. As the other nine men ran from the burning aircraft, Olynik, who had also been wounded, decided it would be better if he left the others and so turned off to continue alone. He soon encountered a French woman who suggested he head for the local town but he ignored that and hid himself in some bushes for the rest of the afternoon. He set off again at about six o'clock that evening, making his way across fields and woods but didn't get very far before he had to stop and rest his feet – he was still wearing his flying boots and heated shoes, having left his GI shoes in the aircraft. After a short nap, he carried on walking, getting directions south from a farmer, who also gave him some of the turnips he was picking. Later that evening, Olynik saw a girl on a bicycle who was whistling "It's Long Way to Tipperary" (which was a common recognition signal for the French to use) and when he approached her, she directed him to some woods, agreed another signal and said she would return later. At about ten o'clock the following morning, two men cycled up and gave the new signal, handed Olynik some civilian clothing and took him to where his journey was arranged.

> *Unfortunately, the rest of Olynik's report consists only of Donald Emerson's notes which are particularly challenging in this case, although some of the detail of Olynik's time in Paris can be compared with Lee Gordon's equally hard-to-read account.*

Elise Mangin (of 65 Route de Thionville, Metz) is mentioned, and Olynik being taken by truck to Sampigny (Meuse) and a building where Olynik had two rooms and a kitchen above a cheese-plant to himself. I think he was sheltered there for two weeks by a man called Robert Collin and his wife before spending another two weeks with a family of four (Carchon – query), which included two daughters. Robert Collin then told Olynik that he was leaving for Paris, and on 11 November, Olynik was taken by truck to Lérouville to catch a train for Nancy, where he stayed overnight in some kind of deserted building – and met Lee Gordon (#434).

Gordon says that he and Mike Olynik left Nancy on 12 November, taken (second class) on an early morning train to Paris by the 22-year-old woman who had brought Olynik from Lérouville, and her husband, a heavy-set man aged about 40, about 5 feet 6 inches tall, balding and with his remaining hair combed back. They had no problems on the train to the capital but then had to wait around near the station until a man called Jean-Claude (fairly tall, aged about 27, with blond hair and a long moustache) arrived. Jean-Claude took them to 9 avenue Niel, Paris XVII where Olynik says there was a man who sold pianos (there are still shops on the ground floor of the apartment building today). Olynik and the girl's husband walked, and the other three took the elevator, to an apartment six floors up. This was the home of Germaine Royannez – described by Olynik as being about 52 years old, 5 feet 5 inches tall, a nurse in the last war – who told the two Americans they would probably be staying for about a month. There was also a maid named Simone, and a big tall French boy called Lucien Thibaut living there.

Mlle Germaine Royannez (born April 1906) (aka Françoise) says that in the spring of 1943, she was the intermediary between "groupe Brossolette" (BCRA agent Pierre Brossolette) and the Morin family at Napoleon's Tomb (Les Invalides) (see later). Of more immediate relevance to this story, she also worked for SOE agent Henri Frager, "chef du groupe Jean-Marie" (known in London as the Donkeyman circuit), and gives his address as 13 boulevard de Montparnasse, Paris VI.

She first became involved in evasion activities in July 1943 when Frager asked her to collect three American airmen from the Rambouillet area where local resistance chief Jacques Gotkovsky was sheltering them in some woods near his home, La Bourbonniere, at Les Essarts-le-Roi. They were 1/Lt James Munday (#104), T/Sgt Francis Green (#105) and T/Sgt Edward Ruby (#108) – the pilot, left waist-gunner and radio operator of B-17 42-3330 which was shot down on 14 July 1943. Doctor Maurice Racine (of 11 rue Gounod, Paris XVII) at the Faculté de Medecine (where I think Mlle Royannez worked) supplied an ambulance, complete with driver and stretcher bearer, to take her and Frager to Les Essarts-le-Roi. At one point they had to stop and explain to the ambulance crew why they wanted to detour around Trappes and avoid German inspection, gaining their enthusiastic support for the venture when they did so. They found the three airmen, and because they were then too many to fit in the vehicle, Frager took Green and Ruby by train while Mlle Royannez went with the injured Munday in the ambulance back to avenue Niel. She sheltered the three Americans for about three weeks (Munday being treated for his injuries by Dr Soulier) until they were passed on to Bourgogne.

In October 1943, while Henri Frager was in England – he left by Lysander the night of 20-21 October – it was another man from groupe Jean-Marie (only identified as Jean-Claude), who asked Mlle Royannez to take on two more Americans, Lee Gordon and Mike Olynik, who were coming from Nancy.

During their stay at avenue Niel, they met a man called Bernard, who was some kind of benefactor, and Alex – who may have been an American civilian but I haven't managed to decipher anything else about him. They also met Doctor Joseph Gorjux who came with his wife and daughter. On 4 (query) December, they received a visit from a man called Pierrot (written as Perot), who said he was going to England by aircraft and would take Gordon and Olynik with him. Pierrot also brought his wife who apparently helped escapers from the Marseille area. Olynik describes Pierrot as being about 35 years old, tall, with dark curly hair and a pimply face. On 8 December, Pierrot returned with his boss, Maho (written as Maro) who said the departure was off for a few days.

Next day, Mlle Royannez was warned that the Gestapo knew about her benefactor, Bernard – this followed on from a warning a week earlier to keep an eye on Lucien as he was apparently no good – Olynik says that he asked too many questions – and although Mlle Royannez maid said she thought he was crazy rather than a spy, Mlle Royannez was getting increasingly worried about keeping him. Jean-Claude came to the apartment carrying a .32 revolver that he said he would use on Lucien that night, and Bernard went with them that evening to Chartres, returning the following morning to say that the deed had been done in the swamps off a lonely road near Chartres. Jean-Claude returned three hours later with Lucien's papers in his pocket, and showed them an empty cartridge case. Later that day, Mlle Royannez found that seven 5,000 franc notes had gone missing from her jewellery box, and although they searched Lucien's room, no trace was found of the money.

Next day, the Gestapo were spotted following Bernard's mother, and that night Bernard, Gordon, Olynik and Simone left the Royannez apartment and went to stay overnight with one of Mlle Royannez friends, a grey-haired woman with a kitchen and bedroom on the second floor (this was Mme Marlier, concierge at 45 boulevard Ornano, Paris XVIII, and the mother of another of Frager's agents). Next morning, everyone left except the two Americans but that evening, Bernard's mother returned to take them to an apartment off the rue du Laos where she, Bernard, Germaine Royannez and Simone were staying with Doctor Gorjux.

Joseph Marius Etienne Gorjux (born April 1889) and his wife Yvonne Marguerite (born Oct 1893), who are listed as logeurs by Marcel Cola, lived just off rue du Laos at 2 Square Theodore Judin. They had two children, Pierrette (born Mar 1916) and her younger brother Guy Henry, who lived at La Cellete, Correze. Joseph was a highly decorated military doctor (Medecin Colonel) with responsibilities in the French colonies. The doctor and his wife were arrested on 3 August 1944 and deported to Germany – Joseph survived Buchenwald but Yvonne died of typhus at Bergen-Belsen in March 1945.

Gordon says that Doctor Gorjux had sheltered four Americans before, including James (?) Greene, a bombardier from Boston. The bombardier was 2/Lt Roscoe Greene (#87) from Maine. Greene was evading with S/Sgt Lawrence Templeton (#86), tail-gunner from the same aircraft as Joe Cornwall (mentioned later), when they were sheltered overnight (19-20 July 1943) with Therese Fabre in her hôtel de l'Ouest at 28 boulevard du Fort de Vaux. Next day, Mlle Helene Rochefort (aka Marthe, of 91 rue Lemercier, Paris XVII), took them to Dr Gorjux on rue du Laos (sic) where they stayed from 20 July to 5 August, and where Templeton says they met 1/Lt William Wetzel (#88) and 1/Lt Ralph McKee (#89), the pilot and navigator of B-17 42-5053 Bloody Tangier Show. McKee says that he and Wetzel arrived in Paris on 3 August and went by Metro to Dr André Lwoff's apartment (at 69 avenue de Suffren). The following afternoon, they were interrogated by a Colonel Brunet, Jean Brunet, Helene Rochefort and another doctor. That night they met Greene and Templeton at the second doctor's house, and two nights later, all four airmen left for Spain – crossing the border from Peyrehorade on 10 August. Note that the only likely IS9 entry for Brunet is a Jean Brunet but with no address given. Note also that avenue de Suffren (where Dr Lwoff lived) is at the end of rue du Laos.

Mme Vve Therese Marie Fabre (born Feb 1892 (to French parents) in Dolores, Argentina) was the proprietor of the hôtel de l'Ouest at 28 boulevard du Fort de Vaux, Paris XVII (where she lived with her 25-year-old daughter

Emilienne). She is credited by IS9 with sheltering some fifty Allied evaders, and recommended for an MBE.

Mme Fabre first became involved with helping evaders in April 1943 when friends in Normandy brought 2/Lt Edward T Logan and 2/Lt Homer H Mohr (co-pilot and navigator of B-17 42-5232 Available Jones, shot down 4 April 43) to be sheltered for ten days while they tried to contact an organisation. Mme Fabre says that she was never part of any organisation or network herself, although MIS-X describe her hotel as being a centre for Liberation-Vengeance where practically all evaders handled by that group were sheltered. Like Doctor Gorjux, she is listed by Marcel Cola, and Doctor Lwoff by Mary-Rose Zerling, as being a lodger (logeuse) for reseau François.

Bernard and Simone lasted about eight days at the doctor's apartment before going back to the avenue Niel apartment to pick up a radio and other things they had forgotten to bring with them. On their return, Simone reported that the concierge had told her that two men had been asking about Mlle Royannez, one of them speaking French with a German accent (Mlle Royannez says that Simone told her that the concierge was from Alsace and heard them speaking German, a language that she spoke fluently). Gordon seems to say that he had also seen two (presumably suspicious looking) men walking past the doctor's house, at which news, Mlle Royannez, Bernard and Simone left Paris for self-imposed exile in l'Eure-et-Loir.

On about 14 December, Pierrot had returned to tell the two Americans that they would leave soon by aircraft, a message that was repeated a few days later, but on 20 December they heard that an English radio operator had been caught by the Germans and shot.

Following the problems of Operation Envious IIb the night of 1-2 December, Pierrot had brought Sub-Lt Michael Pollard (1651) from MGB 318, and RAF evader Sgt Thomas H Adams (1650) to Paris – Adams says on about 10 December. Pollard and Adams understood that Pierrot was hoping to send them back to England by Lysander but "that did not materialise" and they returned to Brittany on about 22 December.

At about this time, Gordon says that he told Doctor Gorjux that he would like to see some of the sights around Paris and his report includes military information from around the city, and damage assessment of several places that had been hit by Allied bombing, including the Hispano-Suiza works.

The date isn't stated but Gordon and Olynik both mention Mme Denise Morin – Olynik saying that she came to say she would try and get some friends of hers to help them. Mme Morin told them that her daughter Yvette was engaged to an American sergeant named Joe who had left by plane, and about five other evaders she had helped, two English and three Americans, including an Englishman called Tony, Harry, Roy (?), and a tall Texan – and Gordon says that he "wrote his name under theirs at Les Invalides".

Joe was S/Sgt Joseph Cornwall (#125), who was sheltered in the Morin home at Les Invalides (where they were the caretakers) in July 1943 and later flown to England by SD Lysander in October on an operation organised by Pierre Hentic. Tony, Roy and Harry were Sgt James Trusty (1449), W/O Roderick Scott (1556) and S/Sgt Harry Eastman (#112), all sheltered by the Morin family in August 1943. The tall Texan was probably S/Sgt Lester Brown (#52) from Austin, who stayed at Les Invalides for eight days in June-July, along with S/Sgt John Houghton (#53).

Georges Julien Morin (born Aug 1898), his wife Denise (born December 1898) and their daughter Yvette (born October 1921), of 2 avenue de Tourville, Paris VII, were arrested on 5 July 1944. Georges was deported to Buchenwald on 15 August 1944 and died in captivity. The two women survived Ravensbruck, Torgau, Buchenwald and Marckleberg to be repatriated to France in the summer of 1945. Mme Denise Morin was recommended for an MBE and Yvette for a KMC.

Gordon then met a woman called Jacqueline – her father was apparently a French colonel or general who had gone to England. Jacqueline was slim, about 5 feet 8 inches tall, and when she visited, she brought her mother – she told Gordon that her brother was a successful lawyer, and they were all crazy about Americans.

Gordon also reports meeting a "mademoiselle" and her mother, neither of whom were in the organisation, and a doctor's daughter called Naomi (or maybe Nanni) who knew the Gorjux son. He also met Henri, the English-speaking boyfriend of Pierette Gorjux (about 26 years old, well built, with brown hair) – he was a lawyer and separated from his wife, and Gordon was taken to his house near the Citroën factory (at Quai de Javel, now Quai André Citroën) a couple of times. Apparently Henri and seven other men were (or had been) involved in some kind of action against the Germans involving the theft of documents and four million francs, which resulted in two Frenchmen and three Germans being shot – and Henri having to change his address.

Both reports become rather confusing at this point but in addition to references to two men, known only as Perot (sic) and Jeannot, there is also a man they call the Optician. I mentioned at the beginning of this book that it has been a collaboration and this example (chosen from many) should serve to illustrate the point. While the names Perot and Jeannot were too common to identify by themselves, reference to the Optician was new to me. I put the question out to my contacts, and within twenty-four hours, veteran researcher Michael Moores LeBlanc gave me the name Marcel Petrucci, saying that he was linked to Doctor Gorjux – and to a Mme de Larminat. The name de Larminat was familiar as a contact of Denise Morin, and a quick search of my records also showed reference to her in "Tant qu'il y aura des étoiles", the 2006 book by Pierre Hentic. She is only mentioned briefly but on the same page were the identities of Pierrot and Jeannot.

Pierrot was Pierre Tissier, and Jeannot his cousin, radio operator Eugene Lorion. Both men worked with SIS agent Pierre Hentic (aka Maho), who says that Tissier was his first recruit into the Jade-Amicol network.

Marcel Petrucci (aka l'Opticien) (born June 1908) of 128 rue de Tolbiac, Paris XII, was arrested in June 1944 and deported, sent to Buchenwald in August on same train as Pierre Tissier, Joseph Gorjux and Georges Morin. Marie-Madeleine de Larminat, was arrested on 6 June (Pierette Gorjux says 13 July) 1944 but released on 11 August.

Note that in December, the idea of Gordon and Olynik being picked up by aircraft had been a real possibility as Pierre Hentic (aka Trellu) had organised several Lysander pick-ups, including (as already mentioned) one that collected American evader Joe Cornwall. However, with bad weather hampering air operations (four Lysanders were lost that month), Hentic was otherwise occupied with sea evacuations from the north Brittany coast, and shortly after his return to Paris in early January, he was arrested.

Hentic says (in his declaration dated 24 May 1945) that it was Mme de Larminat who first asked him to help evaders when she told him she had lots of airmen on the Brittany coast near Vannes and Quimper. Hentic radioed London on behalf of Mme de Larminat and agreed to try and help with their evacuation. Hentic had heard that some of the escape lines taking airmen to Spain had been infiltrated by the Germans, and so rather than risk them being caught by going that way, decided to use his intelligence network arrangements to send them out by sea.

Following the failed operation Envious on 3 November (caused by appalling weather, combined with a lack of radio communication between MGB 318 and the shore party – something that was never really resolved) which saw numerous evaders being returned to their helpers in and around Brest, Hentic took one of his own Lysander flights to England (Op Salvia from a field near Reims on 11 Nov 43) to receive instructions from his MI6 bosses, and discuss the problems they had encountered. He was returned to France by MGB 318 on the otherwise failed Envious II(a) on 26-27 November – bad weather again disrupting communications but Hentic and a folding Folboat canoe were finally landed at Resservor, a tiny island west of Aber-Benoit.

The subsequent Operation Envious IIb of 1-2 December was again hampered by the weather, with seven evaders returned to the UK but six RN personnel (from two of the surf-boats) left behind, and "complete catastrophe" being only narrowly averted.

Some of the airmen brought to Brittany for evacuation by sea had earlier been helped by the MI9 Possum escape line, which was based in Reims. Hentic had a contact in Reims – BCRA agent Henri Bertin – and through him, met Possum organiser Major Dominique Edgard Potier and his radio operator, Conrad Lafleur. This must have been on or before 11 November, when Hentic (as already mentioned) was flown to the UK. A week later (the night of 16-17 Nov), Potier flew to London (along with 1 RAF and 4 US aircrew evaders) on the same double Lysander Operation Magdalen II (Verity & McCairns) that landed Dumais and Labrosse.

SIS officer Tom Greene says of Pierre Hentic (in a letter dd 1 September 1945 to MI9 boss Norman Crockatt) "that of all the agents I have come into contact with during this war, none ran more risks, had more successes, was more honest, and certainly less assuming, than Hentic."

Pierre Tissier and Eugene Lorion were in England at this time, finally evacuated on Operation Felicitate II from Ile Guennoc by MGB 318 on

Christmas Day 1943. Tissier and Lorion both returned to France (no details found), with Tissier organising his first of several Lysander operations on the night of 2-3 March – including Operation Silene the night of 6-7 May which brought back P-47 ace (21 kills) Major Walter M Mahurin (#617). Pierre Tissier (born 1 September 1915) was arrested on 29 June 1944, and deported to Buchenwald on 15 August, where he died. Pierre Hentic, writing in "Tant qu'il y aura des étoiles", says that Eugene Lorion only narrowly avoided a similar fate.

On 2 February, Lee Gordon left Paris by overnight train to Quimper (Finistere) with four other airmen (F/O John Watlington, F/Lt John Pilkington, 2/Lt Roy Davidson and S/Sgt Fred Kruger), where they were met by Yves Le Hénaff (aka Fanfan) in a truck. Next day, Gordon was one of seven Allied evaders taken (along with Buland Khan (1852) and Ralph Hall (#1246) – see later) to join a group of Frenchmen, which included Emile Bollaert, Pierre Brossolette and Emile Laffont, on board a small fishing vessel called the Jouet des Flots. The operation was organised by Yves Le Hénaff with the intention of sailing to England (some reports say to rendezvous with another boat) and they set off from Ile-Tudy (south of Quimper) that evening. But it seems the waves wanted their toy back, the weather turned against them and the boat was wrecked and sank when they tried to run her ashore at Feunteun Aod in the early hours of 4 February.

This was a desperate venture – the Jouet des Flots (which came from Douarnenez) had not been used for some time and was in less than ideal condition (she leaked like a sieve), and then damaged by hitting a rock on the approach to Ile-Tudy. While they had little choice – Bollaert and Brossolette for example were in imminent danger of arrest – it was a disaster. Emile Le Bris (from Ploaré), who had worked with Yves Le Hénaff to acquire the vessel and organise the operation, and was on board with his son, says that sixteen people (of the thirty-two passengers and crew) were caught – they included Le Hénaff, Bollaert, Brossolette and CND member Jean Bernard, who were stopped by a German patrol as they were leaving Audierne in Bernard's Simca later that same day – only Bollaert survived the war. Today there is a monument on the cliffs above Feunteun Aod to commemorate the loss of the Jouet des Flots.

RCAF evader F/O John H Watlington (1925) from Bermuda, the 24-year-old pilot of 400 Sqn Mustang AG641 who had been shot down the previous June, reports that they set off at 2130 hrs but the weather turned very rough and the boat began to take on water. Despite their best attempts at bailing, the engine was soon flooded and they were forced to turn back. They came ashore in a small bay near the Pointe de Feunteun Aod – which is south-west of Plogoff – and says that he met up with Gordon soon after the ship-wreck but then separated again after almost walking into a German patrol. Later that afternoon, he rejoined Gordon, who was by then with members of a "maquis" group, who took them to a house on the Bay of Primelin. The following afternoon, two maquis members with guns took him and Gordon to a chateau near Pont-Croix where they were sheltered with an elderly lady and her daughter-in-law. They spent two nights at the chateau before two of the maquis men took Watlington by bicycle to Quimper. On failing to find Fanfan (Yves Le Hénaff), Watlington went to Paris alone where he contacted one of his previous helpers, Mrs Jeanne Ramsey at 47 rue Dulong, Paris XVII. Watlington was later passed to an organisation in Toulouse and crossed the Pyrenees to Bossost in Spain on 28 March 1944 in the same group as Robert Krengle (#646) (mentioned earlier).

> *"We are at this moment cut off from all escape lines. The Morins had also lost contact. Maho, Pierrot and Jeannot went to Brittany where they were trying to set up an escape route. They promised to take care of our boarders, and suddenly disappeared. In January, Papa [Joseph Gorjux] made contact with "L'Opticien", Marcel Petrucci, 128 rue de Tolbiac. The latter puts us in contact with "Colibiri" who still had 1 free place in a convoy. Lee Gordon, being an evading prisoner from Germany, had the priority and left for Brittany towards the middle of January. A fishing boat .." (my translation from Pierret Gorjux statement dated 25 July 1945, in Gorjux NARA file)*

This seems to explain why Gordon was sent to Yves Le Hénaff and his Dahlia organisation (although the name Colibiri is new to me) but then Olynik says that he was supposed to follow Gordon a few days later. I don't see how that would have worked, regardless of whether the operation had been successful or not, since Le Hénaff himself (along with two of his lieutenents) was also on the board the Jouet des Flots.

Denise Morin had been passing evaders on to Gabrielle Wiame and the Bourgogne organisation but in September 1943, for some unexplained reason, became suspicious of Mme Wiame and was reluctant to hand Joe Cornwall on to her. She tried contacting a Polish colonel for help, but was then advised by her friend, Maurice Cottereau, that the colonel (known as l'Oncle Georges) couldn't be trusted either. On 16 October, the whole Morin family took Cornwall to the gare d'Austerlitz and handed him over to a contact of Pierre Hentic, who sent him to England by Lysander two nights later. It must have been after Gordon left for Quimper that Mme Morin was first put in touch with Marcel Cola and reseau François – probably by Dr Gorjux who seems to be the only contact they had in common.

Gordon stayed at the chateau near Pont-Croix until 10 February, when a young man known as Mickey took him and evader James Quinn (#433) on an early morning bus from Audierne to Quimper. Mickey wanted to take them to Brest and then Rennes but Gordon insisted on going straight to Paris, and that evening, they caught an eight o'clock train to the capital.

When Gordon and Quinn arrived at gare Montparnasse on the morning of 11 February, there was an argument with Mickey about where to go next, and while they were in a park discussing this, attracted the attention of two gendarmes. When they were asked for their ID papers, Mickey walked away and it was left to Gordon to deal with the policemen. Despite his limited French, Gordon seems to have been successful because although the gendarmes pointed out that his carte de travail was invalid, they let the Americans go.

Gordon had been intending to return to Doctor Gorjux but with the gendarmes still watching, he took Quinn in the opposite direction, towards Les Invalides. The doctor, who had been a witness to all this, caught up and took them by a circular route, back to Square Theodore Judin. Mike Olynik was still there, and Mickey came to join them.

Two days later, Denise Morin brought Marcel Cola, the Frenchman with the Canadian accent who told the Americans they would be leaving in the next few days – Gordon was to go with Belgian Spitfire pilot Leon Harmel, and Olynik to follow with James Quinn. Gordon explains at this point that both he and Quinn had caught dysentery and that the doctor (Gorjux) had given them some medicine, and while Gordon was up again the next day, Quinn took three days to recover.

At about eight-thirty on the evening of 23 February, Marcel Cola arrived at the apartment with a woman (in her late twenties) and Leon Harmel. Cola gave Gordon 10,000 francs and the woman took Gordon and Harmel to Montparnasse station where they were handed over to an English-speaking guide. Denise Morin was also at the station and she gave Gordon a letter from her daughter Yvette to be sent to Joe Cornwall.

They seem to have picked up two more men on the train, Gordon refers to one of them as Julien, who may have been Canadian – he was about 5 foot 5 inches tall with a protracted chin, black hair and eyes – but they are not mentioned by anyone else and I have no idea who they might have been.

Their train left Paris at ten o'clock that evening, arriving at Saint-Brieuc the following morning where they changed for Guingamp. At Guingamp station they failed to find their contact, and after waiting for two hours, Harmel wanted to return to the capital – he suggested they could stay overnight in a hotel ready to meet up with the next group of evaders who were due to leave Paris the following morning.

Gordon says there were four of them at Guingamp station and that when they failed to spot their contact (and their English-speaking guide having taken a train back to Paris – Huguen says this was Mr Dussy, who needed to get back to his job at Ford), Julien suggested they try and contact the local abbé for help and so Gordon and Harmel went into the town. They started by having a glass of wine at the Blond Cheval café where they were told that all the rooms had been requisitioned by the Germans. At a second café, a woman suggested they try a third place, somewhere near the theatre – this was the Theatre du Champ au Roy at 1 place du Champ au Roy. Before they could get there, they seem to have found the abbé, who took them back to his house, but when Harmel explained that they were evading airmen, the abbé was too frightened to help them. They then tried a hotel near the theatre before going to yet another bar. I am guessing this was the Café du Cycle referred to by Huguen where they were spotted by Georges Le Cun and Fernand Trochel. Gordon says that he saw a man wearing what looked like an American A2 leather flying jacket, and on hearing them speaking in English, the man came over and asked if they had just come from Paris. Gordon told him yes and showed the man his papers. They were told to wait, and fifteen minutes later, an older man came and said that he had been at the station but had expected to meet four men – which might suggest that Julien and his friend were perhaps too obviously not military evaders. Three men then walked Gordon and Harmel to the home of an elderly couple (Desire and Francine Laurent), Gordon says that he had been a policeman, where they met a black-haired, good-looking fellow, medium build and in his early twenties who seemed to have met Harmel before in Paris – this was obviously Jacky du Pac.

Next morning, another man arrived from Paris (query) – he had black hair and was a couple of years older than Jacky. There seems to be another Canadian reference but I think this was to his coat (une Canadienne) rather than his accent – and he can't have been Marcel Cola as both evaders would have recognised him. There is also mention of the man playing chess but his identity eludes me. Gordon also mentions a girl that Olynik and Quinn knew – Louisette (query).

That evening, the man who was supposed to have met them at the station (Mathurin Branchoux), took them to a garage. They were loaded onto a truck and driven to a chicken hatchery where they collected another seven men, and they (and the girl – query) were driven to Plouha.

Lee Gordon and Leon Harmel took a train from Paris on the evening of Wednesday 23 February, leaving Mike Olynik and James Quinn with Doctor Gorjux. The following evening, Marcel Cola brought his friend Raymond Mauret, who took Olynik and Quinn to Montparnasse station, where they joined two more Americans, Louis Feingold and Warren Tarkington, on the train to Saint-Brieuc.

2/Lt Louis Feingold (#419) and **2/Lt Warren C Tarkington** (#420) were the navigator and bombardier of 95BG/336BS B-17 42-30674 Destiny's Tot (Smith) – see earlier. They landed near Saint-Just-en-Chaussée (Oise) where they were helped by the head of the local resistance organisation, Jean Crouet, and spent the night of 30 December in his house at 7 rue de Catillon. Next day, M. Crouet took them to the factory where he made camouflage paint for the Germans – he was a chemical engineer for Ford – telling the airmen that the paint had been sabotaged and offered no protection from aerial photography. The airmen were hidden in a tunnel under the factory until noon when they had lunch in M. Crouet's office. Feingold and Tarkington spent that night and all of New Year's Day in the office while "truckloads of Germans" searched the town for them. M. Crouet explained that the entire crew of a B-17 had been spirited out of the town just a month earlier (although I am unable to confirm that) and the Germans had since announced they would shoot anyone they found involved with helping Allied airmen. That night, they were taken to Leon Hary, a baker on the main street (rue de Paris), where they stayed for two days with him and his wife Idamir before returning to stay overnight with Jean Crouet. The following night, they were moved again, this time to stay with Georges and Helene Rousseau, also on rue de Paris.

Jean Crouet (born April 1903), engineer and chemist of 7 rue de Catillon, Saint-Just-en-Chaussée, was married to schoolteacher Madeleine (née Serouet Sept 1909). He is credited with sheltering, feeding, clothing and convoying at least 12 Allied evaders – Feingold and Tarkington being the first two. Most of the evaders he helped were brought to him by Dr Edmond Caillard – and knew him as Jean Weeks. Crouet says his chef de groupe was Maurice Georges Jauneau – see "Captain Jacques" earlier.

On 6 January, Feingold and Tarkington followed Jean Crouet out of town on foot until they were picked up by truck. Before he left them, M. Crouet gave Tarkington his own shoes and coat and Feingold, another overcoat. The truck driver took them about two miles before dropping them off beside two parked cars. The two airmen got into one of the cars while the other car led them to Clermont (Oise). They stayed with Odette Sauvage, her son Edmond and an ex-POW named Gaston Legrand, at their home on rue du Chatellier, where they met 2/Lt Edward Donaldson (#460) (see later). Feingold says that Odette's husband was a collaborator who had gone to Germany in 1935 so she was living with Gaston Legrand, a black-market butcher who spent much of his free time shooting collaborators.

Odette Sauvage (née Grigaut June 1906) owned a dairy and fish business (Chez Odette) at 28 rue de la Republique, Clermont. Gaston Legrand (born April 1912) had been captured at the fall of France but escaped and crossed the demarcation line to obtain his discharge from the French army before returning to Clermont, where he joined Odette. Odette and Gaston lived in a rented house on rue de Chatellier, along with Odette's teenage son, Edmond Sauvage. They worked with Gilbert Thibault, and Odette and Gaston are credited with sheltering 23 (named) Allied evaders – many of whom were passed to Bourgogne before they became involved with Shelburn, and others after Shelburn – all of whom returned safely to the UK except Glenn Camp and Jarvis Cooper (see below) who were captured, and 2/Lt Wendell McConnaha, who died whilst crossing the Pyrenees in December 1943.

During their stay at Clermont, Feingold and Tarkington were visited every other evening by a woman only identified as Mlle Bernadette – she was a dressmaker and organisation member who spoke English, having been a governess in Scotland, and she brought them books. They also met Lucien and Maurice Leclercq, sons of one of Clermont's biggest businessmen and so exempt from the German labour draft – the boys brought them food, and their mother Suzanne sent new sweaters and shoes. On 8 January, they were joined by Donaldson's pilot 2/Lt Glenn E Camp Jnr, navigator 2/Lt Jarvis H Cooper, and gunner Sgt Neelan Parker (#461) (see later).

Belgian-born Benoit Leclercq, his French wife Suzanne and their two (French-born) sons, Lucien (born Jan 1921) and Maurice, lived at Breuil-le-Sec where Benoit owned a saw-mill and timber yard. Edmond Sauvage says they helped his family enormously with food and supplies when they were sheltering evaders, and Gilbert Thibault says that Lucien worked for him as convoyeur between January 1943 and August 1944. The Leclercq house was later destroyed in an American air-raid, and Mme Leclercq badly injured. Benoit Leclercq's brother Camille (born June 1901), who lived in Auneuil and also owned a saw-mill and timber yard, was also a convoyeur for Gilbert Thibault.

On 20 January, Mlle Bernadette told them that four men could leave next day and the other two, the following Tuesday. Feingold, Tarkington and Donaldson had been there the longest and Parker won a card-draw for the fourth place, so the next morning, with Lucien Leclercq patrolling in his car, they walked to the station. They thought they were supposed to go to Beauvais but were taken instead to Creil.

In Creil, Feingold and Donaldson were sheltered overnight with engineer Marcel Gerardot, his schoolteacher wife Renée and their young daughter at 107 rue Henri Pauquet while Tarkington and Parker stayed overnight with Paul and Marguerite Toussaint at 15 rue Charles Somasco. Next morning, the four Americans were taken back to the station and Edmond Sauvage and their guide from the previous day took them by train to Noailles.

There was a car was waiting for them at Noailles station, and Edmond and the guide passed the airmen over to the driver who took them to Robert and Marthe Eckert's farmhouse on rue Mignon. Two days later (24 January), they were taken by truck to Auneuil where they stayed with

Gilbert Thibault, who Feingold and Tarkington describe as being a justice of the peace and chief of the local organisation. A barber (probably Hilaire Lemaire) gave them all haircuts and Thibault made them identity cards but only after Donaldson had been taken into Beauvais to have a new photograph taken as his old one showed him with a moustache which he had shaved off the previous day.

On 26 January, they were joined by T/Sgt Ray Reeves (#729) and the following morning, the five airmen were driven to the station to be taken to Paris by Gilbert Thibault and the barber. They went by Metro to stay with Marguerite Schmitz at 87 rue Rochechouart where they met "Olaf" and RAF Typhoon pilot F/Sgt Richard Aitken-Quack. They spent the day there and Tarkington soon told Thibaut that he thought Olaf was an imposter – and Aitken-Quack agreed. Feingold says that Aitken-Quack told him that Olaf had been posing as Norwegian until he found that the multi-lingual Aitken-Quack spoke Norwegian, at which point Olaf claimed that his parents were actually Dutch and that his father was in charge of a radio station in Norway.

F/Sgt Richard W Aitken-Quack, a veteran of the Spanish Civil and Russo-Finnish wars, was flying 609 Sqn Typhoon JP924 on 1 December 1943 when he was shot down near Valenciennes. After being helped by the Chauny-Dromas organisation, he was passed on to Marguerite Schmitz in Paris on about 18 January. T/Sgt Ray P Reeves (#729) was a cameraman on board 44BG/68BS B-24 42-7635 Ram It-Damn It (Howington) which was shot down on 21 January. Mentioned again later, he was eventually passed to the Belgian Comète organisation and taken across the Pyrenees to Spain in May 1944.

Claudette (Mary-Rose Zerling) arrived at dinner (lunch) time and told them she had already handled Richard Smith (#349) and William Booher (#350) from their crew – see earlier. After the meal, Claudette took Tarkington into one of the bedrooms to ask him about Olaf, telling Tarkington that the organisation thought he was probably a Dutchman trying to get to England and that they thought him too stupid to be a spy. That afternoon, she took Donaldson and Parker by Metro to Bertranne d'Hespel's apartment at 7 rue Maspero (see later), before returning at seven o'clock that evening to collect Feingold and Tarkington and take them by Metro to stay with Mme Jeanne Kocera-Massenet at 10 rue Ernest Renan. Claudette told them that she was going to the north of France and would be back on 8 February. Later that evening Claudette also delivered Ray Reeves to Yvonne Diximier at 8 rue Jean Moréas, Paris XVII.

Feingold and Tarkington say that they stayed with Mme Kocera-Massenet and her son Jean for four weeks, during which time, Claudette visited twice to bring them cigarettes, the last time being on 3 February when she also took them to a small shop with an automatic machine to have their photographs taken (again).[20]

On 11 February, they were interrogated by Marcel Cola who said that he was their new contact man as Claudette had been arrested after Olaf had got away from Mme Schmitz. Cola knew nothing about Parker, Donaldson, Reeves or Aitken-Quack but Mme Schmitz had also been arrested. On 14 February, Jean Kocera-Massenet and Raymond Mauret brought S/Sgt Robert Fruth (#462) and T/Sgt Harold Vines (#457) (see both later) to Paris, and Feingold and Tarkington saw them for half an hour before they were taken to stay in another apartment in the same block. Marcel Cola returned on 21 February to take their photographs (yet again) and tell them that they would be leaving for the coast that Wednesday or Thursday.

Feingold and Tarkington left Paris on the evening of Thursday 24 February. Jean Kocera-Massenet led them on foot the short distance to gare Montparnasse where they met Jean's friend Raymond Mauret, who had brought Mike Olynik (#431) and James Quinn (#433), and they got on the overnight train for Saint-Brieuc where, next morning, they changed for Guingamp.

At two o'clock in the morning of 5 February, ten soldiers and civilians came to 87 rue Rochechouart and arrested Marguerite Schmitz, Richard Aitken-Quack and Olaf/Fred. They were taken to 101 avenue Henri Martin and the horrors of the Masuy gang where Mme Schmitz was tortured for information – only finally relenting in the apparent belief that she was too old and too stupid to know anything. Meanwhile the Germans set up a trap (souricière) at her apartment which resulted in the capture later the same day of Marie-Rose Zerling. The arrest and torture of Marie-Rose Zerling led to other names being found and a series of consequent arrests followed – including Mme Jeanne Huet who had sheltered Norman Cufley and John Harvey in January.

20 I'm not sure that Jean Kocera-Massenet actually lived there – IS9 give his address as 16 rue de Saint-Senoch, Paris XVII, and Arthur Steinmetz (#233) – who stayed at 10 rue Ernest Renan, along with William Harnley (#182) in September 1943 – comments on Jean's tall attractive Norwegian wife and their two young children visiting them.

Marguerite Schmitz was condemned to death on 26 April 1944. She was held at Fresnes and only ill health prevented her deportation to Germany. She was freed with the liberation of Paris. Marie-Rose Zerling was condemned to death on 28 April 1944 and deported to Germany. She was repatriated to France on 4 August 1945.

Contrary to the opinions of some of the evaders, Mme Schmitz was not convinced that Olaf/Fred was a German agent and believed that she was actually denounced by an associate of her ex-husband, Marcel Schnerb – himself arrested on 7 February. The fact that the first questions asked of Mme Schmitz were about her ex-husband, would seem to support this.

Mary-Rose Zerling (Claudette) first encountered Olaf Hansen (aka Fred) in October 1943 when she was asked to collect him from Gaston Lepine at Sebourg, just outside Valenciennes. Olaf's story of being a Norwegian working for the BBC and escaping from a camp near Hamburg sounded suspicious but Claudette's then boss, Capitaine Dumay (query) decided that Olaf was genuine. After taking James King (#343), Walter Sentkoski (#348) and Joseph Birdwell (#471) to Paris, she returned to collect Fred who was subsequently lodged with her parents at rue Saint-Ferdinand, with Mme Wallerant at 87 boulevard de Courcelles (the same apartment building as Claudette's aunt, Marcelle Hiaux), with Marie Maziliat at 15 rue Montrosier, Neuilly-sur-Seine and finally with Marguerite Schmitz at 87 rue Rochechouart. The fact that of those helpers, only Marguerite Schmitz, and Claudette's parents and aunt were arrested (the latter almost certainly because Claudette herself was caught when she visited Mme Schmitz apartment), would seem to suggest that Olaf was not that helpful to the Germans.

Mme Jeanne Henriette Kocera-Massenet (born Jan 1885) of 10 rue Ernest Renan, Paris XV. No NARA Helper file has been found for her but there is one for her brother, Roger Massenet (born Sept 1895). He lived at 221a Route de Colmar in Strasbourg, and sent (amongst others) 2/Lt William Harnly (#182) and 2/Lt Arthur Steinmetz (#233) to be sheltered with his sister in Paris, supported by a second brother, Henri Massenet, at 25 avenue Mozart, Paris XVI.

Jean Yvan Kocera-Massenet (born April 1908 in Sarmato, Italy) of 16 rue de Saint-Sénoch, Paris XVII is credited with taking evaders to Brittany from his mother's home in Paris as well as collecting evaders from the suburbs. He also took wireless sets and other equipment to various parts of the country.

It seems generally assumed that most evaders brought out on the Shelburn line travelled via Paris. If that had been the case then this book would have been much easier to write – and quite a bit shorter. In fact, the other twelve airmen evacuated on this second Bonaparte operation all evaded in Brittany and (with the exception of James Quinn) were taken direct to Guingamp.

S/Sgt Harry L Minor (#421) was the right waist-gunner of 379BG/525BS B-17 42-29876 Battlin' Bobbie (Hoyt) which on the way to Nantes on 16 September 1943, and half an hour from their target, when they were hit by either flak or fighters – accounts vary. Co-pilot Norman Schroeder reports that the wings were covered in holes, and engines #1 and #2 were set on fire. Being unable to keep up with their formation, and with the situation rapidly deteriorating, pilot Elton Hoyt ordered his crew to bail out and the aircraft was abandoned to crash, probably somewhere near Guipry (Ille-et-Vilaine).

The 27-year-old carpenter from Pittsburgh was one of eight men from Battlin' Bobbie to evade successfully: pilot 1/Lt Elton Hoyt III (#409), co-pilot 1/Lt Norman C Schroeder (#329), navigator 2/Lt William J Cook Jnr (#410), bombardier 2/Lt Louis H Glickman (#370) and radio operator S/Sgt Herbert W Dulberg (#390) were all helped by the Bourgogne organisation and crossed the Pyrenees in various parties in December, January and February, while waist-gunner T/Sgt William J Miller (#636) and tail-gunner Sgt Edward R Shaffer (#637) were passed to the Dutch-Paris organisation in Paris and crossed the Pyrenees together in March 1944.

Minor delayed his jump from about 20,000 feet, pulling his rip-cord at about 3,000 feet just as he entered cloud, and landed in the middle of a wood where the trees broke his fall. He had hurt his back when his parachute opened, which caused some severe pain, but apart from that he was uninjured. He was still pulling his parachute down when he heard a voice calling and after leaving the chute and crawling a short distance to investigate, found a Frenchman who was obviously looking for him. They were soon joined by a small group of women and children who gathered up Minor's parachute and other flying gear and led him to a thicker part of the wood. Minor waited while some of the women went off to see where the Germans were and eventually Minor was led to a nearby farm.

Minor was hidden in a shed where he immediately had to lie down because of his back. When he explained the problem, a girl brought liniment and gave him a massage. He was also given some food and strong alcohol – the latter being what he says in his report he needed the most.

During the night of 19 September, men arrived, taking Minor on foot to a crossroads where he was collected by truck. Minor was surprised to find two other Americans, 1/Lt John Beilstein (#557) and S/Sgt Cyril Koval (one of the waist-gunners from B-17 42-29901), already on board and they were driven to a farmhouse. Unfortunately, security on the farm was non-existent and too many local people knew they were there and came to visit, which was pleasant enough for the Americans but obviously very dangerous for all concerned. Three days later, the three airmen were moved and the rest of their journey arranged.

On 22 September, Minor, Beilstein and Koval were taken to the abandoned servants' quarters of a nearby chateau where Minor says that "We were given an orientation talk in excellent English by an old count – he always wore a red beret. The chateau belonged to a very old marquess who did not know of our presence but the comte was a friend of the marquise and they were handling us. They had no trust in the servants and kept us hidden the whole time. They stole food for us from the pantry but it could only be cooked in the fireplace at night because of the smoke."

About a week later, they were taken by car to a rendezvous where they got on a bus which was driven just a short distance before stopping again. About five minutes later, they were joined by four men from Minor's aircraft – Elton Hoyt, Herbert Dulberg, William Miller and Edward Shaffer. A Frenchman on the bus had a note from 1/Lt Dwight Fisher (#338) saying that he could be trusted, and they followed a small car to a large house, La Fontaine at La Buzardiere, just outside Saint-Malo – home of Roger Pansart (born Oct 1902) and his wife Aimee (born Dec 1900) of Paramé – where they joined Fisher.

A week later, they received word that the driver of the lorry that was supposed to be collecting them was working for the Gestapo, and the eight Americans were immediately moved to a monastery (le chateau de la Guerche) at Saint-Hélen (Ille-et-Vilaine, about 20 kms south of Saint-Malo). Beilstein, Koval, Fisher, Miller and Shaffer left after three days – one of the priests drove them to Trigavou, Côtes-du-Nord (now Côtes-d'Armor) to be sheltered with an elderly retired French naval officer – leaving Minor, Hoyt and Dulberg to continue in their role as philosophers. Minor says that one of the priests, who did much of his work in plain clothes, was the guiding spirit at the monastery while many of the other monks were not in the picture at all. It was presumably a group of these latter priests who were so startled to find the Americans shooting craps in the woods. Minor stayed for a week at the monastery before he and the others were moved – Minor, Hoyt and Dulberg being taken to a mill house where they posed as Russians. They were supposed to stay for a while but the lady of the house was nervous of their presence and they were moved on next day to a small farm where they stayed with a young couple who were expecting a baby. They tried carrying on with their Russian act but were soon caught out when they asked the farmer's sister about whisky. From there, Minor and Hoyt were taken to Dinan where they rejoined Fisher and Beilstein, had their photographs taken and were told they were changing organisations.

On about 16 October, they were driven to a house about halfway between Dinan and Malestroit where they met Emile Guimard, head of the local organisation which was supposed to be organising their evacuation by boat. After a meal, they were taken to a house on the other side of Malestroit where they joined their navigator William Cook (#410). Cook, Hoyt and Beilstein were billeted in one house while Minor and Fisher stayed in another house on nearby rue des Ponts with a merchant named Pierre Philipot. On 23 October, Henri Mallard and gendarme Raymond Gloux visited Minor and told him that he could move into the Gloux household, which was on the edge of town and safer. That Sunday evening, Minor moved to the Gloux house where he stayed for a month, only returning to M. Philipot for two days while M. Gloux's father-in-law came to visit, and spending three days with Mme Lapierre (at La Madeleine) after her husband, a watchmaker, was arrested for reasons unknown.

Minor describes Emile Guimard as being about 28 years old and wearing thick, horn-rimmed glasses. He had been wounded whilst serving as an officer in the French army and had only partial use of his right arm. Before the war, Emile had apparently been studying to become a priest like his younger brother. Emile visited Minor twice while he was staying with Raymond Gloux, each time telling Minor that he planned to have him taken out by boat with his comrades. This scheme, which apparently involved bribing some German guards to allow the boat to leave harbour, then blew up with the arrest of Emile's chief with the money for the bribe in his possession.

Emile Guimard (born June 1915) of La Grée aux Moines, Lizio, was living with Marie-Therese Jouan (born Sept 1921), and had a daughter, Raymonde (born 1932) who was away at school. He was the local resistance leader and lists numerous people in his NARA file that he worked with whilst helping evaders (including his brother Joseph, their 62-year-old widowed mother, chauffeur Henri Tanguy and gendarme Raymond Gloux) but only names the very first airman that he helped in February 1943, T/Sgt Claiborne W Wilson (#46) – who he sheltered before taking him to Ploermel and passing him on to BCRA agent Guy Lenfant – and 1/Lt Wayne Bogard, as he did not keep written records.

On about 30 November, Emile Guimard told Minor that he would leave the following evening to take a train to Paris with Hoyt, Cook and Fisher but when he returned next evening, it was to say that he had instructions from Paris not to send Minor after all.

With so many aircrew evaders being sheltered in the area, it had been decided to give first priority to the officers and on about 1 December, convoyeurs Jean Carbonnet and Michele Moet arrived to take Lieutenants Elton Hoyt, William Cook, Dwight Fisher, John Beilstein, Joe Burkowski, Wayne Bogart and George Padgett back to Paris where they were passed on to the Bourgogne organisation – Hoyt and Cook being sheltered by Suzanne and Anita Lemonnier (see later) at 2 rue Ernest Renan, Paris XV.

Emile Guimard drove Minor in his truck to the café Cherel in Ploermel where he found his bombardier 2/Lt Louis Glickman (#370) arguing that he should have left with the other officers for Paris – Minor suggests that Glickman was left behind because he had no dog-tags while Glickman maintains that he was left behind because he never complained and so the French thought he was happy to stay. An hour later S/Sgt John Semach (#422) arrived and Emile Guimard took the three Americans to Lizio, the small village where he lived, although the Americans spent the night in another house. Early next morning they were taken to a farm near Josselin where they were sheltered with Mlle Guillo, an elderly cousin of Emile Guimard and whose brother, the maire of Guehenno, lived downstairs.

On 24 December, Henri Tanguy arrived in his truck, very excited because Glickman, Minor and Semach were going to be taken out by boat that night. He drove them to Saint-Aubin-en-Plumelec but when Emile

Guimard arrived, he told them there was only room for one more American in the party, and as Glickman was an officer (which Glickman dismisses as baloney) it was the two sergeants who were left behind when Glickman was taken to Bédée, about 20 kms north-west of Rennes.

S/Sgt John Semach (#422) was the 20-year-old tail-gunner of 379BG/524BS B-17 42-9893 El Diablo (Jamerson) which on the way to Nantes on the afternoon of 16 September 1943. Their escorting fighters had just turned back when Semach heard his pilot 2/Lt Floyd H Jamerson say "There goes Hoyt – he's on fire" (see Minor (#421) above) and Semach reported seven German aircraft attacking them from behind with rockets. The bomber suddenly climbed, almost colliding with another B-17, before circling and when Semach called the pilot on the interphone, there was no reply. He later learned that the rockets had killed Jamerson and knocked co-pilot 2/Lt Earl H Guyette unconscious, that the bombardier Joe Burkowski was unable to take over the controls as Jamerson was wedged in his seat, and with navigator John Beilstein off oxygen (at 21,000 feet), he was unable to pull Jamerson clear before the aircraft fell out of control. Semach heard Burkowski give the bail-out order and he went out through the already open hatch.

The only other successful evader from El Diablo was navigator 1/Lt John N Beilstein (#557) who, as already mentioned, was helped in Brittany before being passed on to the Bourgogne organisation in December and crossed the Pyrenees from Pau in February. 2/Lt Joseph Burkowski was with Beilstein when they arrived at Toulouse railway station on 3 February 1944 but was one of six American airmen captured in a routine ticket-check.

Semach pulled his rip-cord immediately after leaving the aircraft, seeing one parachute below him and four more above. He made quite a hard landing in a field, bruising his face, before rolling up his chute and hiding it under a tree, and then hiding himself in a clump of bushes. He says that people started to arrive from all directions, many of them wearing extra pieces of clothing which they gave him, and he was soon disguised as a civilian. A man then took Semach about half a mile north, meeting a priest on the way who asked Semach if he were English or German before they joined another crowd that was gathered around his navigator John Beilstein, who was also being given civilian clothing. As soon as Beilstein was dressed, an English-speaking boy, aged about nineteen from the second crowd, led them away to another field where they were given some food while arrangements were made for them to spend the night at a nearby farm. It was only when they got up after eating that Beilstein found he could hardly stand – his parachute harness had been too slack and he was badly bruised in the groin. That evening Beilstein was carried to the farm where the two airmen spent the night and the priest contacted a man who brought them English cigarettes and a map.

Early next morning they were moved into a small wood, and as it rained for most of the time, had quite a miserable day before being taken to a cellar where the priest and the young English-speaking boy were waiting. They told Semach and Beilstein that they would meet some friends next day and leave for Spain, and after a meal, the two Americans were taken to spend the night in a haystack.

At about four o'clock next morning, they were moved back to the woods and that afternoon, the English-speaking boy who had been acting as interpreter brought a French General (Marcel Allard) to them. The general spoke no English but he took them through the fields to a carriage in which the priest was waiting. They were hidden under the seat and taken to a wood at Guipry, south of Rennes. That night, Bernard (Bernard Bougeard – query), head of the Guipry organisation, who had been waiting for them when they got out of the carriage, took them to his house and a little while later, a young girl took Semach to nearby Messac and the home of an elderly couple, M. et Mme Gerard. Semach stayed at La Tertre in Messac with the Gerards from 18 September to 6 October, being joined there on 21 September by 2/Lt Louis Glickman (#370).

Semach and Glickman left Messac with Eugene Justeau, a miller from Pipriac, who drove them in his truck to Saint Jean, a large house near Ploermel and home of cultivateur Julien Moureau. From there, two guides took them, Glickman's navigator William Cook (#410) and El Diablo navigator Joseph Burkowski, by train to Rennes. They stayed with one of the guides and were told there was a scheme to get them and others out by boat but an encounter between Jean-Claude Camors (of Bordeaux-Loupiac) and the French traitor Roger Leneveu, and the subsequent shooting of Camors and Remy Roure outside the café de l'Epoque on 11 October, put a stop to that plan.

Semach and Glickman walked out of Rennes the following morning, intending to head north towards the coast but getting lost and eventually getting a lift, directions and a map to find their way back to Messac and General Allard's house. The gardener told them that the general had gone to Rennes to investigate the shooting but the General's wife Marguerite let them wait until the general returned and he took them to stay with Georges Daniel, one of Glickman's earlier helpers, at La Valle en Messac.

On about 15 October, Henri Tanguy, Raymond Guillard and Emile Guimard took Semach, Glickman, Cyril Koval (mentioned earlier) and a French pilot (query) to the café Cherel at Ploemel where they joined Harry Minor. While Glickman was taken to stay with schoolteacher Mlle Madeleine Travers at 41 rue du General Dubreton, Semach and Minor were taken to a farm near Josselin where (as mentioned earlier) they were sheltered with Mlle Guillo, an elderly cousin of Emile Guimard and whose brother, the maire of Guehenno, lived downstairs – and Semach travelled with Minor from this point.

Harry Minor and John Semach stayed at Saint-Aubin, sheltered in a house over a shop run by the Mlles Yvonne, Marie and Lucie Mallard which was reported by Minor as being the headquarters for many of the local activities, including the distribution of arms, with Emile Guimard's mother, Henri Tanguy, and two other Frenchmen also living there. On 1 January, a man arrived in very bad shape, the Gestapo apparently hot on his heels. All Air Corps souvenirs were buried in the garden and a large picture of Marshal Petain hung on the wall. Later that month, they were joined by two Hindus (sic) who had escaped from the hospital in Rennes where they were orderlies – they were two Indian soldiers, Buland Khan (1852) (see later) and his friend Sgt Shahzaman. On 8 January, a photographer came and took Minor's photograph and that same day, Minor, Semach and the two Indians were driven to a garage in Pontivy where they changed trucks and were passed to (yet) another organisation.

They were taken to a café in Gourin where they met Jean-Guy Bariou and were joined by 2/Lt Ernest Hugonnet, S/Sgt Donald McLeod and Sgt Marion Hall. M. Bariou gave the five Americans new ID cards before they were driven to Concarneau, on the Finistere coast. They were taken to stay with a man named Georges Martin where they joined 2/Lt James Schneider (#432) and T/Sgt James Quinn. They all had their photographs taken again and everyone was issued with new identity cards. Three days later, they were driven in an ambulance to Quimper station where they took a train for Brest.

In case you were thinking that Minor and Semach's adventures weren't complicated enough – Semach having been taken to Rennes where he missed out on a Bordeaux-Loupiac sea evacuation that was abandoned following the shooting of Jean-Claude Camors and Remy Roure in October, and Minor not being taken to Paris and passed on to Bourgogne with the officers at the beginning of December, and then both being left behind when Louis Glickman was taken, first to Bédée and then to Pointe-de-Saint-Cast for SOE Operation Jealous III (although that was aborted when MGB 502 was spotted from the shore and fired upon) – they were about to get worse.

2/Lt Ernest H Hugonnet Jnr (#425), **S/Sgt Donald D McLeod** (#426) and **Sgt Marion A Hall** (#427) were the bombardier, engineer/TTG and ball-turret gunner of 94BG/410BS B-17 42-30200 Slo Time Sally (Born), and returning from Cognac-Châteaubernard aerodrome on 5 January 1944 when they were shot down over Brittany.

They suffered no damage from a fighter attack over the target (despite being the low ship in the low squadron of the formation, and so the most vulnerable) but on the return leg, just before reaching the Brest peninsula, they were again attacked by fighters. They fell out of formation with their #2 engine smoking and the horizontal stabiliser "shot up". The pilot (1/Lt Raymond J Born) called Hugonnet to the cockpit to help him with the controls as the co-pilot (F/O Harold J Erickson) was badly injured and only semi-conscious. The damage was severe enough that Born was preparing to ditch the aircraft when they made landfall near Concarneau, and then when fire broke out inside the aircraft, Born gave the order to bail out. The navigator (2/Lt Norman R King (#494) – see later) released the escape hatch and went out at once with Hugonnet close behind him. Hugonnet says that he jumped at about 6,000 feet and pulled his rip-cord as soon as he cleared the aircraft.

Hugonnet landed with his parachute caught in a small tree and on failing to dislodge it, simply unbuckled his harness. An elderly man with a scythe was watching and very surprised when Hugonnet spoke to him in French, and a small crowd soon gathered, mostly elderly men. Hugonnet took off all his flying gear (apart from heated shoes), leaving just his shirt and trousers, which the Frenchmen recognised as being an American uniform, and a younger man then led Hugonnet to a farmhouse. The family gave Hugonnet a meal while he explained how he came to be there, and gave him some civilian clothes to wear instead of his uniform – Hugonnet carefully transferring the contents of his aids-box to his new pockets. A member of the family then led Hugonnet to another farmhouse about four kilometres away where he was made comfortable and tried (in vain) to sleep. Hugonnet (who spoke good French) explained that he wanted to make his way to Spain and would appreciate a little more help than just directions. One of the younger men told him that another American was near by and that he would bring the other American to him. Hugonnet spent his first night in France in a barn at the back of the house and at about four o'clock next morning, was awoken by the arrival of a Frenchman and Sgt McLeod.

Roger Huguen, in his 2003 book "La Bretagne dans la Bataille de l'Atlantique", says that Hugonnet was found that afternoon about two kilometres from Kergras en Duault by Jean Louis Ruven and Jean Cozic, and taken back to the Ruven farmhouse. Jean Ruven's cousin, Yves Lorinquer, a tailor from Locarn, took charge of providing clothes for Hugonnet, including a beret, and found the American spoke the old-fashioned French of his Norman ancestors.

Donald McLeod had been transferring fuel over the Bay of Biscay when the fighters attacked, damaging two of their engines. The ball-turret was out of action and the gunner (Hall) went to take over the nose position. As McLeod climbed down from his turret, he felt the aircraft go into a dive and heard the pilot tell him to bail out. He was still putting on his parachute when the bombardier (Hugonnet) told him to jump and he went out through the bomb-bay. His shroud lines became twisted (probably because he had put the chute on upside down) and while he was straightening them out, saw his aircraft losing altitude though in level flight, and with the wheels down.

What none of the evaders could have known until later was that newly promoted 1/Lt Raymond Born, determined to try and save the life of his injured co-pilot, Harold Erickson (who was actually a first pilot but just recovered from illness, and making only his second operation), landed Slo Time Sally in a frozen field near Poullaouën, about 8 kms NW of Carhaix. Both men were captured and taken to hospital at Carhaix before being sent to Stalag Luft 1 (Barth) as POWs.[21]

21 Thank you Yvonne Millar – and Mme Phine Goubil, who as a 14-year-old ran, with several of her neighbours, to the downed aircraft.

McLeod landed near a farmhouse on the outskirts of the forêt de Duault and was soon surround by a crowd of Frenchmen, including a 16-year-old boy named Le Lay, and his father. Once McLeod had taken off his parachute and Mae West, the young man indicated that McLeod should follow him but then another Frenchman, this one speaking English (he was a Parisian avoiding STO who was staying with the Le Lay family) greeted him. McLeod told him that he wanted to hide and he was led across some fields, taking off his coveralls and electric suit and handing them to another man who was following them as he went. He was taken to a water-logged "straw shed" in the middle of a marshy field and left there while the Frenchmen went to check for German activity.

About two hours later, a man arrived with a note from the English-speaking man, telling him to follow the man with the note. McLeod was taken to another field, where he was given wooden shoes (presumably to wear instead of his soaked GI shoes) and a "stick and straw bed" was fixed up so he could lie in the sun and dry his clothing. About an hour later, the two Frenchmen returned with some civilian clothes, into which McLeod changed (keeping his GI shoes) before being taken to a wooded area where he was hidden in a patch of ferns. That evening, the two men brought him an overcoat and led McLeod to the Le Lay farmhouse at Lespoul en Duault, where he was given food and civilian clothes, and hidden in the attic. In the early hours of the morning he was woken up, given a complete new set of clothing and driven to Jean Ruven's house in the hameau de Kergras en Duault where he joined Hugonnet.

After a short discussion, Hugonnet and McLeod tried to get some more sleep but were soon taken back into the farmhouse for breakfast, before being hidden in a nearby wood. That afternoon, a man they had not seen before brought them more civilian clothing and took them back to his house where they were joined by Sgt Hall. That evening, several more men arrived, and after being carefully questioned, the three Americans' onward journey was arranged.

Marion Hall confirms that his ball-turret became unusable while they were over the Bay of Biscay and says that he went into the radio room. The bombardier (Hugonnet) was in the cockpit helping the pilot so Hall took over his position on the nose guns. Soon after that the bail-out order was given and Hall returned to the bomb-bay in time to see radio operator (Harold Gilley (#428) – see later) leave from the bomb-bay before the two waist-gunners (Robert Schwartzburg (#429) and Robert Southers (#430)

– see both later) jumped out of the waist door. Hall put on his parachute and followed them, leaving just the two pilots, engineer (McLeod) and bombardier in the aircraft. Hall says that he saw three parachutes behind him and then the tail section of another B-17 (assume 42-31212) floated down quite close to him.

Hall landed in a field and before he could unbuckle his harness, was surrounded by a group of Frenchmen asking for American cigarettes. He says that his nervousness must have been obvious as one of the men cut the harness away with his scythe. A young man asked Hall if he had a gun (he did not) (he may have been asking for gum, which Hall should have had in his aids box but the writing is not clear) then buttoned Hall's flying jacket up around his neck to hide his uniform and led him away across the fields. They were soon intercepted by another man who led Hall back to his farmhouse, produced some maps and asked Hall where they had bombed – Hall understanding that he wanted to be sure that Hall was actually an American. Once the man was satisfied as to his nationality, he took Hall into a nearby field and hid him in a hole that he then covered with straw. That evening, Hall was brought back to the farmhouse to meet some Frenchmen who spoke a little English. They asked Hall where he wanted to go and he told them to Spain, to which they said it couldn't be done as it was too far away. Then another man took Hall to another farm where he was hidden overnight in a haystack. Next morning, he was taken into the house for breakfast and then hidden in a barn. That afternoon, an English-speaking Frenchman brought Hall some clothes and several hours later, another Frenchman arrived to take him to join Hugonnet and McLeod.

Hugonnet says (in their combined report) that all three men landed near Locarn, where they were sheltered in a barn by local farmers. On the third day (8 Jan), a tailor from a small village took them to a house where they were turned over to the local resistance organisation. The three Americans were taken to the maire's house (assume this was Pierre Philippe (born 1898), secrétaire de mairie at Trébrivan) where a large black car, which Hugonnet describes as being like an autobus, was waiting with twelve armed men to take them to Gourin.

The chief of the organisation in Gourin, a chemist named Jean-Guy Bariou, talked to Hugonnet all the way and at one stage, his assistant, Jean Le Crenn, described by Hugonnet as "a perfumed, blond-haired, Hollywood type", pointed a gun at Hugonnet and asked if he knew an American called

James Schneider. Hugonnet said that although not from his crew, he had trained with Schneider in the States, which apparently satisfied the blond who told him that he would be meeting Schneider in a few days time.

Jean-Guy Bariou (born May 1899), pharmacist of Route du Faouet in Gourin, was married to Hortense (query) – they had six children (aged 6 to 20), including their eldest son, Jean Pierre Marie Bariou (born November 1924) who was a law student, and daughter Liliane who took over liaison work from Jean Pierre when he was arrested in May 1944. Jean-Guy Bariou was head of the local resistance group (groupe Vengeance) but he and his son Jean Pierre also helped numerous Allied airmen.

Jean-Guy Bariou first became involved with helping evaders in March 1943 when Georges Jouanjean and Job Le Bec brought RAF evader F/O Gordon Carter (1155) from Paris to be sheltered in Gourin for two weeks (21 Mar to 5 Apr) with Jouanjean's brother-in-law, grain merchant Raymond Cougard at rue de Quimper.[22] *Bariou helped to organise (and probably pay for) the fishing vessel Dalc'h Mad, which sailed for England from Treboul-Douarnenez on 6 April 1943 with Carter and a group of Frenchmen on board.*

Jean Pierre Bariou joined the Corps France Vengeance group in Quimper as a liaison agent at beginning of 1943 – he also helped US evader Sgt Cecil Bell (#85) who left for England on board the fishing vessel Moise from Treboul-Douarnenez on 23 August 1943. The operation was organised by Victor Salez, who left for England himself (along with two more American airmen) on 2 October on a Dahlia operation organised by Yves Le Hénaff (aka Fanfan).

On 9 January 1944, the Bariou family left Gourin because they knew the Germans were looking for Jean-Guy and his son. "He had just sent 12 Americans off by boat (Operation Felicitate) but still had 17 (sic) on his hands." On 20 January, a court in Rennes condemned Jean-Guy Bariou to death in his absence.

Jean Pierre Bariou was arrested in Rennes on 9 May 1944, caught in a souricière at 12 rue de Chateaudun, home of a M. Ladoumergue, and deported to Neuengamme for resistance activities – he was repatriated back to France on 24 May 1945.

22 Jean-Guy Bariou says that Raymond Cougard (born January 1909) took over responsibility for the organisation in Gourin in September 1943. Raymond Cougard was arrested on 20 June 1944 and deported to Germany – he was liberated from Mauthausen on 6 May 1945 and recommended for a KMC.

Jean Le Crenn (of rue du Moulin Madame) spoke some English – after serving for 15 years in the French navy, he had been to America, where he worked briefly for Michelin before he and his wife Marie returned to their two sons in France. Marie Le Crenn says (in Remy) that they sheltered one American airmen (James Schneider) in their attic, and after he left, Mme Marie Le Bris (widow of Jean Pierre Le Bris – tailleur of Gourin who died after being deported) sent them a Hindu (Buland Khan) who stayed for a fortnight. After him came five more Americans, including one who spoke French, and their children visited him in New York after the war (Hugonnet, the only American mentioned as speaking French, was from NY but no evidence found that he actually stayed with the Le Crenn family).

They stopped on the outskirts of Gourin, where they were met by two men, and then walked to Jean-Guy Bariou's house on Route du Faouet. The Americans did a clothes swap and Hugonnet was asked if he would stay in France to help them as a contact man – he being the first American they had met who spoke French. That night, McLeod stayed at Jean-Guy Bariou's house while Hugonnet and Hall slept in a room that had been prepared for them over his chemist shop. Next morning, after the first wash and shave they had had in France, the three airmen were taken to a pub (sic) where they were given ID cards and met Harry Minor and John Semach – and a Moroccan man who had been in a POW camp (this was Buland Khan) – before going on to another pub (sic) where they met fish-merchant Georges Martin. Martin drove the five Americans in his fish delivery truck, overnight through Saint-Yvy and Rosporden to the wharf at Concarneau, and then to his house on the sea front, Villa Fleur d'Ajonc on boulevard Alfred Guillou, explaining that his wife and children had gone stay with his mother. On the first night, 2/Lt James Schneider and T/Sgt James Quinn arrived.

Three days later, Hugonnet, McLeod, Hall, Minor, Semach, Schneider and Quinn left Concarneau for Quimper, taken in an ambulance borrowed from Concarneau hospital, with Georges Martin in the front with its regular driver, and following a man on a motorcycle. From Quimper, they took a train to Brest.

Georges Martin was a lot more than just a fish-merchant, in fact he probably wasn't really a fish merchant at all – Paul Le Baron refers to him as Lieutenant Martin, and Colonel Michel Scheidhauer (see both later) says he was head of the FFI (Forces francaises de l'interieur) in Concarneau. Unfortunately Martin's NARA file tells us almost nothing, noting (in April 1948) that although meriting an award, proper recommendation had never been submitted.

Roger Huguen also refers to Georges Martin as being a fish merchant, or at least a fisherman – which genuinely seems to have been his favourite pastime. However, whilst I am not certain it is the same man, the 2017 study "Les Gendarmes dans la bataille de Normandie" by Benjamin Massieu, published for "the 79th anniversary of the landing", identifies Georges Martin (born April 1905) – married to Hélène, and with a daughter Eliane – as a gendarme (the word comes from gens d'armes – armed people) lieutenant who joined the resistance in 1943, and whose work with groupe Vengeance soon took over his official duties in western Brittany. He was transferred to Caen in February 1944, but following a German rafle at Redon (Ille-et-Vilaine) on 27 May (which Massieu says allowed the Germans to obtain information on Martin's resistance activities), he was arrested in his apartment at the Caen gendarmerie on rue Daniel-Huet the following day. His family never saw him again, and he is believed to have died in German hands a few days later, shot (with other captured resistants) when news arrived of the Allied landings.

2/Lt James A Schneider (#432) was the bombardier of 91BG/324BS B-17 42-29895 Black Swan (Mendelsohn) which was returning from Cognac on 30 December 1943. Flak over the target had damaged one engine but they managed to stay with their formation across the Bay of Biscay and were about ten miles inland over the Brest peninsula when there was an explosion at the front of the aircraft. The explosion blew out the nose section (almost certainly killing navigator 2/Lt Warren L Ellis) and the aircraft went into a dive to crash south of Kernével (Finistere). The only other successful evader from Black Swan was radio operator T/Sgt James Quinn (#433) – see later.

Allied bomber crews did not normally wear parachutes while flying but kept them close to their stations, ready to be clipped to their harnesses but I should perhaps explain at this point some of the differences between the British and American heavy bombers and their crews.

RAF Halifax and Lancasters normally had a crew of seven: pilot, flight engineer, navigator, bomb-aimer, wireless operator, mid-upper gunner and tail-gunner.

In a Lancaster, the pilot sat on the left side of the cockpit with the flight engineer on a folding seat beside him. The navigator sat directly behind them at a table facing to port with the wireless operator, sat facing forward, beside him. The bomb-aimer would normally be lying down when assisting the navigator or directing the pilot to their aiming point, and would have to stand to operate the front gun turret. The mid-upper gunner was seated in the unheated part of the aircraft behind them, with the tail-gunner closed inside a powered turret, also unheated, where he sat at the very rear of the aircraft. The main entrance (and exit) was to the rear of the aircraft with an auxiliary emergency exit above the bomb-bay, and a rather narrow escape hatch in the nose.

In the slightly more spacious Halifax, the crew positions and exits were similar apart from where some of the men were actually sitting, and most models lacked a powered front turret.

The more heavily armed American B-17 Flying Fortress and B-24 Liberators, which flew their missions in daylight and depended on mass formations for their defence against the inevitable fighter attacks, normally had a crew of ten. There were four officers: the pilot and co-pilot, who sat side by side in the cockpit, and the navigator and bombardier, who were stationed in the nose of the aircraft where either man could also operate the front gun or guns, depending on the model of aircraft. The other six crew were enlisted men: the engineer was positioned behind the pilots, where he also operated the top-turret, while the radio operator sat in a compartment aft of the bomb-bay, with the four main gunners, one in the ball-turret, two waist-gunners standing back to back with single .50 calibre machine guns on flexible mounts, and the tail gunner, through another hatch aft of that, sitting in a semi-kneeling position to use his twin guns. Note that the American airmen were able to move about their aircraft more easily than their British and Commonwealth counterparts.

Should the need arise to abandon a B-17, there was an escape hatch below the nose for the navigator and bombardier while the pilots, engineer and radio operator could exit through the bomb-bay, once the doors were opened. Ball-turret and waist-gunners could exit through the main entrance at the rear of the aircraft, and the tail gunner had his own emergency exit. In a B-24 the situation was similar except that when the nose wheel was retracted, access to the front escape hatch was compromised, and there was only one escape hatch at the rear, the waist-gunners also having the option of exiting through the bomb-bay – at least that was the theory.

25-year-old Schneider just had time to pull off his flak-suit and hook on his parachute before falling out of the escape hatch. He pulled his rip-cord as soon as he cleared the aircraft and hit the ground (he says near Rosporden, which is about 12 kms north-east of Concarneau) almost immediately. Seeing no-one around, he unbuckled his parachute and stuffed it into a fence before running "as far and as fast" as he could but a few minutes later, came to a farmhouse. A woman at the farm waved him away but as Schneider went around the building, three men ran up to him. They didn't understand Schneider's request for a decent hiding place and instead brought him some food from the house. Schneider finally found a man who could understand some English, and on getting the message across by writing the word "hide" on a piece of paper, the man took Schneider to a ravine and said he would return that night. Schneider still had his Mae West which he inflated to use as a cushion from the cold ground while he tried to figure out where he was on his escape map.

A group of Frenchman arrived that evening, including Yves Le Gall, an English-speaking schoolmaster of 100 rue de la Gare in Bannalec – he was also sous-lieutenant of compagnie "Guy Moquet" – with blankets and hot food before taking Schneider to a barn. Later that night, civilian clothes were brought and Schneider was moved into a haystack, his helpers explaining that the Germans were making a search for the crew. Unfortunately Schneider's hiding place was discovered by one of the local dogs who kept him awake most the night by howling and barking. Just before dawn, Schneider was taken back to the ravine and told that he should stay hidden there and that someone would come for him that evening.

That night, Schneider was taken to stay in the attic of Pierre Le Noc's farmhouse at Bannalec and next day, Joseph Le Bras (born Sept 1913) of 12 rue Saint-Thurien, Bannalec (not to be confused with Joseph Le Bras of Gourin – see later) told him that his journey was arranged.

On about 3 January, Joseph Le Bras loaned Schneider his bicycle and schoolmaster Yves Le Gall took him via a series of back roads on the long ride to Gourin (Morbihan). They were met by two men, one another schoolteacher, who took them to a chemist shop where Schneider was passed over to Jean-Guy Bariou who took Schneider back to his house on Route du Faouet. Schneider was visited by a woman from Brest who said she was married to an American Engineer Corps major named Harold Cockburn – they had a fifteen-year-old son – and she asked Schneider to contact her husband to tell him that she was well. On 5 January, Schneider was taken to stay overnight with hairdresser Jean Le Crenn (on rue du Moulin Madame), before returning next day to Jean-Guy Bariou's house. He was collected from there by Georges Martin who drove Schneider by truck to his home in Concarneau where, two days later (on 8 Jan), he met 2/Lt Ernest Hugonnet (#425).

Schneider also reports that M. Bariou's "right-hand man" was caught shortly after he left and that Schwartzburg (#429) knew about it. Doctor Henri Bahier (of Grande Rue, Gourin) says that Mr Bariou brought Buland Khan to his house on 8 January, to spend the night. That evening, his daughter Marie Therese arrived with false ID cards for numerous airmen being sheltered in the area, and passed them on to Mr Cadic. Eugène Cadic was arrested that same night (and afterwards shot), and early next day, the Gestapo raided the town.

The doctor's son (also named Henri), knew there was an airman (Ralph Hall) staying with Mr Bariou, and he went and brought him back to the doctor's house. The doctor and his son then took him and Khan to Langonnet where they stayed overnight with the maire, Charles Michel. The doctor returned next day, knowing their refuge wasn't safe, and his son Henri, along with Frederick Cloarec and a M. Cosperic (query), took the two evaders to be sheltered by Jean-Pierre Calvez in Crach-en-Gourin, where (he says) they stayed for the next two months (sic) – until they left for Ile-Tudy and the Jouet des Flots episode of 3-4 February.

T/Sgt James N Quinn (#433) was the radio operator of 91BG/324BS B-17 42-29895 Black Swan (Mendelsohn) which was shot down on 30 December 1943 – the same aircraft as James Schneider (#432) – see above.

Quinn says that he bailed out from the bomb-bay at about 1,000 feet, pulled his rip-cord immediately and the next thing he knew, hit the ground. He was still taking off his parachute when a crowd of Frenchmen arrived and led him to a farmhouse. One of them advised Quinn to stay at the farmhouse with the Poupon family until the Germans arrived, that the war would be over soon and that the Germans would treat him well. Quinn decided to ignore that suggestion and ran out the door. He was followed by a boy who took him through the fields to a small wood where he left him. Quinn set off walking down the road and soon had a somewhat bizarre experience when he suddenly encountering a German soldier sitting on a motorcycle. The two men stared at one another and then, because the 22-year-old New Yorker already had an unlit cigarette in his mouth, he asked the middle-aged German (in English) for a light. The soldier didn't seem to understand the question but some simple hand signals made the request clear enough and he obligingly struck a match. After lighting his cigarette, Quinn (who was still wearing his heated suit and green coveralls) continued on his way. After walking another kilometre, Quinn caught up with a group of men carrying bundles of wood. As soon as he tried speaking to them in English, they asked if he were an American. On hearing the affirmative, one of the men (Huguen says this was Louis Nicolas) took Quinn to a bakery shop at La Croix-Lanveur, just outside Kernével, where Pierre Kersulac lived with his wife Françoise and their daughter. Later that same day, two young men arrived to take Quinn to a farmhouse near Rosporden, from where his journey was arranged.

Quinn stayed overnight with Pierre Kersulac's cousin, groupe Vengeance member Alain Créo (of Ferme de Trolan, Kernével), and next morning, he was taken to the gendarmerie at Rosporden, where he stayed for two days, visited by a young English-speaking man who was brought to reassure Quinn that no-one else knew he was being hidden there. Then Georges Martin arrived and he drove Quinn to Concarneau where he was sheltered for five days by Albert Gloaguen in his jewellery shop, overlooking the harbour at 10 avenue Pierre Gueguin.

Huguen (2003) has a slightly different version, saying that Quinn stayed two nights with Alain Créo before Créo and Jean Garo took him to SNCF employee Bertrand Petit on his farm at Coat Morn en Rosporden. Bertrand Petit gave Quinn a railwayman's green and red armband as a laissez-passez, and drove him to the gendarmerie at Rosporden, where a gendarme named Ricco passed him off to his children as a visiting uncle. After four days with the gendarme and his family, Quinn was taken to Vengeance member Albert Rivier, who contacted Georges Martin, who took Quinn in his camionnette back to Concarneau to be sheltered by Albert Gloaguen at quai d'Aiguillon.

Quinn says that another English-speaking man came from Brest – this was Paul Le Baron – where Colonel Scheidhauer was in charge. He told Quinn that he would see his two waist-gunners (S/Sgts Abraham R Lieberman and Rollin E Gater) the following day – however, next day Georges Martin told him that both waist-gunners had been captured, along with a priest (Abbé Joseph Tanguy) and his housekeeper (sic) at Pont-Aven.[23]

Quinn reports that it was Georges Martin who arranged for his bombardier James Schneider to be taken to his house in Concarneau next day, and when Quinn visited Schneider, he also met Ernest Hugonnet, Donald McCloud, Marion Hall, Harry Minor and John Semach. Quinn stayed at the jewellers until Hugonnet came to visit and that night, Quinn moved to join the other Americans at Georges Martin's house on the seafront.

On about 10 January, Georges Martin and a salt merchant named Le Floch, took Hugonnet, McLeod, Hall, Minor, Semach, Schneider and Quinn by truck to Brest. They were met by two young men, Paul Le Baron (described by Hugonnet as being about 5 feet 7 inches tall, dark, smokes, always wore a raincoat and fireman's boots – he had a sister who knew nothing about his work) and René, a cousin of Mme Callarec – this was her 23-year-old nephew, Raymond Le Bourhis, who used the name René Callarec when helping evaders.

Hugonnet, McLeod and Hall stayed with Dr and Mme Yvonne de la Marnierre on rue Traverse where Hugonnet reports that they had four daughters, and were very wealthy – the airmen enjoying ten days of luxurious living with ample food. Paul Le Baron visited every day and on the first day, they also met "the chief of the organisation which was handling the boat deal" (about 5 feet 8 inches tall, medium build, with a very square, small face, a slow talker and great friend of the Colonel) who said he was "hot" and couldn't help them.[24]

Minor reports that he, Semach, Schneider and Quinn stayed nearby at 1 rue Neptune with Colonel and Jeanne Scheidhauer, where their daughter, Christiane Magne, acted as interpreter. They were supposed to leave on 19 January but the organisation chief and the woman who lived in the house that was his headquarters had disappeared, and the servants at the house arrested. Because the Colonel, Dr de la Marnierre and Christiane Magne were often seen at the house, they assumed the Gestapo would soon come for them as well.

23 Felix Le Bris, who sheltered Gater (at least) at Kerros en Bannalec before passing him/them to the abbé, was also arrested at the home of the Cure de Pont-Aven. Felix survived but both the abbé Joseph Tanguy and his vicaire Francis Tanguy died in German camps.

24 I have not yet been able to identify this man – obviously not Pierre Hentic.

Michel William Scheidhauer (born March 1877) was a retired infantry colonel who lived with his wife Jeanne (née Legot April 1880) at 1 rue Neptune, Brest. They had four children: Michel (born Dec 1903), Christiane (born Dec 1912), Ghislaine (born June 1914) and Bernard (born Aug 1921). Recruited by their younger daughter Ghislaine Niox in 1943, the colonel and his wife fed and sheltered some thirty Allied evaders at their home (including some of those evacuated on the Suzanne-Renée, mentioned earlier), as well as having regular contact with numerous other members of the organisation in Brest – notably Doctor and Mme de la Marnierre, and Paul Le Baron.

Colonel and Jeanne Scheidhauer worked with Jean-Claude Camors (Raoul) of Bordeaux-Loupiac until his death in November 1943, and then with SIS agent Pierre Hentic (Maho) of the intelligence network Jade-Fitzroy when he became involved with helping evaders – their daughter Ghislaine leaving for England on board MGB 318 (McQuoid-Mason) with a group of evaders on Christmas Day 1943. After Hentic was arrested in early January 1944, they and their group continued helping evaders under Yves Allain (Gregoire) of Bourgogne, who made the connection with Mathurin Branchoux at Guingamp.

Bernard Scheidhauer was a fighter pilot with the RAF who crash-landed his 131 Sqn Spitfire on Jersey on 18 November 1942. He was a POW at Stalag Luft III and one of those recaptured and shot after the "Great Escape" in March 1944.

Mme Jeanne Scheidhauer died on 9 September 1944 in a catastrophic fire inside the Sadi-Carnot bomb-shelter on boulevard de la Marine which killed an estimated 370 French civilians and 500 to 600 German soldiers.

Roger Phelippes de la Marnierre (born December 1892) lived with his wife Yvonne (née Rousseau-Dumarcet June 1899) on rue Traverse (later at 17 rue Voltaire after their house on rue Traverse was bombed – and post-war at 76 rue Victor Hugo), Brest with their four teenage daughters – Christiane (aka Titane), Monique, Marie Louise (aka Maryse) and Françoise (aka Soizic – her Breton name). Roger (who was known as Butch by the evaders after they learned his false identity card gave the surgeon's occupation as a butcher) had permission to drive his car to visit patients, many of whom lived in the country and paid in food rather than cash, something which proved particularly useful when it came to feeding hungry servicemen. The de la

Marnierres also had the use of Chateau Kerouartz, about 25 kms north of Brest, overlooking the Aber Wrac'h river near Lannilis, which was loaned to them by the marquis of Kerouartz. A large group of evaders were brought to the chateau following the failed Operation Envious on 3 November 1943 when the rendezvous point off Aber-Benoit with MGB 318 was changed, and Yvonne and the girls were staying there when their home in Brest was destroyed by a bomb, Roger being lucky to survive. Maryse de la Marnierre says that her parents were originally recruited by Jeanne Callarec, who was working with Pierre Hentic and the Jade-Fitzroy intelligence network at that time.[25]

Evaders brought to Chateau Kerouartz after Operation Envious included RAF sergeants Harold Nielson (1649) and Thomas Adams (1650), and 1/Lt Lionel Drew USAAF (#288), who had been sheltered in Brest by the de la Marnierre family earlier – they stayed at the chateau overnight before Mme de la Marnierre took them back to Brest. After also failing to leave on Envious IIb at the beginning of December, they returned once more to the de la Marnierre home. They were eventually evacuated by MGB 318 (McQuoid-Mason) on Operation Felicitate II on Christmas night, along with 10 more Americans, 6 Royal Navy crew left stranded by Envious IIb, and 8 French agents. The full story of these maritime operations probably deserves a book of its own.

Historic note: Two generations earlier there were two siblings – Marie Phelippes de la Marnierre, and her younger brother Daniel. In 1867, Marie married Ludovic du Bourblanc. In 1896, their daughter Jeanne du Bourblanc, married Robert de Mauduit and it was their son Henri (born 1898) who married Scottish-born American Roberta (Betty) Laurie in January 1928. While Henri de Mauduit was in England during the war, it was Betty who sheltered so many of the Oaktree evaders in their Chateau du Bourblanc at Plourivo until her arrest in June 1943. Meanwhile, in 1877, Marie's brother Daniel had married Marthe Rassart. They had eleven children, the youngest being Roger, born 1892, who went on to marry Yvonne Rousseau-Dumarcet.

Mme Vve Jeanne Marie Callarec (born February 1885) of 82 bis rue Victor Hugo, Brest, was the widow of François Callarec, who had died in combat in 1917. They had two children, Suzanne (34), whose husband was a

25 My thanks to Maryse's son Roger McKeon for his help here.

POW, and Guy, who was killed by a German car on the streets of Brest in 1940. Originally recruited by Ghislaine Niox, she began her evasion work in November 1943, sheltering evaders for Bordeaux-Loupiac. She took on more evaders for Pierre Hentic (including three stranded seamen from MGB 329), and when Hentic was arrested, continued with Colonel Scheidhauer and Paul Le Baron. Herman Schafer (#291) who was sheltered by Mme Callarec for a month, describes her as being about 5 feet tall, a very nice looking, grey-haired old lady.

Paul Jean Le Baron (born August 1924) of 2 rue Traverse de l'Eglise in Brest, was recruited by Ghislaine Niox (aka Jo/Geo) in June 1943, working for her as an intelligence agent with Jade-Fitzroy, under the orders of a Mr Leconte (query). In October, the teenage Le Baron became involved with helping evaders for Bordeaux-Loupiac and the evacuation of nineteen Allied airmen on board the French fishing vessel Suzanne-Renée from Camaret-sur-Mer. With the death of Jean-Claude Camors, he continued to work under Mme Niox and the Jade-Fitzroy evacuations from l'Aber Wrac'h. Following Operation Felicitate II, when Mme Niox left for England, another maritime operation had been planned for 19 January but the arrest of organiser Pierre Hentic left the seven Americans (Hugonnet et al), stranded in Brest. Le Baron says that he then came into contact with M Feroc (assume Roger Yves Feroc of 30 rue Branda, Brest) and through him, met Mathurin Branchoux.

I think it was Thursday 20 January when the seven airmen were moved out of Brest after the housekeeper of one of the Colonel's friends was arrested and there was fear of her talking. They were taken to the station by Christian (son of a wealthy perfumier, he was a temporary guide) and Titane, one of the de la Marnierre daughters. Christian took Hugonnet, McLeod and Hall to Landerneau while Christiane Magne took Minor, Semach, Schneider and Quinn to Saint-Nic, near Chateaulin.

Hugonnet, McLeod and Hall were met at Landerneau by Berthe Guivarch and the maire, Jean Rolland, the two sergeants staying with M. Rolland, and Hugonnet with Mme Guivarch, who had previously sheltered 2/Lt Raymond Bye (#287), at 16 rue Plonery. Two days later, McLeod joined Hugonnet after word began to spread about the two men staying at the maire's house, and then as a further precaution, all three Americans were taken to stay with school-teacher friends of the maire – his nephew was married to one of their daughters.

Date not given when Jean Rolland and Mme Guivarch took Hugonnet, McLeod and Hall to a rendezvous with Roger de la Marnierre who took them back to Brest. They couldn't stay at the de la Marnierre home because friends had told Mme de la Marnierre it was understood that her husband was helping evaders, so after a meal at the doctor's house, they were taken to stay with Mme Jeanne Callarec, who lived alone at 82 bis rue Victor Hugo. Mme Callarec – described by Hugonnet as being "a distinguished Frenchwoman who holds the Legion d'Honneur" – told Hugonnet that she was only (!) a shelterer for the organisation – 2/Lt Raymond Bye (#287) and 2/Lt Herman Schafer (#291) (both evacuated on Operation Felicitate II) had stayed with her previously – and that she had no visitors apart from a young French couple, who were not connected to the organisation.

After Hugonnet, McLeod and Hall left the train at Landerneau, Christiane Magne had taken Minor, Semach, Schneider and Quinn on to her summer cottage at Saint-Nic. The de la Marnierre's eldest daughter Titane came for the weekend but on the Monday, Mme Magne received a telegram from Yvonne de la Marnierre saying it was necessary that she return to Brest with her little ones immediately. They left next day, Mme Magne buying their railway tickets because she knew the station mistress. They changed trains at Chateaulin, where there was a seven-hour delay which they spent in a church. Titane apparently wanted to show she wasn't afraid by insisting on speaking English all the time.

When Minor, Semach, Schneider and Quinn arrived back in Brest, Paul Le Baron and Yvonne de la Marnierre met them and explained that a woman in Rennes had a plan and that they should wait until they received word from her – this was probably Antoinette Mace. That afternoon, a telegram arrived ordering them to Quimper. Their guides were two 19-year-old boys, and because Mme de la Marnierre was concerned they might miss the rendezvous, she went with them as well.

It was about 26 January when Yvonne de la Marnierre came to Jeanne Callarec's house and told Hugonnet that a boat deal from Audierne had been arranged and Hugonnet, McLeod and Hall left Brest for Quimper. Paul Le Baron and Christian took them to the station where they joined Mme de la Marnierre, Minor, Semach, Schneider, Quinn and the two young boys. They were met at Quimper by Jean Barrossi (described by Hugonnet as being about 22 years old, with thick dark hair, about 5 feet 4 inches tall, well-built – a tee-total, non-smoker after his father died of TB) and while Minor says he stayed overnight with Michel Mehu and family, the other Americans spent the night at Jean Barrossi's house near the river at 1 Route de Penhars (query), which he shared with his mother and another woman.

Jean Barrossi was the elder brother of Paul Barrossi who escaped to England in June 1940, joined the RAF and was KIA in 340 Sqn Spitfire MJ853 on 29 February 1944 – today there is a rue Paul Barrossi near his home in Quimper. Jean was also an old school friend of Yves Allain, who says he established a Breton sub-network of Bourgogne with family and friends, naming Jean Barrossi, along with Paul Le Baron, as members.

Next morning, the airmen had a rendezvous in a park with Christian and Mme de la Marnierre, who introduced them to a man called Mickey, and (according to Hugonnet) Jean-Pierre, a young Parisian who spoke excellent English and desperately wanted to get to England.[26]

Mickey took charge of the party, and he took them by train, via Douarnenez, where they changed trains, to the fishing port of Audierne – Mme de la Marnier assuring Minor (who makes no mention of Jean-Pierre until later) that their guide was young but brilliant, had a good plan and they were to obey his orders – Minor wasn't sure which one of them she was trying to convince. Mickey was about 24 years old, wore glasses, and said that because the Gestapo were after him for some organisation work he had done in Rennes, he planned to go to England with them. Paul Le Baron (who was not a fan), says that his name was Le Droff, and that he had presented himself to Mme de la Marnierre as being on a mission from London.

"There was a mix-up at Audierne and when it was straightened out, I (Lt Hugonnet) went with Lt Schneider to a Frenchman's home accompanied by Jean-Pierre. The other airmen were dispersed to other homes. Schneider and I lived with Mlle Pensec for eight days while plans went forward on the boat deal. Mickey seemed to be one of the chief planners in connection with the obtaining of the boat. We were to be hidden aboard a wine merchant boat that would be making a trip to Nantes. After it as out of the harbour, we were to take it over and bring it to England. Lt Schneider and I were to do the navigating. The day before the plan was to go into operation we heard of a

26 Hugonnet says that Jean-Pierre's real name was Pacquet but I have not found any confirmation of that nor managed to otherwise identify him.

boat filled with Canadian, American, French and British evaders beaching in the Audierne area. It had sailed from Concarneau (sic). This boat had beached at Plogoff and a woman collaborator had called the Germans. This area became so hot we had to make a hasty departure about 5 February, as there was a house-to-house search of the area." (Hugonnet MIS-X #425)

While Ernest Hugonnet simply says there was a "mix-up" at Audierne, Harry Minor, who (along with John Semach) must have close to despair by this time, reports on the events at Audierne in more detail.

Harry Minor, John Semach, Ernest Hugonnet, Donald McLeod, Marion Hall, James Schneider and James Quinn, along with the two young boys and Mickey, arrived in Audierne (on the south coast of the Cap-Sizun Peninsula, at the mouth of the Goyen river) at eight o'clock in the evening (Minor says 20 Jan but more likely about 27 Jan – as per McLeod). They were not met at the station as expected so Mickey took them in small groups to the centre of town to wait while he went to investigate. The two young boys became worried and led the Americans south, out of the town, over a bridge and up a hill to a chateau. At the gates, they began searching for something and after a while, a man came to the gate, surprised to see such a large party of men standing there. As soon as he left, the boys started to panic and everyone looked for somewhere to hide, going down to the river where there were some boats, and generally frightening a man who came to look at his boat. The boys confessed that they had panicked and took the party back to the town where they found Mickey, who had met his contact, and treated the episode as a huge joke. Minor says that he went with Mickey and Quinn back into the centre of Audierne where they met a boy on a bike before he ran back to join another boy who was with Semach, Hall, McLeod and the "panic twins".

While the situation in Audierne was being sorted out, Hugonnet says that Jean-Pierre took him and Schneider by train to Douarnenez where they stayed with Mme Alberte Pensec and family at 21 rue Louis Midi. Meanwhile, Minor, Semach, McLeod and Hall were taken on foot, following the river Goyen inland, to Pont-Croix where an elderly couple took them in. The man's name was Guillaume Audren, described by Minor as being over sixty years old, he wore half-moon glasses and was a well known contact in the town. McLeod says that he, Hall, Minor and Semach stayed with M. Audren from 27 January until 5 February, and it was while they staying at Pont-Croix that Minor says Mickey came to visit, bringing two comrades with him – one a young Parisian named Jean-Pierre, who spoke good English and was desperate to get to England – and it was at this point that Mickey explained the plan.

Apparently there was a boat leaving for Nantes with a cargo of salt and Mickey was supposed to have talked the crew into hiding the Americans on board when it sailed. Once they left port, the group would tell the captain that they were taking the boat to England, with or without his help. Mickey then admitted that he hadn't actually spoken to the crew, only the engineer who assured him they could hide on the boat easily enough, and then if it came to it, Mickey had a gun so they could kill the captain and any other crew who tried to stop them. It also turned out that Mickey had no idea about navigation and assumed that Hugonnet or Schneider, as bombardiers, would be able to take care of that. Two days later, Mickey arrived with the news that the engineer had changed his mind after hearing about another boat with British and American evaders on board, which had sunk nearby and the Germans were combing the area for survivors. This was the Jouet des Flots (mentioned earlier) which left from Ile-Tudy the night of 3-4 February but foundered near the Pointe du Feunteun Aod in the early hours of the morning.

They were due to leave Pont-Croix next day but failed to make a rendezvous at the railway station with Hugonnet and Schneider. A man they met at the station took charge of Hall and McLeod, and they left the station separately, and Minor and Semach had just settled back into the Audren house when Mme Audren rushed in to tell them that Hall and McLeod had been arrested. Everyone ran out through the timber yard at the back of the house but were soon caught by Guillaume Audren who explained that Hall and McLeod had now been released. They had been stopped by two Germans on bicycles, and the Frenchman who led them from the station had left them to it. However, Hall and McLeod managed to bluff their way through the inspection and had made their own way back. That night, they all returned to the house and were hidden in a wood-shed. Next day, German soldiers came to search the house but failed to find the Americans.

Minor says they were told that a young man from Pont-Croix would take them to Rennes. The plan was for them to go in the baggage car to Douarnenez where they would wait for the Quimper train. However when they went to the station a certain amount of chaos seems to have ensued with various misunderstandings between the Americans, Jean-Pierre and their guide from Pont-Croix over the different trains, all of which were running late, and they were separated from Jean-Pierre when he went to buy their tickets and was then not allowed back onto the platform. The situation was not helped at Douarnenez, where Hugonnet and Schneider joined them but had different tickets from the other four, nor when they finally arrived at Quimper and the Americans became separated on leaving the station. Things were further complicated when Minor saw that he was being pointed out by a couple from the train, and decided to head away from the others in order to try and lose the couple, while the others, not realising what was going on, followed him. The couple trailed behind the Americans as far as a park where the airmen sat in the pouring rain, at which point the couple apparently lost interest.

Harry Minor says that Mickey had washed his hands of them by this time, and it seemed that Jean-Pierre had nowhere to take them and was checking some addresses that Mickey had given him. In the end, they decided to go to Jean Barrossi's house for help. Hugonnet was left in the park to wait for Jean-Pierre and then on the way, Semach and Schneider encountered two Frenchmen they had met at the Barrossi house. One went ahead to warn the Barrossi family while the other stayed to guide the airmen.

While they were at the Barrossi house, they learned that Paul Le Baron had arranged "a boat deal". This was apparently good news for Jean-Pierre who had doubts about whether the organisation Rennes would really be able to help them, and he went on to Rennes alone, leaving Jean Barrossi to look after of the Americans until Paul Le Baron arrived.

Minor, McLeod and Hall stayed with Jean Barrossi and before he left, Jean-Pierre took Hugonnet, Schneider and Semach to M. and Mme Albert Forget at 5 rue Valentin, who sheltered Hugonnet and Schneider while Semach stayed in a house across the street with a family connected to the Post Office.

Paul Le Baron was sent for and was "dumbfounded" by their story. While the Americans were having their adventures in Finistere, Paul Le Baron had been put in contact with Lucien Dumais, and learned about the gunboats leaving from Plouha. After checking with his boss Yves Allain, Le Baron agreed to bring the airmen to Mathurin Branchoux at Guingamp, where they would be sheltered until it was time to take them to the coast. He told the Americans that a boat was leaving soon from Guingamp (sic) and that he would get them all places – he came back three days later and told them he could only get places for five.

Meanwhile, James Quinn was having a separate adventure of his own, although the hand-written notes of his report are hard to decipher.

Quinn was separated from the others when he went with Mickey to try and find a friend of Mickey's called Germain. They took a bus for the ten kilometre ride to Plogoff, where Mickey left Quinn to spend the night in a house where (apparently) the Germans had caught a woman. He was moved next day to spend two days alone in another house before Mickey returned to take him by bicycle back to the house where he was staying. Next day (query) they cycled to Audierne where they met Jean Pierre, who told them that the boat deal was off and Quinn returned to the house in Plogoff. The following day (assume 5 February), they heard about the Jouet des Flots sinking nearby, and Quinn spent the next four days hiding in a hay-shed as every house in the district was being searched. He then spent two days on a farm with Mickey's friend Germain before being taken by two young girls, on an early morning bus back to Audierne, where he met Mickey – and S/Sgt Lee Gordon (#434), one of the survivors from the Jouet des Flots ship-wreck.

Mickey and two women then took Quinn and Gordon by bus to Quimper, where Mickey told them he was going to take them to Dr de la Marnierre in Brest, but Gordon didn't want to go to Brest, he wanted to go to Paris. There was something of an argument about this but in the end, Quinn and Gordon gave Mickey the money for their tickets and on 10 February, Mickey took the two Americans by overnight train to the capital.

On their arrival in Paris on 11 February, Quinn says that Mickey went to see his sister before taking them to "a house that Gordon knew about". Following an encounter in a park with some gendarmes (see earlier), Quinn and Gordon went to 2 Square Theodore Judin where Doctor Gorjux was still sheltering Mike Olynik. Quinn and Olynik stayed with the doctor for the next two weeks, during which time they were interviewed by Marcel Cola. Quinn says that Mickey stayed on in Paris, and comments on him picking up an American P-38 reconnaissance pilot from Wisconsin – this was 2/Lt John McGlynn (#502) who was being sheltered by Georges Prevost at boulevard Sebastopol at this time – see later.

As mentioned earlier, on the evening of Thursday 24 February, Ramon (Alain Raymond Mauret) took Quinn and Olynik to join Louis Feingold and Warren Tarkington on an overnight train to Saint-Brieuc, where they changed for Guingamp.

Harry Minor and others at Guingamp and Pommerit-le-Vicomte

On about 11 February, Paul Le Baron took Harry Minor, John Semach, Donald McLeod, Marion Hall and James Schneider to Guingamp where Minor and Schneider stayed with André Chareton and his mother Louise at 54 rue du Grand Trotrieux, and Semach with André's sister Yvonne (address unknown), while McLeod and Hall were sheltered with Desire and Francine Laurent.

A week later, a blond man named Pierre Cottin drove them all north by truck to Pommerit-le-Vicomte to be hidden in a wood-shed, and next day (query), Minor and Semach were taken to stay with a "poor widow" – who I have yet to identify. Three days after that, it snowed and Minor says it was so cold in the house that they had to leave, joining Hugonnet and Schneider, who were sheltered with Mme Anais Diouris, for the last three days until 25 February, when they were taken by truck to Plouha.

Ernest Hugonnet had stayed on in Quimper, sheltered with a Mme L'Haridon (query) and her sister for about a week, receiving visits from Paul Le Baron and Jean Barrossi, until Jean Barrossi took him to Guingamp. He spent the first night at the home of a man who worked in a garage and seemed to be the chief organiser – this was presumably François Kerambrun. He then "passed through the hands of several Frenchmen" before Pierre Cottin (about 23 years-old, well built, blond with a round face and long nose – he spoke some English) took him to Pommerit-le-Vicomte. Hugonnet says the Americans were scattered about the village and that he was taken to stay with Anais Diouris, where he joined McLeod, Hall and Schneider, while John Semach and Harry Minor were sheltered with a neighbour. After seven days at Pommerit-le-Vicomte, Pierre told them that "a Canadian captain" was coming to visit them.

When the Canadian captain (assume Jacky du Pac – Huguen agrees) arrived, he interrogated Hugonnet in a room alone. Hugonnet told the Canadian about his crew and their evasion, and how he knew Schneider and then answered questions about Bing Crosby's leading lady in his last movies. All Hugonnet learned about the Canadian was that he had lived in

France for seven years and gone to school in Los Angeles. He was about 5 foot 10 inches tall, well-built with dark features and a "French" face, and wore a silver French ring on his left hand for good luck.

On 25 February, Jean Trifol arrived in François Kerambrun's gazogène Citroën lorry, and in it were other evaders, including a Belgian and a Frenchman (this was actually Lee Gordon who comments on being mistaken as French in his report), and three men from Hugonnet's crew, Sgts Harold Gilley, Robert Schwartzburg and Robert Southers.

Sgt Harold O Gilley (#428), **Sgt Robert A Schwartzburg** (#429) and **Sgt Robert C Southers** (#430) were the radio operator and two waist-gunners of B-17 42-30200 Slo Time Sally (Born) which was shot down on 5 January 1944 – see Hugonnet, McLeod and Hall earlier.

"When I heard the pilot order the bail-out, I slipped on my English, chest-type parachute and jumped into the bomb bay. I stood on my left leg, the right was painful from four hits, and reached for the salvo handle. The doors fell out from under me. I pulled the rip-cord about a second after I left the ship … I think I went out at about 10,000 feet." (Gilley MIS-X #428)

"When the Me109s attacked us, the left waist-gunner (Southers) was badly wounded in the left arm. The radio operator (Gilley) had two pieces of 20mm in his right leg. The tail-gunner (Sgt Arlie L Thompson) dragged him back from the tail wheel. When the tail was blown off, the pilot ordered us to bail out. In another German fighter attack, the tail-gunner was hit in the left arm and side. 20mms were breaking through the waist, one apparently hitting the tail-gunner in the stomach. The other waist-gunner (Southers) tried to help him to the escape hatch … he fell out of the tail of the ship … Some 20mm opened my chute and it became tangled around Sgt Southers neck. After he untangled himself, I didn't know what to do … I knew I had to bail out, so I said a prayer and jumped holding my parachute in my arms. I looked over the country a bit and released the guide chute first. My parachute opened, and in about 30 seconds, I hit the ground." (Schwartzburg MIS-X #429)

"When the order came to bail out, I pulled the emergency on the waist escape hatch and kicked out the door. After Sgt Schwartzburg jumped, I looked back in the radio room and saw one man there. The plane was losing altitude fast. I jumped out head first." (Southers MIS-X #430)

Harold Gilley landed badly and the 21-year-old was unable to run from the crowd of French people who soon surrounded him. They asked if he were Boche, American or English and when he told them he was an American, they carried him to a nearby house and gave him some food. They also took his clothes, bandaged his leg, called a doctor and told Gilley they could get help to have him taken back to England shortly. When the doctor arrived, he removed some flak splinters from Gilley's leg, rebandaged the leg and gave him some medicine – he refused to take any of Gilley's money.

After a number of people had come to visit, Gilley was taken out and buried in a haystack for the rest of the day. That evening, he was brought back into the house and kept up until midnight trying to hold a conversation via an French-English dictionary before being taken to spend the rest of the night in a neighbouring house. Next day, he was returned to the haystack until lunch-time, when he ate at the first house. At about one o'clock, Sgt Schwartzburg was brought to join him and they spent the rest of the afternoon in the haystack – and an ex-soldier named René (aged about 23) who brought them some clothes, is mentioned at about this point. They had their evening meal in the house again followed by another long session with the dictionary before retiring to the haystack once more. Next day, they were told that too many people knew they were there and they were moved to another place, where their journey was arranged.

Robert Schwartzburg made what he describes as "rather an easy landing near a stream" but it then took the 25-year-old a good ten minutes to free himself from his American chest-pack parachute. He ran to a pile of bushes to hide his chute and flying gear before starting his escape but soon encountered a French family. He says they probably wanted to help him but he didn't realise that at the time so he ran on for several miles before stopping to hide in some woods. He set off again at nightfall, heading east and intending to get off the Brest peninsula before turning south for Spain. He stopped at about midnight and tried to sleep but despite still having all his flying clothes, still felt pretty cold. He set off again in the morning, not seeing any farmhouses he could approach, and finally heard someone cutting wood. He approached the man who then took him to a farmhouse and brought him some food. He was told that a comrade was nearby and was led to a haystack where he found Harold Gilley.

Robert Southers was winded when he landed in the mud with his parachute caught in a tree near a wagon-road between the fields. A group of about ten Frenchmen soon gathered, pulling his parachute down from the tree as he struggled out of his too-tight harness. They posted some boys as guards around 24-year-old Southers while he retrieved his first-aid kit from his parachute, removed some pieces of shrapnel from his left arm and applied a bandage. One of the boys indicated that a patrol was coming so one of the men gave Gilley a jacket which he put on over his uniform ODs before heading off in the opposite direction. Using his escape kit compass, Southers set off south but soon realised he was heading towards the wreckage of his aircraft. Then a man appeared who led Southers back to his house and gave him some food. Southers told the man that he wanted to go to Spain and the man advised him to head for Brest but either way, it was clear that Southers couldn't stay so he set off once more. Southers headed generally south and east, by-passing a town and a village until about ten o'clock that night when he came to Lanrivain. On the other side of the town, on the road to Saint-Nicholas-du-Pélem, a Frenchman with a young boy spoke to him and after some hesitation, Southers told him he was an American, which his little boy understood.

Gilley, Schwartzburg and Southers are another example where their combined basic report, in Gilley (#428), from which most of the above is taken, is typed but the Appendices (Gilley and Schwartzburg are combined) with their evasion details are particularly hard to read – and it is a similar situation with Milton Church and Kenneth Blye (see later), who evaded for part of the time with them.

Southers was taken to a house in Saint-Nicolas-du-Pélem where his arm was bandaged and he was given some civilian clothes. There seem to have been other people in the house, an aunt and cousins, and a man, aged about 28, came to see Southers – he had been a lieutenant in the French army, and he brought a French-English dictionary. I think that Southers was taken to the lieutenant's house in Lanrivain and a room over a barn. Southers possessions were taken, leaving just his underwear, and he says he slept "in a cold sweat" all night. Next day (6 Jan), Southers was taken to the lieutenant's aunt's house, where Southers stayed overnight with the aunt and a cousin, and was told they had found a comrade – he was also visited by a doctor who dressed his arm – and later brought him some more clothes.[27]

27 Roger Huguen says the doctor was Dr Joseph Thomas, and that Southers was also helped by M. and Mme Rolland of Kerivoal, and the Le Tanou family (of Quinquis Saliou).

Early the following morning, Southers met Noel Cozic (of Plounevez-Quintin) (his father was a harness maker) and he took charge of Southers. I think M. Cozic found a local man called Olof who had been to New York City – a short, ruddy fellow, nearly bald, about 5 feet 5 inches tall, about 45 years old – but he said he couldn't help. Southers also mentions a Mme Tinis (query), aged about 40, "had been attractive", with a 19-year-old son, and a daughter who lived in Brest – her husband was a naval officer who worked for Frigidaire (query) and had been arrested by the Gestapo.

It's not clear from his report who sheltered Southers for the next two nights (probably M. Cozic) but it was decided that he should be moved to Pontivy (Morbihan). Noel Cozic (who, according to a report in the NARA file of Jean-Guy Bariou, had consulted with Pierre Sibiril and Yves Loyer of Maël-Carhaix) took Southers to Pontivy on his motorcycle and delivered him to a plumber. Presumably connected to the local organisation, the unnamed plumber (a short, fat man aged about 35) passed them on to a local butcher, who told them that Southers navigator, Ernest Hugonnet, and three other airmen were being helped in Gourin.

That afternoon, Noel took Southers to a priest's house about 4 kilometres from Saint-Nicolas-du-Pélem (Southers thinks in Plounévez-Quintin) where they stayed that night – this was probably Noel Cozic's own home because Southers reports that the mother there was afraid that Noel would be put in prison for helping him, and that Mme Tinis came and reassured her.

Next morning, Noel took Southers into town on his bike, where he saw a French lieutenant directing movements, and people that he'd seen before, although he didn't speak to any of them.

Noel Cozic told Southers that British Intelligence had said that he would have to get rid of his dog-tags – they argued about it but Noel insisted that the new organisation would not help him with dog-tags, and took them away. Noel then took Southers on his bike – Southers thought towards Rostrenen – to a watch-shop (bijoutier Louis Michel) to meet a man who had "taken care of Hugonnet's boys", Milton Church and Kenneth Blye (see later), plus Ralph Hall, where Noel left him. The new man (assume Jean-Guy Bariou) is described by Southers as wearing thick glasses, and being about 35 to 40 years old, balding, with slick black hair – and he had a younger, dark-haired man with him.

According to a report in Jean-Guy Bariou's NARA file, Noel Cozic had intended to pass Southers on to M. Bariou but with the Gestapo in Gourin, Southers was instead passed to friends in the "maquis de Conveau", about 4 kms from Gourin. Next day (sic), Simon Le Bras took Southers to butcher Yves Bourlès at Saint-Hernin, where he joined Gilley, Schwartzburg, Church and Blye, and on 22 January, all five Americans were taken to be sheltered by Robert de Boissier at Kergoat – where they stayed until 26 February, when Yves Bourlès took them in his vehicle to Guingamp.

Southers own report doesn't quite agree with that, saying a new fellow took him by bicycle to a tavern at Glomel (south-west of Rostrenen, on the road to Gourin), where they heard that the Germans had carried out raids in Gourin, and so his guide took Southers to a "terrorist camp" in the forest about four kilometres away, with all sorts of firearms. He lived in a tent for three days – he thought Church and Blye had stayed there previously – before Simon Le Bras took him (again by bicycle) to Saint-Hernin from where his journey was arranged, travelling with Sgts Gilley and Schwartzburg.

Harold Gilley and Robert Schwartzburg each say they landed about 22 kms south-east of Gourin (which is plainly wrong) and that someone (a farmer and Pierre – query) took them to Saint-Michel. Next day, they were taken by taxi to Gourin, where they met some of the Le Bras family, including Simon, his older brother Joseph, and their parents, Simon and Simone – Schwartzburg also mentions three sisters.

I am fairly confident it was François Le Tanou and Roger Duffrin who found Gilley and Schwartzburg somewhere close to their homes at Quinquis Saliou (a small commune about 4 kms SE of Locarn, and 4 kms NE of Maël-Carhaix) and passed them on to a farmer named Goubil who hid them in his barn. I think they may then have been sheltered briefly with the secrétaire de mairie of Trébrivan, Pierre Philippe (born 1898) and his wife, Marie Augustine, principal of the girls' school at Trébrivan, in their house attached to the school. I say briefly because, according to Georges Le Cun, it was two o'clock in the morning of 6 January when François Follezou took the two Americans to Gourin in his taxi.

Schwartzburg stayed with Simon Le Bras on place de la Victoire, Gourin – where Simon's parents were also living – for three days until they received news that the Gestapo was in the town, and Simon and his brother Joseph (chemisier of place du Marche, Gourin) took Schwartzburg – along with Milton Church (#423) and Kenneth Blye (#424), who had been sheltered with coiffeur Robert Dérégniaux – on foot to the little village of Saint-Hernin.

Simon Le Bras (born Dec 1875) and his wife Simone had come to Gourin from Lorient after their home was bombed, and were living with their son, also named Simon, at place de la Victoire. They had 11 children, including Simon Victor Marie (born June 1920), a champion cyclist. Both Simon and his brother Joseph are credited with helping Milton Church (#423), Kenneth Blye (#424), Harold Gilley (#428), Robert Schwartzburg (#429) and Robert Southers (#430) – plus Jack McGough (#475), Ralph Patton (#476), Glenn Johnson (#493), Norman King (#494) and Isadore Viola (#495) – all brought from Mr Bariou, "representait a Gourin l'organisation qui s'occupait du repatriement des aviateurs", except Southers who came from a maquis unit – and all passed on to Paul Le Baron.

Simon Le Bras says that on 6 January, he was asked (by Jean-Guy Bariou) to take two Americans into his home – he was very cramped, being a refugee from Lorient (and living with his son, also named Simon) but accepted one of them, Robert Schwartzburg – a tall and charming boy from Milwaukee. He stayed four days, until Sunday (9 Jan) morning when "they" came to tell them the Gestapo was in Gourin and knew something "was in the wind". Mr Dérégniaux also had two Americans (Church and Blye) in his home, and then two more (query this) came to join them .. his sons Simon and Joseph left with them, taking the Americans through paths in the mountain to the safety of the little village of Saint-Hernin. Simon stayed with them for two months .. they remained longest with Mr de Boissier, Chateau Kergoat – fed by Mr Bourlès, butcher of Saint-Hernin.

Robert Dérégniaux (born Jan 1899) coiffeur of Grande Rue, Gourin, was married to Marie Louise (born in Belgium Jan 1900), and they had three children. They sheltered Church and Blye for two days until 9 January when the Americans had to be moved from Gourin because of a German search.

Louis Yves Gestin (born Dec 1899), cultivateur of Roz Mael, Saint-Hernin, was married to Marie Anne, and had two young children. He is credited with sheltering Church, Blye, Gilley and Schwartzburg for two days and one night, all received from Simon Le Bras, and passed to Yves Bourlès on 11 January.

Yves Louis Bourlès (born Aug 1911) was a butcher who lived at 2 Route de la Montagne, Saint-Hernin, where he had a shop and café – he was married to Marie Louise and they had two young teenage children. He says he was recruited by Simon Le Bras (aka Tonton) and that he sheltered Gilley, Schwartzburg, Southers, Church and Blye – received from Simon Le Bras who brought them from Louis Gestin (of Roz Mael) where they had spent the night – before Bourlès took them to Robert De Boissier. He also names Lucienne Nicholas (nf) of Saint-Hernin as helping the airmen. Note that Southers was brought to him separately from the maquis camp, not from Louis Gestin.

Schwartzburg reports that "While in Gourin, the young men of the town had received cards to report to Brest for work with the Germans. None reported and in turn are now in hiding from the Germans."

While Robert Schwartzburg stayed with the La Bras family on place de la Victoire, Harold Gilley was taken to another house where he was sheltered overnight with a woman called Jeanne (attractive, spoke broken English). I think the house belonged to her father, who Gilley says was aged about 52 with grey hair – he ran two slate mines 5 kms NE of Gourin, was the second richest man in town and lived next to (query) the mairie. The following afternoon, Mrs Chunn came to visit – she spoke excellent English, having spent 10 years in the US, and was married to an Englishman. Her brother-in-law worked for the National Cash Register Company, and she asked Gilley to look him up (presumably in Dayton, Ohio) and tell him that she was safe and well for the present. I think that Mrs Chunn then took Gilley back to her house on rue de Scaer where he stayed until the morning of 10 January when he was moved to Saint-Hernin, and joined Schwartzburg, Southers, Church and Blye.

From Saint-Hernin, the five Americans were taken to be sheltered by farmer Robert de Boissier in a small house that he owned in the woods of his grounds at nearby Kergoat – and while they were there, Simon Le Bras (son) says he contacted Georges Martin at Concarneau and Paul Le Baron in Brest.

Robert de Boissier (born September 1896) of Kergoat, Saint-Hernin was a farmer – married to Emmanuelle, they had four children – Sefanio (sic), Paulette (translated and typed report has both Pondette and Gondette), Louise and Ernest. Robert was recruited in June 1943 by Job le Bec, of the Moulin de La Pie, who he sheltered, along with Georges Jouanjean, Dr Pierre Joseph Lignon (of Kerampoix, Quimperlé), Etienne Le Bihan and Robert Froger (see below), when they were being hunted following infiltration of the "Pen Called" group by Roger Leneveu.[28]

Robert de Boissier says that Church, Blye, Schwartzburg, Gilley and Southers were brought to him from Gourin on 5 January (although this date is wrong) 1944 and he hid them in a small house in the middle of his woods – his daughter Paulette would go into town every day to get food which they would prepare in their own house and take out to them hot. The five Americans stayed with him until 27 (sic – 24) February, when Mr Bourlès of Saint-Hernin came to take them to Guingamp.

On 8 June, eight young men from the local resistance group were arrested at Lampret, about 4 kms north of Carhaix, and hanged along the side of the road. Because none of them would betray their group's leaders, the Germans carried out a reprisal raid on Kergoat the next day, and the de Boissier family was arrested. I don't think they were deported but their home was ransacked and destroyed.

Note that NARA De Boissier file only contains already translated and typed pages, complete with multiple small errors and spelling mistakes – and that some of the evader reports (and so IS9) credit Robert Froger (himself a fugitive) with sheltering them.

Robert Jean Joseph Froger, tradesman of 6 place d'Aiguillon in Carhaix, had been involved with resistance activities since 1940 when he formed a small group with Etienne Le Bihan, François Le Maigre (aka Marsouin) and Jean Solu. Their first targets were local collaborators but in 1942, they joined the Breton equipe "Pen Called", working with the Pat O'Leary organisation. His (rather confused) IS9 recommendation for an award says that he and his wife Marthe sheltered and fed three Allied evaders between Jan and Feb 44. Later housed, fed and clothed a further six men, sheltered with him in small house in the woods. From there, a trusted friend collected them and took them by car to Guingamp.

28 "Pen Called" translates from Breton (and Welsh) as "hard heads", reflecting the stubborn resistance of Bretons against the German occupation.

Robert Froger was arrested following a parachute drop of weapons the night of 14-15 May 1944 and deported – he was last heard of at Brunswick (Braunschweig) hospital and is believed to have died in Germany.

2/Lt Milton L Church (#423) and **T/Sgt Kenneth O Blye** (#424) were the navigator and radio operator of 94BG/331BS B-17 42-31212 (Johnson) which was on a morning raid to Bordeaux-Merignac on 5 January 1944. Pilot Glenn Johnson says they had just dropped their bombs and were turning away from the target when they ran into a flak barrage which damaged their tail. The aircraft began vibrating and it took both pilots to hold course. They were just rejoining their formation when they were struck by a stray round from the tail-gun of a B-17 ahead, and then they were attacked by fighters. The aircraft started to climb steeply and Johnson used his microphone to order everyone to bail out, although he didn't think the interphone was actually working by that time. Johnson could see the men at the front of the aircraft putting on their parachutes and when the aircraft went into a spin (Church says that an explosion near the rear escape hatch cut off their tail), he released the bomb-bay doors. The co-pilot (Ralph Patton) went out the nose-hatch and Johnson followed the engineer (Ralph Hall) out through the bomb-bay at about 6,000 feet.

Five other crew also evaded successfully: bombardier 2/Lt Jack McGough (#475) and co-pilot 2/Lt Ralph K Patton (#476) were evacuated on the third operation Bonaparte, and pilot 1/Lt Glenn B Johnson (#493) and waist-gunner S/Sgt Isadore C Viola (#495) on the fourth (see later) while engineer/TTG T/Sgt Ralph Hall (#1246) wound up with Yves Le Hénaff for the Jouet des Flots episode.

Hall's rather vague report doesn't give many details apart from saying that he contacted the French underground at Gourin on 7 January, and that he and an Indian were sent to Douarnenez, where the Indian was picked up by the police. After getting ashore from the wreckage of the Jouet des Flots, Hall was sheltered in Douarnenez with Mlle Marguerite Seznec at 3 rue Emile Zola for nearly seven months until 22 August when he was taken to Plouha. Hall was met by Captain James Harrison (Dumais) who took him back to the "beautiful house" he had appropriated at Saint-Brieuc before arranging transport to Rennes where Hall rejoined American forces.

Ball-turret gunner S/Sgt James L Stubblefield, waist-gunner S/Sgt William A Monson and tail-gunner S/Sgt Carlton V Coleman were killed, and today there is a monument to them, and Slo Time Sally tail-gunner Sgt Arlie L Thompson, at Kergrist-Moëlou.

Milton Church says that the centrifugal force of the spin made it hard for him to reach his parachute pack, and then when he did, and tried to leave, it caught on the edge of the escape hatch. When the 27-year-old finally cleared the aircraft, he pulled his rip-cord almost immediately, having time then during his descent to wave to a couple of German pilots in circling Messerschmitts, who apparently waved back. Church made quite a hard landing in a field, and while a small group of French farmers were helping him take his parachute off, Sgt Blye arrived.

Kenneth Blye also struggled to get out of the spinning aircraft. He says that as they went into a spin, the ball-turret gunner (S/Sgt James Stubblefield) came up from his turret to bail out but then as the aircraft dived, they and the two waist-gunners (Viola (#495) and S/Sgt William Monson) were "raised to the ceiling and then thrown in a pile at the back of the ship. One man (Viola) sailed through the back end of the ship and pulled his parachute".

Blye, who was just two weeks away from his twenty-second birthday when he bailed out, landed on his stomach in front of the waist escape-door. The emergency release failed but turning the handle opened the hatch only for Blye's back-pack parachute to get caught in the doorway. It took a good kicking from Blye to get the hatch clear, the door finally falling off and Blye following it out of the aircraft. When he opened his parachute, he was just a few seconds in the air before hitting the ground – he says he was the first man of their crew to land. Blye came down in a field where a Frenchman helped him roll up his parachute before taking it away, leaving Blye to watch as Church landed a couple of fields away and then hobbling (his leg had been injured in the aircraft) to join him.

A crowd soon gathered around the two airmen and Blye took out his escape purse to distribute some money. Two young men (Appendix C seems to say peasants with ferrets) were singled out to help them and they took Church and Blye to hide in a clump of bushes, and food (cider, cold pork, bread and butter) was brought to them. A couple of hours later, they heard whistling – it was the two Frenchmen. They measured the airmen and then brought civilian clothes, and as darkness fell, took them to a place from where their journey was arranged.

The above is taken from their basic reports, which are typed, but the combined Appendix C with their evasion details is a set of notes which become progressively more difficult to decipher.

Church and Blye both say they landed near Saint-Nicolas-du-Pélem but I think it more likely they came down much closer to the crash-site at Kermorou, about 2 kms south-west of Kergrist-Moëlou. Yves André (a cousin of Robert Le Tanou, son of François) told Douglas Doig in September 2018 that a Mme Conan at Kervénal saw parachutes, and Annie Le Du of Quinquis Saliou (who knew the story from her parents) pointed east in the direction of Kervénal (just west of Kermorou) where parachutes were seen. Yves André says that one parachutist landed at the Moulin de Kersault (which is about 1,500 metres northwest of Kervénal), and another man, 300 metres north of him. I can't be certain these men were Church and Blye but they do seem the most likely of the 13 Americans who landed in that general area on 5 January 1944.

Church describes how the two returning Frenchmen (both teenagers) whistled "It's a Long Way to Tipperary" as a signal to the airmen they were friendly. I think he says they were brothers and that the older one was called Robert. It was the younger of the two boys who stayed with the airmen while the other went to collect civilian clothes, Church receiving a complete grey suit. Their flying gear and uniforms were put into bags, and at nightfall, Church and Blye were taken about 5 kilometres to a house where they were given a meal. The notes are rather scrambled at this point but Church mentions someone called Edouard (possibly the younger brother), who brought a dictionary to help with communications, and someone called Stephen La Tour (query). It is not clear if they stayed at the house (or stable) overnight but it was probably the following day (6 Jan) when Edouard took the Americans to a tavern about 5 kilometres away where they met some "Patriot-Terrorists".

Church says the tavern was evidently a terrorist hang-out, with many of the men there carrying guns. The Americans were given tobacco to smoke, and a man who spoke English was brought. They told him they wanted to go to Spain but he said it was too far away and too expensive. When it got dark, the leader of the group took them to a wooded area where they settled down in a tent but were woken again at about two o'clock with the warning of "Boches". Everyone packed up and left, the Americans helping by carrying blankets and firearms as they made their way to another camp, about 8 kilometres away, where they went back to sleep.

When they woke, they met a commander wearing a black felt hat who brought them shoes and told them they would "partir tout suite pour Angleterre". He and another man (a fellow with horn-rimmed glasses, about 5 ft 8 inches tall) took them to another little tavern about 3 kilometres away where they picked up two more Frenchmen. It's not clear from their report exactly what happened next but they seem to have been taken to Gourin in a big red bus, driven by the Gourin chief of police (assume Jules le Gall) in civilian clothes.

In Gourin, Church and Blye were taken to a tobacco and wine shop where they met the local organisation chief and five or six others, including three men who were being hunted by the Gestapo. Church describes the chief as a short, heavy-set man who always had couple of days growth of beard (he had heavy dark eye-brows, and wore his leather coat cape-fashion) and says that Hugonnet knew him – this was Jean-Guy Bariou. The chief took their dog-tags and told them their photographs were no good, and that they would need new ones. They also met Mrs Cockburn, who spoke good English and was the organisation's interpreter. She told them that her husband was in Saint Joseph, Missouri, and she asked them to send him a message saying that she was "Well and safe, son okay".

Church and Blye were then taken to a barber-shop on place de la Victoire to be shaved and given more clothes. The man at the barbershop, Robert Dérégniaux, also took their photographs and sheltered the two Americans while they were in Gourin.

Church reports on the arrest of the fellow with glasses and four others. Church was told that he was carrying photographs of the Americans and that when he refused to talk to the Germans, he was shot – this was Eugène Cadic. It was at this point that Jean-Guy Bariou had to leave Gourin, and Church says that their subsequent dealings were with Simon Le Bras. He also mentions Simon's brothers Joseph and Louis, who showed him pictures of Lorient and Nantes after they had been bombed, and described the damage done to Saint Nazaire.

At about eleven o'clock on Sunday 9 January, Simon Le Bras brought Robert Schwartzburg, and with Simon's brother walking ahead to check the route, the three airmen were taken to a farm a few kilometres from Saint-Hernin, apparently one of the wealthiest farms in the neighbourhood, to stay with Louis Gestin at Roz Mael. Church and Blye slept upstairs while

Schwartzburg and Simon Le Bras stayed on the ground floor. Next day, they were joined by Harold Gilley – Church says that he arrived with the fellow who had sheltered him and another fellow, although I'm not sure that's quite correct (see Gilley earlier). That night however, having decided that too many people knew about them, the four Americans were moved to a room in the hotel (sic) run by butcher Yves Bourlès.

During their stay with the Bourlès family, the four Americans were visited by various people, including Mrs Cockburn (who had seen them arrive the previous evening), local baker Emile Clec'h (or Le Clech), schoolteacher François Caro (who was not in the organisation) and Hernin Vitry (who was) – Caro and Vitry were both in hiding to avoid STO – and on 13 January, Simon Le Bras brought Robert Southers from the maquis camp to join them.

A week later, the Germans raided Saint-Hernin and although they failed to find the five American airmen, it was decided best to move them once more.[29]

Church, Blye, Gilley, Schwartzburg and Southers were taken to Kergoat where they were sheltered with Robert Froger and his wife Marthe. Church says they stayed with the Froger couple (in a little house at Kergoat belonging to Robert De Boissier – the Froger couple were also being sheltered there) for five weeks to the day, that every precaution was taken, the Americans not being allowed out of the house, and that only the De Boissier family – and someone called Stephen Bion, who was living under an assumed name (this was Etienne Jean Le Bihan, aka Belchasse) – knew they were there. They finally left on 24 February after (according to Church) Robert De Boissier's daughter Paulette made an arrangement with local butcher Yves Bourlès to drive the five airmen to Guingamp – Paul Le Baron says he organised the journey, travelling with them to Guingamp. They were passed on to Mathurin Branchoux, who says (in Remy) that "they" took their eighteen (sic) boys through "l'allée du chateau du marquis de Kerouartz" (Chateau des Salles) as far as a chicken farm and hid them in a chicken house – where they were joined by American escaper Lee Gordon and Belgian fighter pilot Leon Harmel.

29 Includes additional information on the people of Saint-Hernin from Yvonne Millar and Doug Doig after talking to Saint-Hernin resident Robert Callonnec in May 2018.

Leon Harmel and Lee Gordon's unexpected appearance in Guingamp caused a certain amount of alarm among the helpers (see earlier) but the arrival next morning of the other four airmen brought from Paris went according to plan, and they spent just the day there before being taken to Plouha that evening.

Louis Feingold, Warren Tarkington, Mike Olynik, James Quinn and their guides, Jean Kocera-Massenet and Raymond Mauret, had a reserved compartment to themselves on the overnight train from Paris to Saint-Brieuc, where they changed trains, arriving at Guingamp at about nine-fifteen the following morning, Friday 25 February. They carried folded newspapers as a signal to those meeting them and were soon handed over to a young girl called Louisette (Olynik gives her name as Marie-Louise and says that she spoke a little English) and a man that Olynik says was her father. Louisette took Olynik and Quinn while the man took Feingold and Tarkington into a house across the road from the station (probably with Charles Sirey, owner of the hôtel de la Gare (now hôtel de l'Arrivée) which had been requisitioned by the Germans in 1941). The couple returned an hour later and took them to the Chareton home at 54 rue du Grand Trotrieux, where they rejoined Olynik and Quinn, and were told they would probably leave that night. During the afternoon, they were interrogated by a Frenchman (sic) who they say was called "the Captain" (Dumais) and at eight o'clock that evening, were taken to a garage and loaded into a lorry.

Milton Church, Kenneth Blye, Harold Gilley, Robert Schwartzburg, Robert Southers, Lee Gordon and Leon Harmel were already on board the lorry, having been collected from the chicken hatchery (see earlier) – and the girl went with them to Pommerit-le-Vicomte where they collected Harry Minor, John Semach, Ernest Hugonnet, Donald McLeod, Marion Hall and James Schneider, before driving on to Plouha.

I suspect that the girl was Louisette Lorre, the woman that Dumais describes as being his assistant, and who he says in his book, he poached from Henri Le Blais in Saint-Brieuc.[30] *Louise Lorre was born in April 1923 at Langueux, which is just outside Saint-Brieuc. After the war, she joined the army and was gravely wounded in an engagement in Indochina – she died in Hanoi on 10 July 1951. There is now a rue Louise Lorre in Langueux.*

30 Lucien Dumais (1975) "The Man Who Went Back" Leo Cooper.

For this second Bonaparte Operation, all seventeen airmen were collected from their temporary lodgings in Guingamp and Pommerit-le-Vicomte, and delivered to Plouha late in the evening of Friday 25 February (the day before their departure) where they were sheltered for the rest of that night and following day at three locations around the town.

Feingold and Tarkington report that a group of nine men were dropped off before the lorry driver took the rest of them to a second rendezvous. However, there was no-one there to meet them so they returned to the town until "contact was re-established". The remaining eight airmen got out of the truck and walked about eight blocks to a deserted house on a farm where they found mattresses and blankets. They stayed at the house overnight and all next day until dark. The lady who was looking after them said they would have news that evening at either seven-thirty or nine-thirty, and at a quarter past eight, came to tell them they would leave that night.

Hugonnet (who was with Feingold and Tarkington) describes their lodgings as being a three-story house belonging to an elderly lady who told him it had been built in 1747, and often been used by the organisation for shelter.

Louis Feingold, Warren Tarkington, Ernest Hugonnet, Donald McLeod, Marion Hall, Harold Gilley, Robert Southers and James Quinn were sheltered overnight at Ville-Dé with Françoise Monjaret, while Mike Olynik, Milton Church, Lee Gordon and Leon Harmel stayed with Germaine Couffon and her mother Anne Marie at Kerisajo, and Harry Minor, John Semach, Kenneth Blye, Robert Schwartzburg and James Schneider with Leonie Le Calvez.[31]

Milton Church describes a visit they received the following evening from a Canadian in a leather coat and beret, and another fellow who went to the beach with them – this was François Le Cornec. They all shook hands before the Canadian (Dumais) produced a pistol and told Harmel to put his hands in the air. The Frenchman searched him and Church was told that the Belgian was a prisoner and was going back to England whether he liked it or not – one false move and he was a dead man. The Canadian said that Church was to be in charge of him and not to let him out of

31 In their report, Feingold and Tarkington say they stayed at the same place as their pilot Richard Smith and others of their crew the previous month, although as mentioned earlier, while Booher, Mele and Eshuis were sheltered with Francoise Monjaret, Smith actually stayed with Leonie Le Calvez.

his sight. He also gave Church some papers that he said should be turned over to Intelligence, to pass on to Captain Windham-Wright on arrival in England.[32]

Kenneth Blye says that Marie-Thérèse Le Calvez told them they would be leaving at about nine o'clock, and a man with a leather coat came and warned them not to trust the Belgian (Harmel) before Marie-Thérèse led the five Americans to another house where Dumais briefed them on what to expect next.

Louis Feingold describes how two men arrived to take his group of eight on a three kilometre walk to rejoin the nine men who had left them earlier, including one Belgian (Harmel) who had his hands bound – and they met the chief, a short, dark-haired Canadian who collected up their money, telling them that the organisation could make good use of it. They were then led in single file by a man and a girl down to the beach, each man holding the hand of the next in the darkness, but on finding the tide was too high, climbed back up one cliff and then down another to where they waited to be picked up.

Lee Gordon confirms that the chief who Harmel had seen in Paris (Dumais) came to the house and told Harmel to put his hands up before tying them together. He told the three Americans that Harmel was under arrest and that they would be responsible for him. They were then taken across fields to a house where all the evaders were gathered, along with a man with a machine-gun and another with a pistol. The chief explained that they would be going down a cliff in single file to wait for a boat. Marie-Therese and Dumais went down with them, and at about a quarter to two, four rowing boats arrived at the beach to take them out about a mile to a gunboat.

On the first operation, guides had been able to take the evaders from Jean Gicquel's house to the beach at l'Anse-Cochat via a reasonably accessible gully, just below the present-day Shelburn Commemorative site. However, for the subsequent evacuations it was decided that increased patrol activity by the Germans made that route too dangerous, and they would have to take the more direct, but hazardous, route down the steep and crumbling cliff.

Church reports that they boarded the gunboat at about 0230 hrs, and arrived in Dartmouth at about 0815 hrs, where they tied up to a larger

32 This seems an oddly melodramatic scene when you remember that Dumais had already interrogated Harmel in Paris and should have satisfied himself then that Harmel really was the evading RAF fighter pilot he claimed to be.

boat – the depot ship Westward Ho! They were met by Captain Windham-Wright and an RNVR lieutenant who warned them against speaking in front of the crew. They stayed on board the depot ship until nightfall, when they were taken ashore and driven by truck the short distance to Kingswear railway station and put on a train for London.

Paul Le Baron

Paul Le Baron sums up the situation regarding his involvement with the evaders brought from Brittany in this extract from his (typed and already translated) statement made to Capitaine Lefort of the DGER *(Direction général des études et recherches)* in Paris on 8 November 1944:

> *"After the departure of the 25th, another was planned for 19 January, but in the meantime, Maho was arrested.*
>
> *In Brest there were at this time 7 aviators; 4 at Colonel Scheidhauer's, 3 at Dr de la Marnierre's who were previously sheltered at Lt Martin in Concarneau, and who were brought to Brest by him and M Le Floch.*
>
> *In February the Gestapo charged in. The three aviators at de la Marnierre's were hidden at Mme Callarec's, then in Landerneau at M Rolland's (I was assisted in the convoyage and other things by R Le Bourhis). The 4 aviators at the Colonel's, left for Saint-Nic for Mme Magne's (convoyed by herself).*
>
> *Mme de la Marnierre, who had several times shown herself to be imprudent, fooled by Le Droff who announced himself as being on a mission from London, took it unto herself to regroup the aviators at Brest (4 at the Col's and 3 at her place), and to try to have them leave via Audierne. The whole business, very badly planned, was a failure and it was only through the intervention of an agent at Quimper, Jean Barrossi that they escaped the Gestapo and police barrage (these airman were sheltered at J Barrossi's in Quimper, 1 rue de Penhars. Present address Ecole de Pennanguer, Route de Pont l'Abbe). They were now only six, the 7th having gone back to Guingamp, going through Paris.*
>
> *In the meantime, I had come into contact with an agent of the I.S. (Canadian Leon) who was in charge of departures by means of fast launches, through the mercies of Mr Feroc of Brest and Mr Branchoux of Guingamp. In agreement with Gregoire, my boss, it was agreed that the aviators I had on hand should be evacuated by means of the planned operations at Plouha.*

It is thus that I brought 18 aviators to Guingamp – 6 from Quimper, helped by J Borrocci – 6 from Gourin helped by R Le Bourhis – 5 from Carhaix – 1 from Rennes. The last obtained from Mlle Mace, pseudo Mlle Vincent – 83 avenue du Mail in Rennes.

For information on the aviators from Carhaix, Gourin, refer to Mr Le Bras, place du Marche in Gourin, and Mme Froger, place du Marche in Carhaix, and also on the three Frenchmen, (Lt Roger Dhen, escaped from Germany – Raymond le Bourhis and le Droff, supposedly on a mission).[33]

To learn of the places of shelter, refer to Mr Branchoux who, helped by Mr Le Cun, took very active part in the departures from Plouha; it is on him that rested a large share of the responsibility regarding sheltering, convoying towards the coast, security teams and especially the operations themselves." (NARA Le Baron, with the spelling of some names corrected)

33 The six men brought from Quimper were, as already mentioned, Minor, Semach, McLeod, Hall, Schneider and Hugonnet – the men from Gourin (actually five) were McGough, Patton, Johnson, King and Viola (see later) – the five from Carhaix were Gilley, Schwartzburg, Southers, Church and Blye – and the man brought from Rennes was John McGlynn (see later).

SIS/MI9 Operation Bonaparte 3 (16-17 Mar 1944) MGB 502 (Peter Williams)

With the first two Bonaparte operations running so well, and the number of evaders ever increasing, Dumais decided to try and fit three evacuations into the next moonless period – a decision he attempted to reverse following the problems encountered during Bonaparte 3 but which took place anyway. From an operational point of view, the situation would have been helped by the unusually dry and mild weather conditions over southern England and northern France at the end of March 1944.

This was the only one of the five Bonaparte operations carried out by Lt-Cdr Peter Williams and MGB 502, with 503 tasked with the SOE (DF) Var line Operation Septimus to Beg-an-Fry the following night. MGB 502 would also return to the beach at l'Anse-Cochat in July for the second of the Crozier operations.

The other change in routine was that instead of Guingamp, the twenty-two evaders brought from Paris for this third Bonaparte operation were taken to Châtelaudren.

It's not clear why Mathurin Branchoux decided the men should be taken to Châtelaudren, a small country village about half way between Saint-Brieuc and Guingamp, with a population of about 1,000 people (as against the 9,000 odd in Guingamp), and the little-used railway station is not in the village itself but about a kilometre south.

> *"While Guingamp seemed perfect as a reception centre, for some reason that could not be properly explained, Mathurin Branchoux decided he wanted the evaders to get off the Paris-Brest train (sic) at Châtelaudren. Georges Le Cun cycled over there with his German shepherd dog (Fifi) and immediately saw a problem – the station was deserted. There were two French gendarmes waiting for passengers because, unlike Guingamp, Châtelaudren was in the restricted, coastal zone and visitors needed special papers to get off the train there. Plus, when the train arrived, it was only the ten (sic) evaders and their guides that got off the train, there were no crowds to hide in. Georges Le Cun could hear the gendarme commenting "another one for Plouézec" (a*

small village north of Plouha, between Lanloup and Paimpol) as the eighth (sic) airman showed his ID card and German pass." (lightly edited from my translation of Huguen 1976)

This would have been particularly evident on 14 March when Manuel Rogoff, Shirley Berry, Russell Paquin, William Campbell, Frank Moast, Bill Spinning and their guides stepped off the morning train just twenty-four hours after Harold Vines, Edward Donaldson, Neelan Parker, Robert Fruth, Charles Winkelman and Joe Birdwell. But then, incredibly, the charade was repeated next day when Philip Capo, John Amery and Kenneth Christian alighted on the morning of 15 March, followed a few hours later by Everett Stump, Carlyle Van Selus, Carl Mielke, William Lessig and Dean Tate that afternoon.

The Organisation in Châtelaudren and Plouagat

Mme Vve Rosalie Cardinal (born October 1892), restaurant owner at 1 rue Sainte Magloire (now L'Auberge du Goélo), Châtelaudren. She says she helped Joseph Birdwell (#471) and five others, brought to her by Le Friec, and passed to Georges Le Cun and François Le Cornec. Mathurin Branchoux, in Rémy's "La Maison d'Alphonse", says she had a café restaurant at place de l'Eglise – this is the same place.

Alphonse Le Friec (born September 1903) (menagere) and his wife Maria (mechanicien) and their three chidren (18, 16 and 18 months), of 34 place de la Republique, Châtelaudren.

Jean-Marie Le Sommier (born January 1895) of la ferme de Kerjagu, just outside Châtelaudren at Plouagat, was recruited by Christophe Jezegou on behalf of Mathurin Branchoux. He later sheltered Branchoux for two months after he was "brulé" and his wife Marie taken in retaliation – Mme Branchoux was released with the liberation of the area.

Mme Gourio (or Goriou) of the Grand Café in Châtelaudren. Not listed by IS9 but named by Le Sommier and Rémy, and described by Robert Lorenzi (#489) (see later) as an ex-collaborator. Today, Le Grand Café is at 15 place de la Republique.

Sgt Dennis Brown (1848) was the 22-year-old flight engineer of 625 Sqn Lancaster ND461 which was returning from Berlin in the early hours of 28 January 1944, and over France when they were hit by flak. Two engines and fuel tanks were hit and although the crew managed to extinguish the resultant fires, the aircraft was out of control. The crew jettisoned everything they could from the aircraft and in the confusion, rear-gunner Sgt Jack Ringwood DFM accidently threw his parachute overboard. Brown understood that the mid-upper gunner, Sgt R V Weller, opted to share his parachute with Ringwood, and Brown was later told that two men (believed to be Ringwood and Weller) were found dead on the ground. In fact Weller baled out and survived – he was captured along with three other crew – while pilot P/O Roy James Cook DFM kept the aircraft flying for another hour before running out of fuel and crashing with he and Ringwood still on board – Brown was the only successful evader.[34]

Brown landed in a field near Gournay-en-Bray (Upper Normandy) at about two o'clock in the morning, buried his parachute and Mae West, and hid in a nearby barn for the rest of the night and following day. That evening, he approached a farmhouse where he was given some food, and after another night in the barn, set off walking south. Later that same day, Brown stopped a passing cyclist who took him back to his home and put him in touch with an organisation.

The cyclist was a tailor named Ballet (assume Ernest Ballet) and he took Brown back to his bungalow, about three miles west of Gournay-en-Bray where he gave Brown some civilian clothes. That evening, M. Ballet took Brown to his Paris apartment (assume at 16 rue Ganneron, Paris XVIII) where Brown met his wife and daughter. Brown stayed for two weeks with the Ballet family, during which time he met several of their friends and members of a resistance group, all of whom spoke English. After about a fortnight, M. Ballet brought an unnamed woman who was a member of an escape organisation and she took Brown to stay in another house about two miles away. Two days later, Brown was taken to a Metro station and passed on to two more women who took him to a bootmaker's shop at 18 rue Daumesnil, Vincennes where he stayed with Pierre and his wife Hannah (sic) for four weeks.[35] Whilst he was there, he was visited

34 See W R Chorley (1997) "RAF Bomber Command Losses – Volume 5" Midland Publishing.

35 I think this was Lucien Plumereau (listed by Marcel Cola as a logeur) and Mme Anna Henry.

several time by Maurice Girard, an elderly English-speaking Frenchman (slightly built with greying hair, wore glasses) who lived opposite (at No 11) and told Brown that he had been an interpreter during the last war. On his first visit, M. Girard brought a Red Cross form which Brown refused to fill in as he was not sure that M. Girard was a genuine helper. Brown was also visited by a Frenchman who spoke English with a Canadian accent who questioned him in some detail and asked about the last film he had seen in London, and the name and address of his girl-friend (Kay Taylor). This was Marcel Cola, and two weeks later Cola moved Brown to stay overnight (13-14 March) with Jean Charles Pradal (described by Brown as being about 65 years old, with a full beard, he wore glasses and spoke English) and his dog Tout Suite at 6 Villa Auguste Blanqui, 44 rue Jeanne d'Arc, where he joined American evader, Charles Cregger.

Sgt Charles W Cregger (#470) was the 25-year-old left waist-gunner of B-24 42-7548 Bull O' The Woods (Heskett) which was abandoned to crash between Compiègne (Oise) and Soissons (Aisne) on 30 December 1944 – see Donald Heskett (#347) earlier.

Cregger says that after the bail-out signal was given, he was the first man to jump from the rear escape hatch, passing out and only coming round again after his parachute had opened. He landed in a field near Pasly (just outside Soissons) and several men watched as he struggled to fold his parachute in the high wind. After burying his parachute under some rocks, he ran over a hill to a wood where he hid in the undergrowth for the rest of the day. He spent an uncomfortable night on the hill, and then much of the following morning lying in the sun, watching life go on in the nearby village. That evening, he approached a dairy farm but opted not to approach it straight away and so spent a second uncomfortable night in a field. It rained for much of the following day and that evening, Cregger went to the farmhouse and knocked on the kitchen door.

> *"I was first given help on 1 January at a farmhouse in Pasly. The farmer, Felix Brefort (aged about 50, 6 feet tall with blue eyes and a fair complexion, bald but with a moustache) and his wife (aged about 47, about 5 feet 7 inches tall with black hair), a boy aged 11, three daughters (aged 14, 20 and 22), and a young baby. They appear to be a wealthy family, the Bottin [a sort of French Who's Who] lists Felix as "a leading farmer in the county." (Cregger MIS-X #470)*

None of the Brefort family spoke any English but next day, Cregger was visited by a schoolteacher (aged about 48, 5 feet 11 inches tall with a fair complexion and dark hair) who did, having been in England before the war. He arrived with a man (stocky, about 5 feet 5 inches tall, dark complexion with black hair and brown eyes, aged about 35) (Julien Lefevre from nearby Vezaponin – query) who told Cregger, via the schoolteacher, that he had taken his ball-turret gunner, S/Sgt Stanley Langcaskey (#691), to Paris the previous day (although according to Langcaskey's report, that's not quite true) and he gave Cregger an address in Paris for him to go to. Cregger explained that he couldn't go to Paris on his own as he didn't speak French and eventually it was decided that the man would take Cregger on the Tuesday (4 January).

Two days later, Felix Brefort and one of his daughters drove Cregger to Soissons station where the man was waiting to take him to Paris. They took a seven-thirty train to Compiègne where they had wait a couple of hours before catching a twelve o'clock train to the capital.

Cregger and the man arrived at the gare du Nord at about one-thirty in the afternoon and took a taxi to an apartment building near the Palais Royal. They went to an office on the third floor where Cregger met a lawyer (a short man of medium build, with dark hair, a round face, aged about 30) and his wife (aged about 30, with brown eyes and hair, slim build – she also seemed to work there) and she took one of Cregger's RAF photographs to make him an ID card. That night, Cregger was taken by Metro to Mme Alexandre at 11 bis rue Valentin Hauy[36] – her husband spoke a little English and they had a son of about 21 who visited that night and told Cregger that he was employed by the Nazis. Next day a tall, attractive, dark-haired, fair complexioned woman, aged about twenty-six, came to the apartment – she was apparently connected to the French Embassy in Madrid – this was Odette Drappier (born February 1914 in Tunis) who also lived at this address. That evening a young woman who asked to be called Rivoir (about 19 years old, small, thin, with dark blonde hair) gave Cregger an ID card and took him to the fifth-floor apartment of M. and Mme Chautagnaut at 5 rue Jeanne d'Arc. M. Chautagnaut was an elderly man, a lawyer at the Banque de France who had sheltered three American airmen the previous autumn (1/Lt Phillip E Higdon, 2/Lt Louis E Ritt and S/Sgt Willard J Cronin, all from B-17 42-3459 Jolly Roger). After having dinner with the Chautagnauts, Rivoir took Cregger to stay

36 IS9 has Gaston Dickmann at this address.

with Jean Charles Pradal at 6 Villa Auguste Blanqui, 44 rue Jeanne d'Arc, Paris XIII.

Jean Pradal is described by Cregger as being as an elderly gentleman, fifty-five years old, of average height, slim, with a light complexion, grey hair and a very long, almost white, beard – he had helped some Frenchmen escape to the country but not sheltered an American before. He was working as a mechanical engineer, leaving the apartment early each morning and returning at about one o'clock. At one time, he had been a private secretary and interpreter for a French general, and for the week before Cregger left, worked from home, preparing to return to his previous occupation of teaching physics.

Cregger lived with Jean Pradal and his dog Tout Suite for ten weeks, with his meals cooked by the maid while M. Pradal was at work, during which time, in addition to Mme Chautagnaut and Rivoir coming to see him several times, he was visited and questioned by a couple called Gallay (he sold hats and lived across the road from the Chautagnauts), Lt Fleury (aged about 35, he was a lieutenant in the Fire Department) and his wife, who was a teacher, another teacher called Mme Schindler who had spent four years in America and heard about Cregger from Fleury's 18-year-old daughter – and Marcel Cola, apparently an important man in the organisation who took Cregger's details and brought a photographer to take his picture for a new ID card. On 13 March, Marcel Cola brought Sgt Dennis Brown (1848) to stay overnight and early next morning, M. Pradal took Cregger and Brown to Montparnasse station. Marcel Cola was there to give them their new ID cards before he passed them on to a young man who took them by train to Saint-Brieuc, where they changed for Châtelaudren.

On 7 January 1944, the 389BG B-24 Liberators 42-40747 Heavy Date (Mattson) and 42-63977 Los Angeles City Limits (Cooper), and the 93BG B-24 42-7614 (Carnahan), were returning from a raid on Ludwigshafen when they were shot down by fighters south of Paris.[37] Harold Vines from LA City Limits bailed out and landed near Pithiviers (Centre). Manuel Rogoff, Shirley Berry and Russell Paquin from Heavy Date landed about 15 kms south-east of Pithiviers, near the little village of Egry (Loiret). Robert Fruth from 27614 landed some distance away but was soon helped, and on 14 January, taken to Egry where he found Rogoff, Berry and Paquin, and was joined there by Vines three days later.

37 The aircraft appear to have strayed further south than seems logical – compare with the return route used on the 30 December operation to Ludwigshafen described earlier.

2/Lt Manuel M Rogoff (#455), **2/Lt Shirley D Berry** (#456) and **S/Sgt Russell L Paquin** (#458) were the bombardier, co-pilot and ball-turret gunner of 389BG/567BS B-24 42-40747 Heavy Date (Mattson). At one-thirty in the afternoon of 7 January 1944, about forty-five minutes into the return leg from Ludwigshafen, they were attacked by fighters coming in on their two o'clock, low position. The hydraulic accumulator for the nose-wheel exploded and started a fire and as they began to lose altitude, Berry sounded the alarm bell (one continuous ring) and the aircraft was abandoned to crash south of Vrigny (Loiret). Tail-gunner S/Sgt Keith W Sutor (#536) was the only other successful evader from Heavy Date – see later.

> *"Our ship was burning when I bailed out at 21,000 feet. I was temporarily blinded by the flames and pulled my rip-cord after counting ten. My chute opened with a considerable jerk but my harness was tight and I was not hurt by it. On my way down I noticed about 50 people running to meet me. I landed in a ploughed field and several of the men helped me to my feet and took my chute. After some discussion one of the men motioned me to follow him and we went to an old stone barn a few hundred yards away. There he spread butter on my face, which was very painfully burned.*
>
> *I was taken to a house and all identification removed except my dog-tags. My friends kitted me out with a beret, a heavy leather overcoat and a pair of white shoes. They pooled their money and got together 1,250 francs which they gave me. Then they treated my burns again with more butter and I followed two of the men out.*
>
> *We skirted fields, and one of my helpers stopped once to pick up RAF leaflets, and one of them found an American flying jacket, which he kept. In about twenty minutes we came to a peasant's house, where I was given brandy and put to bed.*
>
> *For the next month or so I was blind and helpless. I was moved about from house to house and was under the constant care of physicians, to whose skill I probably owe my sight. In spite of my conspicuous injuries, my helpers did not relax their care and successfully arranged my journey as soon as I was able to see." (Rogoff MIS-X #455)*

One of the men who helped Rogoff was Henri Vallici and he sent for a girl known as "Miss English Spoken" to come and see Rogoff, and at about seven-thirty that evening a young girl came in. She was the local schoolteacher and confirmed that she spoke good English, although slowly, as she explained to Rogoff that he was in the little village of Nancray-sur-Rimarde, that the first man was a macon (bricklayer), that the second (Henri Vallici) was a baker (at the Boulangerie des Granges) and that they were all comrades. She told Rogoff that M. Vallici said that in three or four days, when his face looked better, they would take his photograph and make an identity card that would say he was deaf and dumb. She also said that the macon would take him to Bordeaux where another man would take him to Spain.

Ten minutes after the teacher left, M. Vallici took Rogoff on foot to a small house on the outskirts of the town where a woman aged about thirty lived with her mother. They washed Rogoff's hands before giving him a meal of steak and eggs. At about nine-thirty that evening, Vallici came back with a doctor (a big man) who cut open the blisters on Rogoff's swollen hand and applied a "pommade" to his face and hands before M. Vallici undressed Rogoff and put him into bed.

At four-thirty next morning, M. Valllici came to check on Rogoff, who was totally blind at this point, before leading him out to a truck. Having placed Rogoff inside, M. Vallici drove for about half an hour to a little farmhouse where an elderly peasant couple directed Rogoff to bed – they put a hot brick in to warm it. Rogoff stayed in bed all the rest of that day (Saturday) until Monday afternoon, disturbed only by M. Vallici on Sunday night when he brought another man, who said he was known as Fiffy (sic). Rogoff describes him as being mysterious, aged about 33, with black hair, and a mole on his face – he spoke English having apparently worked in the Malay States.

Next day, Henri Vallici collected Rogoff in his truck and drove him back to the woman in Nacray and told Rogoff that he would be leaving on about Friday by plane. Rogoff was put back into bed but a few hours later, the young schoolteacher came upstairs to tell him he would leave by plane that evening. When M. Vallici dressed him, he put a message in Rogoff's sock and asked him to deliver it to an Intelligence Officer in England – Rogoff was told in Paris by Jean (assume Jean Kocera-Massenet) to destroy the note but Rogoff says he knew it by heart anyway: "Pour le croque-mort tout va bien, faux nom des chefs de groupes."

Henri Vallici put Rogoff into his truck and drove him for about 10-15 minutes to a small house in the nearby village of Saint-Loup-des-Vignes where he left Rogoff with a clergyman (Armand Chenu) who could speak

German. When Rogoff asked the clergyman if he was leaving, he said no and gave Rogoff something to eat. A little later, Rogoff was taken outside and put into a car where he was joined by his ball-turret gunner S/Sgt Russell Paquin and bombardier 2/Lt Shirley Berry.

Paquin had landed in a field next to a house about a mile from Nancray-sur-Rimarde. In addition to a wounded right arm and leg, his hands and face were badly burned and he says that he could hardly see. A young farmer (aged about 25) who watched him land, helped Paquin with his parachute. By this time, several other people had come out of their houses to watch but the man ignored them, took Paquin to a small farmhouse a few hundred yards away and hid him in a haystack behind the house. That afternoon, the farmer brought Paquin some bread and corned-beef, and some whisky which Paquin used on his wounds to try and prevent any infection. At about seven-thirty that evening, the farmer brought a note from his co-pilot Shirley Berry and Paquin wrote back to say that he was okay and hiding on a nearby farm. Half an hour later, a man they refer to as a country doctor, and describe as being small (this was Dr Maurice Rousse), arrived in a car with a man named Pierre Charié, and the doctor drove them about three-quarters of a mile down the road where they picked up Shirley Berry.

Dr Maurice Rousse (born April 1882) of Beaune-la-Rolande was married to Flore (née de la Boixiere), with a daughter Fanny (born April 1929). He was arrested on 12 July 1944 and deported to Buchenwald, which he survived to be liberated on 30 April 1945. In addition to Pierre Charié, Dr Rousse names the whole Perret family of Beaune as helpers, although none are listed by IS9.

Shirley Berry, who also suffered burns to his face and ankles, says he landed in a field about 5 kms west of Saint-Loup-des-Vignes and 5 kms south-west of Egry. He was soon found in woods just 200 yards from where he landed by a boy (aged about 17) with a dog. The boy took him to a group of men, women and children who looked glad to see him. One of the older men gave Berry a pair of trousers (he appeared to be wearing several pairs) and another his coat, and another a hat before taking Berry to the farmhouse of a man who seemed to be their leader. Berry was told that Russell Paquin was in a nearby farmhouse and Berry wrote him a note. Later that evening, Dr Maurice Rousse arrived in his car with Paquin already on board, along with a man named Pierre Charié.

The doctor drove them to Saint-Loup-des-Vignes where he delivered Paquin and Berry to a priest's house – the priest, (Armand Chenu) was about 5 feet 10 inches tall, aged about 55, with white hair – and the airmen gave him all their belongings, Berry keeping just his identity bracelet in his pocket. During their stay, they were visited by a schoolteacher called Yvette (a nice-looking, rather stout girl, about 5 feet 5 inches tall with brown eyes and black wavy hair – she was a good cook) who took care of them, and Yvette gave Berry a letter to post to the wife of S/Sgt Robert Rugh in Ohio that she had from another helper. The letter described how their waist-gunner Rugh had been wounded in the aircraft and that although his helper had done her best to treat his injuries, she had to call a doctor for him on the Saturday night who told her to take him to a hospital, where he was captured.

On 10 January, a man the airmen refer to as Petit Roger, a small stocky man, aged about 35, with brown wavy hair (this was Roger Mercier of Sceaux-du-Gâtinais), came in a car with their co-pilot Rogoff and Dr Maurice Rousse already inside, and Roger drove them all to Pierre Charié's home the little village of Egry.

Pierre Charié (born January 1915) of Egry (Loiret) (son of Paul and Georgette) was primarily involved with intelligence gathering and later, armed resistance. He first became involved with helping evaders when 1/Lt James Shilliday (#481), 1/Lt Roland Marean (#482) and T/Sgt Halleck Hasson (#619) from B-17 42-30203 Shack Up (Mohr) – which was shot down on 6 September 1943 – were brought to him.

Pierre Charié lived over a wine warehouse near his family house, off the main street in Egry, opposite the cemetery, and the three Americans were sheltered in large apartment on the second floor (first floor for British readers) where Pierre normally lived alone. There was also a worker named Clotaire Prochasson who lived on the main floor. Rogoff describes Pierre Charié as being a man of about 28, with brown hair and brown eyes – he was very athletic, very active and enthusiastically pro-Allied. Pierre told them that the day they were shot down, he had watched their plane with binoculars and jumped on his motorcycle to reach them. He found Paquin first. He says that he saw five parachutes come down out of their plane and seven from another plane (assume LA City Limits). He was definite about this information. He was unable to give Rogoff information about their tail-gunner, S/Sgt Keith W Sutor (#536) (see later) and waist-gunner S/Sgt Robert E Rugh (see earlier) but he told them that eight Americans had been hidden in the vicinity of Egry, Orléans, Montargis and Puiseaux.

> *"Pierre said that he sent messages to England through Paris and he listens to answers on the BBC. He had many radio sets in his house. He always listens to the BBC, liked to show off and use the *** intelligence service. He had had two bundles dropped on a tennis court in the forest near Egry, the bundles contained American hand grenades, ammunition and arms calibre 9.7 (sic). He would like to play with camouflaged parachutes and *** *** he picked up in the forest. Pierre's father was the maire of Egry. At first he didn't know we were hidden at Pierre's place, when he knew he did not seem to approve of Pierre taking such risks. Pierre's mother knew nothing of us. He did not want to tell her so she would not worry." (Rogoff MIS-X #455)*

S/Sgt Robert K Fruth (#462) was the right waist-gunner of 93BG/328BS B-24 42-7614 (Carnahan) which was returning from Ludwigshafen on 7 January 1944 and abandoned to crash south of Paris near Milly-la-Foret (Seine-et-Marne).

Two other crew also evaded successfully: radio operator S/Sgt Willis E Spellman (#484), who was helped by Bourgogne and crossed the Pyrenees in March, and co-pilot 2/Lt Edward C Miller (#693), who I think was helped by the Françoise Dissard organisation before also crossing the Pyrenees in March.

Miller reports there being something wrong with their aircraft that day and they had difficulty in keeping up with their formation. They were hit by flak near the target and lost one engine before turning and being hit again. He says they thought they could get back on two engines but were unable to maintain altitude and began to lose contact with the formation. They were hit again as they passed over Paris, and with one of their engines on fire, the aircraft was abandoned.

21-year-old Robert Fruth, who had flown thirteen missions before, was not expecting to fly that day and so missed the briefing. He was called up at the last minute to join a crew he had never seen before, except for engineer/TTG S/Sgt Warren H Long, and without even knowing what their target was. He says they lost #2 engine near the target and #4 on the way back, and despite throwing all excess equipment overboard, they continued to lose altitude. They were hit by more flak before the radio operator (Spellman) came and told them to bail out, just as the aircraft went into a spin.

Fruth says he jumped at about 4,000 feet and opened his parachute immediately on leaving the aircraft. He landed in a large tree near the little village of Saint-Sauveur-sur-Ecole (SW of Melun), having to leave his parachute tangled in the branches as he scrambled down in full view of a group of people standing by a farmhouse. As they started to run towards him, Fruth headed to where he had seen other chutes landing before coming to a road where he ducked into a dry ditch to avoid more men who were looking into the woods on the far side. He ran along the ditch and then stopped to smoke the only cigarette he had with him, hiding the now empty the cigarette case which had his squadron number on it. He then carried on until he reached a high wall which ran around a large country house. When the radio operator had told him to bail out, Fruth was sure he said they were over Holland, an impression that was reinforced when he saw a man wearing wooden shoes come out of a greenhouse, so he was pleasantly surprised later that evening when he found a road-sign that said "Paris 47 kms".

He carried on walking that night, heading towards the capital, passing through one village and reaching another at about one o'clock in the morning where he stopped to sleep in a barn. Next morning, he could see men working near the barn and so stayed hidden until the afternoon when he finally decided to get out his language-card and ask for help. The man he approached asked Fruth if he were American and when he said he was, asked Fruth to wait while he got pencil and paper. Fruth wrote down several questions, such as what was the best way to get to Spain, and asking for civilian clothes and he man wrote back that he would return later that afternoon. However, after waiting until seven that evening, Fruth decided to start walking south. Unfortunately, Fruth only had his electric shoes which soon began to hurt his feet so he waited at a steep hill until he was able to catch onto the ladder of a large slow-moving truck. Fruth stayed on top of the truck, going through a forest until they reached the town of Souppes-sur-Loing (Seine-et-Marne), at which point he jumped off and resumed walking.

Fruth was looking for somewhere to spend the night when he went into a cellar of a small house on the edge of the town, finding some old clothes, a pair of hob-nailed boots, a few potatoes and a bottle of wine. Taking his booty with him, Fruth walked another few kilometres to a little stone hut where he spent the rest of the night on a bed of branches and dry grass. Next day, because his escape map showed few towns to the south, he decided to head back north, and a few kilometres later, was stopped by a man on a bicycle. Fruth used his phrase-card to tell the man he was hungry and the man signalled Fruth to follow him. The man was a gatekeeper and he took Fruth back to his cottage where he and his wife gave Fruth a meal and showed him a GI belt and an Eighth Air Force patch they had been given by an American airman who had stayed with them previously. They also gave Fruth a loaf of bread and showed him on his map a better way to get to Spain. Later that afternoon, Fruth encountered another man on a bicycle, this one being a railway-crossing gateman, who took Fruth into the nearby town of Nemours where the railway ticket-seller spoke some English. After questioning Fruth, the ticket-seller took him to a house where he had supper before being moved to another house, home of a M. Paillard (nf), where his journey was arranged.

M. Paillard was in the jewellery business and had a large house in two acres of ground near the railway station. The house was unfinished and so he lived with his wife, young daughter and mother-in-law in the caretaker's cottage. Both M. Paillard and his wife spoke good English and it seemed to Fruth that the wife (aged about 37-40) ran things. That evening, she brought a short, heavy-set man to see Fruth. He was the local hairdresser and apparently in touch with an organisation. Late next day, a butcher (no name given) came and took Fruth to his shop about three blocks away where he was sheltered on the third floor with the man, his wife, small child and father – the other occupants not knowing he was there. Fruth was told to lock the door and only open it in response to a special knock. He was given washing and shaving kit, and later a striped suit, underwear and towels, Fruth only keeping his khaki trousers, sweater and flying gloves. The butcher told Fruth that a member of an organisation would collect him that evening and at about eight o'clock, two men arrived. After saying his goodbyes to the butcher, Fruth was taken to a small car which was waiting a block away.

There was already another man in the back seat of the car when they drove away, doubling around the block and driving round the town to lose any pursuers before setting off down the main road that Fruth had come along the day before. Fruth was then shocked to realise the man sitting next to him was a gendarme in full uniform – none of the men in the car seemed to speak any English. They drove into Souppes-sur-Loing and the home of the driver where Fruth met the man's nephew, Pierre, a young man of about twenty who had been living in Milly-la-Foret but apparently left after some Germans had been shot there. Later Pierre took Fruth to an empty house where they made a fire and beds and went to sleep. Next morning, Pierre's uncle brought food that they cooked for breakfast and spent the rest of the day trying to learn each other's languages. Three days later (on 14 January), Pierre's uncle came to tell them that the Gestapo were coming to town and they should leave that evening. At five o'clock, a closed van took Fruth and Pierre's uncle (the uncle being dropped off about fifteen minutes later in a small town) and Fruth was taken for supper with "Petit Roger" – Roger Mercier at Sceaux-du-Gâtinais. After supper, Roger and his wife took Fruth in their own car, firstly to buy some food, and then on to the little village of Egry where Roger and his wife left Fruth and the food, and Fruth joined Manuel Rogoff, Shirley Berry and Russell Paquin from Heavy Date.

T/Sgt Harold R Vines (#457) was the 22-year-old tunnel-gunner of 389BG/567BS B-24 42-63977 Los Angeles City Limits (Cooper). The D-model aircraft doesn't seem to have been in great condition that day, the interphone failed soon after take-off and their bombs failed to drop over the target (they were finally dumped after leaving the target area). However, they were still in formation on the return leg and just south of Paris when they were attacked head-on by fighters. A shell exploded in the waist of the bomber and immediately afterwards, Vines reports three more explosions from the front of the aircraft. The waist windows were blown out, there was smoke and sparks and as the aircraft began to dive, Vines bailed out from the waist window opening.

Two other LA City Limits crew also evaded successfully: tail-gunner S/Sgt George H Stillwell (#371) and waist-gunner S/Sgt James P Cobbs (#372) who crossed the Pyrenees to Andorra together later that same month.

Vines landed in some trees on the edge of the Foret de Fontainebleau at about one-thirty in the afternoon of 7 January. He stuffed his parachute and flying gear under some leaves and went about 200 yards to hide under some bushes. A young man on a bicycle was apparently looking for him, whistling and shouting, and Vines whistled back to get his attention. They then spent some time retrieving Vines' parachute, which he guessed the man wanted for the silk. The man was Maurice Brugger, he was Swiss and aged about twenty-five, who used sign-language to tell Vines to hide himself again and that he would come back for him that evening. Just before eight o'clock that evening, Maurice came back with a man called Jean Cerisier (nf), both on bicycles, and they took it in turns to carry Vines on their handlebars for the long ride to Pithiviers where they lived, and where they had a beer before Vines was taken to stay at a hat shop run by Maurice's French wife.

Jean Cerisier lived with Maurice Brugger and his wife, who Vines refers to as "Mme Brilliant", although none of them seemed to be members of any organisation. Vines stayed with the Bruggers for ten days and says that he was treated very well, given new clothes and plenty of wine. He also had lots of visitors including, on the second day, a man and his wife who spoke English who told him that one of the girls in the hat shop knew someone who might be able to help him. Next day, the girl brought a man who questioned Vines and told him that an American named Rogoff was being hidden in the neighbourhood and that he had been burned. He also said that five US airmen had been killed when they came down near Vrigny, about ten kilometres away, and were going to be buried the next day (10 January). Maurice and another man took Vines to the cemetery at Vrigny where he saw three graves with painted boards – T/Sgt David H Neilson, 1/Lt Carl A Mattson and S/Sgt Irvine J Balsam (all from Rogoff's aircraft). The other two airmen were not identified and simply had boards saying "Aviateur Americain". There was a big crowd there and a priest but no Germans in sight. On the way back, they stopped at a village where Vines had cake and champagne, and a couple who ran a beauty parlour cut his hair.

That evening, Vines was told that he would be taken to Orleans by train and out through the Pyrenees but nothing happened until the morning of 17 January when Marcelle (the girl from the hat shop) took him back to her house. At about noon, Pierre Charié arrived on a motorcycle to take Vines back to his home in the little village of Egry.

While the five airmen were staying with Pierre Charié, they had several visitors. One of the first was a specialist doctor from Paris who came with a nurse and X-ray equipment and operated on Paquin. He only stayed for one night and left insisting he had done this only as a favour to Pierre.[38] The

38 I think this was either Pierre's brother Georges (of 5 Place Voltaire, Paris XI) or possibly the same Dr Francis and his wife Simone that James Shilliday (#481) met at Pierre's house the previous September.

little county doctor, Maurice Rousse, who had treated Paquin and Berry at Saint-Loup-des-Vignes, came to see them several times, and the big doctor who had taken care of Rogoff at Nancray-sur-Rimarde came once. Rogoff and Paquin also received regular visits from a pharmacist from Puiseaux named André Bressin, a small thin man who always wore knickerbockers, had grey hair, a red complexion and spoke German and English. His hobby was photography and he had a complete set of photographic equipment – he took moving picture film of the airmen as well as lots of photographs. There was also a grocer from Puiseaux, Raymond Bourdois (average height, stocky, aged 30, with straight brown hair) and his wife Huguette (also aged 30, with straight brown hair and blue eyes), and a tall priest called Georges who came to stay the night a few times – he was escaping from the Germans and dressed as a farmer, he had red cheeks, sandy hair and a moustache. Yvette, the schoolteacher who took care of Paquin and Berry at Saint-Loup-des-Vignes, came on her days off, and the chief of police at Montargis who always warned Pierre of the Gestapo movements, also visited. Two other regulars were Clotaire Prochasson, who worked in the warehouse and brought them meals, and Pierre's brother-in-law who lived somewhere nearby. There was also a young man called Roger Perret (named by Dr Rousse, along with the rest of his family, as a helper), a friend of Pierre who had false papers and often came to spend the day although he slept at Beaune-la-Rolande, few kilometres south-west of Egry.

On the third week (that Rogoff was there), Pierre told them that he was waiting for the full moon and a message from the BBC to take them to a clearing in the forest near Vrigny where they would take a plane to England. He explained to Rogoff the signal system – "three red lights facing the *** N-S and three white lights E-W".

On the fourth week, Rogoff and Berry visited the grocer Raymond Bourdois and his wife Huguette at Puiseaux. She told them about having lodged James Shilliday (#481) and showed them his photograph, on the back of which he had written his New York address and a note which read "To the best entertainment I have ever had. The grocers seem thrilled to help American aviators".

On 14 February, the five airmen left Egry, taken by truck to the Bourdois home in Puiseaux. They were given identity cards, and that afternoon, three guides took them by train to Paris. They were split into groups with one guide taking care of Rogoff, another looking after Berry and Paquin, and the third with Fruth and Vines.

One their arrival at the gare de Lyon in Paris that evening, Rogoff's guide directed him to follow Berry and Paquin on the Metro, and Marcel Cola took the three of them to Genevieve Schneegans apartment at 62 rue Tiquetonne. Leaving Berry and Paquin with Mme Schneegans, Maurice Cavalier and Jean Pivet then took Rogoff to Maurice's apartment at the Lycée Saint-Louis, 44 boulevard Saint-Michel, Paris VI.

Maurice Louis Cavalier (born October 1895) and his wife Marguerite (born July 1898) were denounced and arrested in June 1944, and deported to Germany. Maurice was condemned to death but later reprieved, and both returned to France after the war, and each (according to the IS9 Helper List) was recommended for a KMS.

Mme Genevieve Delphine Schneegans (née Vernianjal) was 33 years old – her husband (who was later arrested by the French government for smuggling) had left her in January 1944. She was recruited by Maurice Cavalier – with whom she is thought to have been having an affair – and shared her home at 62 rue Tiquetonne with Mme Olympe Vasseur (née Strouken).

Jean Pivet (born March 1917) (aka Michel but known to the evaders as Jean Kotier) lived at 41 boulevard Saint-Michel, Paris V. He was a student, with a baccalaureat de philosophie and certificate de licence en droit, studying at various lycées and collèges in Paris but principally at the Lycée Saint-Louis. In November 1941, he began working for CND (Confederation Notre Dame) and had been involved in various resistance activities ever since. In December 1943, in addition to his commitments to the intelligence network Zero France, he was put in contact with reseau François through Ernestine Labarthe, proprietaire du Café Le Biarritz at 39 boulevard Saint-Michel (arrested on 6 June 44, at the same time as the Cavaliers), to provide forged papers for evaders. Pivet says he worked directly with Paul Campinchi, Henri Bois and Marcel Cola, along with logeurs M. and Mme Solange Mellet of 62 rue Sainte Beuve, Paris VI, Maurice and Marguerite Cavalier, and Genevieve Schneegans – and with convoyeuse Marie-France Geoffroy-Dechaume of 4 Square du Vaucluse, Paris XVII.

Rogoff stayed with the Cavaliers for four weeks – he says that Maurice was the "économe" of the Lycée, and his wife Marguerite worked in a girl's high school. At the end of the first week Rogoff was joined by 2/Lt William Spinning (#477). Jean Kotier (Jean Pivet) (who he describes as being of average height, very thin, with sandy hair, pushed-in teeth, he was a chain-smoker) often visited, and Rogoff understood that he held a high position in the organisation.

> *"Jean had a big set to make false identity cards (he would make them for many Frenchmen in trouble). He was *** bombing result of American raids. Visited the Le Bourget, Villacoublay [aerodromes]. Had been in the organisation two and a half years and devoted to it all his time. His legal address is the hôtel Saint Louis (on the boulevard Saint-Michel, above a shop named Travaux-Photo) across the street from the Lycée. Sometimes he slept overnight at the Lycée, other times at the Café Biarritz nearby on the boulevard Saint-Michel. For 2 days during February the Germans stopped everyone on the Blvd Saint-Michel for identity checks and Jean stayed in the Café Biarritz. Jean showed us a photograph of a new German tank." (Rogoff MIS-X #455).*

Berry and Paquin stayed on with Genevieve Schneegans at 62 rue Tiquetonne, learning that her husband was apparently in Morocco for stealing some money, and deciding that she was probably not a member of the organisation but simply helping her friend Maurice Cavalier. They also saw Marcel Cola, and who told them that he had spent 12 years in the US and Canada, and that his sister Marguerite Jonnet (sic) was married to a university professor in Canada.[39] They describe Cola as being of average size, with a dark complexion, dark eyes, straight black hair and moustache – he was always carefully dressed and very meticulous in his manner – and they thought (correctly) that he had worked for Ford in Paris.

On 13 March, Berry and Paquin were taken to Maurice Cavalier's apartment at the Lycée Saint-Louis where they rejoined Rogoff, and that night, were taken to the station and put on a train to Saint-Brieuc – where they changed for Châtelaudren.

The guide who brought Fruth and Vines to Paris (on 14 February) was Jean Kocera-Massenet and he took them by Metro to the flat where his mother, Mme Jeanne Kocera-Massenet was sheltering Louis Feingold (#419) and

39 Marcel Cola's sister Marguerite was married to Dr Edouard Sonet at the University of Alberta in Edmonton.

Warren Tarkington (#420) (see earlier) at 10 rue Ernest Renan, before going on to a building a few doors away, and the third-floor apartment of Anita Lemonnier and her mother Suzanne. Vines says that the Lemonniers had previously lived in England and Germany and spoke both languages very well, and that Anita had the job of taking "boys" to the coast. He describes her as being 31 years old, although she looked younger, nice looking, medium height with dark hair dyed reddish. She worked as a confidential secretary at an electrical instrument plant nearby, and was engaged to a medical colonel in the French army.

Alice Suzanne Anita Lemonnier (born September 1898) (elder sister of film actress Meg Lemonnier) and her widowed mother Marie Suzanne Lemonnier (born February 1875) (both of whom also spoke fluent English and German) sheltered many evaders in their apartment at 2 rue Ernest Renan. They first became involved with helping evaders in late November 1943 when their neighbour, Jeanne Kocera-Massenet asked them (via a M. Lacroix, who lived in the same building as her) if they would shelter airmen brought to Paris by Jean Carbonnet and Michèle Moet of Bourgogne. In February 1944, Jean Kocera-Massenet and Marcel Cola recruited them to shelter men for reseau François as well, and Anita became one of the guides who took evaders to Brittany.

Robert Sidders (#1056) (mentioned later) and F/O Stuart K Barr (#1061) were sheltered in the Lemonnier apartment from April to June 1944, by which time Shelburn could no longer evacuate men by sea, so they were taken to the MI9 camp at Chateaudun (Freteval) by Pierre Robert of Comète. On his return, Pierre Robert asked the Lemonniers to shelter himself and Jean-Yves Deplanche, their apartment becoming a temporary headquarters for Comète. Anita (using the name Anne) then became responsible for checking the identities of airmen, as well as guiding many of them to and from Paris. According to her mother, Anita continued with her evasion work until twelve days before the liberation of the city, when she went to help nurse the wounded men at the Hopital de la Pitié who had been abandoned there when the Germans left.

Marcel Cola came on the second day to interrogate Fruth and Vines, asking for their ASN, squadron number, group etc. A week later he returned to tell them they needed new identity cards in order to get to the coast, and took them to a large department store where they had their photographs taken.

They were also visited by Jeanne Kocera-Massenet who brought Louis Feingold (#419) and Warren Tarkington (#420) to spend the evening with them.

Marcel Cola returned the next day to tell them that Feingold and Tarkington would be leaving the following day (they left Paris on 24 February – see earlier) and that they would go on the next trip, probably on the Friday (10 March) or Saturday. Charles Winkelman (#468) came for dinner on the Saturday (11 March), and Fruth and Vines left the following night when they were given identity cards, passes and food, and Jean Kocera-Massenet and Anita Lemonnier took them to the station. At gare Montparnasse, they joined Edward Donaldson, Neelan Parker, Charles Winkelman and Joseph Birdwell. They were not asked for papers and just showed their tickets before going to a compartment where they had reserved seats on the overnight train to Saint-Brieuc. They left Paris at ten-thirty that evening and arrived Saint-Brieuc at seven-thirty next morning (13 March), where they changed trains for Châtelaudren.

2/Lt William H Spinning (#477) was the 22-year-old bombardier of 351BG/509BS B-17 42-29863 Kentucky Babe (Carson) which was on a morning raid to Frankfurt on 11 February 1944. Everything was going well until they approached the target, at which point flak knocked out their #3 engine and smashed the top turret, injuring the engineer/TTG. Another barrage took out their interphone and elevator controls, jammed the bomb-bay doors open and set light to their #4 engine. The undercarriage was lowered as a sign to the rest of the formation they were in trouble while the crew reached for their parachutes and released the escape doors. They were reluctant to bail out so close to their target (for obvious reasons) so they jettisoned everything they could and aimed for France. By three-thirty in the afternoon, they were getting close to the English Channel but down to 6,000 feet when they were attacked by German fighters. Losing altitude fast, the aircraft was abandoned to crash in the Bois de la Commanderie, about a kilometre north-west of the little village of Neuville-Coppegueule (Somme).

Five other men from the Kentucky Babe also evaded successfully: navigator 2/Lt Henry Heldman (#543) and engineer/TTG T/Sgt Joseph R Haywood (#544) were helped by the Marie-Odile organisation and crossed the Pyrenees to Andorra together in March, and co-pilot 2/Lt Merlyn I Rutherford (#695), radio operator T/Sgt John R Landers (#696) and combat-cameraman Sgt Stanley A Sokolowski (#697), who were helped by the Joe Balfe organisation at Hornoy (Somme) before being passed to Bourgogne in Paris and crossing the Pyrenees from Pau in April 1944.

Spinning wrote "Missing in Action" in 1945, a personal account for his family and friends, from which some of the details below are taken. He says that Kentucky Babe had flown a record 46 missions without aborting – three more and she would have been the first ship ever to complete 50 missions. Additional information about the first three days of Spinning's evasion come from the detailed investigations carried out by Jean-Pierre and Michèle Thuillier of Aumale who helped Mary Shier retrace that part of her father's journey in 2017.

Spinning came down in a ploughed field about a mile from his burning aircraft – his report says near Abbeville but more accurately, just north of Neuville-Coppegueule. Landing safely, he reached for his personal escape kit and GI shoes, which he had attached to his parachute harness, only to find that both had been lost in the jump. He had just gathered up his parachute and hidden it in a manure pile when a young man ran up, led him to a nearby field and indicated that he should hide in some bushes while he went off the try and find the rest of Spinning's crew. Rather than follow the instructions of a stranger, Spinning decided to hide some distance away but where he had a clear view of the place suggested. A group of German soldiers soon appeared and it was obvious they could see other members of his crew not too far away, and when the soldiers headed towards them, Spinning was able to make his escape. He crawled to a nearby road, which he crossed in clear sight of a woman walking one way and a farmer driving a horse-drawn hay wagon the other, and into a ravine. Although he had lost his personal kit, he still had his issue escape kit, complete with Benzedrine tablets, maps, compasses and some French currency.

Spinning made his way along the ravine towards a farm in the valley below and then waited until dusk before approaching a small farm near Le Quesne. The elderly farmer seemed quite happy to find an American airman at his door and went to fetch his mother. Spinning was taken into the house and fed while both parties tried to understand one another. Using the maps from his escape kit, Spinning decided he was about 15 miles SSE of Abbeville, and after spending the rest of the night in their barn (the only payment the man and his mother would accept being an

American cigarette each) he set off early next morning, almost retracing his route from the previous day and intending to head towards Spain.

He hadn't gone far before he saw the man who had hidden him in the field the day before, and via sign-language, Spinning understood that eight parachutes had landed and five men been captured. The man also confirmed directions for Spain and Spinning continued heading that way. At about noon, he encountered a man and boy who gave him lunch and warned him about a nearby German camp, which Spinning was able to avoid. That evening he approached another farm, at la Rosiere, outside Bouafles (Seine-Maritime), where a woman ushered him into the cellar and he was given some food before being warned that there were collaborators in the house. It was dark by this time and Spinning left the cellar to spend an uncomfortable few hours sharing the remains of a haystack with an irate rat. Finally giving up on trying to sleep in the sub-zero temperature, Spinning set off at about four o'clock next morning, his electric shoes and flying boots hurting his feet but aided slightly by a long pole he found, which was heavy enough to be used as a club should the need arise.

He began travelling south, fording the river Bresle and crossing a railway line but soon turned west to avoid the town of Vieux-Rouen-sur-Bresle, and after a long hard day of crossing fields, and having developed a cold and a fever, Spinning found himself in a wooded area near Saint-Martin-au-Bosc, and so desperate for food and rest that he approached a man he heard chopping wood. It could have gone horribly wrong, the man was strong, and with what Spinning describes as the "coldest, cruellest eyes" he had ever seen, but after careful scrutiny, the man decided that Spinning was a genuine American airman (rather than a German imposter sent to trap local helpers) and hid him while he went to get food. Spinning was soon able to fill himself up with sausage, bread, jam, coffee and wine after which the two men smoked and drank toasts to their respective countries. The man gave Spinning advice on the best direction to go in order to avoid German troops, and insisted that Spinning take his coat before sending him on his way.

Spinning never knew the woodcutter's name but in his memoire, he describes him as being the spitting image of Akim Tamarov, the Armenian-American actor (1899-1972) best known at the time for his role in the 1943 film "For Whom the Bell Tolls" where he played the Spanish Republican guerrilla leader Pablo. Jean-Pierre and Michèle Thuillier printed a photograph of the actor and showed it around the village where he was quickly identified as Médéric Couet – and Jean-Pierre and Michèle met his son François, who still lives in his father's house in Saint-Martin-au-Bosc.

Spinning resumed his more or less southerly course, past Richemont, where a woman directed him south-east, advice that Spinning largely ignored, and that evening, spotted a small barn near the little village of Bernompré where he promptly fell asleep in the hay, dreaming at one stage that someone had locked the barn door behind him. Next morning, he found the door had indeed been locked (by the farmer's son, Lucien) but broke out easily enough using his trusty walking pole. He didn't get far though before realising that he was being watched by two men from the nearby farm. They called Spinning over and took him into a four-room farmhouse where the older of the two men, Marcel Defecque, lived with his wife Fernande and their three young children. Spinning was put in front of the wood-burning stove and given hot drinks, feeling warm for the first time since landing in France three days earlier. The younger man was aged about 30, tall and well built – he was a relative from Paris who had come with his wife Hermance to get provisions. Spinning soon understood that he worked in some kind of intelligence service with an underground organisation, and that his name was Arthur Lanciaux.

Spinning told them he wanted to go to Spain but M. Lanciaux insisted he should go to Paris. The couple had apparently helped an RAF airman earlier in the war and Arthur had been held in prison for six months but released for lack of evidence. Everything moved very rapidly from that point – one of Spinning's passport photographs was used to make him an identity card, numerous neighbours provided shoes and civilian clothes to replace the full officer's uniform he was still wearing – all offers of payment being flatly refused – and after a second meal, Marcel Defecque took Spinning and the Lanciaux couple by horse-drawn cart to the railway station at Aumale.

They caught an afternoon train to Paris, travelling third-class and sharing their compartment with two German soldiers. From the gare Montparnasse they walked about 20 minutes to the Lanciaux's four-room apartment on the third floor at 44 rue du Chateau d'Eau, Paris X. The following evening, when Arthur returned from work, he brought a Mme Marcoux and her children, André and Christine. André and Christine studied English at school and could understand much of what Spinning said so long as he spoke slowly enough. A week later (on Monday 21 Feb), Arthur brought Marcel Cola and two other men, referred to as "John" (assume Jean Kocera-Massenet) and "Comrade P" (assume Jean Pivet). John (5 ft 7 inches tall, brown wavy hair, ruddy complexion, medium build, well (expensively) dressed and a chain-smoker) and Comrade P, who was stocky with black curly (unruly) hair, 5 ft 8 inches tall, 170 pounds, quiet, poorly dressed, very observant and untrusting. Marcel Cola interrogated Spinning before Comrade P took him into the other room and photographed him. As soon as the interview was over, John took Spinning on a guided tour of the sights before crossing the Seine and stopping for a drink in the Café Biarritz at 39 boulevard Saint-Michel where Spinning soon realising that everyone there recognised him for what he was. From the bar, John took Spinning the short walk (across the street) to the Lycée Saint-Louis at 44 boulevard Saint-Michel where John was a boarder (query) and he met Lt Manuel Rogoff (#455).

Spinning was sheltered for three weeks with Maurice Cavalier (who Spinning describes as being well educated, 5 feet 8 inches tall, 180 pounds, with a rugged complexion and dark curly hair) and his wife Marguerite (5 foot 6 inches tall, blonde, fair complexion, athletic and well educated, she spoke English and German fluently) (IS9 says she was a university professor) at the Lycée Saint-Louis, sharing with Rogoff until Monday 13 March when they were joined by two other airmen, Shirley Berry and Russell Paquin, both from Rogoff's aircraft. At seven o'clock that evening, "John" and an older woman (aged about 50) took the four Americans to an apartment near the station – I assume this was Jean Kocera-Massenet's mother Jeanne, and that she took them back to her apartment at 10 rue Ernest Renan. Two hours later, they were taken to the gare Montparnasse, where Spinning had arrived from Aumale, and "John" put them on a train with the two Frenchmen who would accompany the four airmen to Saint-Brieuc. Just before the train left, they were joined by two more Americans, 2/Lt William Campbell and S/Sgt Frank Moast, both of whom Spinning knew from his training days.

2/Lt William T Campbell (#473) and **S/Sgt Frank J Moast** (#474) were the bombardier and engineer/TTG of 94BG/333BS B-17 42-37815 Miss Lace (Porter). On the morning of 26 November 1943, they set off to bomb a ball-bearing factory at Ivry-sur-Seine, near Paris but just before reaching their IP, they were hit by flak and attacked by fighters which knocked out their #3 engine before more flak took out #2 engine. Fighter attacks then hit the ball-turret, set fire to the bomb-bay and nose, and killed the navigator (2/Lt Angelo Rivera). The interphone also failed and the aircraft went into a dive before levelling out in cloud at about 7,000 feet, and then dived again, at which point Campbell decided it was time to leave and went out the nose escape hatch.

Moast heard Campbell call out that the navigator had been hit, and the ball-turret gunner (Sgt Frank A Walancus) reporting his turret out of action before an explosion blew the canopy of his own turret away. After checking with the pilots (2/Lt William D Porter and 2/Lt Henry R Pohl), Moast followed Campbell out of the nose escape hatch – they were the only two successful evaders from Miss Lace.

Campbell and Moast have good hand-written reports in their MIS-X files, and I have added some extra details to Campbell's story from a personal account kindly sent to me by his daughter Patti Marcellus in 2012.

24-year old Campbell made a delayed jump (although perhaps not intentionally as he had put his parachute on upside down which put the D-ring on the wrong side), pulling the rip-cord (with his left hand) at about 1,200 feet. He drifted over the village of Charny (Seine-et-Marne) before landing in a farmyard where he was immediately hidden by the farmer, a younger Belgian farmhand and a young boy. That night, the Belgian took Campbell to his house in Charny and then to the café of Mme Jeanne Gardeaux. Three days later, a French ex-captain of tanks, who owned a local chateau (query) took him to stay with Lucien Bontemps (nf), a grain-dealer at nearby Claye-Souilly. On Monday 6 December, Roger (an ex-French navy submariner) and another man took Campbell by bus to a Metro station in Paris where Campbell was passed over to a construction engineer named Maurice Thomasset, and a blonde woman. Maurice and the blonde woman took Campbell by Metro to the south-western suburb of Issy-les-Moulineaux and then walked to an apartment at 21 rue Ernest Renan, where Campbell was sheltered with Henri Robert. On 24 December, Henri Robert and Maurice Thomasset's 18-year-old son Claude, took Campbell to the northern suburb of Aubervilliers, and the Thomasset's third-floor apartment at 96 avenue Victor Hugo. Campbell was sheltered by the Thomasset family for eight weeks, during which time he was joined (on 15 January) by his engineer/TTG, Sgt Frank Moast.

Maurice Edmond Thomasset (born October 1890) of 96 avenue Victor Hugo, Aubervilliers was married to Germaine Louise (born July 1896). Maurice was arrested at his home on 31 March 1944, and on 26 July, deported to Germany – he was liberated from Buchenwald on 11 April 1945.

20-year-old Frank Moast landed in a ploughed field, about fifty feet from a road. He dragged his parachute to the roadside ditch and then found that his hip had been hit by flak and that he couldn't walk. He threw his parachute, Mae West and boots into the ditch before following them only to find (too late) that the ditch was full of water, despite which, he decided it was a good hiding place, and he stayed in the ditch until found by some men who were obviously looking for him. Moast was told to stay where he was and that they would come back for him that evening. At about five o'clock, a man appeared with some food and a bottle of whisky and at eight-thirty, one of the men who had first found him returned, along with his wife and two other men. They had brought civilian clothes, into which Moast changed immediately, and then led him to a house in Charny where Moast was washed and fed and Moast spent his first night in France in a barn.

Next day, a man named Paul Bourgeois (of Vinantes par Juilly, Seine-et-Marne) took Moast by train to Paris where he was sheltered by throat and lung specialist, Dr Francis Triboulet in his apartment near the gare Saint-Lazare (query this as his home address is given as 101 rue de Prony, Paris XVII). On the third night, Dr Triboulet took him to a large apartment on rue de Piccini where the doctor's mistress, Helene Laurencet, lived. Moast stayed with Mlle Laurencet for nine weeks, during which time Dr Triboulet told Moast that a message had been sent to England reporting he was safe. He also brought a man from Rouen called Raymond (this was Raymond Valtat of Chateau de Bosc-Nouvel, Valmartin par Cleres (Saint-Ouen-du-Breuil), Seine Inferieure) who told Moast he would get him to England by boat, although this plan fell through. Ten days after this episode (on 15 January), a man called Roger told Moast that he could join his bombardier William Campbell, and he took Moast to a café in Aubervilliers where he met Campbell – and from that point, Moast says their stories are the same.

On 20 February, Maurice Thomasset and his son Claude took Campbell and Moast into central Paris and 24 boulevard des Capucines where the concierge, Albert Poncelet, sheltered the two Americans in an apartment on the top floor. Belgian fighter pilot Leon Harmel (1807) was already staying there but he left for Brittany a few days later (see earlier).

Campbell and Moast stayed with Albert Poncelet for three weeks, during which time they were visited by Marcel Cola (described by Campbell as a Canadian British Intelligence Officer who shaved off his moustache the night that Campbell left) who sent Campbell out with two gendarmes to have his photograph taken before providing ID cards for the two Americans. On Monday 13 March, Marcel and a woman took Campbell and Moast to the gare Montparnasse where they were put on a train to Saint-Brieuc with four other Americans (Rogoff, Berry, Paquin and Spinning) and from that point, Campbell's story is the same as Rogoff and Berry.

2/Lt Edward J Donaldson (#460) and **Sgt Neelan B Parker** (#461) were the bombardier and right waist-gunner of 379BG/527BS B-17 42-29963 Judy (Camp) which was on a morning raid to Ludwigshafen on 30 December 1943. Just after they dropped their bombs, the oil pressure failed on #1 engine and caused a propeller runaway. As they dropped out of formation and lost altitude, pilot 2/Lt Glenn E Camp Jnr told them to prepare to abandon the aircraft. At about 1430 hrs, they were attacked by fighters and after the third attack, and with the controls gone, Camp ordered his crew to abandon the stricken bomber, and Donaldson followed navigator 2/Lt Jarvis H Cooper out of the nose escape hatch.

Two other crew also evaded successfully: waist-gunner Sgt Douglas J Farr (#509), who was helped by Bourgogne and crossed the Pyrenees from Pau in January, and radio operator S/Sgt Milton M Mills Jnr (#689) who was helped by the Joe Balfe organisation in Hornoy, Somme before being passed to Bourgogne and crossing the Pyrenees in April.

19-year-old Donaldson was met on landing by two young men, 17-year-old Maurice Louis and his friend Bernard Jasmin, and while Bernard took Donaldson's boots and parachute, Maurice led Donaldson back to his family home in the hamlet of Bonvillers, near Cauvigny, where he lived with his parents, François (born August 1885) and Louise. When François came back from work that afternoon and found the airman in his house, he went to fetch a man who could speak English. The man explained to Donaldson that he would stay at the farmhouse that night, be collected by car next day, and be in England within two days. Early next morning, a French couple who had arrived while Donaldson was still sleeping, took him on foot to a house near a mill at Saint-Félix, where François' daughter, Marguerite Wiotte lived.[40]

At about nine o'clock, the couple left and shortly afterwards, local OCM member Louis Tanguy arrived, as did Gaston Legrand on his motorcycle, and Gaston took Donaldson to Clermont. Unfortunately, Gaston's motorcycle broke down on the way and they pushed it to a house on the outskirts of the town, home of a dressmaker identified only as Mlle Bernadette (mentioned earlier). Donaldson describes Mlle Bernadette as being 30 years old, very small, she wore glasses and spoke perfect English – she acted as a messenger between the Clermont and Paris organisations. From Mlle Bernadette's house, Gaston and Donaldson walked to Odette Sauvage's shop at 28 rue de la Republique where Donaldson was given a meal and put into a back room for the rest of the day. He was visited by Odette's son Edmond Sauvage, and Mme Suzanne Leclercq (see earlier). Just before closing time, Gaston Legrand returned to take him to the house on nearby rue du Chatellier where he lived with Edmond and Odette, and Donaldson stayed there for the next three weeks.

Six days after Donaldson arrived, Gaston brought Louis Feingold (#419) and Warren Tarkington (#420) to join him (see earlier), and about a week after that, Donaldson's pilot 2/Lt Glenn Camp, navigator 2/Lt Jarvis Cooper and waist-gunner Sgt Neelan Parker were brought in a truck. Mme Leclercq sent clothes for Donaldson to travel in, and he also met a medical student called Alain who studied in Paris. The organisation sheltering them could only take four men and on about 21 January, Donaldson, Parker, Feingold and Tarkington were taken by train to Creil by two men they hadn't seen before – one of whom had a little finger missing.

When Neelan Parker heard the bail-out order, the 20-year-old Texan car mechanic just had time to shoot down one of the fighters attacking them and see the pilot bail out before he jumped, closely followed by his radio operator S/Sgt Milton Mills (#689). Parker delayed opening his parachute until about 1,000 feet and landed in a ploughed field. Having disengaged his parachute, he ran into small wood nearby where he hid the parachute under some bushes, and then ran to a railway line which he followed toward a larger wood about a quarter of a mile away. However,

40 Donaldson was taken to Saint-Félix because Francois Louis' son-in-law (and OCM member), Marcel Martin (of 32 rue des Fontaines, Clermont) was told that it would be impossible to take him to Clermont because of the Germans – however ..

before he could reach the wood, he saw two Frenchmen helping Mills, who had injured his leg, and Parker went to join them.

The Frenchmen took Parker and Mills to a house in the wood where Parker had hidden his parachute, gave them some wine and made them understand they were to stay in the house and keep quiet. A little while later some other people brought their navigator Jarvis Cooper to join them. About half an hour after that, Parker's original helpers returned and they took him and Cooper deeper into the wood where they were told to wait until dark. They came back at about nine o'clock that evening, carrying the injured Mills, and took all three airmen to a farmhouse in the hamlet of Chateau-Rouge, Cauvigny, home of Marcel and Marcelle Stopin (born July 1920), in the very centre of a German encampment.[41] Their helpers took anything that could identify the airmen except their dog-tags (which the Americans put in their shoes) and the compasses and edible items from their aids boxes – everything else was burned. Civilian clothes were produced for Cooper, who was then taken away but they explained that Mills would have to stay until they could bring him a doctor. A quarter of an hour later, Parker was taken to another house about a quarter of a mile away where he was given civilian clothes, and then moved to a third house where he spent the night.

Next morning, Parker found that he could hardly move, had developed bad cold and a painful cough. Some other people arrived in a butcher's truck and drove him to the home of butcher Felicien Fermier (born Sept 1896) at Cires-lès-Mello, where Parker was put into bed in a room above his shop. He was given food and Dr Charles Andrieu came to examine him before leaving him to sleep. When Parker woke up, he found the Bonvillers chief of police, a man named de Gaulle and believed to be a relative of the General, standing at his bedside. He also received a visit from his navigator Jarvis Cooper. Next day, Dr Andrieu came and collected Parker in his car and took Parker back to his house at 39 rue de Paris in Neuilly-en-Thelle where he stayed with the doctor and his wife Marie Genevieve. Parker saw Cooper again there and they were joined by their pilot Glenn Camp. After two days at the doctor's house, they heard that the Germans were likely to be calling next day so Dr Andrieu took the three Americans to nearby Crouy-en-Thelle where they stayed with blacksmith Augustin Malingue – Dr Andrieu visiting Parker there each day. About a week later, two men,

41 Marcel Stopin was amongst a group of local men executed by German soldiers on 27 Aug 1944 in reprisal for a maquis attack.

one described as fat, came with what Parker calls a covered car and took Parker, Cooper and Camp to Clermont, Dr Andrieu coming part of the way with them. They were delivered to the home of Gaston Legrand and Odette Sauvage on rue du Chatellier where their bombardier Edward Donaldson was being sheltered, along with Louis Feingold and Warren Tarkington.[42]

As mentioned earlier, on 21 January, Donaldson, Parker, Feingold and Tarkington were taken to Creil where Donaldson and Feingold were sheltered overnight with Marcel and Renée Gerardot at 107 rue Henri Pauquet, while Parker and Tarkington stayed with Paul and Marguerite Toussaint at 15 rue Charles Somasco. Next morning, the four airmen were taken back to the station, and Edmond Sauvage and their guide from the previous day took them by train to Noailles where they stayed with Robert Eckert and his family. On about 24 January, Gilbert Thibault drove the four Americans to Auneuil, where Donaldson and Parker were sheltered next door to Thibault with blacksmith Pierre Nouges and his wife Madeleine at 124 rue de Saint-Léger, and a couple of days later, they and T/Sgt Ray Reeves (#729) were taken to Paris.

A young blond man met them at gare Saint Lazare and he took the five airmen by Metro to Mme Schmitz at 87 rue Rochechouart where they met English Typhoon pilot F/Sgt Richard Aitken-Quack and a supposed Norwegian called Fred (or Olaf). Mary-Rose Zerling (Claudette) arrived the same day and made them fill out questionnaires, and that evening, she took Donaldson and Parker to 7 rue Maspero where they were sheltered by Bertranne D'Hespel for the next six weeks.

Donaldson reports that while they were at rue Maspero, "Fred (Olaf) betrayed Claudette and Mme Schmitz to the Germans". With their connection to the organisation apparently lost, Bertranne d'Hespel contacted her friend Marie France Geoffroy-Dechaume who contacted Marcel Cola. Cola brought new papers for Donaldson and Parker, and told them that a British agent would come to see them. The agent, known as Captain Short (aka André) (Dumais) duly arrived to interview them and the following Sunday (12 March), Bertranne d'Hespel took Donaldson, Parker and Joe Birdwell (#471) to the gare Montparnasse where they were passed on to an unnamed guide who led them into a reserved compartment. Another guide brought Harold Vines, Robert Fruth and Charles Winkelman to

42 Dr Charles Andrieu (born Sept 1903) was arrested on 8 July 1944 and deported to Germany – he died at Buchenwald in March 1945.

join them on the overnight train for Saint-Brieuc, where they changed for Châtelaudren.

2/Lt Charles B Winkelman (#468) was the 22-year-old pilot of 100BG/351BS B-17 42-30035 Torchy and flying only his second mission on 3 September 1943. There were three possible targets for the early morning operation: two in the Paris area – Villacoublay aerodrome and a factory on the outskirts of Paris that made aircraft parts – but cloud cover prevented them seeing either of them so the formation headed for their third target, the airfield at Chartres. They were flying at about 23,000 feet when flak took out their #1 engine and set fire to the wing, and as they lost altitude, Winkelman told his crew to stand-by to abandon the aircraft. Then they were attacked by fighters which set fire to the bomb-bay and the crew bailed out. Winkelman was still clipping on his parachute when another fighter shot the bottom out of the pilot's cabin and he dropped out through the trap-door as the bomber went into a spin at about 19,000 feet.

Six other Torchy crew also evaded successfully: waist-gunner S/Sgt Michael F Darcy (#167), who crossed into Spain near Bielsa in October, bombardier 2/Lt Howard M Harris (#258) and waist-gunner S/Sgt Alfred J Zeoli (#259) who were helped by Bourgogne and crossed from Quillan in November, while co-pilot 2/Lt Ralph D Smith (#271), navigator 2/Lt William H Booth (#272) and engineer/TTG T/Sgt Thomas E Combs (#303) were all helped by the Belgian Comète line, Smith and Booth crossing the Pyrenees together in November, and Combs the following month.

Winkelman delayed pulling his rip-cord until "traffic pattern altitude" (about 1,000 feet), losing his maps, aids-box and everything else in his pockets when his parachute opened. He landed somewhere near Gironville-sur-Essonne, coming down in a ploughed field about 100 yards from some woods but then found his knee and hand were injured and he had to "hobble" to the wood where he cut off his parachute and left it, his helmet and oxygen mask, under some brush. According to his watch, it was nine o'clock in the morning when he tied his belt around his wounded leg to stop the bleeding, and his handkerchief around his hand. He only just managed to avoid being found by a large party of German soldiers who were making an organised search and then decided to wait in the woods until nightfall. At about eight-thirty that evening, Winkelman made his way into an orchard, where he picked and ate some apples, before struggling to the top of a small hill where he spent the rest of the night and all next day.

The following evening, Winkelman came down off his hill and started looking for a farmhouse. He says he walked about five miles but found nothing suitable and spent the rest of his second night in France, not getting much sleep, in another wood. Next morning he approached two young men working in a field and although neither spoke English (or German) an older man came over who seemed to understand the word "parachute" and soon grasped the fact that Winkelman wanted something to eat and drink. He was left hidden in some trees while the men brought him bread, meat and wine and indicated they would return that evening. In the meantime however, there was another raid (6 September to Stuttgart) and parachutes began falling all around him – one of the Frenchmen came to warn him that the Germans would be coming so Winkelman left the area as quickly as he could.

The next day, Winkelman approached a farmer in a field and explained that he wanted to get to Spain. The man went to his house and produced a musette bag with coffee, chicken, bread and wine and hid Winkelman in the woods but that night, the Germans came to the nearby village with dogs, and the farmer told Winkelman he would have to move on. On his fifth day in France, Winkelman reached a village where he met a farmer who turned out to be Dutch, and Winkelman was able to talk to him in German. The Dutchman advised Winkelman to head for Paris so Winkelman headed north for the next three nights, hiding each day in woods. On 11 September, he reached Montlhéry with its racetrack (L'autodrome de Linas-Montlhéry) and a German radio station. Winkelman by-passed the town, and waded along a stream until finally coming to a farmhouse where he asked an older woman for help. She could not speak English but brought a dictionary and Winkelman was able to explain that he needed food, which she gave him before he went to spend yet another night sleeping rough. Next morning he returned to the farmhouse where he met the woman's daughter. She spoke fluent German and so Winkelman was able to make himself understood, and she took Winkelman into the house where she persuaded her parents to help Winkelman.

The girl's father was Auguste Kerysaouen, and he and his family sheltered Winkelman at the Ferme de Mesnil Forget, between Montlhéry and Nozay, for three months (during which time Winkelman learned to speak French) until it was finally decided that he had to move on.

On 23 December, M. Kerysaouen's nephew, Jean Lenez, took Winkelman on foot to Saint Georges (query) railway station where they caught a train to Paris (gare d'Austerlitz), and then went by Metro to a M. Berger's apartment. A Dr Formestieux told Berger that too many people knew about Winkelman and next day, took him to the hospital where he worked (Hôpital Saint-Louis – query). Winkelman, who had been a premedical student in the US, spend the day posing as a visiting Swedish intern and watched various operations being performed, and although Winkelman couldn't stay at the hospital, he did return next day to have Christmas dinner with some of the staff. In a café that evening, Winkelman met a Canadian sergeant called John who claimed to have helped his waist-gunner Michael Darcy (#167), something that a Frenchman with them apparently confirmed by having the Canadian identify Darcy from some photographs he carried – although Darcy makes no mention in his report of meeting a Canadian sergeant. Next day, Winkelman was passed on to a man known variously as M. Blanc or M. Robert.

Robert was supposed to be working with both the Gestapo and the organisation and Winkelman says that although he didn't trust him, he seemed friendly enough. He was about 32 years old, with a high forehead, brown eyes and dark wavy hair. He lived near La Santé Prison (Montparnasse) and had a wife, mother and sister living in Paris, who Winkelman later met. Robert took Winkelman on a sight-seeing tour of the capital, taking the Metro and walking down the Champs-Elysées to the place de la Concorde where he pointed out the American Embassy. Robert told Winkelman that if they were stopped, he had papers as a secret agent and Winkelman was to say that he was in Robert's custody. Later they went to watch a play called "Murder in Paris".

Winkelman was taken to stay with a woman who had an apartment on the outskirts of Paris, near the Renault factory. Later, Robert sent Winkelman to stay with another chief of the organisation, M. Lecoeur at 2 rue de Poissy (Paris V), near Notre Dame – Lecoeur, who had a badly broken and crooked nose, worked for the Renault company. Winkelman stayed there for ten days and they had a big New Year's party, and Winkelman finally got an ID card. On 9 January, Robert returned from a trip and said that he had arranged for Winkelman to be taken out via Switzerland. He moved Winkelman to the home of a Paris fireman named Langlois, just off the rue de Poissy, near the police barracks, and a few days later, Winkelman was told that M. Lecoeur had been arrested. On 21 January, Robert's wife took Winkelman to a Chinese café on boulevard Saint-Germain where he met a crippled man who lived south of Paris, apparently at a place called Clayton (?). Winkelman stayed with the crippled man and his woman for five days until they took him back into Paris and an apartment at 22 avenue de la Grande Armée. The concierge there arranged everything and there were (apparently) several other Americans hidden there. Then Winkelman was passed on to a young Frenchman who lived with his mother in an apartment on rue Pigalle, near the Moulin Rouge. He worked for the clandestine newspaper "Defense de la France" while his mother ran some sort of clinic for refugees.

One of Winkelman's visitors was a girl called Marie Fosse (query) who told him that she would get him out through Spain. Her husband was already in England and she spoke good English. A few days later, she came running in to tell Winkelman that the Gestapo were after the people he was staying with. They left immediately, meeting Germans on the stairs as they left the building. Marie Fosse took Winkelman to stay with a Belgian called M. Petit who lived near Luna Park – he was supposed to be on the board of directors of the resistance movement. About a week later, Marie Fosse came to say that they had found out that Robert really did work for the Gestapo and that he had given away all the "Defense de la France" people.

Marie Fosse took Winkelman to stay with a girl named Milly Geoffroy (this was Marie-France Geoffroy-Dechaume). Winkelman says she lived near the place de Clichy and worked with the organisation, supplying clothes for the airmen. One weekend, Milly took Winkelman to Valmondois (Val d'Oise) where they stayed with her father, Charles Geoffroy-Dechaume, a well known painter who had lost a leg in the 1914-18 war.

Marie-France Geoffroy-Dechaume (born June 1919) of 4 Square du Vaucluse, Paris XVII worked as a librarian at the Bibliothèque Nationale. In her (very brief) Helper file, she is credited with helping three evaders, including Winkelman. Another was Sgt Anthony Reynolds (1835) – Marie-France took Reynolds, S/Sgt William Kiniklis (#508) and Sgt Douglas Farr (#509) to stay at her father's house for two weeks in January 1944 before returning them to the capital. The third named evader is a Canadian called Bergeron (Leonard Bergeron (#488) (see later) was born in Canada but no indication found that he was helped by Marie-France). The file suggests she delivered him or them to a farm near Guingamp but makes no mention of the six men that she and Georges Rouet took from Paris to Châtelaudren and ferme Kerjagu at Plouagat on 19 March – see later.

On 1 February, Milly took Winkelman to stay with Mme de Cormont, a "well-to-do woman" who lived in a large house on the rue de Calais (Paris IX) – Winkelman is referring to the mother of Simonie de Cormont. She knew many Americans having worked with Americans in the First War and now her house was a resistance headquarters. She was a widow, with a son a PW in Germany. On 5 February, just as Winkelman was finishing his breakfast, police knocked on the door and German agents searched the house, not finding Winkelman, who had been hidden by Mme de Cormont in small closet in the kitchen but arresting her daughter, Simonie. As soon as the Germans left, Mme de Cormont got Winkelman out of the house and Mme Henri Tronville took him to a large apartment building at nearby 21 boulevard de Batignolles where she was the concierge, and put him into one of the apartments.[43] Winkelman says that the house was full of people working for the resistance movement or some organisation, with papers being forged, sabotage planned, and radios and other equipment being repaired. While he was there, Winkelman worked on identity cards, and helped translate directions on radio sets that had been dropped by parachute. A former army officer known as Toto (assume capitaine Vellaud of reseau TR jeune) told Winkelman about the way parties of men were taken off the beaches in Brittany by gunboats and said that he would try and get Winkelman sent out that way.

On 11 March, Milly brought two men, one of whom "went to England" (assume Joe Birdwell), and the other, Marcel Cola, who took Winkelman to an apartment at 2 rue Ernest Renan where Robert Fruth and Harold Vines were staying with Anita Lemonnier. Cola quizzed Winkelman about baseball and next day, Winkelman, Fruth and Vines were taken to the gare Montparnasse and put on an evening train for Saint-Brieuc, where they changed for Châtelaudren.

2/Lt Joseph A Birdwell (#471) was the 27-year-old navigator of 390BG/569BS B-17 42-3306 Phoenix (Lawrence) which was abandoned to crash near Sainte-Marie-Kerque (Nord-Pas-de-Calais) on 15 August 1943 following a mid-air collision with another B-17 which cut off their tail – see Sentkoski (#348) earlier.

43 Marie Mathilde Glaub (born July 1889) and Henri Tronville (born 1892 – query) were the concierges at 21 Boulevard de Batignolles, and listed as logeurs by Marcel Cola. Mme Glaub was denounced and arrested in July 1944. She survived imprisonment but was crippled for life by the brutal treatment she received.

Birdwell says the aircraft was in a flat spin when he fastened his parachute, and that the two pilots, bombardier and engineer had already left before he dived through the escape hatch, injuring his leg in the process. He delayed pulling his rip-cord until "traffic pattern height" and landed seconds later in a ploughed field. He was still gathering in his parachute when two men ran up, one taking care of his parachute while the other man helped Birdwell to a nearby farmhouse. Because his aircraft had crashed nearby, Fernand Pouilly and his wife were obviously worried about a visit from the Germans but Birdwell was fed and put to bed, and when German troops did arrive, they apparently believed Fernand when he told them he hadn't seen any parachutists. Next day Birdwell, still in his uniform, was moved to a barn for the day before returning to be sheltered in the house, where a French army doctor came and put his leg into a cast. He was also visited by two men from the organisation in Armentieres who questioned him and said they would take care of him.

A few days later, two more organisation men arrived in a car to take Birdwell to Bourbourg where he stayed overnight with an undertaker before going on to Cassel for another night. The following morning, he was taken to Armentieres where he spent the day with local organisation chief Robert Pouille at 70 rue Jean Jaures. That evening, Birdwell met several members of the organisation – a grain merchant from Armentieres, a chemist and his wife, a man called Jean Pierre, a professor from Lille named Maurice who ran an underground newspaper, and an Englishwoman (sic) whose mother, Mrs E Hollingdale, lived in North London – before being taken to Frelinghien, to stay with Robert Demagt and his wife Cecile at 15 rue d'Armentieres, where he joined his engineer Walter Sentkoski (#348) (see earlier).

Hollingdale is an unusual name to find in France but this was Lucienne (Lucy) Marie Eléonore Hollingdale (née Gantier February 1895), a Frenchwoman who married British army veteran Henry (Harry) William Charles Hollingdale (born c.1881) in September 1921. The Hollingdales, who lived at Houplines (less than 2 kms from Armentieres), were denounced for helping evading servicemen and arrested on 22 August 1943. Harry died shortly afterwards as a result of his interrogation but Lucy survived deportation and was liberated from Waldheim on 6 May 1945. She was awarded the BEM for her escape line work, and died in 1984.

After ten weeks with the Demagt family at Frelinghien, Mary-Rose Zerling (Claudette) took Birdwell and Sentkoski to Villereau near Le Quesnoy where they were sheltered with Emile Ducarne and his wife.

Birdwell says it was Saturday 28 November when Claudette took him, Sentkoski and James King to Paris, where they spent the night and following day with her parents at 12 rue Saint-Ferdinand. Birdwell reports that he met Count Bernard d'Havrincourt (to whom Claudette gave military intelligence), Roger Asselineau, and Claudette's friend, schoolteacher Henri Bois. Bernard d'Havrincourt took King to stay with Bertranne d'Hespel at rue Maspero (where the count was also being sheltered) and Asselineau took Sentkoski to stay with Lucienne Mansienne at rue de Geoffroy Marie.

Roger Asselineau (born 1915) of 50 rue Maurice Bokanowski, Asnieres-sur-Seine (later convoyeur for groupe Claudette) was arrested on 16 February 1944 and condemned to death. He was due to be deported to Germany on 18 August but freed with the liberation of Paris.

Birdwell stayed on with Claudette's parents for three weeks (her mother Hélène was a private secretary for Standard Oil, and her father Armand a retired oil engineer), and on the weekend after he arrived (4-5 December), Claudette brought Olaf (or Fred). Olaf only stayed one night before Claudette took him to stay with Mme Wallerant, who lived in the same apartment building as her aunt, Marcelle Hiaux, at 87 boulevard de Courcelles.

Claudette was looking for a more permanent place for Birdwell to live and on the Tuesday took him to stay temporarily with Marie Maziliat, a general's widow at 15 rue de Montrosier, Neuilly-sur-Seine. They then heard that the Germans had acquired an address book (belonging to MT – query) which would have Claudette's address, and so on the Sunday before Christmas (19 December), she moved – and at the same time Birdwell was taken to stay with Marie Louise Dacremont at 12 rue de Dobropol. He couldn't stay there for very long either as Mme Dacremont's grandson was wanted for STO and so while Claudette's aunt Marcelle Hiaux was away, Birdwell moved into her apartment where he stayed with Claudette for the weekend. While he was there, Birdwell saw Fred (Olaf) and spent the day with him before moving once more, this time to stay with Louise Fournier at 10 rue Claude Debussy, Paris XVII – she was married to First

War veteran Edward Fournier who was in England with the Red Cross at Richmond, Surrey.

It was while he was staying with Mme Fournier that he says he went with Claudette and stood in for the British Intelligence Officer "who was out of town" to identify Morton Shapiro (#353), who was staying with Jacques Aude at 28 rue George Sand, Paris XVI, and later to boulevard Pereire to check on William Booher (#350) and Jerry Eshuis (#352), who were being sheltered with Rose Coulon.

Birdwell says that he expected to leave Paris on 15 January but due to the escape from Brittany of two prisoners they wanted to check on – one English (with a broken foot) and one Russian – who had arrived in Paris, he stayed behind to make sure they weren't working for the Germans – this was (obviously) Val Williams and his Russian friend Ivan – see earlier.

He also reports on Claudette hearing about an RAF evader who had been brought to Paris but with his helper having nowhere to keep him, been passed on to a peculiar man who refused to hand him over to her – apparently he wanted money and some kind of official recognition for his efforts. Birdwell went to meet him in a café, explaining that he was an American navigator and that Claudette could be trusted but he still refused to pass the airman over – I suspect this was Gilbert Asselin of 8 rue du Jour, who was "sheltering" F/Lt William C Dallin, the pilot of 35 Sqn Halifax HR798 (see earlier).

Shortly before the "first boat boys left Paris" (on 18 January), Birdwell met Typhoon pilot Richard Aitken-Quack (who was being sheltered with Marguerite Schmitz) and told him what he knew about Olaf/Fred.

On about 20 January, Birdwell went to stay with Lucienne Mansienne at 10 rue Geoffroy Marie (where King and Sentkoski had been sheltered earlier). Her son had tried to leave France but was captured near the Spanish border and put into a German camp, and she wanted someone to stay in his room.

> *"One time Claudette took me to Mme Schmitz where Olaf/Fred was staying. Mme Schmitz had a godson who ** ** ** Olaf petrified. Claudette was supposed to come and see me on Saturday, she had been in the country with her mother getting food but was delayed by sabotage on the railway line and didn't come by until the Tuesday. Mme Mansienne had been trying to contact the count (Bernard d'Havrincourt) and he came to see her on Thursday while she was at work. He told her that he had spoken to Claudette's mother who*

told him that Claudette had been arrested – something about the "Norwegian" turning her in, although he didn't have the details." (my interpretation from the hand-written notes in Birdwell's report, although the days and dates are not to be trusted – Mary-Rose Zerling was arrested on the afternoon of Saturday 5 February when she went to Mme Schmitz apartment, and her parents were arrested at their home two days later)

It was while Birdwell was staying with Mme Mansienne that Claudette was arrested, and next day (6 February), comte d'Havrincourt took Birdwell to stay with Xavier Eid – a Belgian from Brussels with four cousins in the RAF – at No 1 avenue Emile-Deschanel, Paris VII. The count told Birdwell to go and see Claudette's mother, having found out that Claudette's aunt, Marcelle Hiaux had also been arrested, and asked Birdwell to go with him to warn other friends whose addresses Birdwell knew but the count did not. Mme Dacremont was arrested at about the same time as Mary-Rose Zerling, and the count told Birdwell that Mme Dacremont's daughter, Mme Beltrude, had also been arrested – Mme Schmitz says that Mme Beltrude was caught at Claudette's parents house (as was Louise Fournier). On Sunday (sic – this must have been Monday 7 Feb) comte d'Havrincourt and Bertranne d'Hespel came to take Birdwell (who didn't speak French) to warn the others, the count telling him that Claudette's parents had just been arrested – he had been to their house that morning and seen the Gestapo there.

They went first to boulevard Pereire, where Booher and Eshuis had been sheltered with Rose Coulon, and told her about Claudette's arrest. Mme Coulon said she thought she could notify the British IO through another contact, and Mme d'Hespel said she would check back with her later. Birdwell thought that Olaf (who they were assuming was responsible for the arrests) probably didn't know where Mme Fournier lived, so he went to rue Claude Debussy to warn her. Birdwell used the agreed signal on her door-bell but there was no answer, and an elderly neighbour, Professor Paul de Cohen, a Russian pianist who played on Radio Paris, told him that he thought (correctly) the Germans may have been there already. From rue Claude Debussy, Birdwell and d'Havrincourt went to Neuilly-sur-Seine to warn Marie Maziliat, the general's widow at 15 rue Montrosier – Olaf had stayed there and again, there was no answer, although this time none of the neighbours were aware of any German activity – Birdwell and the count tried again two days later and left a message with an Irish lady who lived in the same building to warn Mme Maziliat not to go back to her apartment. Then they went to Bertranne d'Hespel's apartment on rue Maspero where Birdwell met Edward Donaldson (#460) and Neelan Parker (#461) before returning to Xavier Eid's apartment on avenue Emile-Deschanel. A few days later, Birdwell went with the count to Courbevoie to warn Mme Dacremont's nephew (query writing) at 86 boulevard de la Defense (now avenue du General de Gaulle, and home of M. and Mme Schrub – named as logeurs by Mary-Rose Zerling) but they were unable to find him.

Birdwell says that he went to see Donaldson and Parker several times, and that Mme d'Hespel and count Bernard were trying to get in touch with another organisation. He also mentions that one day Marie (her middle name) d'Hespel took him to her apartment where he met a girl from another organisation. She was very good looking, with long legs and a clean complexion, somewhere between fair and dark, about 5 ft 5 inches tall, about 120 lbs and aged about 25 – he thought she was from a military information group. This was Marie-France Geoffroy-Dechaume (born June 1919 and mentioned earlier), who had been working with BCRA agent Jean Ayral (aka Robert Gautier) – and is said to have had "beauty in her family".[44]

Birdwell returned to rue Maspero a couple of days later to have his picture taken by one of Mme d'Hespel's friends – the photographer was about 5 foot 11 inches tall, with light wavy hair, slim with sharp features, about 23 or 24 years old. A few days later, Mme d'Hespel told him that she had contacted another organisation and that they should be taken out in a few weeks time. On the way to his next visit to rue Maspero to receive some "very good news", he met the same girl coming out of the Metro – she was with a "Frenchman from Canada" who was taking over from Claudette – this was obviously Marcel Cola. He also mentions Mme d'Hespel telling him about Americans being taken to Switzerland but that most them had been caught – I am assuming this was a reference to the John Carter organisation. Cola took more photographs and had new ID papers made, and that afternoon, a British officer (Dumais) arrived and told him about Lee Gordon and a Belgian fighter pilot. He also said that he knew which prison Claudette was being held in.

On the evening of 12 March, Bertranne d'Hespel took Birdwell – along with Edward Donaldson and Neelan Parker – to Montparnasse station where they joined Robert Fruth, Harold Vines and Charles Winkelman.

44 Claire Cherillon (1995) "Code Name Christianne Clouet" Texas A&M University Press.

They were taken to a compartment on the overnight train to Saint-Brieuc along with their two guides – one about 5 ft 10 inches tall, heavy boned (query), athletic, with light wavy receding (?) hair, tan complexion, about 175 lbs, the other guide smaller, about 145 lbs with dark complexion and hair.

Jean Vaina (born Istanbul in June 1914, naturalised as French in April 1938) of 6 rue du Débarcadère, Paris XVII was recruited as a guide by Henri Bois in late November 1943 after being introduced to Bois by his friend Jean Kocera-Massenet.

His NARA file is rather confusing when it comes to naming evaders helped – on one page the IS9 Finance Section says that Vaina claims to have helped Feingold, Tarkington, Rogoff, Berry, Vines, Paquin, Fruth and Spinning. Another page adds William Harnly (#182) and Arthur Steinmetz (#233) (both Bourgogne, in September 1943).

MIS-X credit him as being the Jean who took Feingold and Tarkington to the station where they met Raymond Mauret who had Mike Olynik and James Quinn, and took them to Guingamp on 25 Feb. MIS-X also say that Vaina and Mauret were probably the two unnamed guides who took Rogoff, Berry, Vines, Paquin, Winkelman and Birdwell to Châtelaudren on 12 and 20 (sic) March.

T/Sgt William C Lessig (#466) was the 22-year-old engineer/TTG of 379BG/525BS B-17 42-29633 (Beam) which was on the way to Frankfurt on 8 February 1944 when they were were attacked by fighters. Lessig says that the flight over was normal until about 10.30 or 11.00 hrs "when all hell broke loose". A German fighter came in from dead ahead and blew a big hole in the nose, set #2 engine on fire, started a fire in the oxygen system and shot off the left side horizontal stabilizer. The aircraft went into a steep dive and then when it levelled off, Lessig bailed out.

Three other crew evaded successfully: bombardier 2/Lt Dean W Tate (#467) with Lessig (see below), and ball-turret gunner S/Sgt John F Bernier (#537) and waist-gunner S/Sgt David G Helsel (#538) – see both later.

Lessig says he jumped from about 10,000 feet, delayed opening his parachute until about 800 feet and landed in a field about three kilometres from a German airfield. He hid his flying kit and started walking west through a small swamp. After crossing a field, he turned south, keeping to wooded areas wherever possible and at about five o'clock that evening, hid up in a clump of bushes for the night. Next morning he set off again, and at about noon met a Frenchman with a load of horse manure (not specified but presumably on a cart). Lessig asked him the way to Paris and he pointed in the direction that Lessig was already going. The man asked if Lessig was an American and when Lessig said he was, asked if he was hungry. Using sign-language, the man told Lessig to hide himself in some nearby woods and said that he would come back with some food at four o'clock. The man duly returned with both food and a bandage for Lessig's injured foot and then told Lessig to stay where he was and that he would come back again later and take him into the nearby village to spend the night. At about six o'clock, several other Frenchmen appeared with a selection of civilian clothes for Lessig to put on before taking him to a barn just outside the town (Lassigny) where they met the first Frenchman. Lessig climbed into the hayloft where he slept until about eight-thirty that evening when two of the men returned and took him to the house where his bombardier Dean Tate had been the previous evening. Lessig had supper there, and then at about ten o'clock, was taken to a farmhouse where he joined Tate and met Sgt Carl Mielke.

Sgt Carl W Mielke (#465) was the 20-year-old tail-gunner of 305BG/364BS B-17 42-40020 Good Pickin (Stuckey) which was also on the operation to Frankfurt on 8 February 1944. At about eleven o'clock they were attacked by a fighter which Mielke says shot up the cockpit, knocked out their controls and started a fire in the electrical system. He also believes that two of their engines were on fire as the aircraft went into a dive before starting to level out again. When he saw the waist-door go past him, he knew it was time to bail out so he crawled into the waist area and followed waist-gunner Sgt Arthur B Jones (#662) out of the aircraft at what he believed was between 800 and 1,000 feet.

Jones was later passed to the Bourgogne organisation to cross the Pyrenees to Spain at the end of March, as was radio operator Sgt Lee R Frakes (#661) a few days later. The other waist-gunner, Sgt Odis R Pickering (#1280), was sheltered by the Chauny-Dromas organisation until the area was liberated in September 1944.

Mielke landed at Thiescourt, near Lassigny (Oise) – he says that he followed the advise of a paratrooper who had given them a lecture the previous day, controlling his drop and avoiding a patch woods only to land on the roof of a house on rue Mélique. The woman of the house, a prominent member of the local organisation (who Mielke was later told was Mme de Gaulle but was actually postwoman Mme Rosa Cecile Delnef), was standing in the yard when Mielke landed and she ran inside, screaming for her husband. The husband soon appeared to ask Mielke if he was "Deutsch" and when Mielke shook his head and said "American", they smiled and took him into their home. His parachute and flying gear were taken away and Mielke was given a jacket and top-coat to go over his ODs, and after a meal, was taken to a nearby deserted farm. That evening, an unnamed man led Mielke to his house about two miles away and gave him supper and a pair of shoes in place of his flying boots. The man was a former soldier who had been captured by the Germans and developed TB. At ten-thirty that evening, 2/Lt Dean Tate arrived with a woman who could speak some English – her husband was apparently a famous pilot – and the following morning, Mielke and Tate started out on their arranged journey.

2/Lt Dean W Tate (#467) was the 23-year-old bombardier of B-17 42-29633 (Beam) – the same aircraft as William Lessig. They were on the way to Frankfurt on the morning of 8 February 1944 when, at about eleven o'clock, they were were attacked head-on by fighters. With their instruments shot away and the aircraft on fire, the bomber went into a dive, and when it levelled off, Tate bailed out.

Tate says that he opened his parachute almost immediately on leaving the aircraft, eventually landing in the churchyard of a small village. He says the whole town turned out to meet him, taking his parachute and flying gear and hiding him on a farm. Doctor Byer (from Lassigny) came and gave him what Tate assumed was a tetanus shot, and then returned an hour later with a selection of civilian clothes. The doctor then drove Tate out of town, to a steep hill, and they and a woman (Mme Pellieu) walked up to a woodman's shack where the doctor left them. At about seven o'clock, a man arrived to take Tate back to his house where his wife spoke some English, and gave Tate an excellent supper. At about ten o'clock, the man took Tate to another house (at Le Cessier, Somme – just south of Beuvraignes), where he met Sgt Carl Mielke, and their journey was arranged.

> *"At seven the night of the eighth, a man who had been a French pilot came in to help me. In the last war he won a British DFC and other decorations, among them Russian and Serbian medals. He was a friend of Glenn Martin and Wilbur Wright [aviation pioneers and founders of the short-lived Wright-*

Martin Aircraft Company] and had flown around the world several times. He took me to his house, passing an airport on the way. His wife spoke English slightly. At about 1000 (sic) that night we walked to the house in which Sgt Mielke (#465) was staying. I believe that these houses were either in or in the vicinity of Le Cessier (410265) sheet 129. At 0430 hrs next morning we were taken to the deserted farmhouse in which Mielke had been the previous day. Sgt Lessig (#466) joined us that night the 9th at 1100.

We stayed here 2 more days and one more night. While there a lady who could write English came and wrote on a pad we would leave soon with a guide. She also had written conversations with a man named Jones (same aircraft as Mielke) [this was waist-gunner Sgt Arthur B Jones (#662) who was being sheltered in nearby Ville] and an RAF man whose name we don't know [Jones makes no mention of an RAF man]. At 9:30 the evening of 11th the ex-soldier (Mielke report) came in and hustled us away (query) making us understand that there were Germans in the area. We walked about 2 miles uphill until we came to a cave [at Plessier-de-Roye] that had been used as a fort in 1914. Next night at 8:30 some people took us to meet the French pilot (indicated earlier). We did so, meeting him by a big power line, and went to his house. There two men and a girl were waiting for us. One of the men, and the girl, was Belgian. The girl's name was Godelieve, she has a sister named Clarisse, and two brothers named Willis and Jean. Jean worked at an airfield in Roye (see Appendix B) [missing]. We went to Godelieve's house about 6 kms away. She and her family had helped before.[45] Clarisse, who had some connection with the Germans, told us that the Germans had recently captured nine men evading. About two that afternoon an Englishman named Edward Butler came in and gave us a message to take to his wife at the Manchester Arms, Brighton. He told us to say "I am doing my duty". The people we were with did not seem to trust him completely however." (Tate MIS X #467)

Tate, Lessig and Mielke left the Van Laere home at Canny-sur-Matz on the evening of 15 February, taken to Lassigny where they caught a train to Creil, guarded all the way by a man named Maurice. Tate and Lessig stayed overnight with draftsman André Bataillard (born November 1910) and his family at 5 rue Albert-Thomas – I don't know where Mielke stayed – and next morning, they caught a train to Beauvais. They were taken to a wine

45 René and Marthe Van Laere of Canny-sur-Matz, their daughters Godelieve and Clarisse, son Jean and a 6-year-old nephew called Willy. (Dominique Lecomte)

shop on rue de Clermont for a meal (where they were told that thirteen Americans had been the day before), and then moved across the street to a house at number 24 (home of Lucien Revert and his wife). That afternoon, they were told that the man they were supposed to meet in Paris had been caught (assume André Bureau), and at seven o'clock that evening, Gilbert Thibault drove them to a small inn at Ons-en-Bray (a village about 10 kms west of Beauvais), Tate reporting that Sgt David Warner (#540) was in the car with them.

S/Sgt Everett E Stump (#463) and **Sgt Carlyle A Van Selus** (#464) were the engineer/TTG and ball-turret gunner of 92BG/326BS B-17 42-37984 (Shevchik). They were returning from an aborted operation to Frankfurt on the morning of 8 February 1944 when, at about ten-thirty, they were attacked by a mixed group of German fighters which knocked out their #2 engine, damaged #3, and shot out their instruments. The bomber went into a right-hand glide, the bail-out order given and the aircraft abandoned to crash near Catheux (Oise).

Of the ten-man crew, only bombardier 2/Lt Donald J Periolat was captured – the other nine men evaded successfully: navigator 2/Lt James E Williams (#668) and tail-gunner Sgt Francis F Higgins (#825) were helped by the Bourgogne organisation and crossed the Pyrenees to Spain, Williams in April and Higgins in June 1944. Radio operator S/Sgt Robert E Sidders (#1056) was helped by reseau François in Paris before being taken to the MI9 camp at Freteval, and four more with François-Shelburn – see later.

22-year-old Stump says he landed at Auchy-la-Montagne (Oise), which is about five miles south-east of Crèvecoeur-le-Grand, where he was helped immediately and directed to a nearby farm, meeting his pilot 1/Lt Milton Shevchik (#527) along the way. At about 1300 hrs, they were joined at the farm by their co-pilot 2/Lt James Thorson (#528). That evening they were taken to Domeliers where they saw their tail-gunner Francis Higgins (#825) and radio operator Robert Sidders (#1056) who were being sheltered at another house nearby. The following night, Stump, Schevchik and Thorson were moved to Crèvecoeur-le-Grand where Stump stayed with schoolteachers Henri and Severine Villette on rue de Grandvilliers while Schevchik and Thorson were taken to another nearby house. On Friday 11 February, Stump was told to pick a partner for the onward journey and so he went to see Shevchik. With him was a navigator from their squadron, 2/Lt William Hoffman (#530), who told them that when his aircraft was shot down he had thrown the wounded bombardier (2/Lt Sidney Scheiman) out and was later told that he was dead. Next day Stump saw Shevchik, Thorson and Hoffman, and this time Francis Higgins and Robert Sidders were also there. On 16 February, they were joined by their ball-turret gunner Carlyle Van Selus, who had also been sheltered nearby, and Stump joined him.

21-year-old Van Selus had followed Stump out of the aircraft but landed some distance from him. After hiding his parachute and Mae West, he began walking south but didn't go far before stopping to rest in a clump of bushes. On hearing some people talking nearby, he crawled to the top of a bank and saw a man and two children. Van Selus approached the man and told him that he was an American in need of help. The man was Gaston Dubois and he took Van Selus back to his home in Francastel where he lived with his wife Madeleine and children André and Odette. The Dubois family fed Van Selus, gave him civilian clothes and sheltered him for the next four days, during which time a man known as "the Chief" visited and took his photograph. On 12 February, M. Dubois took Van Selus in his truck to Crèvecoeur-le-Grand where he stayed with "a lady who ran a boarding house" and where, four days later, he was joined by Stump.

On 18 February, Van Selus and Stump were driven to Beauvais, along with S/Sgt George Buckner (#539) (TTG from Hoffman's aircraft – see later) – and that evening went on to Ons-en-Bray where they met 2/Lt Dean Tate.

Tate reports that next day, Higgins (#825) and Sidders (#1056) came in for an hour, and the following morning (20 Feb), 21-year-old André Duval took Tate, Stump, Van Selus, Mielke and Lessig on foot for about two miles to Les Trous Nonos, the farmhouse where he lived with his parents, cultivateurs Maurice and Héloise Duval, brother Pierre and sister Rolande.

The airmen were told there were about 30 Americans at Beauvais and 40 at Crèvecoeur-le-Grand, and on about 8 March, they were interrogated by a British IO (assume Jacky du Pac). Two days later, they all got new ID papers and were taken to Beauvais station, where Stump and Van Selus saw Sgt Francis Wall (#529) from their crew, and 2/Lt William Hoffman (#530).

Tate, Stump, Van Selus, Mielke and Lessig were taken to Paris by René Loiseau and Alain Fleury. Their train was delayed by sabotage on the tracks between Beauvais and Creil, and they had to get off and walk half a mile to Creil and a second train to complete their journey, which resulted in them arriving in Paris after curfew, and having to sleep on the train. Next morning, at about six o'clock, they took the Metro to Lavallois-Perret and then walked two blocks down rue Baudin to number 5, a five-story apartment house. Tate says they went up to room 23 where Stump, Van Selus and Mielke stayed with the owner of the apartment, a girl named Margot (Marguerite Di Giacomo), taking their meals in the next door apartment of Yvonne Latrace, while Tate and Lessig stayed across the street at 4 rue Baudin with Jacky du Pac and René Loiseau's parents, Alfred and Suzanne.

Marcel Cola gave the five Americans papers which allowed them to pass into the coastal Zone Interdite, and early on the morning of Wednesday 15 March, René Loiseau took them to Montparnasse station and put them on a train to Saint-Brieuc, where they changed for Châtelaudren.

The B-17s 42-39784 Cabin in the Sky and 42-31380 were also on the 8 February raid to Frankfurt but they were shot down over Normandy.

T/Sgt Kenneth P C Christian (#472) was the 25-year-old radio operator of 384BG/544BS B-17 42-39784 Cabin in the Sky (Covington) which crashed about 8 kms south-east of Cherbourg.

The pilot (Royson Covington) says they were returning from the target after being hit by flak and on nearing the coast, were attacked by fighters and then coastal batteries. Their #2 engine caught fire and the whole left wing was burning. They were at very low altitude and he climbed to about 950 feet before ordering his crew to bail out. He continued to climb to about 1,200 feet but then had trouble with the automatic pilot and was back down to about 800 feet when he bailed out himself.

Christian says they had trouble with #3 engine on the way out and were unable to keep up with their formation so they decided to abort the mission, salvoing their bombs once the navigator was confident they were over German territory. About ten minutes into the return flight, they were losing altitude and flying on three engines when they were attacked by fighters, one of which Christian believed hit their wing-tanks. When they flew over the Cherbourg peninsula, they were subjected to heavy flak and the engineer (T/Sgt John J Younker) told Christian to bail out .

1/Lt Royson T Covington Jnr (#743) was the only other successful evader from Cabin in the Sky – he was passed on to the Bourgogne organisation and crossed the Pyrenees from Montrejeau in May. Covington reports that the French told him all eight other crew were captured, seven within five hours of landing and the other (thought to have been tail-gunner, S/Sgt Aleck M Wasilewski) two days later.

Christian landed in a field somewhere east of Cherbourg at about 1415 hrs, being clipped on the ankle by flak during his descent. He cut the parachutes shrouds clear and carried his chute to a barn about 300 yards away. There was a woman with a young girl and two children standing near the barn and Christian produced his phrase-card to tell the woman that he was an American. She immediately took him into the barn where he was hidden in the hay, along with his parachute. Several German soldiers arrived a few minutes later and questioned the woman but did not search the barn. Once they had left, Christian got out his escape map and the woman helped him to find his position. Christian then asked her for civilian clothes and was supplied with trousers, a coat and beret. He kept his heated suit on under the civilian coat and cut the tops from his heated shoes. The woman then urged Christian to leave the farm and so he made his way down the road, passing several German soldiers who were searching for the crew.

Late that afternoon, Christian approached a farmer who took him into his house and after about an hour, a Frenchman who spoke some English was brought in. Christian was given a meal and then hidden in a haystack for the night, having been told they would buy him a train ticket to Paris and that he would leave early the next morning.

The following morning his promised guide failed to appear and Christian was told it was impossible for him to take a train anyway as there were too many Germans around. He was advised to walk to a nearby town (assume Valognes), which he reached at about five o'clock that afternoon, where he went into a café and declared himself to the owner as an American airman. He was then locked in the café while the proprietor (an elderly lady) went away, returning fifteen minutes later to take Christian to another building where his subsequent journey was arranged.

Christian was taken to a Red Cross unit at Valognes which was housed in a large chateau. The nurse at the unit spoke excellent English and she questioned Christian about his identity. He spent the next three days and nights in a large ground-floor room in the chateau – the upper rooms apparently being used as a German headquarters. The nurse (whose name Christian never knew) got him an identity card and arranged for him to go to Evreux.

He was driven to Valognes station and took a four-thirty afternoon train to Evreux, arriving there at nine o'clock that evening. His left hand was bandaged as an identification for someone to meet him but no-one was there so he spent the night at the station. Next morning he went into the centre of Evreux and declared himself to the proprietor of the Café de Paris as an American airman. He was told to sit down, and about an hour later a unnamed man who spoke English, having been a waiter in Houston, Texas, was brought in. He then went to look for the man that Christian was supposed to have met the previous day but was unable to find him. The people at the café assumed that Christian was 2/Lt Phillip Capo (who was expected that day) and on finding he was not, subjected him to some "severe questioning" to confirm his identity as an American. Later that day he was joined by Capo and from there they travelled together.

2/Lt Philip A Capo (#459) was the 23-year-old co-pilot of 385BG/548BS B-17 42-31380 (Pabich). They knew there had been several bursts of flak exploding directly under the aircraft but were not aware of any damage being caused until they were about forty miles from the French coast when their #3 engine stopped through lack of fuel and they found the transfer pump wouldn't function. They were over the English Channel when #4 engine stopped, and with the fuel gauges for engines #1 and #2 reading empty, Pabich turned inland and ordered his crew to bail out, leaving the aircraft to crash on the southern bank of the Seine near Pont-Audemer (Eure).

Six other crew also evaded successfully: pilot 1/Lt Francis F Pabich (#717) and navigator 2/Lt Edward J Carey (#718) crossed the Pyrenees together from Peyhrehorade at the end of April, and engineer/TTG T/Sgt Joseph I Gorrono (#1010), waist-gunner S/Sgt Emmett W Bone (#1011) and tail-gunner S/Sgt Donald Hoilman (#1052) were liberated from the MI9 camp at Freteval on 13 August 1944. Radio operator T/Sgt George Solomon (#1217) was also at Freteval but he and 2/Lt Abraham Wiseman (#1193) left the camp on 29 July and crossed the Pyrenees from Halsou to Spain on 12 August.

Capo says that when they found they couldn't make the French coast, they turned south and levelled out, the pilots holding the aircraft steady at about 10,000 feet while the crew bailed out in order. Capo was the next to last man to leave the aircraft, delaying opening his parachute until about 1,000 feet and making a good landing, somewhere south-west of Rouen at about two-thirty in the afternoon.

Capo's landing was witnessed by a farmer who immediately came over, shook Capo's hand and helped him take off and hide his parachute and Mae West. The farmer warned Capo about "Boches" and so Capo decided to hide until it got dark, and after giving the farmer some money from his escape kit, hid himself in the middle of a stubble field. That evening the farmer's son took Capo back to his cottage where he gave Capo a meal and a bed for the night. Capo stayed at the house all next day until evening when the son took him by bicycle to the nearby town. The son talked to some people, obviously all in French, which Capo didn't understand, before returning them the farmer's house for the night and next day. The farmer gave Capo a beret, jacket and blue denim trousers and Capo left him his uniform, keeping just his dog-tags. That evening, one of the men he had seen the previous evening took Capo to a place from where his journey was arranged.

> *"The house to which I was taken was next to a big chateau. Three men came to see me, one of whom was called Alphonse. He furnished me with a carte d'identité on which I used my GI photo. Two of the men spoke English, including Alphonse who claimed to have spoken it only for six months. We slept that night in a barn, and Alphonse said he would return to take us to Paris the next day. We biked about ten miles and took a train at Montfont [Monfort-sur-Risle]. At the station was a RR official who was one of the men with Alphonse the night before. Alphonse and I got off at Evreux where we were met by three young Frenchmen (the oldest about 27). We had supper in a café. Man 27, who was well-dressed and spoke fair English, was reputed to be head of an organisation. By truck we went about 12 kms to home of Alphonse's brother-in-law. It appeared to be a lodge, of which the brother-in-law was caretaker [about 12 miles from Claville (Eure), Francis Pabich (#717) was later sheltered there as well]. Staying there was a Frenchman about 35. He had been a lieutenant in the army, and was head of a Paris organisation, hiding there temporarily. Walked to a prosperous farm and spent a week there. A boy was there who spoke a little English and who was studying to be a priest (Jean Jacques ?). Joined by T/Sgt Christian." (Capo MIS-X #459)*

A man named Barbat (of 34 rue Lépouzé in Evreux) took Capo and Christian north by truck to the little village of Hondouville where they were sheltered by Jacques Roger (of Moulin du Valtier). Capo says that they had expected to go straight to a "second-class hotel in Paris run by a woman" (assume Therese Fabre – see earlier) but there was "a delay due to police troubles with her". Finally, their host went to Paris and made arrangements for them, and early on the morning of 13 March, they were taken by train to the capital. They spent the day at a café in the Clichy district, and stayed overnight in an apartment belonging to a 35-year-old woman called Annie. Next day they were supplied with new identity cards by Marcel Cola, and that evening, a French girl and a man called John (who worked for the Ford Motor Company, and wanted a Mrs J Offord of Fernleigh Road, Winchmore Hill in London to be told that he was well) took them (and John Amery – see below) by overnight train to Saint-Brieuc, where they changed for Châtelaudren.

Sgt John T Amery (#469) was the 23-year-old engineer/TTG of 100BG/351BS B-17 42-5997 Heaven Can Wait (Smith) which was returning from Ludwigshafen on 30 December 1943 when it was shot down by fighters and crashed near Monthois (Ardennes). Amery says they were nearing their rendezvous with a P-47 escort when three Fw190s attacked them from the clouds below. He says that when the pilot (2/Lt Francis P Smith Jnr) yelled for everyone to "get out of the ship" he dropped from his turret and grabbed his parachute – the bulkhead was a mass of flame and the left wing was on fire. The co-pilot (James Law) shoved the bombardier's hatch open and fell through with Amery close behind him.

Seven other crew also evaded successfully: bombardier 2/Lt Clyde S Manion (#577), waist-gunners Sgt John W Runcel (#567) and Sgt Conrad P Stumpfig Jnr (#568), and tail-gunner Sgt William Wertz (#576) crossed Pyrenees together to Bielsa in March, radio operator S/Sgt John L Swenson (#726) crossed in April, and ball-turret gunner Sgt Alvin C Little (#850) in June. Navigator 2/Lt Saul Hershkowitz (#2415) was flown back to England by 161 SD Hudson (Operation Failsworthy) in September. Co-pilot 2/Lt James P Law evaded for about three months until he was captured outside Paris.

Amery had been off oxygen for almost five minutes before jumping and so he pulled his rip-cord as soon as he cleared the aircraft for fear of passing out. While he drifted down, he was able to watch as his own burning aircraft passed below, and saw another B-17 dive vertically into the ground while the three Focke-Wulfs circled around him. He finally landed in a ploughed field somewhere north of Montfaucon-d'Argonne, Lorraine, twisting his leg on the stony ground and then was further abused when the wind caught his parachute and dragged him another three hundred yards. Once he'd unbuckled his chute, he made his way to a nearby wood where he bundled the chute under some stones (forgetting his first-aid pack which was attached to the harness), removed his flying boots and electrically heated shoes and put on a pair of moccasins that he had brought with him – he later evaluated the moccasins as being very satisfactory, though conspicious. He then took out his compass and used it to head west, not knowing at the time whether he was in Germany or France.

Because he wasn't sure which country he was in, Amery avoided some men he heard working in the woods, walking on for another fifteen minutes before stopping to bury his flying clothes and boots, leaving him with just his ODs and coveralls, which had the seat burnt out of them from the aircraft. He took out his maps but was unable to orientate himself and so continued west though the woods until dusk when he came upon two elderly wood-cutters. Amery declared himself to them but while they shook his hand, they didn't seem to understand his requests for assistance. However when Amery posed the question "Francais" to which they replied "Oui" and then "Paris" to which they pointed west, and then "Deutschland" and they pointed north and east, Amery was fairly confident that he was at least in the right country.

On leaving the two men, Amery made his way along a road heading south. Soon though a passing car frightened him enough to leave the road and start out across the fields and about a mile later, he came to what he describes as a "rickety" house. Presently, one of the same wood-cutters he had encountered earlier appeared and Amery asked him for water. Amery was made to sit while some bread, apples and wine were produced but when Amery asked if he could sleep in the haystack, the man said "Chateau" and pointed to a house in the distance. Amery walked to the chateau and saw that it was boarded up but then a child appeared, and seeing Amery, called his father. The man turned out to be the caretaker of the estate and when he understood that Amery was an American airman, he took Amery into his cottage and gave him food and wine. While Amery was eating, the man's daughter went to bring a young man who took Amery back to his own house (near Le Fohe, just south of Grandpré, Ardennes) where he lived with his parents, and after inspecting Amery's dog-tags, put him to bed.

Early next morning, the young man gave Amery a civilian jacket, a scarf, some sandwiches, a tin of British rations and a large-scale map on which he traced a route for Amery to follow. After warning Amery to avoid the roads after eight o'clock because of the curfew, he took Amery to the road and sent him on his way. Amery walked for the rest of the day, not having much luck when he asked for assistance and spending his second night in France in a haystack. Unfortunately it was so cold that night that Amery was unable to sleep so he set off again at about four o'clock, soon losing his way in the dark and finding himself inside a vineyard from which he could only escape by climbing over an "immense" fence. He made his way into the hills where he found pools of water to fill his bottle, adding Halazone tablets from his escape kit to purify it, before walking through a large town, over an unguarded canal and into a wood where he changed into some dry socks that (like the moccasins) he had brought with him. Amery (who had obviously thought this through in advance) explains in his report that he had three pairs of socks that he wore two at a time with the third pair drying about his body. He also wore a towel instead of a scarf and used that to dry his feet when he changed his socks.

> *"Amery walked all that day 30 Dec (sic) stopped at l'Espérance Ferme (south of Auberive) where a woman with two children gave him wine. He slept out that night near Les Petites-Loges. The third day (sic) he walked to Gionges where at evening a woman at the first house as you enter Gionges on the highway from Oger (south of Avize) took him in and gave him a bed (this woman has five children, and her husband is dead or POW). In the late afternoon of fourth day he stopped at a large farm just off Highway 33 at Vouchamps. Here a young man gave him food, medicine for his cold, a razor and a bed. The young man tried to find a friend to help Amery but failed and so gave him a note in French saying "This is an American aviator. Help him and show him the way to Paris". (MIS-X #469 Amery)*

Amery carried on in this fashion, with his injured leg getting worse, sometimes getting food and shelter and sometimes not, until the morning of the seventh day when he finally reached the outskirts of Paris.

In his tired and dirty state, Amery knew he had to keep to the back-streets – he was looking for a small café or restaurant where he might be able to get some much needed food. At the first empty café he tried asking the owner simply for wine but when the man asked what kind he wanted, Amery was unable to answer and so tried showing his flying wings but then four men entered and Amery left immediately. About an hour later,

Amery tried another place and this time the proprietor, who was rather deaf, called his wife. Amery managed to convince them that he was an American airman and that he was hungry – he was given food and wine and told to stay while the husband went to find a man who could speak English. When they returned, Amery's journey was arranged.

The English-speaking man took Amery to an apartment at 31 rue Charlot, Paris III where a large blond police inspector named Jacques Lefort lived with his wife Mariette. Jacques had three helpers, Paul (a young man with blond wavy hair who lived with the Leforts), André (a short man with brownish, wavy hair) and a mulatto named William Edwards. Amery stayed with the Leforts from 5 January to 11 February, during which time he was given clothes and shoes, and received medical attention from a Dr Roget (or Roger) who came to treat him. The Tuesday after he arrived, Amery was taken to meet a man named Claude Jolly (nf), another police inspector. Amery also reports a man called Guy coming to check Amery's identity which he apparently confirmed by radio to England. Amery says he was a sports commissioner and head of the organisation, and that when the Germans raided M. Guy's office and detained his wife, he went underground in Paris, and when he left for Algiers, Lefort took over from him.

On 4 February, Lefort received a phone call saying that the guide who had been due to collect Amery the next day had been arrested with all of Amery's papers on him and so Amery was hidden under the mansard roof of Lefort's apartment building. On 11 February, Claude Jolly was arrested and Amery was moved to Clichy and sheltered with Andrée Buizzone (query) on rue d'Alsace where he stayed for two weeks before returning to the Leforts for several more weeks – spending some of the weekends with Jacques Lefort's mother at Villiers-sur-Marne.[46] Finally Lefort contacted a Joe Lucien (query) who put him in touch with a Canadian Captain (Marcel Cola) who interrogated Amery and came on 13 March to say that Amery would be leaving the following night.

Jacques and Mariette Lefort, M. Roger, a coiffure who was Lefort's lieutenant, and a Mme Suzanne, who worked for Roger and did a lot of the organisation's leg-work, took Amery to gare Montparnasse the following evening. The Canadian Captain pointed out his guides who took Amery into a compartment on the train where he was soon joined by two more

46 IS9 has Jacque's parents, Fernand and Amelie Lefort, at 56 rue Mathilde Lapeyre, Chennevièressur-Marne.

Americans, Philip Capo and Kenneth Christian, who were brought by a man and a woman. They travelled overnight to Saint-Brieuc, where they changed for Châtelaudren.

Châtelaudren, Plouagat and Plouha

The first fourteen men to be taken off on this third Bonaparte operation were brought from Paris to Châtelaudren in three groups over two days, then driven to Plouha on the evening of Tuesday 14 March to be sheltered in and around the town for two nights until the evening of departure. The other eight men were brought to Châtelaudren in two groups the day before departure – they were sheltered overnight at two locations in nearby Plouagat before being driven to Plouha on the Thursday evening, along with two more Americans, Jack McGough and Ralph Patton.

Robert Fruth, Harold Vines, Edward Donaldson, Neelan Parker, Charles Winkelman and Joseph Birdwell arrived at Châtelaudren station at about nine-thirty on the morning of Monday 13 March. They passed through the control to be met by Georges Le Cun, a sandy-haired man wearing glasses. He led the six Americans along rue de la Gare, past the police station, to Rosalie Cardinal's café at 1 rue Sainte Magloire where they spent the rest of the day. That night, Fruth, Vines, Winkelman and Birdwell stayed at the café while Donaldson and Parker slept in Alphonse Le Friec's bicycle shop at 34 place de la Republique. The following afternoon, Georges Le Cun returned with "une splendide chien berger allemand" (Fifi), and instructed the six Americans to follow Alphonse's daughter Alice, who led them out of the village in pairs, while Le Cun and Fifi went back to the station to collect a second group of airmen. Alice led the six Americans a little way out of the village to an embankment at le Bois-de-la-Salle where they waited until a truck arrived with the second group.

Manuel Rogoff, Shirley Berry, Russell Paquin, William Campbell, Frank Moast and William Spinning arrived at Châtelaudren station in the early afternoon of Tuesday 14 March. Their overnight train from Paris had been delayed for an hour leaving the capital and they didn't reach Saint-Brieuc, where they changed to the small local train for Châtelaudren, until mid-day.

They were met by Georges Le Cun on a bicycle, and Fifi, the Americans having been told that their guide would be wearing a white raincoat and have newspaper in his left pocket, and as they got off the train, he would stroke his hair as a sign of recognition. The hand-over worked perfectly although as it was just the six Americans who got off at the little country station, Spinning says that they felt rather conspicuous.

Georges and Fifi led the six airmen through the western outskirts of Châtelaudren, where everyone but the two Germans sitting outside the police station seemed to know who they were. They took the Guingamp road as far as Plouagat then turned right and over the railway line to la ferme de Kerjagu, where Jean-Marie Le Sommier gave them lunch – it is not recorded what reception Fifi received from Jean-Marie's two dogs. At about three-thirty that afternoon, they were collected by a man in a small truck and driven to an embankment where they picked up Fruth, Vines, Donaldson, Parker, Winkelman and Birdwell before going on to a wood where they were dropped off to wait while the truck went back to collect two more airmen. Huguen says that while they waited at the Bois de Beauchamp, Rogoff, his burned face disguised with dark glasses and a wide-brimmed hat, kept himself amused watching Fifi as she jumped over obstacles.

> *Huguen (1976) also says that Christophe Jézégou (from Plouagat), who worked with Mathurin Branchoux, and local Resistance chief Alphonse Le Friec, were involved in guiding some of the airmen but I am basing this story around the evader reports, and I'm not really certain who took who, or exactly where they may have taken them.*

Dennis Brown and Charles Cregger left Paris by early morning train on Tuesday 14 March, arriving at Saint-Brieuc station a few minutes after six that afternoon, just in time to catch a 6.30 local train to Châtelaudren.

At Châtelaudren they showed the papers given to them by Marcel Cola that allowed them to enter the coastal zone, and simply walked out of the station behind their guide. There was a new guide waiting for them who signalled his presence by putting his hand over his hair. They followed the new guide, who spoke enough English to ask them if they wanted beer or cider, and a few minutes later, he led them into a café.[47] The proprietor directed them to a back room where they had a drink and some food, and were joined by their guide from Paris and some other men that Cregger thought were probably members of the organisation. The proprietor seemed to keep a roster of all the escapers who went through there because

47 Probably not Mme Cardinal's café at 1 rue Sainte Magloire as she makes no mention of them.

he came over to the guides with a notebook and talked to them. Brown and Cregger were told to hurry their meal and just before half past seven, they jumped into a truck to be driven north for about three miles before stopping at the top of small hill in the woods. Somebody whistled and a girl (Alice Le Friec) and twelve more evaders climbed into the truck. They waited for another half an hour until it got dark before driving to somewhere near Plouha where they all got out again.

On their arrival at Plouha on the evening of Tuesday 14 March, the fourteen airmen brought from Châtelaudren, were met and divided into three groups.

Rogoff, Donaldson, Parker, Campbell, Most and Spinning went with Alice Le Friec to a dress-makers shop. Spinning describes it as being "a large house at an intersection, across the road from a railway line". Their hostess ran a dress-making business on the ground floor and the airmen were hidden in a room that had been prepared for them on the upper floor. Germaine Couffon, who had four young girls working for her, was about fifty years old, with dark curly hair, and a very ruddy complexion – she stood about 5 feet 7 inches tall, was stout, and wore glasses. Germaine and her mother looked after the Americans until the evening of 16 March when, at about seven o'clock, they were collected by Pierre Huet and taken on foot to another farmhouse. They met some armed Frenchmen and the chief, who gave them instructions, and then walked "several kilometres" to the beach. Two more men arrived and they were asked about sentries. The evaders' money was taken before they were led down to the beach, where they waited for about two hours until the boats arrived to take them off.[48]

Berry, Paquin, Fruth, Vines, Winkelman and Birdwell went with Marie-Thérèse Le Calvez back to her mother's house where they stayed until the evening of 16 March when two men came and led them across the fields for a mile to a farmhouse.

Fruth reports that they stayed in the house all of Wednesday and Thursday, chatting and reading books, and listening to the radio. On the Thursday evening, they heard the radio message saying they were going that night, and were told to be ready to move at nine o'clock. They were taken to a barn in the fields where they joined another group of airmen, and an English-speaking guide who took all their money – he also gave one

48 Cregger (#470) is quite clear in saying it was the girl who rode with them on the truck who took the first six Americans while Marie-Thérèse Le Calvez says that she met Kerambrun's truck from Guingamp (or wherever) each time. None of the evaders mention Marie-Therese until meeting her at Plouha, and she doesn't mention ever going to Guingamp or Châtelaudren herself.

of the party a suitcase with secret papers and a bottle of brandy, together with instructions that it was to be destroyed rather fall into enemy hands.

Dennis Brown and Charles Cregger went with a man who had been with the twelve Americans waiting in the wood. He took them past the house (Kerisago) where Alice took her six men and on for another mile and a half to a policeman's house. The policeman lived with his wife and young son, and two other women but unfortunately, none of them spoke any English. Brown and Cregger stayed at the policeman's house until the Thursday evening when their guide returned with an older woman to take them to an "assembly point" where they joined the other evaders.

> *"The owner of the hotel [at Châtelaudren] then took us in his lorry towards the coast. After we had gone some way we got out and walked for several miles to a farmhouse where we met 14 members of the USAAF. Cregger and I spent the night at another farm and in the morning we were joined by three more Americans. That night six more Americans arrived. The following day (16 Mar) we were told to be prepared to leave.*
>
> *At about 2000 Cregger and I were taken by our host to an unoccupied barn still nearer the coast where the other 22 Americans had already congregated. With them was man who spoke good English who immediately started questioning us. He took away all the French money in our possession. I gave him 1200 French francs. He then led us in single file by a circuitous route to the coast, just north of Plouha. After we had waited on the beach for about an hour and a half four rowing boats came into the shore. I got into a boat with six others. It was manned by a two Naval ratings and a Naval officer who had a wireless transmitter. About three miles out we were transferred to a gunboat. We were told we were likely to run into German E boats. This did not occur although we passed a convoy which star shelled us but did not open fire. We disembarked at Dartmouth." (Brown WO208-5583/1848)*

The eight men brought from Paris to Châtelaudren (in two groups) on 15 March, stayed at nearby Plouagat overnight before being driven to Plouha on the evening of their departure for England.

Philip Capo, Kenneth Christian and John Amery arrived at Châtelaudren station on the morning of Wednesday 15 March. They were met by a guide (Le Sommier says this was Christophe Jézégou) who took them to the ferme de Kerjagu, near Plouagat where Amery describes Jean-Marie Le Sommier as being an oldish man who had been in the last war, with a son of about fourteen. Amery, Capo and Christian stayed at Kerjagu that night, and the following evening a truck arrived with two other Americans (McGough and Patton – see later) already on board. They drove to a canyon (sic) where they picked up three (sic) more Americans (assume Tate, Stump, Van Selus, Mielke and Lessig – see below) before driving to a back road and a house where they were given a meal. At 2245 hrs they were all taken to another house where they were interrogated by a short man with a moustache (Captain Short – André) (Dumais) before walking down to the beach where they were picked up by boat.

Dean Tate, Everett Stump, Carlyle Van Selus, Carl Mielke and William Lessig arrived at Châtelaudren station on the afternoon of Wednesday 15 March. Tate is the only one who gives any detail about the rest of their story, the other four reports all refer to his (which appears to be in his own hand-writing), and says they changed at Saint-Brieuc to a local train "for Guin (?)" – from which I am guessing that Tate never actually saw the name of the station where they got off. He says they were met by a guide who walked them four miles to a catholic school (assume l'Ecole Sainte-Thérèse at Plouagat) where they met two Canadian B.I.O.s (British Intelligence Officers), and spent the night there. Tate records that "At 1030 next morning, Thursday, we were briefed by one of the B.I.O.s who was a tremendous big man (Labrosse) who had been dropped in France by parachute several times (sic), once with two bicycles. The other B.I.O. (Dumais) said he thought that the Brest peninsula could be taken by a battalion of men."

Tate gives no details of how they got to Plouha, and then simply says that they "walked to the coast, saw no guards along the way. Climbed down a steep bank to the water and rowed out to the boat waiting for us at about 0130 hrs. Landed Dartmouth Mar 17, 1944."

The last two men brought out on this third Bonaparte operation were already in Brittany.

2/Lt Jack McGough (#475) and **2/Lt Ralph K Patton** (#476) were the bombardier and co-pilot of 94BG/331BS B-17 42-31212 (Johnson) which was returning from a morning raid to Bordeaux-Mérignac aerodrome (home to the Fw200 Condors of KG 40) on 5 January 1944 when they were shot down. Patton, McGough and their pilot 1/Lt Glenn Johnson (#493) all landed near to one another, probably not far from where their navigator Milton Church (#423) and radio operator Kenneth Blye (#424) came down (see earlier), and close to where their aircraft crashed at Kermorou, Kergrist-Moëlou.

Additional details are included from a post-war account written by Ralph Patton for his family in 1992, along with other correspondence between Patton and some of his war-time helpers, all kindly sent to me by his daughter Beverly Patton-Wand. Most of the previous references to Roger Huguen have been to his 1976 book "Par les nuits les plus longues" but for this section, I have again used information from his 2003 book, "La Bretagne dans la Bataille de l'Atlantique".

Glenn Johnson says that he bailed out at an estimated 6,000 feet and counted to five before pulling his rip-cord, seeing his aircraft crash into the ground as his parachute opened. He landed in an open field where a Frenchman (Huguen says he was the son of the local maire, Etienne Philippe) immediately tried to speak to him but Johnson could not understand what he was saying. The man took Johnson's parachute, which he hid in a hollow tree at the edge of the field before making a gesture that Johnson understood to mean he should go on his way. Johnson then spotted another airman running across the next field to a second airman in the adjoining field, and Johnson went to join them – they were his co-pilot Ralph Patton and bombardier Jack McGough.[49]

Jack McGough says that having heard the bail-out bell, when the aircraft levelled out, he opened the nose escape hatch and went out head-first. The Texan 28-year-old delayed opening his parachute for fear of hitting his own spiralling aircraft, and when he did, saw nine American and one German chute in the air. He made a good landing close to his burning aircraft, took off his parachute and began running towards two men who were nearing the ground. He saw that one of the parachutes was caught in a tree, and as he ran to help, recognised his co-pilot Ralph Patton coming towards him.

49 Yves André (now of Locarn) told Doug Doig and Yvonne Millar in September 2018, that he had been working in the fields at the farm of the Moulin de Kersault (about half-way between Locarn and Kergrist-Moëlou) when he saw a low-flying B-17, obviously in trouble. He watched as something fell away from the aircraft and then a parachute opened, and an airman landed just 200 metres away. He ran to where the flier was already rolling his chute up and he motioned to Yves to hide it, which he did, and the airman ran away. Another airman landed at Goaz Tériot, which is around 350 metres due north. I am guessing the first parachutist was Glenn Johnson.

Ralph Patton had only served for slightly less than two years in the Army but the 23-year-old year old clerk from Pennsylvania was already on his ninth mission when he followed bombardier (McGough) out of the escape hatch. He saw his aircraft crash and burn before landing in a tree close to a house where a group of five people stood watching him. On receiving no response to his declaration of being an American, Patton then spotted Jack McGough, and as they began heading out of the area together, they were joined by their pilot, Glenn Johnson.

Roger Huguen says that the three men landed near Petit Paris, which is just west of Kergrist-Moëlou, and then headed towards the bois de Kergrist. 17-year-old Joseph Pampanay, who was looking after some cattle at Kechenez-Argoat, found the three airmen at about four-thirty that afternoon while they were stopped at a white rock near le ferme de Villeneuve, and he gave them a casse-croûte of bread and bacon fat. The Americans then carried on walking, reaching Guernavalou (south-east of Plougonver) that evening where they were spotted by Désiré Géron. Désiré lived in Trémargat but was working at his parents' home in Guernavalou when he went to investigate the furious barking of one of the local dogs. He invited the three Americans into the house where they stayed for about an hour while Désiré contacted the maire of Trémargat, Louis Denmat at the Ferme de Laskibou. The maire agreed to shelter the airmen overnight, and next day, after consulting their escape maps, the Americans decided they would go south through Gouarec towards Pontivy.

During the afternoon of 6 January, they were picked up by a schoolmaster from Gouarec, although he soon left when he spotted a gendarme watching them. That evening, another Frenchman, this one about 24 years old, an ex-army officer from Gouarec, gave them some food and took them to hide in a field near Gouarec. That night they were joined by Norman King (shot down on the same raid as them), and one of their own waist-gunners, Isadore Viola. Next night, the same man took them part of the way to the Abbaye de Langonnet, about 4 kms south-west of Plouray, before leaving them with instructions not to travel at night because of the curfew, and a sketch map with directions to the Abbaye where he said that a friend of his would take them in.

2/Lt Norman R King (#494) was the 28-year-old navigator of 94BG/410 B-17 BS 42-30200 Slo Time Sally (Born) – the same aircraft as Ernest Hugonnet (#425) and others – see earlier.

The gloriously named Norman Rock King describes how they had been hit by flak over the target and then attacked by fighters. They lost touch with their formation and were losing altitude, despite having thrown all excess weight overboard, and were expecting to ditch in the Bay of Biscay when they reached the Brest peninsula. They called for fighter assistance and saw another B-17 in trouble before more enemy fighters appeared and the right waist-gunner (Schwartzburg) called over the intercom to report that the other bomber's tail had been shot off. Then Born gave the bail-out order and rang the warning bell, and King ripped off his head-set and ate his flimsies (secret instructions of the day, generally written on rice paper). They were down to about 8,000 feet and he already had his parachute on so went straight to the escape hatch, pulled the handle and dropped out.

King landed on the side of a small hill (presumably somewhere near Duault – see Hugonnet earlier) and as he gathered up his chute, found a farmer standing about 100 yards away, watching him. King ran to the farmer and while he was asking him to hide the parachute, a dozen or so other people arrived and to tell him that one of his comrades was being helped at a nearby farm. King went with them to the farm where he met Isadore Viola, waist-gunner of the B-17 he had seen in trouble earlier over Lorient. The two Americans were given bread and butter and some cider before being sent on their way.

S/Sgt Isadore Viola (#495) was the 29-year-old left waist-gunner B-17 42-31212 (Johnson). He describes how the aircraft went into a series of violent evasive manoeuvres. He already had his parachute on and when the tail broke off he was thrown back toward the tail with the right waist-gunner (S/Sgt William A Monson) landing on his feet, and as he struggled to free himself, the slipstream pulled him out of the aircraft. He thought they were at about 13,000 feet and he pulled his rip-cord as soon as he left the aircraft, playing dead in his harness when one of the German fighters came close as he drifted down.

Viola landed in the back garden of a farmhouse where the occupant immediately took his parachute and led Viola into his house. The man didn't understand Viola's English but still managed to convey the fact that a "comrade" was coming, and half an hour later, Norman King was brought in. Viola reports that when the Frenchmen started using the word "Allemand", he and King took off.

King and Viola walked east until it got dark, seeing the wreckage of Viola's aircraft smoking on a hillside. They got some food from an isolated farmhouse (Huguen says this was Auguste Bonhomme at Kernevez-Lann, Kergrist-Moëlou, which is south of Petit Paris) before walking on until midnight, when they went to sleep by a haystack.

They were found next morning by a small boy who took them into a house for a breakfast of bread and coffee before they carried on walking. They stopped at another farm at noon to show their silk escape maps and ask where they were. The family had seen their parachutes the previous day and gave the two airmen detailed paper maps of the area. After a meal of bread and butter, the boy took them to a house where the owner spoke some English. Although obviously frightened by the situation, the man gave them hot soup and put them to bed in his loft. Next morning, another man arrived who spent most of the day in an unsuccessful attempt to get them civilian clothes. That night, King and Viola were given a supply of bread and butter and set off walking once more, Viola now wearing a pair of ill-fitting rubber boots donated to replace the single flying boot he had arrived in. They were walking along a paved road – near a farm at Traou Bloavez, not far from Gouarec – in almost total darkness when they realised another group was passing them, and after some confusion, Viola recognised Glenn Johnson, Jack McGough and Ralph Patton as being officers from his own aircraft. They were being guided by a Frenchman, and King and Viola joined them.

The following morning (Saturday 8 January), the five Americans were nearing the Chapelle Saint-Guénin at Plouray when a man stopped them and took them to his house near the church, where he gave them some food. According to McGough, some twenty Frenchmen came in from round about, including François Dorlot, a crippled boy, about 17 years old, who lived in Plouray, and spoke some English. He told the Americans that he would bring them civilian clothes that night and hide them in some woods near Gourin. François then left and the man who had picked them up, hid them in a field near the church. René Le Louarn, son of bicycle-shop owner Joseph Le Louarn, and Joseph Marchadour, the butcher's boy from Plouray, stayed with them. An hour later, Marie Antoinette Piriou, the schoolmistress from Plouray, and Josephine Veley arrived with a young boy, Lucien Quilliou, who had seen the Americans on the road and told Mlle Piriou, his teacher at school, and Mlle Piriou asked them if they knew an American airman named Frank Greene. Jack McGough knew a man of that name (probably from his E&E lectures) and Mlle Piriou said that she had helped him get back to England and would do the same for them – this was S/Sgt Frank W Greene (#51) who was sheltered by Mlle Piriou for a month after his aircraft was shot down and crashed near Plouray in January 1943. At eight o'clock that evening, Mlle Piriou returned with François Dorlot, his father and uncle, and Josephine Veley and her fiancé Marcel Pasco (a sabotier – maker of wooden shoes). Two of the men carried Viola (because of his badly blistered feet) and the rest walked to Mlle Piriou's residence in the schoolhouse where her brother Alain was hiding from the Germans.

> *"All five of us were taken to the schoolhouse, Isadore (Viola) was carried all the way because of the massive blisters on his feet. Jack McGough and I slept in Toni's extra bedroom, formerly used by her brother Alain Kerisit, who slept in the Plouray Hotel, the Lion d'Or, operated by Mons Callac, who was a chief in the local resistance. Isadore and Glenn (Johnson) stayed with the parents of Josephine Veley at 31 rue de l'Elle, in a typical Breton home about 100 yards across the schoolyard from the school. Norman (King) stayed across the street at 28 rue de l'Elle with Marcel Pasco. Marcel had five brothers and sisters so Norman had to arrive after they had all gone to bed, and depart in the morning before they got up. The five of us spent all of our days in the schoolhouse, with three going out each night and coming back early in the morning, being careful not to be seen by anyone. One night it snowed a little and all concerned were worried about the footprints in the snow." (Patton 1992)*

Ralph Patton stayed with Mlle Piriou, and Norman King with the Pasco family, for six weeks. Jack McGough shared with Patton at the schoolhouse for five weeks before being taken to stay with the Dorlot family for a week. Glenn Johnson and Isadore Viola stayed with Josephine Veley and her parents until 13 February, when they were taken to stay with bicycle-shop owner Joseph Le Louarn.

While the five Americans were being sheltered in Plouray (their hair being trimmed by local tailor Charles Nicole, and much of their food provided by Joseph Marchadour's father), Mlle Piriou contacted her elder brother Jean (an ex-naval man and radio operator with an organisation in Auray) who came from Auray with a friend who brought civilian clothes. Jean apparently knew someone in Paris called Lucien but after a further two weeks with no answer, Mlle Piriou went to Gourin, and next day, the maire of Gourin, Alexis Kergaravat, a retired professor (of rue de Scaer), came to see the Americans. M. Kergaravat gave McGough 1,000 francs, and photographs were taken for those Americans who did not have them – he also said that papers would be procured and the Americans would return to England by boat.

Nothing much happened for the next month but then a coiffeur in Gourin – Roger Huguen says this was a M. Lacreu (nf) – whose father was influential in the organisation, came to interrogate the Americans (he had lived in New York for six years) and had new photographs taken. During their conversations, Viola heard that his navigator Milton Church was in the hands of the organisation in Gourin, along with two of King's crew – assume Harold Gilley and Robert Schwartzburg (see earlier) – along with another American they did not know. Meanwhile a quarrel had developed among the helpers in Plouray because Mlle Piriou was keeping them all while the other helpers wanted them distributed among them. During this time the head of a school in Priziac (an ex-lieutenant in the French army) came to Mlle Piriou's house and told her that he had a place to keep the Americans at Priziac. A few days later, a M. Theridaud drove Mlle Piriou, André Letoguenec (a friend of Mlle Piriou's from Pluvigner) and Ralph Patton to explain the situation to M. Kergaravat in Gourin and M. Kergaravat decided that the Americans should go to Priziac as soon as possible.

> *"The next day (Sunday) a young man, schoolteacher from Priziac, came to see Mme Piriou and she explained her troubles to him. This schoolteacher said he would return at 8 am the next day. Sunday afternoon a note came from Kergavanat saying that we should split up and Mme (Piriou) could keep 2 of us. That night they locked the five of us in and all of them went to Veley's for a meeting to smooth things over. While they were gone we heard a knock at the door, which we didn't answer. The man went around and knocked on the windows which we ignored until he gave the knock (the Morse code for V), so we opened the window. We thought he was the hotel keeper who was at Veley's so King told him to go to the door which he couldn't open. When King opened another window, King saw he was a stranger. This man asked for one of the people who were at Veley's so King sent him over to Veley's. Fifteen minutes later he came back with all the crowd from Veley's. This stranger was head of a school in Priziac, an ex-lieutenant in the French army.*

He had a place for us near Priziac. Two of us were to leave Monday night and on Tuesday, the other three were to leave. Sunday night, Patton and King slept in the schoolhouse, Viola and Johnson went to Louarn's and McGough stayed with François Dorlot. On Monday someone came with a note from Kergavanat saying we should stay in Plouray. We stayed until Thursday when André Letoguenec came in a car with two friends. Patton went in this car with Mme (Piriou) and Letoguenec and M Theridaud (the driver of the car) went to see Kergavanat and explained the situation. Patton said they wanted to avoid all trouble. Kergavanat decided that the five Americans should leave as soon as possible and sent a note ordering the others in Plouray to turn the others [Johnson, McGough and Viola] over to Mme (Piriou).

Friday night the five of us met at a party and talked over the plans and we all agreed to leave. Saturday night Patton left with King. Mme's brother (Alain) and Mons Daniel (Mme's assistant teacher) went ahead and arranged things in Priziac. Mme (Piriou) led them half way to Priziac and turned them over to three men from Priziac who took them to a bistro 7 kms from Priziac. Here Patton and King stayed together above the bistro (Jean Viola was responsible for keeping us – had wife, father-in-law, brother-in-law and 2 sisters-in-law 23-25 yrs old)." (Patton & McGough in MIS-X #476 Patton, with the spelling of some names corrected)

"Mme Piriou knew Mons Kergaravat who was a friend of Jean Bariou, a leader of the resistance in Brittany – and Mons Bariou knew Mathurin Branchoux from Guingamp who was part of the Shelburn network.

Mme Piriou had very wisely taken Louisette Penvern into her confidence when we five came to Plouray. Louisette was the telephone operator in Plouray. She was a very pleasant woman of 28 years. One day towards the middle of February 1944, two men came into the telephone exchange asking questions about airmen or parachutists in the region. They were not very specific but Louisette suspected that they were Gestapo and immediately contacted Mme Piriou.

Mme Piriou went to Gourin next day to inform Mons Kergaravat what had happened. She asked me if I would like to go with them. I agreed and we went off in the car driven by Mons Theridaud and drove into Gourin to the house of Mons Kergaravat. Two days later [on Monday 21 February] we were split up and moved out of Plouray. Norman (King) and I went about 5 kms down the road to the bistro of Louis Le Daeff, Louis' daughter Francine had married Jean Violo in January 1943 and was living in the Le Daeff home. Jean Violo was the prime mover in accepting Norman and me but his wife's two sisters (Yvonne and Marie) were in complete agreement and were willing helpers. The father, Louis, wasn't sure that this was a very good idea and was half scared to death during our two weeks here." (Patton 1992)

McGough's report says that he had been separated from Patton in Plouray on 13 February (although I don't know where he went) and a week later, McGough, Glenn Johnson and Isadore Viola were taken to Mlle Piriou's house, from where her brother Alain, M. Daniel and a hotel keeper called Carlac (query) led them as far as the Abbaye de Langonnet. They were handed over to André Le Fieur (nf) and Maurice, proprietor of the hotel in Le Croisty (assume Maurice Nestour), who took them within a mile of Priziac before the three Americans were separated again.

On 21 February, Patton and Norman King went to stay with the Le Daeff family at Keranna en Priziac, while McGough was sheltered in Le Croisty with Joseph Lucas (who had spent four years in the US and spoke fluent English), sharing with a Frenchman from Lorient called Joseph Jacques. Glenn Johnson was taken about 2 kms from Priziac and passed over to a schoolteacher (and local organisation chief) who placed him with cultivateur Roger Le Leannec and his brothers at nearby Le Rest, and Isadore Viola was sheltered with Priziac bistro proprietor Vincent Le Moual.

On 2 March, Patton and King were moved to a hotel directly opposite the Abbaye Notre-Dame de Langonnet (at Saint-Michel) – although they actually slept at Antoine Garnier's house at Tournebride, Langonnet, while the Garniers stayed in the hotel. A week later, they were moved once more, this time to a farm at Restembleye, about two kilometres from Langonnet to stay with Mme Le Naour (who spoke only Breton) and her sons Louis and Baptiste, where they were joined the same day (9 March) by Johnson and Viola.

On Tuesday 14 March, the coiffeur from Gourin (M. Lacreu) and another man came to Restembleye and told Patton, King, Johnson and Viola that they were leaving for England immediately. Baptiste Le Naour led them half a mile across country to a truck where they found McGough waiting.

McGough confirms that André Le Fieur and the coiffeur arrived unannounced at Le Croisty at about two o'clock in the afternoon to take him by truck to a shop in Langonnet where they picked up a boy who took them to collect Patton, Johnson, Viola and King. From there they drove to Gourin (Huguen says with M. Lacreu's sons, René and Désiré) where they missed the train and so spent the night at the coiffeur's house. Next day, they were handed over to a new guide – Johnson says his name was Paul (good looking, with straight, dark-brown hair, small scar high on left cheek, olive complexion, spoke good English) and that he claimed to have taken lots of evaders from Brest – this was Paul Le Baron. They caught the 1620 hrs train from Gourin and rode to Guingamp where they followed their guide off the train and he passed them over to three Frenchmen who were waiting for them.

While one of the men took Johnson, King and Viola (see later) another led McGough and Patton to rue de l'Etang du Prieuré where they were sheltered overnight with Désiré and Francine Laurent. The following afternoon, Mme Laurent told them they would probably leave for England that night (16 March) – which came as a surprise as they had been told they wouldn't be leaving until the twenty-first.

> *"At 1913 hrs a tall blond Frenchman arrived with another man, went in to listen to the radio, and then told them that all was right for their departure. They took Patton and McGough to a truck which was waiting outside, drove to a village where they picked up six (sic) more Americans and then leaving the main road, drove about two hours. The truck stopped in the countryside where a Frenchman met them and led the ten Americans in single file to a farmhouse where they were fed and stayed until 2245 hrs. They were then taken into the cellar of another house where they met another group of Americans and a British intelligence officer who interrogated them. Another American and an Englishman were brought in. They were then all led in single file to the beach where they waited until boats came in and took them aboard." (McGough MIS-X #475)*

The Appendix C of McGough's MIS-X report is nicely hand-written by his interviewing officer (S/Sgt Harold F Cherniss) but he seems to have skipped over a few details. I believe the six (sic) Americans were Dean Tate, Everett Stump, Carlyle Van Selus, Carl Mielke and William Lessig, collected from Plouagat, having already picked up Phillip Capo, Kenneth Christian and John Amery from ferme Kerjagu, to make up the ten Americans taken for a meal. The other American was Charles Cregger, and the Englishman, Dennis Brown.

Several evaders say they were taken to the cellar of a farmhouse prior to going down to the beach and whilst it seems tradition to assume that all evaders went to Jean and Marie Gicquel's house (the Maison d'Alphonse) at Saint-Samson, the Gicquel house (described by Jean Gicquel as being relatively small, consisting of two main rooms separated by a corridor, with an attic) didn't have a cellar. I suspect that many of them were actually gathered in the cellar of another building nearby, possibly the cellier (cellar or storehouse) close to the Ropers home at Camblac'h.

The twenty-four airmen almost didn't get away that night at all. For some reason, shortly before the third Bonaparte operation was due to take place, security along the coast was suddenly increased and local fishermen were prohibited from leaving port. Dumais considered cancelling the operation but there just wasn't enough time for Labrosse to get back to Paris and radio London. Then as MGB 502 was approaching her anchorage site off Le Taureau, and Dumais was able to speak to the gunboat by walkie-talkie radio, there were two explosions. Dumais was told the gunboat was pulling back but would try again later. Several more shots sounded (no-one seemed to know their source) followed by a long pause before the gunboat radioed Dumais to say they had returned. Shortly after that, four surf-boats approached the beach, two of them having to make a return journey as there were so many men to be taken onboard that night. By the time the gunboat was finally ready to leave, dawn was almost breaking and Peter Williams wanted to get away from the shore as quickly as possible but listeners on the beach could clearly hear the gunboat's engines and Dumais radioed for them slow down until they were further out. Fortunately none of the enemy seemed to notice the gunboat's presence and MGB 502 returned safely to her base.

> *"We arrived in the port city of Dartmouth, and were taken alongside an old white excursion boat that had had the engines removed. We were fed, took showers, and our French civilian clothes were taken and we were issued brand new British GI winter uniforms, and was that wool ever itchy. Farewell I said to my well worn striped pants, my somewhat worn gray jacket and my beloved beret. They had served me well. About noon time or shortly thereafter came the daily issue of English Grog, or what was one heck of a good mug of strong, hearty rum. The English Navy has this most wonderful custom, and since this old boat we were on was under the command of the Royal Navy, we were issued the rum too. Now why can't our Armed Forces also have such*

a delightful custom? Sometime later we were taken to the train station and boarded a train for London. We were warned to talk to no-one, and were put in well guarded and locked compartments." (William Campbell (#473) writing in January 1988)

SIS/MI9 Operation Bonaparte 4 (19-20 Mar 1944) MGB 503 (Mike Marshall)

Operation Bonaparte 3 seems to have taken most of the evaders being sheltered in Paris by reseau François. With the next evacuation from Plage Bonaparte scheduled for just three nights later – followed by another, three nights after that – subsequent evaders could be brought into the capital and moved on to Brittany with the minimum delay.

It is worth noting that apart from McGlynn and the four men who evaded in Brittany, many of the other twelve evaders taken out on this fourth Bonaparte operation were sheltered by the organisation in Chauny (Aisne), and all were helped by the organisation in Creil (Oise) before being passed to reseau François.

Also note that both groups of six airmen brought from Paris were taken to Châtelaudren and then walked to ferme Kerjaguat at Plouagat. All twelve were then collected by truck, which already had the other five evaders (brought from Guingamp) on board, and driven straight to Plouha on the night of their departure for England.

Because of the problems encountered by MGB 502, Dumais had decided to abandon any subsequent Bonaparte operations – he told François Le Cornec that he had sent Labrosse to Paris the day before to have the shipments cancelled, although he was still in Plouha himself on the morning of 19 March. François Le Cornec pointed out to Dumais that he had witnessed Labrosse at his house trying to contact London for three consecutive days once before and there was no guarantee he would be able to get through in time. Dumais wanted to get back to the capital and agreed to let Le Cornec make the necessary arrangements should Labrosse have failed to pass the message to London. Dumais took a bus to Guingamp that afternoon (along with Francis Baudet, who went to warn François Kerambrun to have his lorry available), where he stayed until evening when they heard the BBC message confirming the operation was going ahead that night, after which he took the train for Paris.

2/Lt Robert O Lorenzi (#489), **2/Lt Robert L Costello** (#490), **2/Lt Paul R Packer** (#491) and **S/Sgt Edward J Sweeney** (#492) were the pilot, co-pilot, navigator and engineer of 452BG/730BS B-17 42-31325, and the raid to Frankfurt on 8 February 1944 was their first operational mission. The aircraft was hit by flak over the target which damaged the superchargers on #3 and #4 engines, causing them to drop out of formation. They dived for cloud cover when they were attacked by fighters and were down to about 5,000 feet when they realised their chances of reaching England were gone, and so headed for France. As they came out from the cloud, they were hit by the flak defences at Montdider aerodrome, and with the bomber on fire, Lorenzi ordered his crew to bail out, leaving the aircraft to crash near Le Cardonnois (Somme).

Lorenzi was just twenty-one years old when he jumped from the bomb-bay of his stricken aircraft. He landed flat on his face, and because he had been wounded in the foot by flak, and was unable to run and spill his parachute, he began cutting the shrouds with his knife. Before he could finish untangling himself, he was found by Lucienne Mortier and her cousin Charlotte Bizet who took his flying kit and helped him into the village of Pérennes (Oise) and a barn on the Mortier family farm. He was hidden in the straw and given whisky, and one of the women brought him a fried egg. He was told that a doctor would visit him, and that afternoon, he was taken into the farmhouse where Doctor de Léaucourt plied Lorenzi with more alcohol before taking some metal from his foot. That evening, Albert Antoine and Marcel Gibert arrived with a cart to take Lorenzi to the Gibert farm at Sains-Morainvillers where he was given a meal and some morphine and left to rest but after an hour's sleep, was woken up to find his co-pilot, Robert Costello, and navigator, Paul Packer, had joined him.

Costello followed the engineer, Sweeney, out of the nose hatch, landing in open ground but then had a similar problem to Lorenzi in that he was unable to spill his parachute, and wound up being dragged some distance before he finally managed to get out of his harness, the parachute then blowing away and disappearing. He ran towards some woods, with a small group of men in pursuit, picking up his discarded kit as they followed him. One of the men caught up with him, and having established that Costello was an American, ran with him. Costello spotted Packer cutting across the fields and whistled and signalled for him to follow at a distance until they were led to a house.

Packer says the nose of their aircraft "looked like a sieve" as he went out of the front escape hatch, pulling his rip-cord as soon as he cleared the falling bomber. He landed hard next to a clump of trees and was still unbuckling his parachute harness when two Frenchmen arrived to ask him who he was. When he told them he was an American, they grabbed his flying kit and directed him across the field. As he was running, he spotted two other men, recognising one of them as his co-pilot, Robert Costello, and he followed them to a farmhouse.

Pierre Bruyant, who worked at the Gibert farm at Sains-Morainvillers, hid Costello and Packer under a cart-load of hay and had his mare Mousmee take them to Fay Wood in La Morlière Wood. They were told to wait there, and so took it in turns to doze until two Frenchmen brought them some wine, brandy and water. Later that evening, the same two men took the airmen to the Chateau de la Borde where the owner, comte Jacques de Baynast, swopped his fur-lined coat for Packer's leather flying jacket, gave them a meal and asked them to hand over anything that might identify them as Americans. After another short rest, Albert Antoine arrived with his cart to take them to the Gibert farm at Sains-Morainvillers, where they joined their pilot, Robert Lozenzi.

Doctor Edmond Caillard arrived from Saint-Just-en-Chaussée at about midnight to take charge of the airmen. They were delayed in leaving by the presence of a group of gendarmes, curious that lights were on in the house that late at night, but once they had left, Dr Caillard drove the three airmen in his Simca, taking Lorenzi to Lorteil, where he was sheltered with the elderly Raoul and Marie Bilcoq, and Costello and Packer to Pierre Coulon in Bulles, where they were joined by Lorenzi on 11 February.

Sweeney says he jumped from about 3,000 feet and delayed opening his parachute until about 1,000 feet. In trying to avoid coming down near a man he saw running below, he spilled his parachute too much and landed flat on his back with the chute caught on a barbed-wire fence. Two men were watching from a nearby wood but they declined to come over and then when two teenage boys, Jacques Mortier and his cousin Michel Bizet (younger siblings of the two girls who found Lorenzi), approached, Sweeney was unable to understand what they said to him. Sweeney took off his parachute, harness and Mae West, which prompted the two men to run over and grab them, and then a third man, André Durot of nearby

Abbemont farm, appeared and showed Sweeney on his escape map where he was before advising him to head north. Sweeney was faced by a large open field and while he was hesitating, reached into one of his pockets, dislodging a religious medal. On seeing that Sweeney was a catholic, André Durot led Sweeney to a barn, and later returned with his wife bringing food. Sweeney was taken by horse and cart to another barn where he was hidden in the hayloft.

It was dark when a priest named Louis Dutriaux arrived. Dutriaux (aka Berthelot) was head of the OCM group in Maignelay, and he took Sweeney on foot to his presbytery in nearby Ferrieres. Later that same evening, Sweeney was taken to another house in the village where he was sheltered by Noel Jacot des Combes. Sweeney stayed the rest of the night and all next day with Noel Jacot, and that evening, received a visit from Colette de Baynast who told him that Lorenzi, Costello and Packer were also being taken care of locally and were safe. On the evening of 9 February, Noel Jacot took Sweeney to stay overnight with his neighhbour on the same street, racing driver Louis Gerard – Gerard had moved to Ferrieres shortly before the war and set up a chicken hatchery. Sweeney was returned to Noel Jacot's house the following afternoon, and that evening, Noel walked with Sweeney to the Château de La Borde (where Lorenzo, Costello and Packer had rested the previous evening). At about midnight, a doctor (almost certainly Edmond Caillard again) drove Sweeney to Saint-Just-en-Chaussée and 7 rue de Catillon, home of Jean Crouet, where Sweeney spent the rest of the night and following day. That evening (12 Feb), Sweeney was taken to Bulles where he stayed overnight with station-master Edouard Bruerre, and next day joined Lorenzi, Costello and Packer at Pierre Coulon's house.

Much of the finer detail in this account is taken (in consultation, and with permission) from Dominique Lecomte's 2006 book "Tail End Charlie", published by Cercle Maurice-Blanchard of Montdidier, and additional information he has gathered since.

While the four airmen were sheltered in Bulles with Pierre Coulon, they had an unexpected visitor. It was Jacky du Pac, who had come to verify that they were in fact downed American aircrew – he talked about America, deliberately making errors that the airmen quickly realised they had to correct in order to prove their identities.

They stayed with Pierre Coulon for twelve days before being collected by truck and taken to Montataire, just outside Creil. Lorenzi and Packer were sheltered by Marie Dorez and her daughter Jacqueline at 4 rue de Condé – Mme Dorez was a dairy wholesaler – while Costello and Sweeney stayed with Jules and Hortense Duchateau at 21a rue de Condé – Jules was a hairdresser by trade but worked at the local Marinoni factory, and Hortense worked for Marie Dorez, selling produce.

"On the first Sunday that Lorenzi and Packer spent there, Mme Dorez and her daughter Jacqueline went to church. When they came back they were accompanied by Jacqueline's elder sister Genevieve and her husband Edmond Bourge. It was Edmond Bourge who supplied the first false papers for the airmen. Edmond and Genevieve lived with Edmond's mother and her husband Raymond Stubert on rue Henri Pauquet in Creil, who were themselves sheltering two more American evaders, Earl Wolf (#487) and Leonard Bergeron (#488), who one day joined Lorenzi and Packer for lunch." (Dominique Lecomte email to the author)

The NARA file for Mme Marie Dorez (née Horidor) of Montataire doesn't tell us much beyond saying that she was 47 years old, and had two children (aged 19 and 20). Her husband Fernand had been gassed in the First War and in very poor health – he died in 1945. Mme Dorez had sheltered Kenneth Morrison (#690) in January 1944 – and Milton Mills (#689) briefly before he moved to stay with the Duchateau family on the same road. Her elder daughter Genevieve was married to Edmond Bourge (see below). (My thanks to Mme Vve Jacqueline Muller (née Dorez) for the information about her father)

Jules Duchateau (born January 1890) of 21 rue de Condé, Montataire was married to Blanche (née Verkomst) with a son, Paul (born October 1917). They sheltered Milton Mills (#689) from 10 to 25 January 1944, and Robert Costello and Edward Sweeney from 15 February to 16 March 1944 – all received from, and returned to, Mme Dorez (who helped support them) by Edmond Bourge. (My thanks to Nicole Coffin, grand-daughter of Jules Duchateau, who explained to Dominique Lecomte that her grand-mother Blanche was always known as Hortense)

Edmond René Victor Bourge (born May 1921) was married to Genevieve (née Dorez March 1922). They lived at at 61 rue Henri Pauquet in Creil with Edmond's mother and her husband Raymond Stubert – Edmond's father (Edmond Désiré Bourge) had died in 1936 and his mother Suzanne (née Guyard 25 Oct 1897) married Raymond Stubert in May 1938. Like the Dorez family, the Stuberts had a dairy business which they ran from their home.

Often travelling on his motorcycle, Edmond is credited with helping some 25 Allied evaders, guiding some parties himself and recruiting other guides as well as finding safe lodgings and providing false papers – he was recommended for the King's Medal for Courage.

Lorenzi and Packer stayed in Montataire with the Dorez family, and Costello and Sweeney with the Duchateaus, for four weeks until 16 March when Marie Dorez and her son-in-law Edmond Bourge, drove the four airmen to Creil. They were joined by 1/Lt Earl Wolf and S/Sgt Leonard Bergeron, and 2/Lt Clyde Richardson and 2/Lt Richard Schafer who had recently joined Wolf and Bergeron at the Stubert-Bourge home on rue Henri Pauquet. At the railway station they met René Loiseau and Genevieve de Poulpiquet who had come from Paris to collect them. René Loiseau took Lorenzi, Packer, Costello and Sweeney, while Wolf, Bergeron, Richardson and Schafer travelled with Genevieve de Poulpiquet, on the train to the capital.

1/Lt Earl J Wolf Jnr (#487) and **S/Sgt Leonard F Bergeron** (#488) were the co-pilot and right waist-gunner of 306BG/423BS B-17 42-31388 (Di Betta) which, according to Wolf "got lost" on the way to Frankfurt on 11 February 1944. In such circumstances, they had been instructed to bomb any suitable city in Germany, but on dropping their bombs on a "good-sized town" they were hit by flak which damaged all four engines. They fell out of formation and fired green flares as a signal to friendly fighters that they were in trouble but despite their P-47 escort, were attacked by German fighters, and with the bomber leaking fuel, it was abandoned to crash near Campremy (Oise), about 20 kms north-east of Beauvais.

Four other crew also evaded successfully: pilot 1/Lt Geno Di Betta (#962), radio operator T/Sgt Clyde E Hewitt Jnr (#1058), left waist-gunner S/Sgt Guy H Golden Jnr (#1000) and tail-gunner S/Sgt Eldo C Weseloh (#1001) were all taken (with others) to Clermont before going in various groups to the MI9 Mission Marathon camp at Freteval, from where they were liberated in August 1944.

Wolf says that when Di Betta passed the verbal order to bail out – the intercom and alarm bell having been shot out – he followed the engineer (T/Sgt Fortunate V Chiccarelli) and bombardier (1/Lt Jerrell E Sanders) through the escape hatch. He jumped at an estimated 11,000 feet but delayed pulling his rip-cord until entering clouds at about 2,000 feet before making an "easy" landing in a field. He says that it looked as though the entire population of the nearby town (Wavignies) had turned out to meet him. Wolf's close-cropped hair made them suspect he might have been German but his parachute with USA on it apparently convinced them of his nationality, as one man took his flying gear while another led Wolf to a nearby house. He used his phrase card to ask for civilian clothes, and while he was handing out American cigarettes, they were brought to him. Shortly after that, a man arrived who arranged his journey.

The man was Dr Edmond Caillard, and he took Wolf back to his house on rue Valentin Hauy in Saint-Just-en-Chaussée. Shortly after that, a woman took Wolf to a room above a local café where he was joined by his pilot, Gino Di Betta. That evening, the two Americans were taken back to Dr Caillard's house, and he drove them to Bulles, where they were sheltered with Pierre Coulon, his wife Albertine and their two daughters on rue du Mesnil. Next morning, Pierre Coulon took Wolf and Di Betta to the Café du Bon Coin, where the owner, M. Vanhoudeusden, was a local resistance leader. They were hidden in the cellar until Dr Gaston Redaud arrived later that day to take them to Clermont, and his house on rue d'Amiens where they met his wife and four young children. One morning (date not stated), France-Raphaële Fleury and Gaston Redaud's son Didier walked the two airmen to her parents house on rue de Mouy, where they joined their tail-gunner, Eldo Weseloh.

Georges Charles Adrien Fleury (born January 1890) was the maire of Rémécourt, a small village a few miles north-east of Clermont, and head of the OCM for Centre-Oise. Georges lived with his wife Rachel Clothilde (née Levasseur July 1893) and their two daughters, France-Raphaële and Annette, in a large three-story house set back from the road at 25 rue de Mouy (now rue Pierre Vienot). Their son Alain (mentioned earlier) worked for the organisation as a convoyeur, taking evaders to Creil and Paris.

In addition to those mentioned in this story, other airmen that I know to have been helped by the Fleury family are eight men from B-17 42-3452 – John Wagner (#254), Arthur Vetter (#260), Edward Fontaine (#275),

Warren Lush (#310), James Bormuth (#311), Edward Daly (#653), Hobart Trigg (#654) and Wendell McConnaha – who were joined on 24 September 1943 by William Boren (#194) and Francis Anderson (#309) from the B-26 Cactus Jack, before being taken to Paris the following month.

Leonard Bergeron says that he, radio operator (Clyde Hewitt) and their left waist-gunner (Guy Golden) were all hesitant about leaving the aircraft, 24-year-old Bergeron jumping first from about 7,000 feet, delaying slightly before opening his parachute and landing in a wooded area. He saw two of his crew, who turned out to be Hewitt and Golden, and walked over to join them. They were soon helped, brought food and their journeys arranged.

Bergeron's MIS-X report gives no details of his evasion (and neither Hewitt or Golden give many clues) but a combination of research by Dominique Lecomte, some scribbled notes in Wolf's file, and other evader reports, tells at least part of the story.

Bergeron, Hewitt and Golden all landed close to one another near the hamlet of Wariville, near Litz (about 8 kms NW of Clermont) where they were helped by Pierre Pouly who took them back to his house in Gicourt (near Agnetz) on a trailer behind his tractor. Although not listed by IS9 as a helper, M. Pouly had contacts, including Dr Roger Bouchard who took the three airmen into Clermont to be sheltered with Odette Sauvage and Gaston Legrand on rue du Chatellier – where they joined two black South African soldiers, Donald Retief and David Abrahams, who had been captured at Tobruk, escaped from a camp at Beauvais and had been sheltered by François Louis in Bonvillers.

Dr Roger Bouchard (born July 1897) of 33 place de l'hôtel-de-Ville, Clermont was married to Claire (born July 1903) and had three children, Guy (born August 1927), Arlette (born January 1936) and Yves (born January 1937). Roger was the maire of Clermont, a veteran from the first war and chief of the local OCM group until being threatened with denouncement and forced to leave the area after helping the three Americans. His daughter Arlette recalls that in order to protect the family (who knew very little about his resistance activities at the time) he left a note to his wife telling her that he had abandoned them. Dr Bouchard is also credited with helping T/Sgt

John Wagner (#254), treating his injured ankle while he was sheltered with Odette Sauvage and Gaston Legrand in September 1943.

After about a week in Clermont with Odette Sauvage and Gaston Legrand, Edmond Bourge arrived with a truck to take Bergeron, Hewitt and Golden (along with Wolf, Di Betta and Weseloh, who had been sheltered with the Fleury family), first to Creil, where Bergeron was delivered to Raymond and Suzanne Stubert at 61 rue Henri Pauquet, then Gouvieux (about 10 kms south of Creil) where Wolf, Hewitt and Golden were sheltered with Inocente and Betty Lauro at 1 bis rue de Boran, and then to Vineuil-Saint-Firmin where Di Betta and Weseloh were sheltered with Henri Lestienne for the next six weeks.

It was while Bergeron (who was born in Canada and spoke good French) was staying with Raymond and Suzanne Stubert that Doctor Georges Debray took him to visit the injured T/Sgt Chiccarelli at Creil hospital. Bergeron was able to visit him a second time, the day before Chiccarelli was transferred to a hospital in Beauvais, where he was discovered a few days later by the Germans and captured. (Dominique Lecomte email to the author)

Earl Wolf was only with the Lauro couple for two days before he was taken to stay with a butcher in Gouvieux (possibly Paul Prebay) who lodged Wolf in a room above his shop. About a week later, Edmond Bourge arrived on his motorcycle to take Wolf back to Creil where he joined Bergeron at the Stubert-Bourge home on rue Henri Pauquet. During their stay with the Stuberts, they spent Sundays visiting Lorenzi and Packer at Montataire where (as already mentioned) they were being sheltered with Marie Dorez, and Jacky du Pac came to interrogate them. Shortly before they left for Paris there was a warning that the Germans were going to raid the Stubert home, so the two Americans were moved a few kilometres north-east, to Villers-Saint-Paul, where they were sheltered briefly with Englishman Charles Warren (and his German-born, Jewish wife) on rue des Marquets until Edmond Bourge returned them, one at a time on his motorcycle, to rue Henri Pauquet.

1/Lt Francis P Hennessy (#496) was the 27-year-old pilot of 388BG/526BS B-17 42-3285 Mary Ellen on a morning operation to Frankfurt on 29 January 1944. As they turned away after dropping their bombs on target, their #1 engine failed and the propeller wouldn't feather, causing them to lose speed. As they dropped out of formation, they were attacked by fighters which shot away the aileron controls. With the fighters continuing their attacks, and Hennessy controlling the aircraft with a combination of trim-tabs and AFC, they levelled off at about 3,000 feet. About an hour from their target, they spotted a formation of B-17s and their P-38 escorts, and flew along below them but just before they reached the French coast, were attacked by three German fighters which damaged their starboard wing and put the bomber into a dive. Hennesey pulled up about 1,800 feet, but with three engines stopped and a wing on fire, he gave the bail-out order and the aircraft was abandoned.

Hennessy landed near Le Cateau-Cambrésis (Nord) and a few minutes later found his top-turret gunner, T/Sgt Lewis F Pursley who had broken his leg. Two Frenchmen arrived to take care of Pursley, and Hennessy was told to clear the area as quickly as possible.

Hennessy spent the next three and a half days walking generally south, passing through Busigny, where a crippled young man and his wife gave him a meal and a civilian coat, Bohain-en-Vermandois, where a man gave him a meal and directions, through Saint-Quentin where a farmer also gave him food, and Saint-Simon (Aisne) where he was hidden in a stable and given food while a man went to fetch a gendarme but never returned. Hennessy went on to spend his third night hidden in a hayshed while a railway agent gave him food and shelter for the night. Next morning, he was given coffee, warned him to stay away from the railway lines (which were presumably guarded) before continuing south-west towards Noyon. At about noon on a cold and wet fourth day, Hennessy was somewhere north-west of Chauny when saw some smoke in the woods, and on approaching the fire, found two young wood-cutters. They gave him food and sent for an English-speaking Frenchmen who took Hennessy by truck to a large farm on the eastern outskirts of Chauny.

Hennessy was questioned to confirm his identity then "fed, shaved and bathed". A little while later Jacqueline Boury (daughter of Dr Jacques Boury) and Mme Fourrey (wife of surgeon Jacques-Paul Fourrey) arrived to tell Hennessy that he would be back in England within four days. Mme Fourrey returned at six that afternoon and took Hennessy by bicycle until she passed him on to Mlle Boury, who took Hennessy the rest of the way into Chauny. She took him to 23 rue Camille Desmoulins, home of Emile Gossart, whose wife Irene worked for Dr Fourrey – they were already sheltering Richard Schafer (#499), who confirmed that Hennessey was indeed a fellow American airman. Hennessy was then visited by a man that he calls "the chief" – young, dark and with a wooden leg – this was Etienne Dromas, leader of the Chauny-Dromas organisation, who interrogated Hennessy before having his photograph taken for an identity card. Hennessy stayed with Emile and Irene Gossart for a week – during which time he and Schafer were joined by Paul Dicken (#500) – before Hennessy was taken to the Garage Saint Charles on rue du Brouage to be sheltered by Alfred Logeon and his daughter Ginette, where he met his navigator Clyde Richardson (#497).

Etienne Dromas (born December 1911), who lived with his wife Renée at the mairie in Ugny-le-Gay, headed the organisation in Chauny (Aisne). Founded in late 1942, it was intended as a temporary refuge for evaders until they could be passed on to other lines – notably Comète and Bourgogne, and later Shelburn – but after D-Day, the organisation evolved to shelter men in the local area until Allied forces advancing from the Normandy beach-heads could liberate them. The Chauny organisation is credited with helping at least 87 Allied evaders, and Dromas was recommended for the King's Medal for Service.

2/Lt Clyde C Richardson (#497) was 24-year-old navigator and only other successful evader of the B-17 42-3285 Mary Ellen (Hennessy). He says that when he heard the bail-out bell, he released the nose hatch door and went straight out, seeing his co-pilot (2/Lt Edward I Neft) leaving via the bomb-bay. Like Hennessy, Richardson also landed near Le Cateau-Cambrésis, and about 150 yards from Neft – although he makes no further mention of his co-pilot in his report. Richardson collected up his parachute and Mae West and put them into a ravine before changing into the cadet shoes that he had (very sensibly) attached to his parachute harness.

Over the next three days, Richardson headed generally south. Towards the end of the first day, a young man took him to his home somewhere between Bohain-en-Vermandois and Wassigny where he was sheltered overnight and given civilian clothes. Next morning, the young man's brother walked with him to Wassigny and gave Richardson a map of Aisne. Near Mesnil-Saint-Laurent (just SE of Saint-Quentin), Richardson was given dinner by a Polish couple, and then as he was approaching Quierzy, M. and Mme Brochard took him in. He was sheltered at Ercuis with the

Brochard family, Maurice, Fernande and their two daughters, Denise (22) and Jeannine (18), for two or three days before two men (one of whom, balding and wearing horn-rimmed glasses, spoke English) came in a green car to interrogate him. The two men returned later and drove him to Blérancourt (Aisne) and what he describes as "Morgan's Castle" – where he met Mme Marguerite Morgan (nf) – before being returned to the Brochard farmhouse. Two days later, the same English-speaking Frenchman took him back to Morgan's Castle where he was transferred to an ambulance and driven to the Garage Saint Charles in Chauny. Ginette Logeon asked him if he knew Francis Hennessy, and Richardson gave her one of his dog-tags, and that night Hennessy was brought to the garage to join him.

After a meal at the garage, Richardson and Hennessy were taken to stay with the elderly Mme Vve Bachelet at 22 rue de Noyon, where they were also helped by relatives of Mme Bachelet, butcher René Felix and his wife. They say they were aware of other Americans being helped in Chauny but didn't meet any of them. After two weeks with Mme Bachelet, they were taken to stay overnight with René Felix at 26 rue du Brouage and given identity cards. The following morning, Alfred Logeon took them by train to Creil where, after coffee at a café, they were taken to the home of an unnamed man (with some missing fingers) for a few hours before crossing the road to a bar. They were passed on to Marcel Gerardot, director of a local boiler factory, who took the two Americans back to his house at 107 rue Henri Pauquet, where his wife Renée spoke fluent English.

Alfred Logeon (born June 1890), garage proprietor of 24 rue du Brouage in Chauny, is credited with sheltering and helping some fifty to sixty Allied evaders. Alfred and his wife had three daughters, and he and their eldest daughter Ginette also convoyed several parties of evaders.

René Felix (born November 1903), of 26 rue du Brouage in Chauny, is credited with sheltering 19 Allied evaders, as well as helping many more.

That evening, Hennessy and Richardson were separated, and Hennessy was taken to stay with railway worker François Maizieres and his telephone operator wife at 1 rue des Deux Villes. Hennessy stayed for three weeks with the Mazieres family, during which time he was taken to spend a day with Mme Mazieres' parents, near Lassigny. On 17 March, Mme Maizieres took him to the Stubert-Bourge home (at 61 rue Henri Pauquet) where he joined Elmer Risch, Paul Dicken and William Scanlon, and a young man from Paris took them to the station, Mme Gerardot meeting them on the way and giving them their tickets for the train to Paris.

Meanwhile, Clyde Richardson had been taken to nearby Nogent-sur-Oise to stay with André Marcel Labydt (born July 1913) and his mother Germaine at 74 avenue Claude Peroche – Mme Labydt was a perfumier and chiropodist – where he joined William Scanlon (#501). Richardson and Scanlon had to move from the Labydt home after two weeks as André had been called up for compulsory labour service (STO) and rather than go to Germany, he had "skipped".

Richardson was taken back into Creil on 6 March, and 13 rue Charles Somasco where he joined Richard Schafer (#499) who was being sheltered by Paul Toussaint. One evening, they were taken to a cheese shop (Bourge) at 61 rue Henri Pauquet where they met Lorenzi, Costello, Packer, Sweeney, Wolf and Bergeron. They were questioned by Jacky du Pac in his role as a British Intelligence Officer, and a woman in a large hat (Genevieve de Poulpiquet) before being taken to Paris on 16 March.

2/Lt Richard F Schafer (#499) was the 23-year-old pilot of 389BG/564BS B-24 42-63973 which was shot down on 30 December 1943 – see Morton Shapiro (#353) earlier. They were on the way to Ludwigshaven and still had their Spitfire escort at about ten o'clock that morning when they were hit by flak which stopped their #1 engine. They were then attacked by fighters which sent the bomber into a spiral dive. Schafer gave the bail-out order and waist-gunner Paul Dicken (#500) jumped (see below) before Schafer regained control, pulled out of the dive and cancelled the order. However the aircraft was then flying in circles with engines #2 and #3 running away, the bail-out order renewed and Schafer followed the rest of his crew out of the stricken aircraft at an estimated 1,500 feet.

Schafer's foot was caught in his parachute shrouds when he pulled the rip-cord and on hitting the ground, broke his left leg. He managed to gather up his chute and crawl to a nearby ditch, trying to avoid detection by circling German aircraft, and continuing along the ditch until he was found by a young man who took Schafer back to his house.

Schafer landed south of Noyon (Oise) near the little village of Chiry-Ourscamp, and the young man (about 25 years old, 5 feet 5 inches tall, with black hair and brown eyes) took him to a house just outside the village where four women, three young boys and an elderly man gave Schafer civilian clothes and arranged to have him taken in a coal truck to Chauny. After a visit to the station to have the coal weighed, Schafer was taken to a surgeon. The surgeon initially declined to help Schafer but when they left, he followed the coal truck in his car. Schafer was taken to the home of a Belgian ex-officer where he was put to bed and that evening, the surgeon, Dr Jacques-Paul Fourrey (about 50 years old, fat and balding) came with his wife to see him. They put a splint on Schafer's leg and then drove him to the upstairs apartment of Henri Magne (about 32 years old, 5 feet 5 inches tall, black hair and with a missing leg, he spoke English and was the director of Banque L Dupont). Also in the apartment were M. Magne's wife, mother-in-law and a six-year-old child. M. Magne questioned Schafer about his aircraft and squadron (which Schafer refused to answer) and told him that he had previously sheltered an RAF airman, and a Canadian flyer called Ginger – this was Sgt Wallace E Phillips (1268) who was treated by the surgeon and then sheltered in Chauny from 17 April to 15 May 43, and Sgt John D Duncan RCAF (1388) who was sheltered in Chauny for 8 days in July 43 – both were later passed on to Bourgogne.

Next day (31 Dec), Dr Jacques Boury (described by Schafer as being about 45 years old, 6 feet 1 inch tall with sandy coloured hair) and his daughter Jacqueline (18 years old, 5 feet 3 inches tall with black hair and blue eyes) came to visit. Both of them spoke English, and this time Schafer did answer their questions. The doctor apparently told Schafer that he would be back in England within five days.

Doctor Jacques Boury (born January 1895) of 4 rue de la Paix, Chauny was married to Annette (née Lefebvre) and with a teenage daughter, Jacqueline. His IS9 recommendation for the King's Medal for Courage says that he provided shelter for some 39 Allied evaders, many of whom remained with him and his family for periods of between two weeks and a month – the first four being F/O Stanley Everiss (1271), Sgt John Ford (1327) and Sgt Wallace Phillips (1268) from Stirling BK725, and Sgt Hugh McKinnon from Wellington HE550, all helped by the organisation in Chauny in April 1943. "Whenever necessary he provided prompt and adequate medical attention, doubtless saving the lives of several evaders who were seriously wounded." His Helper file says he used his medical skills to treat 19 Allied evaders, 10 of whom were seriously wounded.

Dr Boury names M. Magne, directeur of the Banque Dupont at Saint Quentin, M. Obled, epicier of rue de la Republique, Chauny, Alfred Logeon, garagiste of Chauny, and Eugene Marlé, garagiste of Damcourt par Chauny as fellow members of OCM (Organisation Civile et Militaire) Secteur 5 – plus other helpers, including Charles Froment of 9 rue Paul Doumer, Emile Gossart of 23 rue Camille Desmoulins and Auguste Navlet of rue Ganton, Chauny.

That night, the surgeon (Jacques-Paul Fourrey) and his wife got Schafer drunk on champagne before setting his leg in a cast – telling him at the same time that they were in desperate need of morphine and sulphur drugs – something that Schafer probably understood rather well at that point. They asked Schafer to have a BBC message send when he got back to the UK saying "Schafer boit du champagne le soir" to tell them that he had returned safely, and Henri Magne asked him to tell the British authorities that he would help any man who came to him with that message.

During his stay with Henri Magne, Schafer was visited by Typhoon pilot Richard Aitken-Quack (see earlier), the postmaster from Chauny who brought him some wine, and a professor who asked that his sister-in-law in England, Mrs Conners, who lived in Sale, near Manchester, be notified that he was alright.

On 15 January, the doctor (Jacques Boury) and the surgeon (Jacques-Paul Fourrey) changed the cast on his leg, and he received a visit from Ginette Logeon (about 20 years old with blonde hair and blue eyes). Ginette spoke enough English to tell Schafer that she and her father (Alfred) were sheltering ten English (sic) airmen, and she gave Schafer some bread tickets.

On 29 January, bank director Henri Magne was to be transferred to Saint Quentin and Schafer was due at the hospital in Chauny to have his leg X-rayed. Dr Fourrey took him in his car but Schafer entered the hospital on his own. A nurse took him to the X-ray department, where she obviously knew who he was because after taking off the cast, she told him that he would have to have his leg re-set in England.

Schafer was then taken to stay with Emile and Irene Gossart at 23 rue Camille Desmoulins in Chauny. Schafer describes Emile as being 59 years old, 5 feet 8 inches tall, a bald ex-officer in the French army – and Irene as 56 years old, 5 feet 5 inches tall, fat with black hair – she worked as house-keeper for the Fourrey family. During his stay with the Gossart family, Schafer met the doctor's son-in-law, and Jean-Paul Chevalier (23 years old,

5 foot 6 inches tall with brown hair) from Creil. He also met B-17 pilot Francis Hennessy (#496) who stayed for four nights before moving to join his navigator, Clyde Richardson (#497) who was being sheltered with Alfred Logeon. Another visitor was the 25-year-old man who first helped him after he landed who explained that Schafer had come down near some munitions trains, and then told him how the Germans had found his flying clothes and parachute, and searched the village for him, even interrogating the children.

On 5 February, Alfred Logeon brought Schafer a slip of paper with the name of one of his crew for him to identify – and S/Sgt Paul Dicken moved in to join him.

S/Sgt Paul F Dicken (#500) was the 23-year-old right waist-gunner, and only other successful evader from B-24 42-63973 (Schafer).

Dicken landed just east of Laon at La Paix, he says near the junction of the Laon-Sissonne and Liesse-la-Maison-Bleue roads, and walked to a farm. A 22-year-old man called Masso gave him overalls, buried his flying gear and took him to another farm at nearby Montaigu where Marcel and Jeanne Bocquet lived with their two daughters, Marie Louise (18) and 14-year-old Yolande. Masso was supposed to take Dicken to Paris next day but in the meantime, Marcel Bocquet went to Saint-Erme-Outre-et-Ramecourt to contact the local organisation member (Julien Chapelet). Masso returned on 5 January to report that 40 (sic) members of the organisation there had been arrested.

Louis Zeid (or Zegre) (aged 38, 6 feet tall with brown hair and eyes), foreman of a large farm on the Marchais estate, came to visit and after "thoroughly" interrogating Dicken (in English), said that he would contact the organisation. Dicken stayed with the Bocquet family for the next month, during which time he was visited by the owner of the farm, Princess Charlotte of Monaco (born September 1898) (5 feet 5 inches tall, with black hair and brown eyes – she spoke English), who brought him some food and wine, and Dicken visited her at the Chateau de Marchais where he also met her 21-year-old son, Prince Rainier.

On 5 February, Louis Zeid took Dicken in his truck to the gendarmerie in Marchais where he picked up a gendarme sergeant who saw them through the German check-points on the way to the station. They eventually met up with Bob (Robert Pique) who took Dicken by bus to Chauny where he was delivered to Alfred Logeon at his Garage Saint Charles. Dicken was told that he could write a letter home, and did so, and was asked to put his name on a piece of paper. The paper was taken to his pilot, Richard Schafer (who confirmed his identity), and that night, Dicken was taken to join him and Francis Hennessy at the Gossart home on rue Camille Desmoulins.

On 13 February, they received a visit from "the chief" (Etienne Dromas) and 23-year-old Jean-Paul Chevalier, who had come from Creil, and the following morning, Jean-Paul and Alfred Logeon took Dicken and Schafer to the station. They met Dr Boury and his daughter Jacqueline, who had brought T/Sgt Elmer Risch (#498) (see later), and Jean-Paul took the three Americans on the 0815 train to Creil.

On their arrival in Creil, Schafer was taken to stay with Armand Wiamont and his wife at 5 rue Ribot while Dicken was sheltered by Paul and Marguerite Toussaint, and their daughter Paulette, at 15 rue Charles Somasco. Elmer Risch was delivered to dentist Georges Budin's home at 39 rue Gambetta, Nogent-sur-Oise, from where Mme Marie Budin took him to be sheltered with English-born Mme André Fauchoix on nearby rue Claude Péroche. Risch says that he supposed to stay for three or four days but was actually there for four weeks and two days, being joined by William Scanlon (#501) on about 8 March.

While they were in Creil, Schafer and Dicken (at least) met Earl Wolf, Francis Hennessy and Clyde Richardson – and were interrogated by Marcel Cola and Jacky du Pac from the organisation in Paris.

S/Sgt William J Scanlon (#501) was the 22-year-old left waist-gunner of 92BG/326BS B-17 42-37984 (Shevchik) – same aircraft as Stump and Van Selus (see earlier) and Shevchik, Thorson and Wall (see later) – which was abandoned to crash near Catheux (Oise) on 8 February 1944.

Scanlon says he reported to his pilot that numerous aircraft from their formation were aborting over Luxembourg, and they had just started back to base when they were attacked by German fighters. Both Scanlon and the other waist-gunner (Francis Wall (#529) – see later) were hit. He says that with their aircraft in a dive, he remembers a shell exploding next to him, and falling against Sgt Wall but nothing else apart from reviving briefly while he was in the air.

Scanlon was unconscious when he landed in a field somewhere near Beauvais and found himself being dragged across the ground by his parachute. Having finally released his harness, he stood up to see that he was about 1,000 yards from a village but bleeding profusely from injuries to his head, shoulders and face. He headed towards the village to try and find some medical assistance, discarding his flying kit as he went. As he started down a road, he was approached by a man on a bicycle who, on finding Scanlon was American, threw his bicycle into a ditch and called to some men standing nearby to come and help. Scanlon was taken to a haystack where he was hidden from the searching German patrols until being taken by cart to a farmhouse.

Soon after laying down in the farmhouse, two gendarmes arrived and went through Scanlon's effects, taking anything that might betray his identity, before driving him to the home of another gendarme in Beauvais. A middle-aged doctor came and examined Scanlon's injuries, returning later with another doctor, who confirmed that Scanlon really needed to be taken to a hospital. That evening, the two gendarmes wrapped Scanlon in a blanket and put him into a car which took him to Creil and the home of a doctor named Dupré (sic), reputed to be the third-best surgeon in France – this was Georges Debray (mentioned earlier) who lived with his wife Lina (who was also a doctor) on rue Gambetta. Dr Debray had two nurses working with him, including Madeleine who spoke good English, and they stopped most of Scanlon's bleeding. After bandaging him up again, Dr Debray dressed Scanlon in brand new civilian clothes and took him to his hospital. Scanlon was X-rayed and operated on that night, the doctor removing shrapnel from his face and shoulder, before taking him to be sheltered with organisation chief Marcel Gerardot at 107 rue Henri Pauquet where Scanlon was confined to bed.

With either Dr Debray or the head nurse from his hospital making regular visits to check on his progress, Scanlon was sheltered with Marcel Gerardot until 21 February when, following of the capture of Chiccarelli, and with Marcel Gerardot's home having been raided twice before, he was moved to Nogent-sur-Oise, on the outskirts of Creil. He was sheltered by Mme Germaine Labydt and her son André at 74 avenue Claude Peroche where, about a week later, he was joined by Clyde Richardson. On 6 March, Scanlon and Richardson were taken to stay with a 35-year-old woman and her 70-year-old husband – this was Paul Toussaint at 15 rue Charles Somasco, who had earlier sheltered Richard Schafer. The woman was a private secretary and Scanlon says that one of her bosses was a collaborator.

Two days later, Schafer returned to rue Charles Somasco and Scanlon was taken to join T/Sgt Elmer Risch, who was being sheltered about half a kilometre away in Nogent-sur-Oise with André Fauchoix and his wife on rue Claude Péroche.

T/Sgt Elmer D Risch (#498) was the 30-year-old (substitute) engineer/TTG of 44BG/66BS B-24 42-7548 Bull O' The Woods – the same aircraft as Donald Heskett (#347) and Charles Cregger (#470) see both earlier – which was abandoned to crash between Compiègne and Soissons on 30 December 1943.

Risch says he had been busy working on the voltage regulators from take-off until after they crossed the French coast and had only just reported to his turret when he heard an explosion and felt his leg go numb. As the aircraft peeled off, he heard the pilot (Donald Heskett) tell the crew to prepare to bail out. Risch went to the bomb-bay where he helped radio operator T/Sgt Eugene Symons open the doors before taking off his flak-suit and putting on his parachute. He saw two parachutes passing under the bomb-bay and when Heskett started to leave his seat, jumped at about 22,000 feet.

Risch delayed pulling his rip-cord until he reached cloud cover and then landed "easily" in a ploughed field. He had seen a man on horse-back following his descent and as he hobbled across the field, the man approached him. Risch pointed to the blood on his trousers while he buried his parachute and the man indicated that Risch should leave the area as quickly as possible. Risch made his way to some railway lines and lay down between the banks, parallel to the tracks. He saw the man ride away before returning on foot with several friends. They took Risch's flying gear and used his own first-aid pack to bandage his leg and foot before leaving him in hiding. Two hours later, a man brought him some food and that night, two farmers came with a cart and took him to a cave. Risch spent the rest of that night and following day on a straw bale in the cave, where he was given food, wine and a blanket. The man with the horse returned to ask Risch what he intended to do and when Risch said he wanted to walk to Spain, advised him to surrender himself to the German authorities instead. When Risch insisted (although his lack of French combined with a New Orleans accent may have contributed to a misunderstanding), the man gave up and left him to it. Then the farmer with the cart returned with more food and wine, and a hunting jacket and trousers, and that night Risch was collected by a doctor (Dr Matry of Folembray – query) who drove him to surgeon Jacques-Paul Fourrey in Chauny. The surgeon and his wife drove Risch to a hospital where he was X-rayed and had the shrapnel removed from his ankle and leg – another piece of metal in his thigh was left because it was judged to be too close to an artery. Risch was then driven back to the

Fourrey house in Chauny, and half an hour later, Dr Jacques Boury arrived to take Risch back to his home at 4 rue de la Paix.

Risch stayed overnight with Dr Boury before being taken to "a small villa (home of a butcher – query) a few kilometres away". However, Dr Boury called next day to tell Risch that the number of visitors to the house made it too dangerous for him to stay and suggested he pretend that his wounds were more serious than they thought. This apparently convinced his hosts and that evening, Dr Boury took Risch to stay with some elderly friends (M. Obled, epicier of rue de la Republique in Chauny), where Risch was sheltered until 14 February – the doctor making frequent visits and Risch in turn visiting the doctor's house on Sunday afternoons and for Thursday dinners. Dr Boury also provided Risch with an ID card and some "really beautiful civilian clothes, and a perfect overcoat" and early on the morning of 14 February, Dr Boury and his daughter Jacqueline took Risch to Chauny station, where he joined Richard Schafer and Paul Dicken to be taken by train to Creil.

As already mentioned, Risch was sheltered just outside Creil, at Nogent-sur-Oise with the Fauchoix family until being taken to Paris with Hennessy, Dicken and Scanlon on 17 March.

Creil to Paris and on to Châtelaudren

On Thursday 16 March, René Loiseau and Genevieve de Poulpiquet took Robert Lorenzi, Robert Costello, Paul Packer, Edward Sweeney, Earl Wolf, Leonard Bergeron, Clyde Richardson and Richard Schafer by train to Paris.

On their arrival at the gare du Nord that afternoon, they gathered at the Metro entrance before René Loiseau took Lorenzi, Costello, Packer and Sweeney to Levallois-Perret and Marguerite Di Giacomo's apartment at 5 rue Baudin.

A man came to take their photographs and the following morning, three men, one of them Marcel Cola, brought identity cards, work permits, residence certificates for the coastal zone, and tickets for the Metro. Cola told them they would be leaving and explained the procedure they were to follow, walking singly but not letting the man in front out their sight as René Loiseau led them back to the Metro. They would be changing trains at Reaumur-Sebastopol in order to get to gare Montparnasse, and simply trust to luck that they weren't picked up in a routine ticket-check. Everything went according to plan, and the four Americans were discretely passed on to Henri Bois, who in turn passed them to two English-speaking guides (a man aged about 24, 5 feet 11 inches tall, he had apparently blown up bridges and shot Germans, and a woman who Wolf says talked too much) who to led them to their reserved compartment where they rejoined Wolf and Bergeron on the overnight train to Saint-Brieuc. The following morning, they changed trains for Châtelaudren.

I don't know where Wolf and Bergeron stayed overnight in Paris – their report says something about a well-built young man avoiding STO taking them to stay with his aunt, and then next day a French Canadian (assume Marcel Cola) took them to the station.

While René Loiseau took Lorenzi, Costello, Packer and Sweeney to rue Baudin, Genevieve de Poulpiquet took Richardson and Schafer to 7 rue Maspero where they were sheltered by Bertranne d'Hespel. On their second day at rue Maspero, they were joined by William Scanlon (whose injuries still required treatment), and Mme Jules Henry, wife of the French ambassador to Spain, arrived with Australian airman Ronald Daniel (1855) (see later). That evening (18 March), Bertranne d'Hespel took Schafer, Richardson and Scanlon to the gare Montparnasse where she passed them over to Marie-France Geoffroy-Dechaume and a young French medical student named Georges Rouet who took them to their reserved compartment. They joined Francis Hennessy, Elmer Risch and Paul Dicken on the overnight train to Saint-Brieuc, where they changed for Châtelaudren.

On Friday 17 March, René Loiseau took Francis Hennessy, Elmer Risch, Paul Dicken and William Scanlon by train to Paris.

The day after Richard Schafer left Creil for Paris with Clyde Richardson, François Maizieres took Francis Hennessy to Marcel Gerardot's home at 107 rue Henri Pauquet, and it was his wife Renée who took Hennessy to Edmond Bourge's home at 61 rue Henri Pauquet where they collected Elmer Risch, Paul Dicken and William Scanlon. René Loiseau, who had just returned from Paris, took them to the station, meeting Renée Gerardot along the way who gave them their tickets.

On arrival at the gare du Nord, they waited for a new guide to arrive, and when he didn't, Loiseau took the four airmen to Levallois-Perret and the fifth-floor apartment of Marguerite Di Giacomo at 5 rue Baudin. They saw Lorenzi, Costello, Packer and Sweeney (who had spent the night in Yvonne Latrace's apartment opposite) before they left for Brittany that evening, and Marcel Cola brought a photographer to take their pictures for new ID cards. Next day, Scanlon was taken to Bertranne d'Hespel's tiny apartment at rue Maspero for some medical treatment, and (as mentioned above) joined Clyde Richardson and Richard Schafer. That evening, Margot and René Loiseau took Hennessy, Risch and Dicken by Metro to the gare Montparnasse. They were given train tickets by Charles Rouet and then he and Marie-France Geoffroy-Dechaume took them to a reserved compartment where, as already mentioned, they joined Richardson, Schafer and Scanlon on the overnight train to Saint-Brieuc, where they changed for Châtelaudren.

Châtelaudren

Lorenzi, Costello, Packer, Sweeney, Wolf and Bergeron arrived at Châtelaudren station on the morning of Saturday 18 March.

Lorenzi (the only one of his crew whose report has any details) says they were met by a woman, aged about 50, who he describes as being an ex-collaborator – she is named by Le Sommier as Mme Gourio (or Goriou) of the Grand Café in Châtelaudren. She walked with them for about three miles, out through the town to a farmhouse on the outskirts, where the owner (Jean-Marie Le Sommier) was an ex-soldier. They were told that the whole coast was alerted, with increased shore patrols.

Wolf comments that on leaving the train at Châtelaudren station, they "damn near walked in cadence – with everyone watching". However, the ticket collector showed no interest and simply took their tickets before they were led out into the country, four or five miles to an "old man's house" (ferme Kerjagu).

The following day, a girl brought another six Americans, and at about nine o'clock that evening, a truck – which already had seven other men on board – arrived to collect them.

Hennessy, Richardson, Risch, Schafer, Dicken and Scanlon had arrived at Châtelaudren station at about nine o'clock on the Sunday morning. They were met at the station by a man on the platform who apparently told their guides they should have stayed on the train as far as Guingamp, and so they reboarded the train. However, when they got to Guingamp, there was no-one there to meet them, so they bought new tickets and returned once more to Châtelaudren.

There was no-one to meet them at Châtelaudren either so Marie-France Geoffroy-Dechaume took them in pairs, through the village to

Jean-Marie Le Sommier's farm at Plouagat, where they joined Lorenzi, Costello, Packer, Sweeney, Wolf and Bergeron. They stayed at ferme Kerjagu until dark, when their two guides left to return to Paris, and a truck – which already had seven other men on board – arrived to collect them.

The other five evaders on this fourth Bonaparte operation were taken, by various routes, to Guingamp.

Buland Khan (1852) was the officer's cook of 22 Animal Transport Company (Mules), Royal Indian Army Service Corps. When the Germans invaded France in May 1940, the company was moved up from Marseille to a small village near Metz, where they were captured on 24 June. After a spell at Stalag VIIIB (Lamsdorf), Khan was moved with his officers to Annaburg (where there was a holding camp for Indian POWs), and then in December 1942, to a prison camp at Rennes. In February 1943, an Indian doctor who had also been moved from Annaburg asked Khan to work as a nursing orderly at the Ecole Premiere Superieure, a hospital for Indians, Morrocans and Senegalese in the town of Rennes itself. One day in March, a girl that Khan names as Lise La Rider approached the hospital and asked Khan if he knew a Senegalese named Kulubali, and when Khan brought Kulubali to speak to the girl, Kulubali explained to her that Khan was a British Indian soldier. On 23 November 1943, Khan says that Lise La Rider helped him and his friend Sgt Shahzaman to escape from the hospital, and took them by train back to her apartment in Paris at 17 rue d'Oleron (address not found).

On 24 December, Ms La Rider took the two Indian soldiers by train to Vannes (Morbihan) and delivered them to 13 rue Saint-Gildas (home of Mlle Marie Louise Lethiec). On 30 December, a man known as M. Emile (this was Emile Guimard) took them to Saint Aubin, and on 7 January, they were moved to Gourin, where they were sheltered by Jean Pierre Le Bris, tailleur of rue du Moulin Madame, and his wife Marie. On 13 January, an unnamed French guide took them to Douarnenez where Shahzaman was arrested in what seems to have a been routine check, probably at the railway station. Khan makes no mention of his adventures on board the Jouet des Flots the night of 3-4 February (see earlier) but shortly after that episode, he was returned to Gourin where he simply says that he stayed in the same house as before.

I think that Khan went back to Jean Pierre and Marie Le Bris but when Jean Pierre was arrested (on 23 Feb), Khan was sent to stay with Jean and Marie Le Crenn, where Mme Le Crenn says (in Remy) that he lived in their attic for a fortnight, only coming down for meals. Khan was then taken to Guingamp (no details found but he says on 14 March) where he stayed with Joseph and Marie-Antoinette Lanoe in their flour mill on rue Chateaubriand until being taken by truck to Plouha with John McGlynn, Glenn Johnson, Norman King and Isadore Viola on the evening of 19 March.

Joseph and Marie-Antoinette Lanoe, millers at rue Chateaubriand (près de la place Saint-Sauveur), Guingamp – a young couple with 2 children. They told Rémy they were recruited by Georges Le Cun, who brought 4 airmen (query this), who stayed 3 or 4 days until Kerambrun collected them – and some more after that (probably Shevchik, Wall and Buckner on 21 March, and Laux and Wright for a few hours on 22 March – see later), including a Hindu (Khan) who came from Gourin, and was questioned at their home by Dumais.

"On 14 March I left (Gourin) with a guide for Guingamp. I left Guingamp on 19 March for a place on the beach. I am not certain of its name." (Khan WO208/5583-1852)

2/Lt John A McGlynn Jnr (#502) was flying 7PRG/13PRS F-5 42-67361 on a photo-reconnaissance operation on 4 February 1944. The 24-year-old was on his third such mission and at about 30,000 feet over Romilly-sur-Seine when he noticed a flak burst low and to his left, immediately followed by another burst, nearer and higher. Having been told that the Germans never fired twice at the same spot, McGlynn turned left, directly into the path of a third shell which exploded in the left engine of his converted P-38 fighter. McGlynn feathered the propeller and carried on but the oil pressure fell, and then the right-hand engine began smoking before stopping altogether.

McGlynn turned all his switches so the aircraft would explode on impact, jettisoned his canopy (at exactly twelve o'clock) and tried to get out while the aircraft was still in level flight. Unfortunately he was caught by something in the cockpit and had to get back in to grab the controls. He then turned the aircraft over onto its back and blacked out as he dropped free. He says he must have fallen some 4,000 feet before pulling his rip-cord, hoping the high winds would blow him clear of the city and far away from where his aircraft would crash.

McGlynn spent a good fifteen minutes in the air and guessed that he drifted about fifteen miles before he landed in the mud of someone's back garden. McGlynn had seen two men running hard to meet him and they immediately asked "Deutsch? Anglais? Americain?" to which McGlynn responded "American". They quickly gathered up his parachute, Mae West and dinghy and hid them before directing McGlynn to run north, away from approaching German troops. McGlynn opted to walk rather than run through the town and attract attention to himself, and covered about six blocks before noticing that the cellar door of one of the houses was open. He decided to hide there and keep a look-out for any patrols, discovering it was in fact a wine-cellar but with only two bottles left. Helping himself to one of the bottles, McGlynn climbed on top of the rack and used some of the wine to steady his nerves while he examined his aids box. After a while, he checked and saw no evidence of pursuit and so, filling his water-bottle with the rest of the wine and leaving 200 francs in the now empty bottle, he left the cellar and began walking down the main street.

McGlynn walked about two and half miles to a main road which he then followed for another four before asking for help. He decided to try an antique shop on the hopeful basis they may have had American customers in peacetime and that as an artistic person, the proprietor might just happen to hate Germans. McGlynn was in luck, as soon as he produced his language card, he was hustled into a back room where he was questioned, given civilian clothes, and a member of an organisation brought to talk to him via a dictionary.

McGlynn was taken by bicycle to the home of Mme Peter Brown – this was Mme Felicie Brown of 6 rue Léon Bernard, Fresnes – which is about half a kilometre away from the centre of Antony – wife of an American who was in prison at Compeigne. She ran a wine-shop over which she lived. McGlynn had just finished a meal when his guide returned with two gendarmes in civilian clothes who looked over his kit and explained that new regulations had been issued that day requiring full profile photographs, and they took him to a photographer that evening. The gendarmes returned the following evening with McGlynn's photographs and said they hoped he would be leaving by aircraft – they also said he would be going to Paris next day. On 16 February, the two gendarmes took McGlynn by train into Paris and the apartment at 20 boulevard Sebastopol where Jean and Genevieve Rocher lived, along with Genevieve's brother, Georges Prevost. McGlynn says that Georges Prevost was the leader of the gendarme symphony orchestra, and was also mixed up in the black market and underground. Georges made ID cards for the Paris area, working chiefly for French POWs in Germany, and always had fifteen to twenty in process – he made five cards for McGlynn to be used at different places. He says that Jean Rocher owned one of the largest wholesale dairy businesses in Paris and that his wife Genevieve was the chief cashier in a Paris business house. He reports that his treatment there was excellent.

On his second Sunday at boulevard Sebastopol, McGlynn reports that he was taken to Vincennes for dinner at the home of M. De Pelwois (query), a wealthy director in Genevieve's business who gave McGlynn a very fine set of clothes. Because the maid was Alsation and not to be trusted, she was told that McGlynn was a gendarme musician who had been frightened out of his mind by the Allied bombing.

McGlynn also met a small man that other evaders refer to as Mickey but who McGlynn (and Prevost) knew in Paris as Michel – with the surname of Dubois from papers that he saw later. Mickey seemed to be the contact between the Paris organisation and the one that got airmen out of France. He spoke German and Italian – and according to McGlynn, Arabic, having apparently lived in North Africa – and said that he and his sister had been German prisoners of war. McGlynn says that Mickey's sister Marguerite always accompanied him when he visited but gives no further details of her. Another man that McGlynn met is described as a French Canadian officer, about six feet tall, with a moustache. He spoke with a clipped accent and talked to McGlynn about baseball in order to confirm his identity. Marcel Cola makes no mention of either McGlynn or Prevost so I suspect that this particular "French Canadian officer" was the French traitor and German infiltration agent, Guy Marcheret.

On 10 March, Mickey took McGlynn by overnight train to Rennes. He was supposed to stay in a house for one day but he and Mickey actually stayed for seven. Five girls working for the underground lived there, one of whom was apparently an escaped POW with a 50,000 franc price on her head for killing Germans, and was by then in charge of all the correspondence for the Brittany underground. She played cards with a German general and collected information – McGlynn describes her as being about 23 years old, short and chunky, with dark hair dyed reddish brown – this was Antoinette Mace (aka Mlle Vincent or Mlle Mothe) of 83 avenue du Mail, Rennes.

On 18 March, Mickey took McGlynn by train to Guingamp and because they were delayed by Allied bombing, arrived at dusk and spent the night with what McGlynn describes as "some poor people" (that I have not been able to identify). At seven o'clock the next evening, a French-Canadian officer (assume Dumais) came and spoke to McGlynn and told him he would leave in three or four days time but less than an hour later, three Frenchmen collected McGlynn and Mickey in a truck, where they joined Glenn Johnson (#493), Norman King (#494), and Isadore Viola (#495).

McGlynn doesn't mention Buland Khan (who was sheltered with Joseph and Marie-Antoinette Lanoe at rue Chateaubriand) and although Johnson (see below) says that he was collected with McGlynn, I think he means at about the same time rather than from the same place.

As related in the previous chapter, **1/Lt Glenn Johnson** (#493), **2/Lt Norman King** (#494) and **S/Sgt Isadore Viola** (#495) evaded with Ralph Patton (#476) and Jack McGough (#475) until their arrival at Guingamp railway station on 15 March, where they were separated into two groups. While Patton and McGough were taken to stay overnight with Désiré and Francine Laurent, Mathurin Branchoux took Johnson, King and Viola to 54 rue du Grand Trotrieux, home of André Chareton and his widowed mother Louise, where they had a meal together.

After the meal, André Chareton took Johnson to nearby 9 place du Centre where he stayed in the second-floor apartment with two elderly women, Mme Yvonne Lefeuvre, who used to teach at a school near Brest, her older sister Mme Renée Martin – and Madeleine, Yvonne's daughter, who had been an artist in Paris until coming to join her mother and aunt at Christmas. Another daughter, Louise, was in England, married to an RAF dentist named Charles Millar.

Rémy and Huguen both say it was John McGlynn who stayed with Yvonne Lefeuvre at 9 place du Centre but it was Glenn Johnson who was "le géant". Mme Lefeuvre's grand-daughter, Yvonne Millar theorises that when Rémy interviewed André Chareton for his book, he would have consulted the list of evaders that his mother had kept hidden under the kitchen table. André then confused McGlynn (who would not have been on the list) with Glenn, while recounting how the 2.02 metre tall American came to their house but couldn't fit into any of their beds and so was taken to stay with Mémé Lefeuvre instead. Rémy, in the chapter "Jean Boulbain, Prêtre", corrects his error.

King and Viola stayed on with Louise Chareton and her son André, learning that André worked in a clothing shop and Louise for a government bureau in Guingamp. Frequent visitors included André's fiancée Anne and her sister Jeanne, who lived in the corner house on rue Gambetta, near the bridge over the railway lines. King and Viola report that two or three Americans had been there before (see Minor, Semach and Schneider earlier), and that they had great food in the best house they stayed at in France.

Mathurin Branchoux arrived on the afternoon of 19 March with a Canadian officer who questioned all three airmen. Johnson describes the Canadian as being a short man with a little moustache, who asked them questions about football, the Flatiron building and something he called "anklets" but insisted were not girls' socks – Johnson also says he spoke good Italian. The Canadian told Johnson he would leave that night and that there would be plenty of cigarettes at the next place.

That evening, two men came to the Chareton home to tell King and Viola they would be leaving in ten minutes. One was another André (aged about 28, about 5 feet, 11 inches tall and with a pock-marked face) and the other, a family friend called Petit Jean (39 years old, 4 feet 11 inches tall, who made horse and carriage buggies – his real name was Jean Turquet). Petit Jean and the two Andrés then took King and Viola to a garage on the main street, Etablissements Kerambrun at 2-6 rue du Vally, where the man on the door, François Kerambrun, was expecting them.

Johnson was eating supper at 9 place du Centre when a tall young priest named Jean Boulbain rang the door bell (with the correct signal) and told him that he was leaving straight away. The priest walked while Johnson took the priest's bicycle (brought along to try and disguise Johnson's great height) to a garage where he rejoined King and Viola.[50]

At the garage, they met Mickey and a French lieutenant named Roger Dhen (Mathurin Branchoux says Dehen and that he had escaped from a camp at Lubeck), and Johnson reports that they were all sitting in a truck in the dark. They were then driven to a house where Johnson says that the

50 The airmen would have had more notice before leaving but Georges Le Cun forgot to give Jean Boulbain the password, and when he went to collect King and Viola, Mme Chareton wouldn't let him in.

Canadian officer came out to say good luck, see you soon on the beach, and John McGlynn and Buland Khan joined them.

Khan, McGlynn, Johnson, King and Viola, along with Mickey and Roger Dhen, were driven out of Guingamp to Plouagat where their driver spent half an hour looking for Jean-Marie Le Sommier's farmhouse where they collected twelve more Americans – Lorenzi, Costello, Packer, Sweeney, Wolf, Bergeron, Hennessy, Richardson, Risch, Schafer, Dicken and Scanlon – and all nineteen men were taken to Plouha.

> *"We had hardly time to catch our breath than a message from London informed us of a new embarkation that very evening. This time no lodgings whatsoever at Plouha had been arranged. Our airmen were coming directly from Guingamp (sic) in Kerambrun's van, which dropped them near the "Maison d'Alphonse" in a little track where we were waiting for them." (Marie-Thérèse Le Calvez)*

Johnson reports that they drove along back roads, sometimes taking the wrong ones and having to turn back, and picking up a Frenchman on a bicycle on the way, until about eleven o'clock when they arrived at a place where two or three men and a girl were waiting for them. They got out of the truck and were formed into groups of six to walk along tracks and trails to a farmhouse, arriving there just before midnight. Johnson says that Mickey then told them to turn in their money, saying that they each had about 2,000 francs and that these poor people needed it as they were not properly paid by the English and Americans – and the girl took the money into the kitchen.

William Scanlon adds a note to his report saying that at Plouha, Mickey told him that he was standing in as interpreter for the chief, who didn't speak any English (assume François Le Cornec) and that he had "come from England to uncover the Paris chief (Dumais) who pockets all the money". He said that the English pay them but the Americans don't, and that they were to turn over all their money to two men at the farmhouse.

The reader may have got the impression by now that Mickey could be somewhat imaginative with the truth, but in this particular case, several of the helpers in Brittany confirm that Dumais did not pay them. Apparently, guides were given 2,000 francs for bringing the airmen but none of those who housed them received anything. Mathurin Branchoux says that he never received anything either (apart from six submachine guns after the last Bonaparte operation), and that even the cost of travelling when he went to Paris to contact Dumais was at his own expense.

In a declaration dated 26 October 1944, Marie-Thérèse Le Calvez says that Dumais created resentment among the people of Plouha from the very beginning – they didn't trust him, thought he was dishonest, and ungrateful for their efforts. She says that following the first operation (when cases containing money were known to have been landed), there was a "heated altercation" with Dumais about the costs of sheltering the evaders, for whom they had to buy food on the black market, after which they decided not to work for him again. However, when Dumais returned to Plouha to organise the second operation, and as they wanted to carry on their work "for the cause", they "stupidly" accepted his conditions, despite continuing to believe (rightly or wrongly) that he kept most of the money sent from England for himself.

The evaders and their guides left the Maison d'Alphonse at about ten past midnight, instructed to keep quiet, not to smoke, to stay close together and if possible to hold hands. They were taken through fields to a steep bank which they slid down to reach the beach. At about one-thirty, four small boats arrived, each crewed by three sailors, and with room for five passengers. The sailors unloaded their cargo, and Johnson comments on two men who disembarked – they were Bourgogne radio operators Michel Bourgeois (aka Maxime) and Martin Mary (aka Jacques). The seventeen evaders, Mickey and Roger Dhen were rowed out to the British gunboat, and a few minutes later, they set off for England.

> *"Near the cases were two men, two officers of the Fighting French Forces coming in on a mission. The arms and munitions were more than on the first embarkation and were accompanied by a radio transmitter which was to be used by the two French officers. As their arrival was not expected they came to stay at Mum's house. I found the two officers at our house. They stayed there for three days, and their presence was a comfort to us, for we learned from them everything which was being prepared for our liberation. They sent out several radio messages, then, when the time of departure came, I took them before dawn to M. Trocquer, at Pludual, from where they would get to their destination. This little journey remains fixed in my mind as a true miracle, since, not only did we have to pass right through a part of the town but, and*

especially, pass under the windows of the German garrison which was under surveillance day and night." (Marie-Thérèse Le Calvez)

Mickey

The young man the evaders knew as Mickey was Georges Le Droff (born Lannilis, Finistere on 17 August 1923) of 20 rue Buffon, Brest where he lived with his mother. On the questionnaire (dated 26 March 1946) in his NARA file, he gives his profession as "sergeant pilot", and the only names he gives as working with him are Mme Jeannic of rue du Lavoir in Plogoff, and Mr F Priser of 2 rue Edouard Vaillant in Brest. He says that he worked with reseau "Elie" in Brest, although I suspect this is a reference to Françoise Elie in Rennes.

In addition to Gordon, Quinn, McGlynn and six other (Shelburn) evaders whose names he had forgotten, Le Droff also claims to have helped Dwight Fisher (#338), Elton Hoyt (#409), William Cook (#410), John Beilstein (#557) Wayne Bogard, George Padgett and Joseph Burkowski – and Hoyt reports a boy (about 5 foot 8 inches tall, straight, good looking, black curly hair, carried a gun) coming from Brest to the chateau near Lizio where he and the others were being sheltered in November 1943. He had brought a note from Françoise Elie in Rennes but there is no evidence of him (Le Droff) providing them with any actual assistance.

I don't know who the girl was that came with Mickey to visit John McGlynn at boulevard Sebastopol – McGlynn says she was his sister Marguerite but Le Droff didn't have a sister.

In an informal interview with Claire Melson at the US Embassy in London on 10 May 1944, Le Droff told her that he had been a medical student when the war began, and immediately engaged in resistance activities. He was arrested, along with a number of fellow students, most of whom, he says, were executed – his own life only being spared because he had saved a German major from a burning aeroplane which had made a forced landing during the "Battle of France" – this would appear to be a reference to the Ju88 that landed (apparently intact) near Plouguerneau on 18 June 1940. After a year in various prisons, during which he had his eighteenth birthday, he resumed his resistance work, specialising in the rescue of United States fliers, and towards the end of March (1944) helped organise the escape of seventeen American airmen with whom he arrived in England.

He says that at the beginning of 1944, he was asked (he does not say who by) to organise the departure of seven American flyers. In contrast to what Harry Minor reports on the incident at Audierne, Le Droff says that a boat was chartered, all necessary supplies were secured and the sailing date set for 3 February, and it was only the increased Germany activity following the ship-wreck of the Jouet des Flots that prevented his operation from going ahead.

The only American he names as giving him any problems was Lee Gordon, who (as mentioned earlier) refused to be taken to Brest and insisted on returning to Paris.

The interview report goes on to describe how, on 10 March 1944, he received instructions to leave Paris with his "brother" (query) and go to the coast with just one airman – he chose to take John McGlynn as he "evidently found him particularly likeable". Le Droff then rounded up three more Americans who were sheltered in a garage, and another twelve on a farm, and took all sixteen in one small car to the coast. The only person he mentions as helping him in this enterprise being a 22-year-old girl with a torch and a revolver who guided them on the last stages to the beach.

In her notes, Ms Melson describes Le Droff as being "observant, intelligent and reliable, and at his best in matters pertaining to the resistance movement."

SIS/MI9 Operation Bonaparte 5 (23-24 Mar 1944) MGB 503 (Mike Marshall)

This final Bonaparte operation took a record twenty-six Allied airmen, all of whom went through Paris before being taken by train to Guingamp. They left Paris for Saint-Brieuc and Guingamp in four parties over three days, only stopping briefly at Guingamp before being taken to Plouha and Plage Bonaparte.

Also included in the party taken to England that night were Jean Tréhiou of Plouha, and Raymond Le Bourhis, whose IS9 recommendation for a King's Medal for Courage says that in addition to his convoying work, he also sheltered three evaders at his home in Brest.

Raymond Le Bourhis (born July 1922) was the son of Commandant Jean and Mme Genevieve Le Bourhis. A student during the war, in 1946, when his NARA file was compiled, he was a lieutenant in the DGER (Direction générale des études et recherches – French Intelligence) and serving in the Far East. He was also the nephew of Jeanne Callarec, who seems to have supplied the details for his NARA report, saying only that he worked closely with Paul Le Baron for SIS, Bordeaux-Loupiac and Shelburn, and that he was known to the airmen as René Callarec.

The Evaders

On Saturday 18 March 1944, Milton Shevchik, James Thorson, John Bernier and David Helsel arrived in Paris by train from Clermont (Oise) with their guide Jacky du Pac.

1/Lt Milton V Shevchik (#527) was the 25-year-old pilot of 92BG/326BS B-17 42-37984 – see Stump (#463), Van Selus (#464) and Scanlon (#501) earlier.

Their mission to Frankfurt on 8 February 1944 was going well until they reached Luxembourg where they were hit by flak and attacked by fighters. Shevchik says that he saw several other aircraft aborting and when there were only six of them left in the formation, got a course from his navigator (2/Lt James E Williams) and headed west at 25,000 feet. A few minutes later they were attacked by more fighters which hit their #2 engine and started a fire in the cockpit and Shevchik put the aircraft into a dive. They still had their bomb-load on board which the engineer (Stump) was trying to dump, and down to 10,000 feet when another fighter fired into their tail, damaging the controls. Shevchik dived the aircraft again to get into some cloud at about 5,000 feet before giving the order to bail out. He says that the gunners went first, and then the engineer and co-pilot (Thorson), followed by the navigator and bombardier (2/Lt Donald J Periolat), with Shevchik following them out at about 4,000 feet.

Shevchik says he saw six parachutes open below him and watched another aircraft (42-31387) crash before he landed in a ploughed field near Domeliers. As he was getting up, a group of Frenchmen came running down a hill towards him but quickly turned back when an enemy fighter flew low over the field. Shevchik took off his flying boots and carried his parachute to a small clump of woods where the Frenchmen came to shake his hand and take his parachute. They pointed to a barn on the other side of the field and started to run there with Shevchik, at which point, Shevchik's engineer, Everett Stump (see earlier) joined them.

At about noon, food was brought to the barn, and while the two Americans were eating, their co-pilot (James Thorson) appeared, already wearing a blue denim civilian jacket, along with the man who had helped him. Wine was also produced and something of a party atmosphere seems to have taken over through the afternoon, with several local people coming to stare at the barn, all apparently aware that the Americans were there.

At about four o'clock that afternoon, a boy brought Shevchik, Stump and Thorson civilian clothes and a little later, a group of men came to take them to a house about a mile away in the little village of Domeliers. An elderly woman gave them a meal of meat, scrambled eggs and more wine, and several people came to see them, including two girls who had seen Shevchik and Stump land. They were also given a razor and some blades and so were able to wash and shave before changing into their new clothes and being taken to another house. At this second house, they met Gilbert Thibault who asked them several questions and said that he would have their identities checked through Paris. They were then were taken across the road to a third house where they spent the night.

Next morning, their helpers came and cooked them breakfast, one man staying with them all day and only allowing Shevchik to leave the house on a brief visit see their radio operator Robert Sidders (#1056) and tail-gunner Francis Higgins (#825) who were being sheltered in yet another house nearby – Shevchik reporting that they were alright although Higgins had sprained his ankle (their reports are almost illegible at this point so I don't know where Sidders and Higgins were staying). More people came to see them later and the airmen were given apple-jack (Calvados) to drink. That evening, a priest named François Leclainche came and told them that it seemed to be safe, and they were taken about five miles by truck to the town of Crèvecoeur-le-Grand, about 20 kilometres north of Beauvais.

At Crèvecoeur-le-Grand, Shevchik was sheltered with carpenter Georges Bourgois, his wife Marcelle and son Maurice at 49 rue de la Rochefoucauld. Shevchik says that he took no special security precautions beyond returning to his upstairs room when the doorbell rang, and that despite there being large numbers of German troops in the village, he often went to visit Thorson and Stump. Shevchik reports that the head of the organisation was André Cocuelle who asked him for his crew-list, squadron and group numbers that Shevchik was reluctant to give, but finally did so.

On 18 February, Gilbert Thibault took Shevchik and Thorson, along with Francis Wall (#529) and William Hoffman (#530) (see both later) by truck to Beauvais – they were given blue denim jackets and told that if they were stopped, they were to pretend they were foreign workers who had thumbed a ride in the lorry.

Shevchik and Thorson were sheltered with coal dealer Emile Vifquain and his wife Marie at 158 boulevard Aristide Briand until 23 February, when one of the men who had visited them at Crèvecoeur moved them to 24 rue de Clermont to stay with Lucien Revert. Lucien worked just outside the town at Beauvais-Tillé airfield, and his wife worked in the post office, where organisation members received all their mail to avoid censorship. Thorson comments that "although the house was a centre of organisation activity, security was poor. They kept rubber stamps used in forging identity cards lying about in plain sight in the dining room". Shevchik and Thorson joined Sgt Ray Reeves (#729) (see earlier) who had been brought back from Paris the night before because the organisation that was handling him had been broken up (sic) – Reeves left Beauvais (taken to Noailles) five days before Shevchik and Thorson but they heard in Brittany that he had not gotten out yet.

A week before they left Beauvais, a man called Jacques came from Paris. He said he was English and working for the British Military Intelligence however he used a French name, and said he would get them to England soon – this was (obviously) Jacky du Pac. That evening, a French cavalry officer who was staying at the house was taken off to Paris but the Americans were left behind. Lucien Revert told them something had gone wrong again and the Americans started to plan a way out through Switzerland on their own, even sharing their ideas with Revert, who went across the street to where Jacques was staying and brought him back. Jacques told them they would never get to Switzerland and then mentioned for the first time the possibility of sending them out by boat from Brittany – which cheered up Shevchik at least.

On 16 March, Gilbert Thibault and "a short man", came to Beauvais in a truck to take Shevchik and Thorson about twenty-four kilometres east, to the town of Clermont. They were (again) told that if they were stopped they were to say they had been picked up on the road and didn't know them. At Clermont, Shevchik and Thorson joined John Bernier (#537) and David Helsel (#538), who were being sheltered with Georges Fleury, his wife Rachel and their daughter Annette at 25 rue de Mouy. Jacques came to visit them again, and he explained that they were supposed to go to Paris the following evening but there had been a raid on Creil and no trains were going through. On the day after that however (18 March), the four Americans did leave for Paris, their train being delayed by two hours by bomb damage at Creil and witnessing another raid as they passed through.

2/Lt James M Thorson (#528) was the co-pilot of B-17 42-37984 (Shevchik) and he says that he saw William Hoffman's aircraft (42-31387) going down to his west as he drifted in his parachute to land in a field on the other side of Doméliers from Shevchik and Stump. There was a man ploughing the field and Thorson's sudden appearance startled his horse, but once he had settled the animal down, he came over to help Thorson roll up his parachute. The farmer indicated that he would take care of the parachute and waved Thorson towards some woods, where Thorson hid his oxygen mask, throat-mike and flying boots. A small crowd soon formed around Thorson's hiding place and his original helper took a blue denim jacket from one of them and made Thorson put it on. He then took Thorson down the road to the nearest town (Doméliers) and into the kitchen of a house where Thorson was given bread and wine. Then the man took Thorson through the town and out into open countryside, meeting a priest named François Leclainche on the way who smiled and shook Thorson's hand, to a barn on a hill about 100 yards from the road where (as already mentioned) Thorson found his pilot Milton Shevchik and engineer Everett Stump.

When Thorson, Shevchik and Stump were taken to Crèvecoeur-le-Grand on 9 February, Thorson was sheltered with Alexandre Dizambourg and his wife Albertine on rue de Breteuil. Alexandre was the foreman of a textile factory and he told Thornson that the entire output of the factory was taken by the Germans, that the workers did considerable sabotage, and the output was only about fifty per cent of peacetime capacity. Thorson could see German patrols passing the house every three hours.

As described earlier, Thorson stayed with the Dizambourg family at Crèvecoeur-le-Grand until 18 February when he and Shevchik, along with Francis Wall (#529) and William Hoffman (#530), were taken to Beauvais where he and Shevchik stayed first with Emile and Marie Vifquain and then with Lucien Revert and his wife. On 16 March, Gilbert Thibault took Thorson and Shevchik to Clermont where they joined John Bernier and David Helsel at the Fleury home, and two days later, the four Americans were taken to Paris.

S/Sgt John F Bernier (#537) was the 21-year-old ball-turret gunner and **S/Sgt David Helsel** (#538) the 23-year-old left waist-gunner of 379BG/525BS B-17 42-29633 (Beam) which was on the way to Frankfurt on 8 February 1944 when they were attacked by fighters. This is the aircraft that engineer/TTG William Lessig (#466) and bombardier Dean Tate (#467) bailed out from (see earlier), and their reports may have given the impression that the aircraft was abandoned – but that's not the case, as Bernier and Helsel explain:

> *"When the ship dropped to 10,000 feet, the bombardier (Tate), navigator (2/Lt Eugene H Gallagher), engineer (Lessig) and co-pilot (2/Lt Bob F Ross) bailed out – and shortly after that the aircraft went into a steep dive. The pilot (2/Lt Doris R Beam) pulled it out just above the tree-tops and crashed into a barn [at Monchy-Humières, Oise] and split in two at the radio room. Four jumped out – Bernier, Helsel, waist-gunner S/Sgt George C Lissandrello and radio operator T/Sgt George C Fotenakes – and the pilot, who had been thrown clear of the ship, joined us. The burning ammunition was bursting*

around us and three enemy fighters were strafing us. The five of us took off our chutes and ran towards a clump of trees. On the way, a Frenchman ran up to us and told us to hide in the wood (Bernier speaks French and acted as interpreter for the others) but the pilot wanted to go to a barn which we saw about a quarter of a mile away in a cemetery. When we reached the road near the barn, the pilot ordered us to cross this road and approach the barn one at a time. He went first, we (Bernier and Helsel) followed him, and Lissandrello and Fotenakes remained where they were. As the pilot crossed the road, a young Frenchman came along on a bicycle, stopped near him and said "Francais, camarade". Just then four German soldiers came up, asked the Frenchman for his papers, and then noticed Lissandrello and Fotenakes. The Germans grabbed them and asked how many of them there were. Lissandrello and Fotenakes said "Two". The Frenchman, as soon as the Germans had moved away from him, came up to us (Bernier and Helsel) and said "Cachez-vous" (hide). We dropped behind the bank at the side of the road. The pilot, who had also dropped behind the bank as soon as the Germans ran over to Lissandrello and Fotenakes, looked up for a moment and the Germans spotted him, ran over and grabbed him, stopping within a foot of us. We lay motionless in the tall grass, rejoiced that our summer flying suits gave us perfect camouflage. When the Germans asked the pilot how many Americans there were, he said "Three". The Germans puzzling over the conflicting statements. Then they noticed a woman running up the road, and they started after her, taking the three Americans with them and stepping right over us as they went." (Helsel MIS-X #538)

Bernier and Helsel stayed where they were for the next two hours before starting to crawl towards the barn but before they could reach it, they saw a man drive up in a wagon. They changed course and headed for a corner of the cemetery at Monchy-Humières where they hid behind one of the tombs. They could hear a tractor being driven around and around the cemetery and later learned it was their French friend looking for them. Later that afternoon, two young girls and their maid came to the tomb where Bernier and Helsel were hiding. As they prayed, one of the girls spotted the two Americans and although obviously startled, made no reaction that might attract the attention of the German troops searching nearby. In between her prayers she told them to remain hidden until her brother could come for them. An hour or so later, a young man came to the grave with a basket, and as he knelt and prayed, he passed the two Americans flasks of cognac and a package of food. That evening, the young man came back with his two brothers, one of whom was their friend from the morning, and they took Bernier and Helsel through the fields to their home, a large farmhouse on rue de Gournay, Monchy-Humières, a few miles north-west of Compiègne.

The brothers were Jacques, Jean and Pierre Vervel, who lived with their parents Gaston and Henriette, and their two (unnamed) sisters, aged 18 and 20. Bernier and Helsel were given food, civilian clothes and 1,000 francs each, along with shelter for the night. Next morning, a priest named François Le Pévédic came to the house and he gave Jacques the key to his presbytery in Francières (about 5 kms SW of Monchy-Humieres) and instructions to take the Americans there. That night, Jacques took the two Americans to Francières where he locked them in the presbytery, and next day, Le Pévédic came and told them that his chief, Henri Doisy, would collect them the following night.

Henri Doisy came with his wife and 14-year-old son Philippe, to take Bernier and Helsel back to their estate at Cressonsacq (west of Francières) where they were sheltered for three weeks before being returned to stay with François Le Pévédic for another three days. On the third day, a man they describes as English, and refer to as Jacques Marcier, or JPM, came from Paris to interrogate them – this was (obviously) Jacky du Pac (Jacques du Pac de Marsoulis). Next day, Henri Doisy took them by camionette to Clermont where they were sheltered with Georges Fleury, head of the local organisation, his wife Rachel and their 18-year-old daughter Annette, in what they describe as "a nice big house with an enclosed garden where they could sit in the sun". Bernier and Helsel were joined on their twelfth day with the Fleury family by Milton Shevchik and James Thorson, and two days later, Jacky du Pac took the four Americans to Paris.

On Saturday 18 March 1944, Kenneth Woodhouse, Milton Rosenblatt, Robert Laux, Phlemon Wright, Thomas Glennan, Abe Helfgott, Rudolf Cutino, Richard Hamilton, Francis Wall, William Hoffman, George Buckner and David Warner arrived in Paris by train from Beauvais (Oise) with their guides Gilbert Thibault and Louis Marin – coming into the gare du Nord shortly after Milton Shevchik and his group from Clermont had left the station.

F/O Kenneth B Woodhouse RCAF (1858) took off from Biggin Hill in 401 Sqn Spitfire MJ119 at about 1330 hrs on 16 March 1944 for a bomber escort mission but before he could reach the rendezvous point, his engine failed completely and the 20-year-old Canadian was forced to bale out.

Woodhouse probably set a record for the quickest return to the UK by any Allied airman from Occupied Europe – just eight days after he baled out over northern France, Woodhouse was brought safely back to England by the Shelburn organisation – Express Delivery. The following comes from Woodhouse's MI9 report with some added details from an account that he wrote many years later.

Woodhouse landed in a field about a kilometre from Rémérangles (just east of Beauvais) where he was met by a farmer named Maurice Rendu who had watched him come down. After quickly hiding his parachute, M. Rendu drove Woodhouse a short distance in his truck (which had his father's name painted on the side) and hid him in a haystack. That evening, Woodhouse was walked to a farmhouse at Le Fay-Saint-Quentin, home of Maurice's parents, Wilfred and Genevieve Rendu, where he joined two American evaders, Robert Laux (#521) and Phlemon Wright (#522).

Next day, they were visited by a gendarme who the two Americans apparently knew (assume Alphonse Rouillard), and later he returned with a civilian (assume Gilbert Thibault) who asked Woodhouse questions that as a Canadian, he had difficulty answering. Early next morning, the gendarme returned, and Wilfred Rendu took them all in his truck to the gendarmerie at Bresles where they collected three (query) more Americans (one of whom had a wounded leg which had been operated on by a doctor – Thomas Glennan (#523) – and Abe Helfgott (#524) – see later). From Bresles, they went on to Rochy-Condé and a house attached to a flour-mill, home of Louis Marin, where they picked up another American (Milton Rosenblatt), before going on to Beauvais. They were taken to an office in a walled compound where those airmen who had photographs with them were given identity cards – including Woodhouse who was also given civilian clothes – and then put back into the truck (with others) and driven to an alley near the station where Wilfred Rendu and the gendarme left them. At Beauvais station, they were given rail tickets, and Gilbert Thibault and Louis Marin led them into a reserved compartment on the train to Paris.

1/Lt Milton L Rosenblatt (#520) was the 21-year-old co-pilot of 44BG/68BS B-24 42-7501 Bing's Big Box (Sobotka) which was on an operation against V1 rocket sites in the Pas-de-Calais on the afternoon of 21 January 1944. They were making their third run over the target when they were hit by fighters which knocked out the intercom, set #2 engine on fire and caused the #1 engine to run away. The aircraft went into a spiral dive at about 12,000 feet, pulled out at about 5,000 feet and then went into a flat spin. The pilot (1/Lt Frank W Sobotka) rang the alarm bell and Rosenblatt followed the engineer (T/Sgt Clair P Shaeffer) out.

Rosenblatt reports seeing three other parachutes on the ground but the only other successful evader was bombardier 1/Lt Abraham Teitel (#728) who was passed to Comète and crossed the Pyrenees in May 1944.

Unfortunately the finer details of Rosenblatt's evasion are in Donald Emerson's usual style and I have only been able to piece together parts of his story, which ends soon after meeting three of the crew from Tenabuv, after which we follow his progress from other evader reports.

The aircraft crashed near Beaussault in Upper Normandy and Rosenblatt, who despite having his parachute on upside down, landed safely, if a little dazed, nearby. He took off his parachute and was running when he spotted a man coming towards him. In order to avoid the man, Rosenblatt changed direction and began walking along a ditch, tearing up his AGO card as he went, acknowledging that bringing his ID on what he thought was going to be a "milk run" was a mistake. After trying, without much success, to get some sleep in a wood, Rosenblatt acquired a bundle of faggots to carry on his shoulder as he walked across a field, pretending to be a peasant. His disguise obviously didn't fool a local French boy who promptly took him back to his house, and Rosenblatt was put into a barn until the man of house told him to "Partir". The man pointed out which direction he should go and Rosenblatt checked with his compass to confirm that he was being directed to head south. After crossing more fields and getting into some marshland, somewhere between the villages of Boutavent and Mureaumont, Rosenblatt encountered a woman who was having trouble with her runaway horse. When he finally caught the errant animal (not bad for a waiter from Miami Beach, Florida), the woman realised he was an American and took him back to her house. The following morning, the woman (Gilberte Bourdon – query) gave Rosenblatt a jacket and trousers (presumably belonging to her husband, who was a POW) before taking him to her mother's house, just outside Boutavent. Rosenblatt explained that he wanted to go to Paris but did not want to take the train so the daughter took him "some distance" by horse and buggy, and he set off walking towards Milly-sur-Thérain. He got as far as Crillon before stopping at a blacksmith's shop to ask if there were any Germans in the area. He was advised to carry on through Bonnières, and just before Milly-sur-Thérain, found a family who, although understandably nervous, gave him a meal. Then a man took Rosenblatt back to his house in Bonnières where he stayed overnight with the man and his pregnant wife.

Next day, a woman who spoke a little English came from Milly-sur-Thérain with her husband, Raymond Peroche (query), who spoke the language pretty well (Rosenblatt thought he was a schoolteacher), and the husband took Rosenblatt by bicycle back to Crillon. Then a man called Foulon (query writing) took Rosenblatt to his home in Vrocourt (about 4 kms away) where Rosenblatt met his wife and their teenage daughter. There was a "big, tall fellow" (Paul Georges – query) there who took Rosenblatt to a shack in a field. After two nights in the shack, Rosenblatt was taken to Héricourt-sur-Thérain, and a couple who had apparently sheltered English and American evaders before, hiding them in their cellar. After three or four days at Héricourt, Rosenblatt was taken by car to a little house on the outskirts of Beauvais where he met an older man and a younger man who had studied English at school, and from where he was collected by Gilbert Thibault.

Note that Gilbert Thibault is the first helper in Rosenblatt's report whose name I have been able to confirm as there are no helpers listed by IS9 as living at any of the villages mentioned above.

Thibault asked Rosenblatt for his dog-tags and photographs before driving him to the other side of Beauvais (assume to Rochy-Condé) where they stopped near a church at what Rosenblatt calls a pub, and met Mme Odette Marin and one of her daughters. Then Thibault took him, first to his own house in Aunueil, and then about three kilometres north-west to be sheltered by Joseph and Marthe Roget on their farm at Hameau de le Croquet, Troussures, where Rosenblatt also met their son and his wife, Christiane.

Rosenblatt says that he was sheltered with the Roget family for about three weeks, and that towards the end of his stay he visited Phlemon Wright (#522), Thomas Glennan (#523) and Abe Helfgott (#524) (from the B-17 Tenabuv – they were being sheltered in Auneuil with Thibault's neighbours Pierre and Madeleine Nouges). He says that Thibault was trying arrange for a French organisation (presumably Bourgogne) to take them to Spain as an American woman, his contact with another group, had been captured – I am guessing this was a reference to the arrest of Mary-Rose Zerling (see earlier).

The date isn't given but it would have been about 17 February when gendarme Alphonse Rouillard took Glennan to a doctor (Glennan was still suffering from injuries sustained when his aircraft was shot down – see later), and Rosenblatt, Wright and Helfgott were moved to Rochy-Condé. The three Americans were sheltered with Louis Marin and his wife Odette, although Helfgott only stayed one night before moving to stay with their neighbour, Mme Xenia Rossi and her 21-year-old daughter Christianne.

Louis Marin (born December 1909) and his wife Odette Raymonde lived at the Moulin de Rochy-Condé, where Louis owned a large mill, making flour for macaroni – they had four children, and a maid named Louisette.

Mme Xenia Rossi (aged 57) and her daughter Christianne are credited with sheltering Rosenblatt (#520), Laux (#521), Wright (#522) and Helfgott (#524) for 8 days in April 1944. Nine other airmen are also claimed for a day in August 1944 but they are not part of this story.

On 11 February 1944, the 381BG/532BS B-17 42-31099 Tenabuv (Laux) was returning from an early morning operation to Frankfurt when it was attacked by fighters. The crew bailed out and the aircraft crashed about nine kilometres south-east of Forges-les-Eaux (Seine-Maritime).

Three of the crew were captured but the other seven men evaded successfully: bombardier 2/Lt Judson F Doyle (#2332) being helped by René Guittard and the Bordeaux-Loupiac organisation in Frevent before being taken to Paris, and eventually to Switzerland, and the other six – Robert Laux, Phlemon Wright, Thomas Glennan, Abe Helfgott, Rudolf Cutino and Richard Hamilton – with François-Shelburn.

2/Lt Robert V Laux (#521) was the 23-year-old pilot of Tenabuv and he describes how they were returning from the target when they were attacked by fighters which set their #3 engine on fire, knocked out the oxygen system, and wounded the left waist-gunner Thomas Glennan

(#523) and tail-gunner Sgt Henry R Barr. As they fell out of formation, another attack knocked out their #2 engine and started a fire in the bomb-bay. They were down to about 12,000 feet when Laux rang the alarm bell and told his crew to get out, and after checking his men had cleared the ship, Laux pushed the two detonators to destroy the internal secrets of their SCR-535 (IFF) radio, in case radio operator Abe Helfgott hadn't already done so, and followed them out.

After what he describes as a "pleasing experience" in the air, Laux made a rather hard landing in a field somewhere south-east of Amiens, and before he could get out of his parachute harness, some Frenchmen were helping him. They indicated that he should run to the nearby woods and leave them to take care of his flying equipment. Laux found a deep gully where he pulled brush over himself and hid for the next couple of hours, hearing shots fired by German soldiers trying to scare him from cover. Once it quietened down, Laux began walking through the woods, hiding from civilians as he did so, until finding an abandoned house, where he spent his first night in enemy-occupied France.

Laux set off early next morning, keeping to the woods wherever he could, until he heard a boy chopping wood and approached him. After Laux used his phrase card to explain that he was a hungry American, the boy brought him some food, a beret and a coat and trousers that Laux put on over his uniform ODs before setting off walking once more, using his compass to head south towards Spain. At one stage, Laux was stopped by a German motorcyclist who raised his hand in what Laux first thought was a salute. He promptly saluted back and carried on his way, repeating the performance when passed by a lorry load of German soldiers later that day. That evening, he approached a farmhouse where he asked to be allowed to sleep in their barn. The farmer brought him blankets and let him milk one of his cows to fill his water bottle, and early next morning, woke him up with a packet of food and sent him on his way. Later that day, Laux approached a woman (who he seems to name as Mme Maison) and showed her his phrase card, and after some consideration, she took him back to her house, from where his journey was arranged.

Mme Maison's husband was a POW, and Laux met their son and his wife (IS9 list Maurice Maison at the Cour d'appel in Amiens). Laux said he wanted to go to Paris and they agreed to get him a railway ticket, for which they refused Laux's offer of payment. They told him that "the underground" had their headquarters in Paris and that he should be able to find them. Laux swapped his flying jacket and sweater for another pair of trousers and a shirt, and was told that the son and his wife would take him to Gisors (Eure) that night. However, that doesn't seem to have happened as the next mention is of Pierre Lemaire, secretary to the maire of Trie-la-Ville, a tiny village just east of Gisors.

Laux says that Pierre (who was aged about 21, and had lost an eye and half his nose in a bicycle accident) gave Laux some more civilian clothes, and asked for casualty information. Laux seems to have stayed with Pierre Lemaire at Trie-la-Ville for a week until being taken by car to Jouy-sous-Thelle, which is about half-way between Gisors and Beauvais. In Jouy-sous-Thelle, Laux was sheltered with Georges Louis Bosset (born Sept 1881), sole distributor for the Bates Stapling Machine Company – Laux says that he had been an interpreter during the last war and had apparently helped two Allied evaders the previous September, one from Johnstown, Pennsylvania, and the other from Florida. Laux stayed with M. Bosset, his wife Andrée and their teenage daughter for about eight days until Georges took him by car to Gilbert Thibault in Auneuil. Thibault told Laux that five other men from his crew were safe and then drove him to Rochy-Condé where he joined his navigator Phlemon Wright, who was being sheltered, along with 1/Lt Milton Rosenblatt, by Louis and Odette Marin.

2/Lt Phlemon T Wright (#522) was the 23-year-old navigator of Tenabuv. When he heard the order to bail out, he waited until the bombardier, Judson Doyle, came back from the rear of the aircraft (where he had been helping waist-gunner Thomas Glennan), gave him his parachute and then followed him out of the escape hatch. He delayed his jump for about twenty seconds before landing in a field and running to hide in some woods. That night, having decided that he knew where he was on his escape map, Wright set off walking south-west through the fields until daybreak when he stopped to rest for the day in a forest. He stayed resting in the forest, living off his aids-box all the next day as well before setting off to walk through the night and then spending the day in a deserted barn. By the third morning he was getting very hungry and that afternoon, he approached two women at a farm. They took some convincing but eventually gave him some food and let him sleep in their barn, and from there his journey was arranged.

Wright slept until about midnight when he woke up to find two faces looking down on him, a man and his son-in-law. They took Wright into the house where he spent the rest of the night and all next day in bed. He doesn't name the family – man, wife and two daughters – but does say that the two women who first helped him were related, and that they had previously helped 1/Lt Abraham Teitel (#728), the navigator of Bing's Big Box, the same aircraft as Milton Rosenblatt (see earlier), shot down on 21 January.

> *Teitel was helped by primary school teachers Roger and Madeleine Cressent at Nesle-Hodeng (Seine-Maritime) before being taken to Formerie (Oise), and then Marseille-en-Beauvaisis where he was visited by Gilbert Thibault. Teitel was later passed to Comète and crossed the Pyrenees in May 1944 but unfortunately his report is even harder to decipher than Wright's.*

Like the rest of the Appendix C of Laux and Wright's combined report, the two pages of covering the first days of Wright's evasion are very hard to read but within a few days, he was taken to Auneuil where Gilbert Thibault told him that everything was okay and that he was with an organisation. He mentions Glennan and Helfgott (and possibly two other men) and that they had been sent next door to stay with a blacksmith and his wife (Pierre and Madeleine Nouges at 124 rue Saint-Léger) – and that he met Milton Rosenblatt there when he came to visit. Wright seems to have stayed four or five days at the Nouges home before being taken to live with retired schoolteachers Raphael and Hélène Lefevre. The pages don't go as far as Wright meeting up with Laux – and Rosenblatt only says that Wright was with him and Helfgott when they were taken to Rochy-Condé – so we have go back to the notes of Laux and Wright's combined report (and other sources) from this point on.

As already mentioned, at Rochy-Condé, Wright, Rosenblatt and Helfgott were sheltered with Louis Marin and his family, although Abe Helfgott only stayed one night before being moved to Xenia Rossi's house. It's not clear exactly when Laux arrived but sometime after that they heard that someone had reported their presence to the Germans. Because it was thought too dangerous for them to stay at the house, Louis Marin took Laux and Wright by car to Fouquerolles (Oise) where they were joined by Rosenblatt (also brought by Louis Marin) next day. I don't know who sheltered them in Fouquerolles (possibly Edmond Caron or Lucien Hardivilliers) but they were there for about two weeks, during which time they were visited by Gilbert Thibault and Jacky du Pac. On 14 March, a gendarme, a farmer and his son-in-law (sic) took Laux and Wright to the farmer's house. This was

Wilfred Rendu at Le Fay-Saint-Quentin, and they stayed with M. Rendu, his wife and daughter, for the next three nights and four days, being joined on the second day by Canadian Kenneth Woodhouse (1858). I think that Rosenblatt was returned to the Marin family at this time.

On 18 March (as mentioned earlier), Wilfred Rendu and the gendarme took Laux, Wright and Woodhouse by truck to Bresles, where they picked up Helfgott and Thomas Glennan, to Rochy-Condé where they collected Rosenblatt from Louis Marin's flour mill, and on to Beauvais. They stopped at a small house on the outskirts of town where they collected George Buckner (#539) and David Warner (#540) from some friends of Louis Marin, and then all eight airmen were driven across town to the home of a tall, slender man and his wife where they had lunch. The man of the house made new ID cards for three of the Americans and then he and Louis Marin took them in another truck to the station where they joined four more Americans – Rudolf Cutino, Richard Hamilton, Francis Wall and William Hoffman. Note that this last part is slightly different from Woodhouse's version earlier.

Sgt Thomas J Glennan (#523) was the 23-year-old left waist-gunner of Tenabuv and he describes how they were just twenty minutes from the French coast when they were attacked by fighters. Glennan was shot through the foot, and the bombardier, Judson Doyle, gave him first-aid before helping him back to his gun just as a second attack set their bomb-bay and left wing on fire. When he heard the bail-out bell, Glennan tapped fellow waist-gunner Rudolph Cutino (#525) on the shoulder before following tail-gunner Henry Barr out of the aircraft.

Glennan landed in a wood about 100 yards from a farmhouse somewhere near Amiens where he says the whole family was waiting to greet him. By this time, the morphine that Doyle had given him the aircraft had reduced him to a semi-comatose condition and the family gave him a cane to help him walk to the wood where his engineer/TTG S/Sgt John E Holton was hiding. From their hiding place, Glennan could see two more of their crew (presumably Doyle and Barr) about half a mile away and Holton went to fetch them but never returned.

That evening, the family brought Glennan civilian clothes and carried him back to their farm where he spent the night in a hay barn – they also brought him food but Glennan was too sick to eat it. The following morning, Glennan was in so much pain that rather then wait for the family, he says he dragged himself to a café in the nearby village that he had seen the day before. He used his phrase-card to explain to the woman there that he was a hungry American and once she was satisfied, she locked the door and called for a young girl to fetch someone who spoke English. While they were waiting, she gave Glennan some cognac and began to cook him breakfast. Before she had even finished cooking, the girl returned with a young man who could read and write English and Glennan wrote a note asking him to get some medical aid as quickly as possible. The woman then washed Glennan's wounded foot and put him into bed. That evening, the woman's husband came home and seemed delighted to meet Glennan, and shortly after that, the young man he had given the note to returned with a friend. They put Glennan on a bicycle and pushed him some five kilometres to a farmhouse where he joined Abe Helfgott.

Sgt Abe A Helfgott (#524), the 25-year-old radio operator of Tenabuv, says he didn't hear the bail-out bell but the bombardier (Judson Doyle) came to the radio room and told him to tell the men in the waist to bail out, which he did. Helfgott then put his parachute on and went to help ball-turret gunner Richard Hamilton (#526) with his parachute before going out of the escape hatch himself.

Helfgott made a deliberately delayed jump and landed in a farmyard where a French couple ran up while he was still taking off his parachute. The man took his chute and hid it while the woman led Helfgott to an outbuilding. She then wrote him a note saying that because there were Germans nearby, they could not hide him on their farm and that he should go into the forest. Helfgott ran to the nearby woods where a young boy soon found him and led him to a small clearing where the boy's mother was waiting but then there was a noise behind Helfgott and the woman signalled for Helfgott to hide himself again. This time Helfgott kept going until nightfall when he came to a house on a hill. He hid in trees close to the house for the night, and early next morning went to the kitchen door and declared himself to the three men and a woman he found there. They gave him some food but again made it clear there were Germans in the area so Helfgott returned to the woods and resumed his walk.

Helfgott soon came to the end of the forest and continued across fields until he came to a farm where he saw a woman entering the house. He followed and told her that he was an American and she called a young man into the room. The young man shook hands with Helfgott, had him sit down, gave him some civilian clothes and money, a map to show Helfgott where he was, and directions to Abbeville. Helfgott followed the directions until noon when he came to a small village somewhere near Aumale, and being by then very hungry, went into a shop to try and buy some food. Helfgott didn't know that food coupons were required and when the proprietor said something to him in French, Helfgott took him to one side and explained that he was an American. The shop owner quickly shoved Helfgott through the door into his kitchen where the man's wife gave Helfgott some food while her husband called a younger man in. When he'd finished his meal, the young man took Helfgott by bicycle to a farmhouse about five miles away where three more young men asked Helfgott for some of the ID photographs he carried. Helfgott was then hidden in a loft, his meals provided by an elderly couple, and at about eleven o'clock that evening, his injured waist-gunner Thomas Glennan was brought to join him.

While Glennan and Helfgott were staying on the farm, a doctor came and treated Glennan's injured leg and fever, and after three days, the farmer (a wounded and decorated machine-gunner from the 1914-18 war) took the two Americans to another farm about three kilometres away where they found their navigator Phlemon Wright, right waist-gunner Rudolf Cutino and ball-turret gunner Richard Hamilton. The five Americans were loaded into two cars, Glennan, Helfgott and Wright with two Frenchmen in one, and Cutino and Hamilton into the other.

Glennan, Helfgott and Wright were driven to Auneuil where they met Gilbert Thibault and went to his house. Thibault then took took them next door to stay with a family of three who kept a shop (Pierre and Madeleine Nouges (maréchal-ferrand) at 124 rue de Saint-Léger), and a doctor (who had been a POW in Germany) came to treat Glennan's injuries. Two days later, gendarme Alphonse Rouillard (born July 1912) arrived to take Glennan back to his apartment in the police barracks (gendarmerie) in Bresles where he was second-in-command and lived with his wife and three young children, and where Glennan reports that he was treated excellently. An English lady, about 60 years old, who was staying next door with her daughter (who was married to another gendarme), acted as his interpreter (possibly a Mme François), and a doctor, a former flight-surgeon with the French Air Corps, came every day to treat his foot. The mayor of Bresles also visited frequently.

When Glennan went with gendarme Alphonse Rouillard, Abe Helfgott and Phlemon Wright were taken – along with Milton Rosenblatt who was collected from the Roget family at Troussures (see earlier) – to stay to Louis Marin at Rochy-Condé. Helfgott was only there for one night before being taken to a neighbour's house where he stayed with Xenia Rossi (wife of a French officer) and her daughter Christianne. A few days later, he was returned Louis Marin's house where Gilbert Thibault passed him on to Gaston Legrand and Odette Sauvage. They took Helfgott back to their home in Clermont where he met Odette's son Edmond, and Gaston's brother, Bernard. After nine days with Gaston and Odette, Gaston took Helfgott on his motorcycle back to Louis Marin at Rochy-Condé and then on to the gendarmerie at Bresles to join Glennan at the Rouillard apartment.

The following week, Glennan and Helfgott were taken to a farmhouse where they rejoined Wright and Rosenblatt, along with their pilot Robert Laux, and were interrogated by a man they refer to as Jacques the IO – Jacky du Pac. Three days later, Glennan and Helfgott were returned to the Rouillard family at the Bresles gendarmerie.

On 18 March, Glennan and Helfgott were collected by truck, driven by farmer Wilfed Rendu with Kenneth Woodhouse, Robert Laux and Phlemon Wright already on board, to Beauvais where they picked up more Americans, and then to another house for lunch. After the meal, they were taken in a different truck (this one driven by Louis Marin), with Gilbert Thibault and others as guides, to the railway station, where they boarded a train for Paris.

Sgt Rudolf Cutino (#525) was the 23-year-old, right waist-gunner of Tenabuv and he followed fellow waist-gunner Thomas Glennan out of the aircraft, losing his aids box and the purse with his escape money, which fell out of his pocket when his parachute opened, and landing in an open field. He hid his parachute before running to some nearby woods where he hid for the rest of the day and following night. Next morning, using the small compass that he always kept in the waist-band of his trousers, he started walking north-west. At about two o'clock that afternoon, he was passing a farm when he was spotted by a woman who called out to him, and when he told her that he was an American, she took him to a shed where she brought him some bread and coffee. A few minutes later, she brought a man who took Cutino to his farm where he was given a proper meal and put into a hayloft for the rest of the day. That evening, the farmer brought Cutino civilian clothes, and after a meal in his house, took Cutino to another farm where he joined his ball-turret gunner, Richard Hamilton.

Sgt Richard C Hamilton (#526) also landed in a field, which he says was somewhere near Conteville (Oise) – which is about half-way between Amiens and Beauvais. After hiding his parachute in some brush, the 21-year-old started running towards another parachute which he saw on the ground. He was met by a group of Frenchmen who gave him a coat and began to lead him away but then two German soldiers appeared, the Frenchmen scattered, and Hamilton was captured. He was taken to a small hut and while the soldiers were apparently waiting for transport to arrive, Hamilton tripped one and hit the other before running off through some scrubby trees. He found the Frenchmen standing on the other side of the trees and they grabbed him and made him run with them to a barn where he was left hidden in a hole under the hay. His rescuers returned at midnight with some food but they wouldn't let him leave the hole until next morning, and then still kept him inside the barn. During the day they brought civilian clothes and that night, Rudolph Cutino was brought to join him.

Cutino and Hamilton stayed in the barn for five days until being taken to a house where they met two Frenchmen who brought their fellow crewmen Phlemon Wright, Thomas Glennan and Abe Helfgott in two cars (see earlier). One of the Frenchmen checked their identities and took their dog-tags before putting them into one of the cars and driving through Marseille-en-Beauvaisis (Oise), where they waited for the second car. When that did not appear, they carried on alone but then got a flat tyre, and Cutino and Hamilton were taken to a farmhouse nearby. After two nights at the farmhouse, one of the Frenchmen returned and took them in another car with two French officers of the "Secret Army" (one spoke Spanish and the other Italian) to a house on the outskirts of Beauvais where they had supper. After their meal the two Americans walked to a house at 13 rue Aristide Briand in Marissel where 23-year-old butcher Charles Choux lived with his wife Ginette (22) and brother Albert, who worked as a cook for the Germans. Cutino and Hamilton stayed with the Choux family for a month until 18 March when the same man who had brought them, collected them in a truck with four other Americans (sic) already on board (Wilfred Rendu with Woodhouse, Laux, Wright and Rosenblatt), and took them to Beauvais station where they joined Glennan and Helfgott – and they say that four French guides took them (and others) by train to Paris.

S/Sgt George P Buckner (#539) was the engineer/TTG and **Sgt David Warner** (#540) one of the waist-gunners of 92BG/326BS B-17 42-31387 (McMurray) which was shot down on 8 February 1944 and crashed near Catheux (Oise) – the same aircraft as 2/Lt William Hoffman (#530) – mentioned above and see below.

Buckner reports head-on attacks by Fw190s which hit the front of their aircraft, smashing oil lines and control cables. The pilot (1/Lt Warren E McMurray) jettisoned the bomb load and dived for cloud cover at about 4,000 feet but was struggling to maintain altitude and the co-pilot (2/Lt Clayton F Fitzgerald) told Buckner to go back and tell the rest of the crew to bail out.

Buckner rolled out of the escape hatch at about 1,500 feet, pulled his rip-cord as soon as he was clear of the aircraft, and says that he saw three other parachutes in the air before he landed in some brush. He had only just finished hiding his parachute when he spotted another chute dragging someone and ran across to find Warner unconscious.

Warner had followed Buckner out of the aircraft but then had trouble controlling his parachute before knocking himself out on landing. Buckner collapsed Warner's parachute and was helping him up when a farmer who had been ploughing a nearby field came over to them. Buckner used his phrase card to ask if the man could hide them and he took the two 22-year-old Americans back to his house. Another man brought them civilian clothes, and their journey was arranged from this point.

Their combined report is almost illegible but the farmer who took Buckner and Warner back to his house was Louis Picard of Fontaine-Bonneleau. Another man came to the house and the two Americans swapped their uniforms for French peasant clothes before two men with a pick-up truck drove them to Crèvecoeur-le-Grand. Warner was sheltered with Marc and Odette Hanniet and their two children at their bakery on rue de Presbytere – Marc was an ex-cavalry veterinarian who also took their pictures for ID cards – while Buckner was sheltered with garagiste André Cocuelle, his wife and their two children at place de l'hôtel de Ville. They stayed in Crèvecoeur for about ten days – during which time they saw Milton Shevchik, Francis Wall and their own navigator, William Hoffman (see earlier) – until Marc Hanniet, took Warner, along with Francis Higgins (#825) and Robert Sidders (#1056), to Beauvais.

Warner, Higgins and Sidders were taken to an abandoned house in Beauvais from where they were collected by Gilbert Thibault. Dean Tate,

William Lessig and Carl Mielke, who had arrived that day from Creil (see earlier), were already in the vehicle, and Thibault drove them all to a café at Ons-en-Bray.

Buckner was driven into Beauvais with Everett Stump and Carlyle Van Selus – who had also been sheltered in Crèvecourt (see earlier) – and after a meal at their driver's house, two other men took the three Americans to a café in Ons-en-Bray where they joined Warner, Higgins, Sidders, Tate, Lessig and Mielke.

Buckner and Warner were sheltered with Camille and Georgette Orliac, garagistes of Hameau du Pont-Qui-Penche (Ons-en-Bray), and their two children, Jean (16) and Jeanette (18). I think they were there for about two weeks before Gilbert Thibault took them, Higgins and Sidders to Noailles.

In Noailles, Buckner and Warner were sheltered with Robert and Marthe Eckert on rue Mignon. They met their tail-gunner Sgt Marion Knight (#1057) there, along with 2/Lt Glenn E Camp Jnr and 2/Lt Jarvis H Cooper, the pilot and navigator of B-17 42-29963 Judy, before Thibault took Sidders, Higgins, Knight, Camp and Cooper on to Chaumont-en-Vexin where they were sheltered with René and Eva Moreau of rue Pierre Budin.

Shortly before Buckner and Warner left Noailles, Gilbert Thibault brought Jacky du Pac to interview them, and on 18 March, Thibault returned in a truck to take them back to Beauvais where they joined a group of airmen (which included Rosenblatt, Laux and crew) to be taken to Paris.

2/Lt William H Hoffman III (#530) was the 25-year-old navigator of 92BG/326BS B-17 42-31387 (McMurray), the same squadron and on the same operation to Frankfurt on 8 February as 42-37984 (Shevchik). Like Shevchik's aircraft, they were attacked by fighters over Luxembourg and turned back with what was left of their formation, losing altitude as the attacks continued until the aircraft was abandoned.

Three other crew also evaded successfully: engineer/TTG S/Sgt George Buckner (#539) and waist-gunner Sgt David Warner (#540) – see both above – and tail-gunner Sgt Marion Knight (#1057) who was taken to Noailles, where he met Glenn Camp and Jarvis Cooper (mentioned earlier), to Chaumont-on-Vexin with Sgt Ray Reeves (#729), and in May, to Chateaudun where he helped with work on the new MI9 Mission Marathon camp at Freteval, and from where he was liberated in August.

Hoffman reports them turning back in formation but losing altitude rapidly. With shells going through their left wing and fuselage, the bombardier (2/Lt Sidney Scheiman) being wounded in the head and the interphone dead, the co-pilot (2/Lt Clayton F Fitzgerald) went through the aircraft telling everyone to bail out. They threw the engineer (Buckner) out and Hoffman saw his parachute open before jumping at an estimated 1,000 feet. Hoffman pulled his rip-cord as soon as he left the aircraft, landing on his back just fifteen seconds later (at 1130 hrs) in a ploughed field north-west of Crèvecoeur-le-Grand.

Hoffman could see a farmer nearby at the edge of some woods, and after taking off his parachute, carried it towards him. While the farmer was helping Hoffman hide the parachute, Mae West and flying boots, a girl arrived, followed by some other people, and she led Hoffman off to the south-west, away from his burning aircraft. She took him about two miles to a small village on the edge of the woods, probably Doméliers, not the one he had seen from the air, and a house where he was given cognac and some food, and the slight wound on his hand was dressed. Then he was moved to another house where a woman brought a French-English dictionary and wrote out some questions, asking his nationality, what he wanted to do and whether he knew of any organisation in the area. Hoffman concluded this last question was a test and he later found out that the woman knew all the helpers in the district. Hoffman told them he wanted to get to Spain, and spent the night in the house but next morning his helpers told him they would arrange to have him sent back to England by air. That night, three men came in a truck and took Hoffman to the larger village nearby (Crèvecoeur-le-Grand) where his journey was arranged.

At Crèvecoeur-le-Grand, Hoffman stayed with Justin Lefranc and his wife Germaine on rue de Clermont. Justin was a book-keeper in the textile factory, and Hoffman describes him as the "first sergeant" of the resistance group in the town. Hoffman was taken to see Milton Shevchik, James Thorson and Sgt Francis Wall – he also saw Robert Sidders and Francis Higgins from their crew, who were in safe hands but did not make the rest of the journey with them. For the last two days of his time in Crèvecoeur, Hoffman stayed with André Cocuelle and his wife Simone at place de l'hôtel de Ville. André ran the local garage and Hoffman says he was the "organisation chief". He asked for Hoffman's dog-tags, saying that their insignia would be taken and buried so they could get them after the war.

Sgt Francis C Wall (#529) was the 21-year-old right waist-gunner of Shevchik's aircraft. Wall, who had been hit in the left eye by a piece of shrapnel over Luxembourg, bailed out at about 3,000 feet, losing his gloves but keeping his aids-box when his parachute opened. As he drifted down, he saw his aircraft crash nearby just as an enemy fighter fired at Hoffman's aircraft, which was also about to crash.

Wall landed in a field about three miles north of Crèvecoeur-le-Grand, where the wind dragged his parachute across the ground before he managed to get it off, and a man working in the field came over and asked him for a cigarette. Hearing an American reply, he took Wall's parachute, harness and Mae West, and two boys ran up to help the man hide them under his coat before taking Wall to hide in some briars in the corner of the field. At about five o'clock that evening, the boys and their father came back with coffee and food, and when it was dark, led Wall about two miles south to a barn. They brought more food, and some wine, and a woman came to wash the blood off Wall's face before leaving him to sleep overnight in the barn. Next morning the woman returned with breakfast, sandals and some civilian clothes, and Wall was taken by truck into Crèvecoeur-le-Grand where he was sheltered with Gaston and Jeannine Plichon.

Gaston Plichon was a teacher and he had a radio on which he listened to English broadcasts. He took care of Wall and had a doctor look at his eye. Wall's radio operator (Robert Sidders) came to see him, and then all the rest of the crew visited except the navigator (2/Lt James E Williams) and bombardier (2/Lt Donald J Periolat). Wall didn't go out much at first because he felt sick but about a week later, he was taken join his co-pilot James Thorson (#528) at the Dizambourg home on rue de Breteuil.

On 18 February (as mentioned earlier), Wall and Thorson were taken to Beauvais, along with their pilot Milton Shevchik, and 231387 navigator William Hoffman. While Shevchik and Thorson stayed with coal dealer Emile Vifquain and his wife Marie at 158 boulevard Aristide Briand, Wall and Hoffman spent their first week in Beauvais with Emile Vifquain's neighbours, an elderly couple, Julien Reusse and his wife, and then on 26 February, they were taken to Marseille-en-Beauvaisis, where they were sheltered by a farmer named Joseph Lesueur. Joseph was eighty-four years old and lived with his wife Marguerite, their son Albert, and his wife Jeanne. Wall says they stayed for 22 days and had a good rest – they got plenty of food and could sit in the sun outside, and sawed wood for exercise. Hoffman says they stayed 24 days, confirms lots of good food and chopping wood – the Lesueurs were very poor people and appreciated anything the Americans did for them. The old man hated the English and

Germans equally but apparently liked Americans. Shevchik and Thorson came once to visit them, as did Sgts Rudolf Cutino and Richard Hamilton from Robert Laux's crew.

They were also visited by an English-speaking Intelligence Officer who asked them questions about baseball. He was a dark, heavy-set man, about 5 foot 10 inches tall who went by the name of Jacques. Next day (18 March), Hoffman and Wall were taken back to Beauvais where they joined ten other evading airmen to be taken by train through Creil to Paris.

By what may have been a coincidence, Graham Brickwood, Russell Barnlund and Kenneth Lussier, also arrived in Paris on Saturday 18 March 1944.

F/O Graham C Brickwood (1854), a 24-year-old Australian who had joined the RAF in December 1938, was flying 2 Sqn Mustang AM188 on a photo-reconnaissance sortie to Oisemont on the afternoon of 29 January 1944. He had just crossed the French coast when he was hit by light flak and crash-landed in a field north-west of the little village of Nibas (Picardy). As he climbed out of his aircraft, four civilians appeared and made signs for him to follow a young boy who was with them. The boy took Brickwood to a wood where he gave Brickwood his jacket and told him to wait there. A short while later, the boy returned with his father and two brothers who took Brickwood back to their house in Nibas. Brickwood was given food and civilian clothing and Dr Eugene Delleville was summoned from Friville-Escarbotin to treat Brickwood's injuries. The doctor left after dressing Brickwood's various wounds but returned soon afterwards with hairdresser M. Roux and his wife (query) who took Brickwood back to their home at Friville-Escarbotin where he was sheltered for the next seven weeks.

During his stay with the Roux family, Brickwood says that he visited Russell Barnlund (1859), Kenneth Lussier (1860), Leslie Lambourn and Arthur Wilby.

F/O Leslie T Lambourn and Sgt Arthur C Wilby (LIB 1534) were the navigator and wireless-operator of 578 Sqn Halifax LW503 (Ormrod) which was shot down near Abbeville on the night of 24-25 February 1944. They were sheltered for two days with mechanic René Pollet at rue Hubert Acoulon in Friville-Escarbotin before being moved to Gamaches. On 15 March, they were collected from Gamaches by an English-speaking man, who was almost certainly a German agent, and driven to Lille where they were captured.

F/O Russell E Barnlund RCAF (1859) and **Sgt Kenneth E Lussier** RCAF (1860) were the bomb-aimer and mid-upper gunner of 408 Sqn Lancaster DS845 (Fillion) on an operation to Augsburg on the night of 25-26 February 1944. However, engine failure forced them to turn back before reaching the target and after jettisoning their bombs, the pilot gave the order to bale out and the aircraft was abandoned to crash near Abbeville.

I believe all the seven-man crew landed safely but that the other five men were caught – certainly F/Sgt P E Fillion, engineer Sgt Robert Gigg (LIB/614) and rear gunner Sgt S Thorvardson. Gigg and Thorvardson were sheltered by M. and Mme Saint-Yves at Longroy (Seine-Maritime) until being collected by a man who drove them to Amiens where they were passed onto another man who was almost certainly a German agent. He drove the two airmen to Arras where they, along with an unnamed American waist-gunner, were captured on 17 March 1944. Gigg later met their pilot Fillion in Brussels, who had been captured in exactly the same way.

Barnlund landed in the back garden of a house in Friville-Escarbotin at about four o'clock in the morning. He hid his parachute and flying gear in a haystack and then hid himself in another haystack nearby where he stayed for the next forty-eight hours, living off the contents of his escape box. On the early morning of 28 February, he set off walking, heading south-west. He met a woman on the road and although not speaking French, managed to make her understand that he was hungry, and she took him to a farmhouse and gave him coffee and a packet of food to take away with him. After leaving the farm, he continued through two villages and had entered a third when a boy approached him and led him to his house. After giving him some food and clothes, the boy took Barnlund to Buigny-lès-Gemaches where he stayed for a few hours, during which time a man asked to see his identity disc, before he was taken by horse and buggy to Saint-Blimont (about 10 kms north, passing Escarbotin on the way). He was given an identity card before leaving the house at nine that evening and his journey arranged. On 28 February, Dr Eugene Delleville and Maurice Sellier took Barnlund to Friville-Escarbotin and Maurice's house at 42 place de Marie, where on 3 March, he was joined by Kenneth Lussier.

Lussier landed in a field a few miles east of Friville-Escarbotin, near the little village of Chépy, and leaving his parachute, ran down the road to a field where he slept for the rest of the night. In the morning he found that he was quite close to a farmhouse which seemed to be occupied by German soldiers, so he hid in a cattle stall. That evening he moved to another farm where he slept in a chicken-coop, staying there for most of the next day until following a man who had come out of the house. Deciding to return to the farm, he encountered two men and so used his knowledge of French to tell them he was an RAF airman in need of food and civilian clothing. They took him back to the chicken coop, and later brought him some clothes. An hour later, two men arrived on bicycles and walked with Lussier through the village to the home of one of the men where he stayed the night. He spent the following day in a haystack, during which time another man came to check his identity and that evening, he was taken by bicycle to a house in Saint-Blimont where he stayed with a man who worked in the nearby sugar factory. A few days later (on 3 March) he was taken to Maurice Sellier's house in Escarbotin where he joined Barnlund.

On 17 March, Barnlund and Lussier were taken to see Australian Mustang pilot Graham Brickwood, who was sheltered in the same village, and early next day, a man who worked for Maurice Sellier took them and Brickwood to Woincourt where they were given railway tickets and put on a train to Abbeville with a man that Brickwood refers to as M. Poilu (poilu is simply an informal term for a WW1 French infantryman), and Barnard and Lussier name as M. Rouen, as their guide. They were met at the station by a woman who took them across the river to the home of Bernard and Marguerite Horen at 33 rue Lesueur. They were supposed to leave for Paris that day but the line had been bombed and they stayed overnight with the Horens before taking a nine o'clock morning train to Paris. They went first to the apartment of a woman called Berthe at 18 rue Demarquay (almost next to the gare du Nord) and then to a restaurant. After a meal, they were walked through the streets to a café near Montparnasse station and a flat belonging to an unnamed man, his wife and their two small boys where they spent the night, all three in one bed.

The following morning, Brickwood was separated from Barnlund and Lussier when their guide returned to take him elsewhere, and Barnlund and Lussier were taken to boulevard Saint-Michel. They were sheltered overnight by Maurice Cavalier at the Lycée Saint-Louis, and that evening, given identity cards and passes to permit them to enter the coastal zone. At seven o'clock the next morning (21 March), they were taken to Montparnasse station where they met four Americans (Rosenblatt,

Cutino, Hamilton and Hoffman) and the young man (query) and woman (Bertranne d'Hespel) who were their guides. Their train left at 0815 and they travelled to Saint-Brieuc in a private compartment before changing to the local train for Guingamp.

Brickwood was taken to 62 rue Tiquetonne, the home of Genevieve Schneegans, where he met American, Keith Sutor (#536) and Canadian, Kenneth Woodhouse (1858). Woodhouse left Paris that evening, and Brickwood joined Sutor and stayed overnight and the following day at rue Tiquetonne, during which time, a photographer came and took their photographs. Early the following morning (22 March), Brickwood and Sutor were taken to Montparnasse station where they made up a party of six men (with William Lock, Charlie Mullins, Alfred Coffman and Robert Rujawitz – see later), and were given their identity cards and permits for visiting the coast before boarding a train to Saint-Brieuc, where they changed for Guingamp.

I'm sure it was no coincidence that Keith Sutor arrived in Paris on Saturday 18 March 1944, brought there from Egry by Pierre Charié.

S/Sgt Keith W Sutor (#536) was the tail-gunner of 389BG/567BS B-24 42-40747 Heavy Date (Mattson) – the same aircraft as Rogoff (#455), Berry (#456) and Paquin (#458) (see earlier) – which was abandoned to crash south of Vrigny (Loiret) on 7 January 1944.

Sutor was probably the last man to jump from the burning aircraft, and as he pulled his rip-cord, it broke. Fortunately he was still at fairly high altitude and had time to use both hands to pull the little piece of cable left before landing in a field near Nibelle (Loiret). Sutor hurt his leg on landing and was still trying to hide his parachute in a ditch when he saw a group of people running in his direction. Two men found him in the ditch and took his parachute and Mae West before one of them pointed to some woods and told Sutor to "scram" – which he did.

Sutor spend the rest of the afternoon hiding under a small bridge in the woods before coming out as it got dark and using his compass to set off walking south, thinking (erroneously) he was heading towards Paris. Sutor spent the next five days walking by night and sleeping in woods and haystacks during the day until the fifth night (12 January, Sutor's twenty-second birthday), when he was on the road just south of Pont-aux-Moines and approached a man (aged about 45, with grey hair and a small red moustache) who was loading wood onto a cart. The man was a wood-cutter and he hid Sutor in the back of his cart and took him to his house outside Mardé where he lived with his wife and small son. Later that evening, a man named Marcel Germain (aged about 40, he was fat, with black hair and heavy stubble)[51] took Sutor to the nearby home of electrician Marceaux Jovilet (26 years old, thin, with black hair, an ex-sailor who had been a prisoner in Germany). Next day, a friend of M. Jovilet, a man named Pierre Berault, drove Sutor about two miles south of Mardé to a farmhouse where a man named Charteret (aged about 50, 6 feet tall, bald but with a big red moustache) lived with his equally tall wife.[52] His wife's mother lived in a little house next door, and his sister-in-law, and her young daughter and three sons in another little house nearby.

While Sutor was staying with the Charteret (Chartraire – query) family, Pierre Berault brought a man from an organisation in Orleons to see him, and after a week, Pierre took Sutor back to his own house. Three days later, Sutor was taken to stay with Marcel Germain, where a doctor visited and removed a bullet from under the skin of his back. There was also an elderly interpreter who often came to talk to Sutor. Maurice was about seventy-five years old and lived with his mother somewhere outside of Mardié. He told Sutor that he had lived in England for thirty-one years, and that his son was a London policeman.

On 22 February, Sutor was taken back to Nibelle where he stayed with the man (aged about 50, 6 feet tall, wore glasses) who had taken his parachute when he landed. Apparently he had not been able to help Sutor the first time because there were so many German troops in the area but he and his wife, a retired schoolteacher, had sheltered two airmen before, one Englishman and one American, and that the American had just left. Next day, a French "country doctor" (a short man, aged about 40) (probably not Dr Maurice Rousse, who makes no mention of helping Sutor) drove Sutor to Egry and delivered him to Pierre Charié.

Sutor only stayed for a couple of hours with Pierre Charié before grocer Raymond Bourdois, his wife Hughette and a miller called Marcel (aged about 32 with black hair, spoke English, walked with a cane) drove him to the Bourdois house in Puiseaux. Sutor received daily visits from the local pharmacist (André Bressin) who showed him motion pictures of his crew-mates, Rogoff, Berry and Paquin – see earlier.

51 IS9 lists Mme Marguerite Germain of Pont-aux-Moines.

52 IS9 lists Mme Heloise Chartraire, fermier at Mardié.

On 18 March, Pierre Charié took Sutor on a two and a half hour train-ride to Paris gare de Lyon where, after some delay as their contact wasn't at the station to meet them, Charié passed him on to a man that Sutor refers to as a dentist (aged about 35, 5 ft 7 inches, black hair, thin body and face) (see below). The dentist took Sutor to rue Tiquetonne where Genevieve Schneegans lived with a girl of about twenty-four named Olympe Vasseur (she had an English father and Spanish mother), and where Sutor met Maurice Cavalier. On 20 March, he was briefly joined by Canadian Spitfire pilot Kenneth Woodhouse (1858) before the dentist took him elsewhere – and English (sic) Mustang pilot Graham Brickwood (1854) arrived.

Woodhouse says in his post-war account, that Sutor's guide, who Sutor refers to as a dentist, was the same man who took him (Woodhouse) to the Lycée, and later made his identity papers – this was Jean Pivet.

On the morning of 22 March, Marcel Cola arrived at rue Tiquetonne to take Sutor and Brickwood to the gare Montparnasse and they were put into a compartment where they joined William Lock, Charlie Mullins, Alfred Coffman and Robert Rujawitz on the train for Saint-Brieuc, where they changed for Guingamp.

The other six airmen evacuated on this final Bonaparte operation – Ronald Daniel, William Lock, Charlie Mullins, Alfred Coffman, Robert Rujawitz and Robert Sweatt – had all arrived in the French capital earlier.

P/O Ronald W Daniel (1855) was the 22-year-old Australian pilot and only survivor of 35 Sqn Halifax HR985 which was returning from Cannes (where their target was the marshalling yards on the main coastal line to Italy) in the early hours of 12 November 1943 when they were attacked by a night-fighter. Despite shooting the enemy fighter down, the bomber's controls were shot away, the aircraft went into a spin and Daniel gave the order to bale out, although the intercom was no longer working.

Daniel says he landed in a field somewhere between Le Sar (assume Le Sap) and La Ferté-Frênel (Orne), hid his parachute and used his compass to start walking south. When it began to get light, he stopped to take off and hide his tunic, keeping only the badges for identification purposes, and carried on with just his navy blue pullover. After being turned away from the first house he tried, Daniel had better luck at the second where a woman gave him something to drink but not the civilian clothes Daniel was hoping for. He carried on walking towards the town of Gacé but quickly retraced his steps when he saw German troops before circling the town and heading south-east to regain the road in an attempt to reach Alençon, where he thought he could get a train going south. Daniel continued on to Echauffour where he went to the railway station to ask about trains running south but was told no such trains went from there. He returned to the town and went to a bakers to try and buy some food. The woman there was unable to understand Daniel and when he produced his phrase card in an effort to get his message across, the woman immediately called her husband. He asked Daniel to wait while he fetched a woman who spoke English. Fortunately the woman, Mlle Noelle Guillou (about 32 years old, medium height with brown hair) managed to convince the baker and his wife that Daniel was an Allied airman, despite his short cropped hair. Mlle Guillou then brought Pierre Desfresne (query) who carefully examined Daniel's escape kit and badges to confirm that Daniel was genuine, after which he took Daniel to a forest and hid him in a hut while plans were made to try and help him.

On 3 December, Mlle Guillou took Daniel to met a M. Gaubet (query), whose father was the maire of Neuilly-sur-Marne. Daniel had to leave everything that might prove his British identity behind at Echauffour when M. Gaubet took him to Paris, something which Daniel says was a "great handicap" on future occasions. Daniel stayed in M. Gaubet's flat in Paris for about three days before moving to a house in the grounds of the Maison Blanche Hospital. Three days later, he was taken in by a M. Cima (query) who had a house in the same grounds, where Daniel stayed for the next six weeks.

On 20 January, Noelle Guillou came to tell Daniel that he would be leaving for Algiers in two days' time. Next day, Daniel received a visit from Lt Sherman USAAF (this was 2/Lt Howard Sherman (#608) co-pilot of the B-17 42-5763 Bomb Boogie) who had been sent by the organisation that was helping him (Sherman was being sheltered in the Parisian suburb of Livry-Gargan at this time before being passed on to Dutch-Paris) to check on Daniel as he had no means of identification. Sherman told Daniel that about 30 Americans had been captured recently in Paris (this is a reference to the eighteen men captured at Eglise de Pantin on 17 December) and he urged Daniel to go with Mlle Guillou as that was his best chance of getting out, and asked Daniel make sure his people were notified if he did.[53]

53 See "They came from Burgundy" for more details.

On about 22 January, Mlle Guillou took Daniel to stay with Mlle Marie-Thérèse Auffray and her cousin Mlle Monique Tarin at 21 rue Gazan, Paris XIV – Daniel says that neither woman was member of any organisation – and it seems they didn't know their neighbours very well either – dentist Dr Jacques Cahen-Delabre, an early contact of Georges Broussine, and listed by Yves Allain, also lived at this address. Daniel was told (again) that he would be leaving for Algiers but his guide failed to appear and after two weeks, Mlle Guillou returned to say they could not get him away after all. Mlle Auffray said she thought she knew a woman who might be able to help and on about 3 February, a woman (no name) came to the house and said that Daniel was to go to Gournay (Indre, Centre) from where he would leave for England by air.

On about 12 February, a M. Trompier (no such name found) took Daniel by car to La Feuille (assume Manche) where he met a dark, middle-aged man called Bailleux (more likely Baillieul) who took him to Morville (assume Manche) and then to a house in the country. Daniel was supposed to met a member of British Intelligence but the only people he did meet were three women, one of whom was the sister of a Mrs Bingley-Day who lived at Hoverigham in Yorkshire. Daniel could see no point to this journey and he returned to Morville where he stayed in a hotel with M. Bailleux for a couple of nights where Bailleux introduced him to his friends as a member of the RAF!

On 14 February, Daniel and M. Bailleux cycled to Auzouville (there are several in Upper Normandy) where Daniel was told he would be picked up by aircraft that night. He stayed in a hotel in the village with an unnamed Belgian who told him the aircraft would arrive the following night. Later he was told the aircraft had come but flashed a message saying it would not be landing that night.[54]

On 16 February, Daniel went to stay with a M. Deschamps (possibly Hubert Decamps of Forges de Sainteny, Manche – later shot) until 22 February, and while he was there M. Deschamps told Daniel he did not trust M. Bailleul – any more than Daniel did by this stage. Daniel asked M. Deschamps to write to Marie-Thérèse Auffray explaining his position and telling her that he wanted to return to Paris. On 22 February, Mlle Auffray collected Daniel and took him back to Paris where he stayed with her for a

54 "We Landed by Moonlight" (Hugh Verity, revised version published by Crecy in 1998) shows Operation Corpus (Wg/Cdr Lewis Hodges in a Hudson – no other details) failed the night of 15-16 January through bad weather.

week while she waited for a de Gaullist friend of hers to turn up. On about 4 March, this woman visited Daniel (she was Mlle Maud, a dark attractive woman of about 28, slim build, about 5 feet 5 inches tall) who said she would get Daniel back to the UK in a few days time.

At about the same time, Daniel was visited by Mme Jules Henry, wife of the French ambassador to Spain in 1935. She asked Daniel if he would write to a Marc Rugart of the French National Committee for Liberation when he got back to the UK to tell him that she was safe and well.

Daniel then became ill and was attended by a woman doctor Huguet (Dr Simone Huguet of 90 avenue Mozart – query) and on 12 March, Daniel went to stay with her. On 17 March, Mme Henry took him to stay with another woman doctor, Dr Heslet (this was Bertranne d'Hespel) at 7 rue Maspero. On the evening of 20 March, Bertranne d'Hespel took Daniel to Montparnasse station where he met three Americans – George Buckner, David Warner and Francis Wall – and Mme d'Hespel passed them over to their guide, René Loiseau. They joined some more Americans (sic) – Kenneth Woodhouse, Milton Shevchik and Robert Sweatt – and René Loiseau took all seven airmen by overnight train to Saint-Brieuc, where they changed for Guingamp.

1/Lt William B Lock (#531) was the pilot and **S/Sgt Charlie H Mullins** (#532) one of the waist-gunners of 92BG/326BS B-17 42-31175 Trudy which was returning from Oschersleben on the afternoon of 11 January 1944. They were about fifteen minutes from the Dutch border when they were hit by flak which set the aircraft on fire, and Lock gave the order to bail out.

Lock, who was on his twenty-fourth mission, and had celebrated his twenty-fifth birthday the day before, says he checked that the men in the rear of the aircraft had left before returning to the nose where he found his officers still on board. He signalled for them to jump and his co-pilot (1/Lt Richard H Sperry) indicated that he would follow Lock and so Lock jumped from the nose hatch.

Top-turret gunner T/Sgt Raymond F Pencek (#1892) was the only other man from Trudy to evade successfully – he was taken to Belgium and sheltered in Brussels until the city was liberated in August.

Lock landed hard in a small orchard close to a house, about half a mile from the Ijssel river, some fifteen miles north of Deventer (Overijssel). His parachute was tangled in a fence so he left it and ran to hide in some woods but before he could get there, was stopped by a boy on a bicycle. Lock tried to explain who he was and the boy waved him into the woods and joined him there. Lock used his language card to tell him that he was an American and the boy left. Lock had no idea if the boy was likely to return and so set off walking south by himself – he later learned the boy did return for him that night. Lock walked for the rest of the afternoon until about five o'clock when he approached a farmer ploughing a field. Lock, who was himself a farmer in Colorado, explained that he was a hungry American but on receiving no offer of assistance, continued until dark and spent his first night in Holland sleeping in a wood.

He set off early the following morning and had covered about four miles before the sun rose and he spotted a haystack where he thought he could warm himself up. That afternoon, an elderly woman came to work in the field, and after watching for an hour, Lock approached her. He was still trying to explain who he was when an elderly man arrived in a carriage and that evening, they took Lock back to their home. Their 35-year-old son lived with them and although none of them spoke English, the son managed to get the message across that he would take Lock to someone who could.

The son took Lock to a "well to do" country house where an elderly, crippled woman lived with a friend of about the same age, and a 19-year-old maid. The woman asked Lock if he wanted to go to Belgium and although he said he would rather head for Spain, she explained that she could only get him a train ticket and papers for the Belgian border. The elderly lady gave Lock a civilian leather jacket, sweater and shirt, and Lock's first helpers brought him some trousers.

On 14 January, a young man (aged about 25) took Lock by a roundabout route to another big house where a large family lived. He was shown the name and address of his engineer (Pencek) by a man who spoke a little English, who wanted to know if Lock recognised the name, and Lock confirmed that he did. Lock was also able to have a shave, and his leather jacket was exchanged for a dress overcoat.

That evening, a woman aged about 25, 5 feet 6 inches tall, rather heavy, fairly attractive with dark hair and a dark complexion (Lock was later told she belonged to an organisation) arrived in a nurses uniform (borrowed from her sister) to take Lock to another farmhouse where Lock saw the young man who had stopped him when he first landed. The woman seemed to know the people at the farmhouse and she wrote a note for the young man saying "Follow me, do as I tell you, I am a friend and will help you" in English. From the farmhouse, the woman took Lock by car back to Deventer where she lived in an expensive house near the river with her sister and their mother. That evening (query) a police inspector in civilian clothes (a tall, thin man with light brown hair) took Lock back to his house where he lived with his wife (aged about 28, five feet 7 inches tall, very attractive) and their year-old daughter. On 16 January, because they were expecting a visit from the wife's family to celebrate their daughter's birthday, another policeman (dark-haired, 150 lbs, 5 feet 7 inches tall) took Lock back to his house. An hour later, his waist-gunner, Charlie Mullins arrived and (next day according to Mullins) the two Americans were taken to an artist's house where they stayed for the next four days.

Charlie Mullins had landed between two roads, half a mile apart, about four miles north-west of Deventer, near Terwolde. Like his pilot, the 29-year-old was also a farmer but from the neighbouring state of New Mexico. After hiding in a hedge for an hour, Mullins approached two boys who seemed to be looking for him. The eldest was about 21 years old, spoke good English and said that he had been training to become a pilot when his country was invaded – he was heavily built, about 180 lbs and 6 feet 2 inches tall, with light-coloured hair – the younger boy looked about 19, had dark hair, was 5 feet 9 inches tall and spoke very little English. They offered to help Mullins, brought him some food and told him to hide until they came back that evening. When they returned, they took Mullins to a barn about three miles away where Mullins spent the rest of the night and next day, the boys bringing him more food there. That night (12 January), the older boy took Mullins back to the farmhouse where his father (aged about 55, 5 feet 10 inches tall, about 140 lbs) lived with his wife and their crippled teenage daughter. Mullins was given civilian clothing and the opportunity to shave, and next morning, Mullins and the boy cycled into Deventer.

Mullins was sheltered by an artist (a tall, slender man, about 32 years old) and his attractive, dark-haired wife. The artist's father was an English teacher who also lived at the house but (deliberately) never saw Mullins because he was afraid of the Germans. Mullins learned that the artist was the head of an organisation that provided food for Dutchmen in hiding, Mullins being the first American he had ever helped. There was also a Dutch Jew living in the house who only ever went out at night – he was a dark-haired man, about 37 years old, whose clothing shop had been shut down by the Germans. The artist wanted to see Mullins dog-tags and one day asked for a description of his pilot, Lock, who also being sheltered in Deventer. Visitors to the house included the young man who first helped Mullins, numerous Jewish friends of the man who was hidden there – they also brought clothes for Mullins – and two Dutch policemen (one was dark-haired, about 5 feet 7 inches tall, 32 years old, the other was a large man, about 6 feet 2 inches tall, aged about 30). On the fourth day that Mullins was with the artist, a woman from Deventer (about 25 years old, her sister was a nurse, they were both in their middle twenties, both heavy-set and with dark hair) came with a photograph, and the name and address of his pilot, William Lock. She also took some photographs of Mullins for an identity card. That night Mullins was taken to the home of the smaller of the two policemen where he met Lock, and the following night, the policeman took them both back to the artist's house.

While Lock and Mullins were staying with the artist (neither evader gives his name) one of his men went to try and find an organisation that could help them – the artist telling them on several occasions that he didn't trust the two sisters. He went to Amsterdam and then Eindhoven where he was put in touch with a Catholic priest who was part of the Dutch organisation which later took Lock and Mullins all the way to Paris. They also received a visit from a woman from Amsterdam – she spoke some English, and she told them that her husband had been a pilot who was killed on the first day of the war whilst trying to evacuate Queen Wilhelmina by flying boat.

On 20 January, a man with detective papers that he said he would use if they were questioned, took Lock and Mullins by train to Eindhoven where they were met at the station by a woman (described by Lock as having dark hair, a very long nose, light complexion, and not speaking any English) who took them to a higher-middle-class house where they stayed with a Catholic family who claimed to have helped many pilots before – the last one being Robert Schuen, a Thunderbolt pilot who was still with the organisation but had a sprained knee. The family was made up of the mother (a very large woman, aged about 75 who didn't speak any English), six daughters and two sons, the youngest, aged about 22 and hiding from the Germans, being the only one in the household who spoke any English. Two days later, the woman who had met them at the station, took them to another house where two men who were pretending to be detectives, took them by train to Roermond (Limburg).

At Roermond they were passed on to another man who took them to another Catholic house. They stayed with an elderly man, his wife, their son Peter (aged about 26, he was a teacher at his father's technical school) and a daughter. Lock comments that the family seemed to be rich and very religious, going to church every evening. Lock and Mullins stayed for five days, during which time an English-speaking man came to take their names, serial numbers and aircraft details. They also visited another house nearby where they met an English navigator from a Halifax which had been shot down over Eindhoven on 20 December, and who had stayed at the same house in Eindhoven as they had. Note that Lock says that both he and Mullins deliberately forgot all names and addresses of their helpers.

The "English navigator" was 36-year-old F/Lt Sydney Smith (LIB/1522) who gives his home address as Sao Paulo in Brazil. Smith was an observer on board 78 Sqn Halifax JN974 (F/Lt James G Smith) (2603) which was returning from Frankfurt on the evening of 20 December 1943 when they were shot down near Eindhoven. Smith landed in a small wood inside the perimeter of a German airfield, where he stayed until the evening of 22 December when he made his way to the village of Oerle. He was sheltered by a farmer at Oerle while one of his sons contacted an organisation, and that same evening, a young schoolteacher and his fiancée took Smith through Eindhoven to Nuren where he spent the night with another farmer. Two nights later, Smith was taken into Eindhoven where he spent the evening with Mr van Bruggen (the Ceramics Master of the Phillips factory) and his family, and the night with their in-laws, Mr and Mrs Oomens at 13 Hugo Verrieststraat. On 27 December, a Catholic priest gave him instructions on how to exchange passwords with a young Dutch CID officer who then took Smith to a tailor's shop near the station where he was passed on to another guide who was supposed to take him to Roermond. However, they missed their train and Smith was returned to the Bruggen household. On 30 December, the CID man took Smith to Roermond, where he passed him over to a Catholic priest who led Smith to Kapellerlaan 233, home of architect Henri Lemmens, his wife and their teenage son.

At the beginning of February, Smith was taken to Maastricht, where he stayed for about a week with a Dutch ex-army officer and his wife in an apartment near the station, during which time he met Liberator pilot 2/Lt Donald Schumann, who was severely burned in one eye and both hands.

On about 7 February, Smith and Schumann were taken across the Maas bridge to a small house about five miles across the Belgian border (assume Vlijtingen), where they spent the night. Next morning they were taken to a small railway station where Smith says they met seven Americans and the two Dutch girls who were their guides, and because he spoke good French, Smith was asked to buy their railway tickets for Brussels. Note that Lock (below) says Smith and the Americans joined him and Mullins in Brussels on 6 February.

On 27 January, the English-speaking man who had asked for their details, took Lock and Mullins by car to Maastricht, leaving them on a street in the middle of town where another man collected them and took them to a house near the canal. They were visited by another man who spoke a little English and he asked them to fill in a questionnaire with their family history, group and airfield details. They refused to give any details of their unit, and Mullins had his photograph taken again.

On 2 February, another man brought them identity cards and took them to another house in the town where they met their two guides (a dark, heavy-set fellow aged about 27 and a young woman who was introduced as his girl-friend – Lock describes her as being aged about 25, an attractive blonde who wore lipstick and jewellery) who would take them to Belgium. The guides took their money, leaving them with just their watches, and then walked with them about five kilometres down the main road out of Maastricht. They crossed the border through a barbed wire fence behind a guard-house, then walked south-west for another five kilometres to Vlijtingen, where they stayed overnight (2-3 February) in a café. Next day, their guides took them by train to Brussels.

Lock and Mullins spent their first night in Brussels at the Old Antwerp Hotel, where the owner (a small, grey-haired woman aged about 50 – her husband had a crippled foot) spoke good English, before going on to a boarding house at number 17 on a street they couldn't remember the name of, and where the owner (another small woman, this one thin, with a red face and red hair) was used to sheltering Dutch escapers but was (understandably) nervous of keeping Americans. Two days later (on 6 February) they were joined by the English navigator, Sidney Smith, and five Americans – Donald Schumann, Clayton David, William Koenig, Kenneth Shaver and John Buckner.

2/Lt Donald C G Schumann was the pilot of 448BG/712BS B-24 41-28593 The Prodigal Son which was shot down on 11 January. 2/Lt Clayton C David (#674) was the co-pilot of 303BG/358BS B-17 42-29524 Meat Hound (Watson), from which the crew were ordered to bail out on 11 January before pilot Captain John W Watson returned the aircraft to the UK. 2/Lt William J Koenig, T/Sgt Kenneth D Shaver (#675) and Sgt John R Buckner, were the co-pilot, engineer and tail-gunner of 384BG/560BS B-17 42-30142 Pistol Packin' Mama (Walker), which was shot down and crash-landed in Holland on 5 November 1943 – all three were captured on landing but made a brilliant escape from a train near Rotterdam a few days later (along with their pilot 2/Lt Roy M Walker, navigator 2/Lt Kenneth L Haines, bombardier 2/Lt Donald G Naughton and an unidentified B-24 waist-gunner).

Although they became separated on jumping from the train, on 12 November, Koenig and Buckner were brought from the farm where they were being sheltered, to join Shaver. All three were then taken to stay with a Dutch naval captain, and a week later to stay for two weeks with Joke Folmer (awarded the George Medal, and one of the nicest people I have ever met) who supplied them with identity cards. They were moved again several times over the next few weeks before finally crossing the border into Belgium at Maastricht and being taken to Brussels, where they met Clayton David. David had also been helped, and taken to Maastricht, by 21-year-old Johanna (Joke) Folmer, but it was another young girl who took him across the border in much the same way as Lock and Mullins, and then having delivered David to a nearby house, immediately returned to bring Donald Schumann and Sidney Smith across to join him.

Note that the route used via Maastricht and the Old Antwerp Hotel in Brussels is "classic" Dutch-Paris (see Emerson post-war comments in MIS Memo to Col Holt dd 30 July 1944, and a report by Major John H White Jnr dd 31 May 1946), with Lock and Mullins (along with Schumann, David, Koenig, Buckner and Shaver) being among roughly half the airmen claimed by that organisation who were actually brought from Holland. Many of the others (like Sherman (#608), Miller (#636) and Shaffer (#637) – all mentioned earlier) were passed to D-P in Paris. In July 1945, John Weidner of Dutch-Paris listed a total of 51 airmen as being helped by them – including 12 who were captured. The list includes three names (Pansy Johnson, Jacob Wallinga and Simon Cohen – so far unidentified) who were presumably also captured.

On 9 February, Mullins, Sydney Smith and Donald Schumann left for Paris, and on 11 February, two guides, the man who had brought them to the hotel and a Dutchman, took Lock, William Koenig, Kenneth Shaver, John Buckner, Clayton David and a Dutch escaper called Jack, presumably following the same route, by overnight train to the capital (note that Clayton David gives slightly different groups and dates). From the gare du Nord, they were taken for a long Metro ride to somewhere south of the Eiffel Tower, near a Catholic church, and down into the basement of an Electric Technical School in the Latin Quarter (this was l'Ecole Normale Supérieure (ENS) on rue d'Ulm, Paris V) where they rejoined Mullins, Smith and Schumann. The concierge was a man aged about 42, about 5 feet 5 inches tall with a dark complexion and curly black hair. He had a wife aged about 40, a daughter aged about 17 and a son aged about 15. That afternoon, French police and Gestapo came in and searched the building looking for young Frenchmen avoiding STO, because (according to Lock) the concierge explained to Smith, they had arrested two professors and three students from the school earlier that morning.

Following the raid, a Dutch priest in a black ecclesiastical robe (he was aged about 43, with a long nose and light reddish hair), moved the evaders that night to a condemned part of the church next to the school, where they stayed from 14 to 26 February, looked after by the concierge from the school, his daughter (described by Lock as being a small, attractive, 17-year-old girl with red hair) and the priest. They were visited by a member of a Dutch organisation who came to get their sizes for clothing for them to wear in the mountains but on 26 February, the priest disappeared with the Dutch boy Jack. That afternoon, another priest, who had heard that the first priest had been arrested while trying to take Jack to the station, came to the church and was startled to find Allied airmen there, rather than the Dutch or French civilians that he expected. He explained to Sydney Smith that the first priest was the only one who was a member of the organisation, and that with his arrest, they would have to leave. David says they were very reluctant to leave but when Smith went to check the building next door he found that it had been searched – he also saw the concierge's daughter through the window, who told him that her father had been arrested.

That afternoon, they were joined by two more priests and taken to the chapel where they posed as members of the congregation. After the service, the eight airmen left the church, walking in pairs (Lock with Mullins, Smith with Schuman, David with Shaver, Buckner with Koenig) trying not to look too obvious and generally heading south and out of Paris. Lock says they left at five-thirty and walked south, using the stars, until about eight o'clock when they came to an airfield (presumably Orly). They turned off the road and into a field where they decided to split into groups, and that night Lock and Mullins lost contact with the other six airmen.

Sidney Smith says that he led the Americans out of Paris, past the Porte d'Italie before the curfew and on to Etamps about 40 kms south of Paris (which seems unlikely and does not agree with Lock or David at all) where the party split up (David agrees leaving via the Porte d'Italie and passing close to an airport but then meeting up at a haystack where they said their final adieus – he and Shaver being the first to leave). Donald Schumann and William Koenig went with Smith, continuing south through the night until they stumbled into an Organisation Todt (OT) camp where they were challenged by the guards. Smith managed to get away but Schumann and Koenig were captured. Smith says that he hid up for the rest of the night in the snow before walking to Dooray (query) where he caught a train back to Paris. He went to see what had happened to the concierge at the school but the daughter spotted Smith through the window and waved him away, making him understand that there were police in the house.

That night, Smith went to the police station at Porte d'Italie where he bluffed the officer in charge into letting him spend the night next to the stove. Next morning, Smith went to the gare d'Austerlitz where he bought a railway ticket for Limoges, the furthest south he could get on the money he had. By the time he got to Limoges, his feet were badly blistered and partly frost-bitten, forcing him to go to the General Hospital, where he was admitted for treatment. On 28 February, Smith was arrested by French police and on 1 March, he was taken to a German prison in Limoges. Three days later, he was sent to Fresnes (where he shared a cell with Donald Schumann) and in May, to Stalag Luft III (Sagan).

Clayton David (#674) and Kenneth Shaver (#675) walked to the village of Sainte-Genevieve-des-Bois and approached the first house they saw with lights on. They chose well, being given a meal by the family and shelter for the rest of the night before they set off again early next morning … After several detours, they were finally taken to Pau and crossed the Pyrenees together in April.

John Buckner was captured but I don't know the circumstances.

Lock and Mullins spent the night in a haystack and next morning walked to the outskirts of a village about ten kilometres south of Paris that may have been Longjumeau where they went to a house and explained they were hungry Americans. The occupants gave them some food but did not seem prepared to help further so they carried on through the next village, Champlan (in which case they're heading north) and on to towards another village, possibly Cassaux-les-Charbreux (like previous suggestions, this is from their interviewing officer – but I think more likely south towards Saulx-les-Chartreux, where IS9 lists Mme Juliette Detry of 321 Allée de Chasse as a helper), stopping half-way to approach a farmhouse. The farmer was understandably reluctant to help but did give them some bread and half a dozen eggs before they continued on their way. About half a mile past the village, they approached another farmer (a little short fellow, bald headed, dark complexion, aged about 40) who hid them in a hut. He brought food and two friends, neither of whom spoke English but that afternoon, an English-speaking man came from Paris. He was about 45 years old, 6 feet tall, 200 lbs with black curly hair, and he quizzed them carefully about the US and England. That evening, one of first two Frenchmen, an ex-marine, took Lock and Mullins to stay overnight at his house. Next day (28 February), they were taken to another farmhouse where they stayed with a tall man, aged about 65 with a large, tobacco-stained moustache and a crippled foot. During their stay, the nephew of the man from Paris came to see them – aged about 20, he had dark unruly hair, and like his uncle, he also spoke good English.

On 3 March, the farmer they had approached in the field, and another man, took Lock and Mullins to a Metro station where they were passed on two other men, one of whom was a French spy. The spy – who spoke good English, having been to the United States, was about 30 years old, tall and thin, with straight, dark hair – took Lock and Mullins into Paris and an apartment on the top floor of an old building, ten minutes walk from the gare Montparnasse, where a large woman (aged about 45 with greying hair) and her husband (aged about 39, with dark Italian features and a small moustache – he was a wine merchant) lived with her daughter (aged about 24, her husband was a POW). The spy explained that the daughter's father was the woman's first husband. There was also a son named Louis, who visited and brought them food, and who seemed to manage the wine store.

On 21 March, the night before they left Paris, a blond man (aged about 30, average size with a light moustache) and a woman (small, dark, heavy-set, aged about 36) came to take their photographs and the following morning, Louis, the wine merchant's son, and the blond man from the night before, took Lock and Mullins to gare Montparnasse. They waited while somebody bought their tickets and were then passed on to their guide (aged about 30, 5 feet 10 inches tall with thick brown curly hair and jovial features), and he and another Frenchman took them – along with Alfred Coffman, Robert Rujawitz, Keith Sutor and Graham Brickwood – on the 0840 train to Saint-Brieuc, where they changed for Guingamp.

2/Lt Alfred T Coffman Jnr (#533) was the 27-year-old co-pilot of 381BG/535BS B-17 42-40025 Touch The Button Nell (Putek). Coffman describes how they were on their way to Nancy on 6 February 1944 when there was one explosion followed by another, and they left formation. As the smoke in the cockpit cleared, there was a third explosion and he saw their #2 propeller windmilling. He heard crackling as if something was burning but the next thing he remembered was regaining consciousness in mid-air, pulling his rip-cord and landing in a small clearing in a wood.

Navigator 2/Lt Conrad N Blalock (#546) says he looked up to see the nose of the aircraft a sheet of flame, and as he turned towards the bombardier (Harvey Christensen) there was a terrific explosion and the aircraft went into a dive. He was fastening his parachute when he heard the pilot (Henry Putek) give the bail-out order, and jumped out through the escape hatch. Blalock crossed the Pyrenees to Andorra the following month with a group which included Henry Heldman (#543) and Joseph Haywood (#544) from Kentucky Babe (see earlier).

2/Lt Harvey L Christensen (#1226) simply says that he followed Blalock out of the aircraft and landed near La Trétoir (Seine-et-Marne), about 5 kms south of Bussières. Christensen was helped by the Possum organisation of Belgian MI9 agent, Edgard Potier (who had been captured in Reims and died on 11 January) and taken into Paris where he stayed with Toussaint Sinibaldi at 2 rue du Dobropol until the city was liberated.

What none of the three officers could have known at the time was that before any of the enlisted men could jump, engineer S/Sgt Lifford E French put the fire out and waved the other crewmen back to their stations. Despite further damage from flak and attacking fighters, 2/Lt Henry Putek, with the badly burned S/Sgt French acting as his co-pilot, then nursed the crippled bomber back to England where they landed at the American Navy base at Dunkeswell in Devon.

Coffman landed near Bussières, and after hiding his parachute, heard the sound of someone chopping wood and walked towards it. He found a wood-cutter working in a clearing, pointed to the sky and told him that he was an American. The wood-cutter hid Coffman in some brush, and that evening some people took Coffman to a place where his journey was arranged.

The wood-cutter was an elderly man, aged about sixty with a grey moustache – he had been gassed in the first war, was slightly built and obviously quite poor. He told Coffman "cachey" (sic) so he went back to hide in the bushes. About 40 mins later, another, much larger, man came along, and Coffman whistled to get his attention. This was Amand Ernould (of Bussières) and although he didn't speak any English, Coffman managed to convey the fact that he was thirsty, and gave him his water bottle. Amand returned with a bottle of wine and three raw eggs. Then the elderly man came back with food and drink, and seeing Amand with Coffman, went to get a bottle of apple brandy and three glasses.

Amand Ernould organised a visit from a doctor at the local sanatorium (Dr Jean Mery – query) to check Coffman over, and once they were satisfied that Coffman was okay, he was left in the woods until evening. M. Ernould returned at about eight o'clock to walk Coffman back to his house in Bussières where he was given supper and allowed to spend the night. Next day, Coffman was taken by car about 8 kilometres to be sheltered with a M. Briant (aged about 72, 5 feet 4 inches tall with white wavy hair and moustache), his wife and their daughter. On 19 February, Amand Ernould took Coffman on foot back to his house in Bussières, where Coffman stayed with him, his wife and three daughters (including 18-year-old Marie-Ange) for next six days. On 25 February, M. Ernould and his wife took Coffman by train to Paris.

Coffman was taken to the home of a doctor (possibly a relative of Mme Ernould), somewhere near the Eiffel Tower, and that afternoon, a Mme Pamier (query spelling) arrived to take Coffman to a church near Napoleon's Tomb where they "picked up" a girl, and a young man (a fish merchant – query) who took Coffman to his home in the suburbs – apparently he had sheltered two other Americans before, one from Philadelphia and the other from New York. Three days later, Coffman was taken by Metro, meeting Mme Pamier along the way, who delivered him to an apartment at 88 rue de Vanves (now rue Raymond-Losserand), Paris XIV, home of policeman Jean Bebengut (born April 1903), his wife Yvonne and their 19-year-old daughter Andrée.

His report seems to say that Coffman was sheltered with the Bebengut family until 15 March when Mme Pamier (who had been supplying him with books and food coupons) arrived with Robert Rujawitz (#534) but this was just a visit and I think that Coffman stayed on at rue de Vanves until 21 March.

T/Sgt Robert J Rujawitz (#534) was the 20-year-old radio operator of 93BG/409BS B-24 42-100345 (Mankin) which was on the way to Frankfurt on 2 March 1944.

> *"We were hit by flak over Abbeville. Number four engine began to smoke. Shortly the engineer (Paladino) came down from the top turret and yelled that the whole wing was on fire. The ship went out of control and the pilot (2/Lt Charles W Mankin Jnr) ordered us to bail out, and hit the alarm bell. The engineer opened the bomb-bay doors and jumped. I grabbed my GI shoes, hitched them to my harness and followed him at about 18,000 feet." (Rujawitz MIS-X #534)*

Three other crew also evaded successfully: bombardier 2/Lt Roy W Carpenter Jnr (#670) crossed the Pyrenees in April with Spitfire pilot F/O Ray Sherk (1891) (who was making his second successful evasion), co-pilot 2/Lt Melvin L Heinke (#732) crossed Pyrenees with F/Sgt Harry Moss (1948) in May, and TTG/engineer T/Sgt Anthony R Paladino (#826), who was helped by Bourgogne and crossed Pyrenees in June.

Rujawitz says that he delayed his jump to about 5,000 feet, and then his parachute wouldn't open and he had to "tear off the pack by hand and throw the silk out" – fortunately he landed with his parachute caught in a tree, which broke his fall. People "came running from every direction" to help him and Rujawitz ran to some woods, where he hid his Mae West and lay down to rest. When German soldiers approached the other side of the woods, a man led Rujawitz to another wood where more local people brought him civilian clothes – and his escape-kit purse, which had fallen from his pocket during the jump. When everyone else had left, the Frenchman took Rujawitz to his barn and gave him a meal before telling him to go back and hide in the woods. Rujawitz took a Benzedrine tablet to clear his head and then spent the night in a graveyard, sleeping in a building where they kept tools.

Next morning, he was brought more civilian clothing, and shown on his escape map that he was in or near the village of Maricourt, Somme.

A boy said he would take Rujawitz to Paris but when they walked the twelve kilometres to Albert, they found there were no trains running, and so returned to the barn in Maricourt. After getting some food from the helpful farmer, Rujawitz and the boy walked to Péronne but again there were no trains running, and at about 0200 hrs, the two separated.

Rujawitz began walking south using his compass, and later that morning, lay up among some hay bales in a barn until detected by a dog. The dog's owner came to see what was going on, and on finding an evading airman, gave Rujawitz a meal. He couldn't shelter the American but he did provide directions, advice on which places to avoid, and a pitchfork to carry as part of his disguise. Rujawitz set off walking once more, taking small country roads as far as Chaulnes. From Chaulnes, he followed some farm carts until they approached the village of Curchy where he spotted a barn that looked like a good place to spend the night. It apparently belonged to one of the cart-drivers who let Rujawitz sleep there, even donating some blankets. Every two hours, a girl brought Rujawitz coffee to help keep him warm, and when he woke in the morning, there was three inches of snow on the blankets. He also found that his journey had been arranged.

The barn belonged to the d'Hautefeuille family, and Rujawitz was the second American airman to be sheltered there (P-47 pilot 2/Lt Charles B Screws (#673) had been helped by the d'Hautefeuille family in January). The girl was the daughter Elisabeth who took Rujawitz that morning by train to Amiens where they changed for Paris. In the capital, Elisabeth took Rujawitz by Metro to a place with steel doors, and a second-floor apartment at 97 rue des Petits-Champs belonging to one of her aunts, who seems to have moved to Lille. Rujawitz gave Elisabeth one of his dog-tags to take while she tried to make contact with an organisation, and that night, a female friend of hers came to the apartment.

Rujawitz says it was a woman that Coffman knew (Mme Pamier) who took him to Porte d'Orleans and a sixth-floor apartment at No 1 avenue du Général Maistre, Paris XIV (about half-way between Porte d'Orleans and Porte de Vanves Metro stations) where he was sheltered by Fernand and Leonie Zimmer. Fernand had been a test-pilot until he was injured in a crash and was now an engineer in an aircraft factory on the outskirts of Paris, while his wife Leonie was a school teacher. Rujawitz was the first American they had helped so they were probably quite pleased that English-speaking Mlle Reine Marie Rose Gonnet (who lived nearby at 10 rue Achille Luchaire and worked for the French Red Cross), visited each evening. About a week before he left, Mme Pamier took Rujawitz to see Alfred Coffman at rue de Vanves.

On 21 March, Mme Pamier took Coffman and Rujawitz by Metro to Odéon, where she handed them over to Jean Pivet who walked them to 44 boulevard Saint-Michel and the Lycée Saint-Louis apartment of Maurice and Marguerite Cavalier. They stayed overnight with the Cavaliers, and Jean Pivet took their photographs and made them new ID papers. They both mention meeting an attractive young woman at about this point – 5 feet 5 inches tall with blonde hair – but I don't know who they are referring to.

Next morning, it was Jean Pivet, along with a blond man and a woman, who took the two Americans to Montparnasse station where they joined four other evading airmen (Graham Brickwood, Keith Sutor, William Lock and Charlie Mullins) and their two guides, and boarded a train for Saint-Brieuc.

S/Sgt Robert H Sweatt (#535) was the right waist-gunner of 389BG/566BS B-24 42-41013 Trouble (Wilhite) which was returning from Ludwigshafen on 7 January 1944. They were just south of Chartres when they were attacked head-on by a Fw190 which fired a BR-21 rocket through the front of the aircraft, almost certainly killing the four officers. Sweatt only remembers a loud explosion and being pushed out of the waist window before finding himself falling through the air – 21-year-old Sweatt was the only survivor.

The following account comes from Sweatt's MIS-X report (nicely written by S/Sgt Harold F Cherniss) with some additional information from a study by Arnaud Théron.

Trouble crashed near Monboissier (Eure-et-Loir) and the badly injured Sweatt came down close to the crash-site. He was soon picked up by Moise Duplant, his father Kléber and Adrien Thion, and taken to be sheltered with Kléber Duplant and his family (father, mother Yvonne, two sons and two daughters) in their farmhouse at Augonville near Montboissier – his injuries being treated by a Dr Duboquet. However, word began to go around that an American was being sheltered and so after five days with the Duplant family, Sweatt was moved to an isolated house near Montboissier to be sheltered with bicycle mechanic Lucien Duneau (born January 1897) (aka Gaston Dunot), his wife Albertine (née Pichot April 1906), their son

Bernard, daughters Huguette and Odette, and Lucien's parents. During this time he was visited by a man described as a sheriff but perhaps chief of police, who gave him an ID card – I suspect this was local resistance chief Jules Gouzy of Bonneval.

On 1 February, a man and his wife came to the house, and the sheriff took them all to the railway station at Moriers. The couple took Sweatt by train to south-east Paris, and a woman who ran a laundry – Arnaud Théron says that Sweatt was sheltered with (metal worker) Alfred Deaudeville of 10 rue de l'Avenir, Maisons-Alfort. Whilst there, he was interrogated by a dark, slightly bald French captain who spoke English and told Sweatt that he would have him out in two or three days.

On 17 February, a man called Roger (35-40 years old, spoke English) and a garage mechanic called Maurice came to see him – they said they would radio England – and took him to Maurice's house in north-west Paris (around Neuilly-sur-Seine) where he lived with his wife Vivienne.

On 20 March, Maurice and Roger drove Sweatt to Montparnasse station where they met the Captain (sic) who said that Sweatt could not be moved until the following night. Next night, Maurice took Sweatt back to Montparnasse and passed him to a guide who led him onto a train where he met Canadian Spitfire pilot Kenneth Woodhouse, Milton Shevchik and others (Ronald Daniel, Francis Wall, George Buckner and David Warner) and they took the overnight train to Saint-Brieuc, where they changed for Guingamp.

It's not clear where, with the exception of Kenneth Woodhouse (see below), the sixteen airmen brought from Clermont and Beauvais stayed in Paris during their brief visits to the capital.

On their arrival at the gare du Nord in Paris on 18 March 1944, Milton Shevchik, James Thorson, John Bernier and David Helsel were met at the station by Marguerite Di Giacomo and René Loiseau who were waiting for twelve more evaders to arrive from Beauvais. Jacky du Pac took them to a hotel somewhere near the Anatole France Metro stop (Levallois-Perret), and a little while later, brought Robert Laux from the second group to join them. Jacky then took the five Americans around the corner to an apartment where they found Marguerite, René and Yvonne Latrace with the rest of the group from Beauvais. They were told that the boat had been shot at (a reference to Bonaparte 3, two days earlier) and that patrols at the coast were too active for them to be sent out right away.

According to Shevchik, they spent that night (18-19 Mar) in a hotel, and next day went to Yvonne's apartment at 5 rue Baudin. Robert Laux says that his party of twelve were taken to the sixth-floor, three-room apartment of a woman called Mme Higgins before he and Woodhouse left with Jacky du Pac and "a lady". He says that while Woodhouse went elsewhere with the lady, Jacky took him to another apartment where he met Yvonne.

Over the next two or three days, some of the airmen stayed in Marguerite Di Giacomo's apartment at 5 rue Baudin, some with her neighbour Yvonne Latrace and others with the Loiseau family across the road – and other addresses as well (Buckner, Warner and Wall for example, spent their last night in Paris at 7 rue Maspero) – until they were taken in groups to Montparnasse station and put on trains for Brittany. All of them met Marcel Cola, who arranged to have their photographs taken for new ID papers, and some report meeting a man that Cutino and Hamilton describe as a French officer who they believed was the head of the organisation, and Laux names as Paul – this may have been Paul Campinchi but I think it more likely to have been Paul Barrelet de Ricou.

Kenneth Woodhouse, Milton Rosenblatt, Robert Laux, Phlemon Wright, Thomas Glennan, Abe Helfgott, Rudolf Cutino, Richard Hamilton, Francis Wall, William Hoffman, George Buckner and David Warner arrived at the gare du Nord shortly after Shevchik, Thorson, Bernier and Helsel left the station.

Woodhouse explains that their train was delayed by about an hour at Creil due to bomb damage on the line but says they were met at the gare du Nord by members of the organisation. In his post-war account, Woodhouse describes how from the station, the twelve airmen were led by an elderly woman to a block of flats and up several flights of stairs to an apartment where a "lovely young woman and a middle-aged man" greeted them. As only Woodhouse and one of the Americans (Robert Laux) had suitable photographs, they were told they could continue while the rest of the party would have to wait for new pictures to be taken. Woodhouse was to follow a Frenchman (Jacky du Pac) while Laux went with a young lady that Woodhouse names as Simone. In the confusion of the crowded Metro, they became separated and it was left to Simone to take Woodhouse to her "rather spacious" third-floor apartment facing the Luxembourg Gardens – Woodhouse says there was a clear view of the Eiffel Tower so presumably this was either on the boulevard Saint-Michel or rue de Médicis. A man arrived the following morning to collect Woodhouse, and after stopping off at a bar where he was obviously well known, took Woodhouse across the Seine to an apartment at 62 rue Tiquetonne where he joined American evader Keith Sutor who was being sheltered by Genevieve Schneegans and Olympe Vasseur.

Next morning (20 Mar), Australian Mustang pilot Graham Brickwood was brought to rue Tiquetonne before his guide from earlier returned to take Woodhouse back across the river to boulevard Saint-Michel and an apartment at the Lycée Saint-Louis that appeared to be a headquarters for making identity cards and passes. The flat was owned by Maurice Cavalier but the documents were made by Woodhouse's guide, Jean Pivet (described by Woodhouse as having been an observer in the French air force, about 28 years old, 5 feet 10 inches tall, of slight build and spoke only French).

That evening, Jean Pivet took Woodhouse to Montparnasse station where his report says he met "the other Americans with whom he had travelled to Paris". The whole group (of seven airmen) had one guide (René Loiseau) when they took the 2215 train to Saint-Brieuc, where they changed for Guingamp.

Note that in his post-war account, Woodhouse says it was the same guide who was with the American (Laux) that delivered Brickwood to rue Tiquetonne, before taking him (Woodhouse) to the Lycée Saint-Louis, while Brickwood himself (see earlier) says it was the guide (M. Poilu) who had brought him, Barnard and Lussier to Paris from Normandy. Woodhouse also says that the guide who started out with the American (Laux) was the same man who collected Woodhouse from Simone the following morning – this is also clearly wrong.

Readers who might like to check some of the escape reports for themselves will notice that the Appendix C of Woodhouse's MI9 report seems to get confused with that of Graham Brickwood (1854) who reports meeting Woodhouse and an American (Keith Sutor) at rue Tiquetonne. Woodhouse's report (which makes no mention of Brickwood) says that Sutor went with him to the college and then the station but Brickwood's report says that he and the American stayed on at rue Tiquetonne until the morning of 22 March – and Sutor confirms staying on there with Woodbrick (sic – Brickwood), an English (sic) Mustang pilot who was shot down on 29 January, who left Paris with him after Woodhouse was taken away by a man that Sutor refers to as a dentist.

Canadian authors Lavender and Sheffe, who either interviewed Woodhouse or used his personal account for their 1992 book "The Evaders", agree the above version of events, although they go on to say that Woodhouse then joined Barnlund, Lussier, Sutor and a wounded American (presumably Thomas Glennan) at the station, and that their guide to Brittany was a young woman – this appears to be a reference to Bertranne d'Hespel who took Barnlund and Lussier in a group of six men to Guingamp – see later. They also say that Woodhouse met Barnlund and Lussier at Maurice Cavalier's apartment at the Lycée. The dates seem to match, Barlund and Lussier's report saying that they went to a flat in a school on 20 March, but they make no mention in their report of meeting Woodhouse there.

Paris to Guingamp

On Monday 20 March 1944, Ronald Daniel, Kenneth Woodhouse, Milton Shevchik, Francis Wall, George Buckner, David Warner and Robert Sweatt left Paris on the 2215 overnight train to Saint-Brieuc (where they changed for Guingamp) with their guide René Loiseau.

René Loiseau explained in a 2008 interview with Dominique Lecomte, that he took Shevchik's group to Brittany himself because he thought that Shevchik was a particularly experienced pilot, having flown some some sixteen missions, more than any of the other airmen he had met previously.

"The sailor [René Loiseau] took me to the Gare Montparnasse where we met other members of the party and were given tickets. The conductor on the train [assume Henri Bois] was an organisation member and we had reserved seats, all together in one compartment (seven Americans (sic) and one guide that is). We rode all night and changed trains at Saint-Brieuc next morning. We felt conspicuous while waiting on the platform there. A lot of Frenchmen stared at us, as well as several Germans. I heard one man say "Don't look at them, they are Americans." Our yellow cards were taken up on the train to Guingamp and we were given other passes, good for the restricted zone." (Shevchik MIS-X #527)

In Lavender and Sheffe's book "The Evaders", Kenneth Woodhouse seems to suggest that their guide on the train was a particularly determined young woman who called for a railway official to evict the "squatters" they found occupying their reserved seats. I think this was Bertranne d'Hespel, but that having settled the airmen in their compartment, she then left the train because Mme d'Hespel certainly didn't travel with them to Saint-Brieuc.

James Thorson would probably have gone with his pilot when Shevchik left Paris for Brittany on the evening of 20 March but because he didn't have any photographs left for an ID card, had to stay on at rue Baudin. That evening, Thorson says he met a blonde American woman, originally from California, who had lived in France for six years and was married to an Englishman (sic) who was high in the underground. She told him she had to report to the Gestapo once a week but otherwise had complete freedom – this was Margaret Barrelet de Ricou.

On Tuesday 21 March 1944, Russell Barnlund, Kenneth Lussier, Milton Rosenblatt, Rudolf Cutino, Richard Hamilton and William Hoffman left Paris on the 0815 train to Saint-Brieuc (where they changed for Guingamp) with their guide Bertranne d'Hespel.

Glennan and Helfgott would presumably have gone with them, taken to Montparnasse with Cutino and Hamilton, but apparently their papers weren't in order and they were returned to rue Baudin, where they joined Laux and Wright – and travelled to Guingamp with them the following day.

Guingamp and Plouha

Ronald Daniel, Kenneth Woodhouse, Milton Shevchik, Francis Wall, Robert Sweatt, George Buckner and David Warner arrived at Guingamp station on the morning of Tuesday 21 March, where their guide René Loiseau handed them over to Mathurin Branchoux. The group were split up and taken to different addresses in Guingamp – Woodhouse and Sweatt to Desire and Francine Laurent at 1 rue de l'Etang du Prieuré, Shevchik, Wall and Buckner to a flour mill (presumably with Joseph and Marie-Antoinette Lanoe on rue Chateaubriand), and Warner and Daniel to an unidentified woman with two children.

That afternoon, Russell Barnlund, Kenneth Lussier, Milton Rosenblatt, Rudolf Cutino, Richard Hamilton and William Hoffman also arrived at Guingamp station where they were also met by Mathurin Branchoux. He took them and their guide Bertranne d'Hespel to a house in the village where they had a meal (almost certainly chez Laurent at 1 rue de l'Estang du Prieuré) before they, and the first group of airmen (Daniel, Woodhouse, Shevchik, Wall, Sweatt, Buckner and Warner) were picked up by truck, and François Kerambrun drove them all to Plouha that evening to be sheltered at various locations around the village for the next two nights.

It's hard to be sure from the evader accounts exactly who stayed with whom and where for the next two nights but this is my best guess:

Daniel, Warner, Buckner and Hoffman went with Marie-Thérèse Le Calvez back to her mother's house at Kerlérot while Woodhouse, Schevchik, Wall, Rosenblatt and Sweatt were sheltered with Marie Tréhiou at Lizandré (actually sleeping in a deserted house nearby). Rosenblatt says there were five of them and that a little Frenchman called Jean, who came back with them, lived there – this was Marie's brother, Jean Tréhiou.

"We were here for two nights and during this time were looked after by a Frenchman who came back with us to the UK. At night (23-24 Mar) we walked to a house still closer to the coast. On the way there was a scare and we had to split up and scatter. We were escorted all the way by a gendarme, and there were women posted all the way along the road to see the way was clear. We congregated in a house about 2 km from the coast. In all our party numbered about 30." (Woodhouse WO208/5583-1858)

Barnlund, Lussier, Cutino and Hamilton were sheltered with Germaine Couffon at Kerisago. They were joined the following evening by John Bernier, and a man that Barnlund and Lussier describe as an ex-captain of the French army who came back to the UK with them – I think this was Raymond Le Bourhis.

On Wednesday 22 March 1944, Graham Brickwood, William Lock, Charlie Mullins, Alfred Coffman, Robert Rujawitz and Keith Sutor left Paris on the 0845 train to Saint-Brieuc (where they changed for Guingamp) with their two unnamed guides. On their arrival at Guingamp station that afternoon, they were taken in groups but all to the same house (probably at 1 rue de l'Estang du Prieuré) where they had a meal.

Robert Laux, Phlemon Wright, Thomas Glennan, Abe Helfgott, James Thorson, John Bernier and David Helsel also left Paris on Wednesday 22 March by morning train to Saint-Brieuc (where they changed for Guingamp) with their guide, an elderly moustachioed man who was probably Henri Bois. Note that while no time for their departure is given,

I am working on the assumption that they left sometime after Graham Brickwood and his party.

On their arrival at Guingamp station, they were met by Georges Le Cun and taken to various addresses for a meal (Wright and Glennan going with a tall man in boots back to his house – Laux, Helsel and Thorson to a flour mill (presumably with Joseph and Marie-Antoinette Lanoe on rue Chateaubriand) – I don't know who fed Helfgott and Bernier.

That evening, they were collected and taken to a garage, Etablissements Kerambrun at 2-6 rue du Vally, where they boarded a truck. They were driven to another house where they collected Brickwood, Lock, Mullins, Coffman, Sutor and Rujawitz, who had (probably) left Paris ahead of them that morning, and François Kerumbrun took all thirteen airmen to a wood near Plouha.

Charlie Mullins describes how, on their arrival at Plouha, the evaders were divided into small groups for the last night. While his pilot William Lock was taken to a house in a group of five, he was taken by two more Frenchmen to a village where he was picked up by the "main boss" (a short man about five feet six inches tall. He had a long broken nose, said he used to be a boxer, was well dressed, knew good English, and must have been about 35 years old), two uniformed policemen (neither of whom spoke English) (assume René Dagorne and Joseph Garion) and another Frenchman (about 25 years old, well-dressed, who spoke good English). They walked 5 miles to a very nice house where a man (about 50 years old, slim, with brown hair – he seemed to be important in the organisation), lived with his wife (about 50 years old, slim, with greying dark hair) and two daughters (one was 25, slim with dark hair, the other was 18, short heavy-set, fleshy with light complexion). The house did not look to be a farm nor did it's occupants.

Mullins was sheltered at Saint-Barthélémy with Mme Vve Marie Le Saux and her daughter Marguerite (aka Guiguite), where he also met Francis Baudet (married to Anne-Marie Le Saux, and with a teenage daughter), who lived at the same address.

Mullins recalls how the boss stayed that night (22 Mar) and all next day, and that on the last evening at about seven o'clock, he turned up the radio and listened to the French news and notices. After the news, he said "Well you are leaving tonight" and then went away. A little later, the man with whom Mullins was staying (Francis Baudet), and the two Frenchmen who had brought him, walked him to another house about a mile away.

In the house they were joined by a French policeman who took the lead and went ahead, checking the woods. They finally arrived at another house where they found twenty-six (sic) Americans and English, and four Frenchmen.

> *"The man (which I have called the boss) gave us a discipline talk, collected our money and led us in single file through fields and down a cliff. We arrived at the foot of the cliff an hour and half later and waited there for the boat. As it didn't come, we walked to the beach, hid in the rocks [they thought they had been seen by Germans] and 45 minutes later, 4 life-boats (sic) came to get our party." (Mullins MIS-X #532)*

Alfred Coffman and Robert Rujawitz (query) went with Marie-Thérèse Le Calvez back to her home at Kerlérot where they joined Daniel, Buckner, Warner and Hoffman. The following night, Marie-Thérèse took the six (query) airmen to a farmhouse near the coast.[55]

Brickwood, Lock, Sutor, Thorson and Helsel were taken to be sheltered with a man that Lock describes as being 50 years old with grey hair, an ex-sailor who talked of being on the Normandie (the SS Normandie, which went into trans-Atlantic service in 1935) and his wife, aged about 45 – they had a 19-year-old daughter, small with medium dark hair, and a 15-year-old son who went to school in Guingamp. This was Georges and Marie Ropers of Camblac'h, and the two youngest of their four children.

Helsel says that the following afternoon, they were visited by a French pilot (Pierre Huet) and after supper that night (at 2200 hrs), a guide came to take them for a twenty-minute walk across fields to the cellar of a farmhouse where they joined the rest of the evaders.

Jean Tréhiou took Laux, Wright, Glennan and Helfgott to stay with his fiancé Jeanne Lesné and her parents Augustin and Julie at Kerverzio – the four Americans actually slept in a house belonging to Mme Lesnés brother, Jean Pen – he was a gendarme at Treguier, and although knowing about it, was not there at the time. The following evening they were told that they were leaving, and Jean Tréhiou and Mme Lesné took them along trails to a house in a field where they rendezvoused with the other evaders, and saw the man (Dumais) who had been at the station in Paris.[56]

55 Note that Marie-Thérèse Le Calvez (in her NARA file) does not include Rujawitz in the men sheltered at her mother's house, in which case, I don't know where he stayed.

56 Laux and Wright also mention "some girl whose brother was in England fighting for France". I am guessing this was Hélène Le Touzé referring to her brother Yves (see earlier).

François Le Cornec took John Bernier to stay with Germaine Couffon at Kerisago, where he joined Barnlund, Lussier, Cutino and Hamilton – and Raymond Le Bourhis at some stage. Bernier says he remained there that night and following day and at 2000 hrs the next night, they were taken to the cellar of a farmhouse where the evaders were assembled.

> *"We all left this house at about 2130 hrs on 23 Mar, being guided by a man who appeared to be in charge of the entire party. He was a man of about 35 years old, with dark hair and a moustache. He was short, of medium build and had a gold tooth. He spoke both French and English fluently. We walked to a farmhouse where the whole party – 30 in number – had congregated. Our guide then took all the French money we had in our possession away from us. We stayed at the farmhouse until midnight and then walked down to the coast. At about 0145 (24 Mar) four rowing boats came into the beach. We boarded the boats and were later transferred to a gunboat, arriving at Dartmouth about 0930 hrs." (Barnlund and Lussier WO208/5583-1859/1860)*

SIS/MI9 Crozier Operations

Following the departure of MGB 503 in the early hours of 24 March 1944, further operations to collect evaders from Plage Bonaparte were suspended due to a combination of shortening nights and the Allied build-up for D-Day. There was however SIS Operation Reflexion on the night of 15-16 June to land three agents (Jean Tréhiou, Jean Hamon and Raoul Parent) and stores to the beach at l'Anse-Cochat.[57] Unfortunately, the three-man landing party from MTB 718 (Lt Ronald Seddon) was left behind when the returning surf-boat missed her rendezvous with the MTB.[58]

This was not a Shelburn operation, and the people of Plouha were not notified in advance but the stranded seamen were found and sheltered by Shelburn helpers before being returned to England. It was then only because the operation to collect the three seamen was delayed by bad weather that eleven aircrew evaders were also taken back with them.

Of particular note is that, unknown to the three agents, the Germans had laid a new minefield inland of the coastal path above l'Anse-Cochat. Local man Jean Tréhiou (who had been taken to England on the last Bonaparte operation in March) led his group up from Bonaparte beach and through the mines, apparently without noticing, and the surf-boat crew, who landed somewhere close by later that night, only found out after crossing a fence and looking back to see a sign reading "Achtung Minen".

> *"Towards the end of April 1944, following an inspection of the coastal defences by General Rommel in February, the Germans started laying mines along the coastline. The resistants in Plouha could only note the impossibility to reaching the landing beach by the usual paths. Access to the minefield was*

57 Reflexion was an MI9 operation for an organisation called Cornwallis, which was intended to be established by Jean Tréhiou (aka Trent) on similar lines to Shelburn but operating further west. It was supplied with stores on Operation Robespierre (14-15 July) by MGB 502 (Williams) but no evaders were brought back from the beach at Grach-Dzu near Clogourouan (Ile-de-Batz), and Operation Robespierre II (12-13 August) by MGB 318 (McQuoid-Mason) failed to make contact. Operation Robespierre III was made in daylight on 25 August by MGB 318, and after the landing party enjoyed lunch ashore, brought back Raoul Parent along with members of two other missions – see Secret Flotillas for more operational details.

58 See Milner, Hamilton & Seddon (2014) "HM MTB 718 Something Special", York Publishing for more details of Operation Reflexion and the landing party's subsequent evasion.

guarded by barbed wire fences. At l'Anse-Cochat (Plage Bonaparte) the average depth of the minefield was at least 800 metres. Huet and Mainguy studied these new defences on the cliff and managed to find a the narrow path through, although even there they discovered five mines, and later, two 203mm shells hidden under the roadway, covered with turfs. These shells were linked to small planks connected to the detonator by a wire – one step on the plank would set off the explosion.

During the night of the 16/17 (sic) June, Pierre Huet was woken by knocking at the door of his house at Dernier-Sou. Very surprised, and very anxious, he opened the door to find Jean Tréhiou, the Shelburne agent who had left for England in March. When Pierre Huet asked him how he came to be back in Brittany, he explained that an MGB had landed him and two comrades Parent and Hamon, at l'Anse-Cochat and they had then used the usual path. Jean Tréhiou had been surprised by the barbed wire but all three had crossed the minefield without incident. Although the British had been told that the cliff was mined, they had still taken the risk of re-using the Bonaparte beach, and landed three French agents there. In the absence of Dumais and Labrosse [who were in Paris], any message they may have sent was not received, but it was surprising to the local organisation that they were not warned about the operation. If the three men had been killed or injured by the mines, and the landing beach discovered, then police investigations which could well have been catastrophic for the whole network.

Jean Tréhiou was on a mission to find a new base in Nord-Finistère in the Lannilis – Ile de Sieck – Santec area where Royal Navy had already carried out several landings (at Aber Wrac'h and Clogouruan) the previous year. Raoul Parent (alias Yves) and Jean Hamon (alias Guy) were sent to collect military intelligence as well as recovering airmen in the Josselin – Foret-de-Quénécan area. They would direct any evaders towards the coast where Jean Tréhiou would organise their evacuation in the event of prolonged hostilities. After a short stay at Lizandré with Jean's sister Marie, the three agents left for their respective missions." (my translation from Huguen 1976)

Some publications about Shelburn describe mines and white handkerchiefs on sticks being used during the Bonaparte evacuations but it was men brought out on Operation Crozier who first comment on them in their escape reports. François Le Cornec says the Germans only started laying mines along the coast after the operations in March, which obliged them to spot the mines on the paths they used. It was then Pierre Huet and Job Mainguy who located and mapped the mines, and during the subsequent operations, marked them with white clothes on sticks.

SIS/MI9 Operation Crozier (12-13 July 1944)
MGB 503 (Mike Marshall)

The Evaders

Sub-Lt Mervin I G Hamilton (2022), the First Lieutenant of MGB 718, **Leading Seaman Alfred H Dellow** (2023), her Second Coxswain, and **Ordinary Seaman Hayward D Rockwood** (2024), were the crew of the SN1 surf-boat from MGB 718 who were stranded following Operation Reflexion.[59]

> *"We landed on the coast about 0500 hrs (16 Jun) and hid in a gorse bush until about 1500 hrs. We found we were in a mine-field just south of Pointe de la Tour which is marked on the seaward side by a plain wire fence about ten yards from the top of the cliff.*
>
> *At about 1630 hrs we met a French farmer and Hamilton, who speaks fluent French, asked him for help and for information about the local defences. The farmer said that he could not help us because of the proximity of German troops. He gave us some food and advised us to get inland to the other side of the main coastal road. He warned us that German patrols would be passing after 2100 hrs.*
>
> *About 2230 hrs we started walking south and in the morning we found we had made a mistake and that we were still north of Plouha. During the course of the morning Hamilton spoke to several Frenchwomen and asked for assistance. As on previous occasions, Dellow and Rockwood hid until Hamilton had found out if the person he spoke to was likely to be friendly ..*
>
> *.. Hamilton had great difficulty in establishing the identities of himself and his two companions, probably largely because of his ability to speak fluent*

59 While MGBs 502 and 503 used PD1 Praam dinghies, MTB 718 carried 14 foot SN1 surf-boats, designed by Lt-Cdr Nigel Warington-Smyth RNVR and built by Camper-Nicholson (hence Smyth-Nicholson) and/or 25 foot SN6 boats. (see HM MTB 718 Something Special)

French. He showed his helpers his identity discs and those of his companions but they did not seem to convince the French. In addition to this, his story was rather thin as owing to the secret nature of the operation, he was not able to tell the truth." (WO208/3320-2022-2024)

"During the morning of 16 Jun, Hamilton was told by an unknown Frenchwoman to get in touch with Pomerite Le Vicomte (sic), the chief of the local Maquis. He was told that the Vicomte lived about 20 miles away from Plouha and given complicated directions to get there. Hamilton did not attempt to get in touch with Le Vicomte" (WO208/5583-2022-2024)

Possibly some confusion here as Pommerit-le-Vicomte is the name of the village (mentioned earlier) north-east of Guingamp where several of the Shelburn evaders had been sheltered in February.

21-year-old Guy Hamilton, who was born in Paris and grew up in France, hence his fluent French, says (in a 2014 statement) that they spent their first night walking to somewhere near Trévros before making their way further south to Kernescop where they first met Marie-Thérèse Le Calvez when she found them hiding in a pit on Eugene Harscouet's farm. That night (18-19 June), Marie-Thérèse took them back to her mother's house in Plouha and later that same day, François Le Cornec took them to Marie Tréhious's home at Lizandré, and then to an abandoned house at nearby Kervenec, Pléguien. The abandoned house had no electricity or running water so on the night of 21-22 June, Job Mainguy took them to be sheltered with Georges and Marie Ropers at Camblac'h.

"In the evening of 16 (sic – 18) Jun, Marie Therese Calvez, a young girl of about 18 years took us to her home in Plouha where she lived with her mother. Marie Therese told us that they had helped numerous evaders and that her brother was in the Fighting French Forces. As the house overlooked a road that was frequently patrolled by Germans, it was decided that it would not be safe for us to remain there. Marie Therese informed François, the chief of the resistance organisation, of our whereabouts, and the following day we were taken to a deserted farmhouse. While we were here we were provided with food by the local farmers.

Hamilton gave François the following message to be transmitted to London: "Beach OK. Am in good hands". He knew that if the message was sent off, he would receive instructions from London. François took this message to the British headquarters at Guingamp. On the morning of 24 Jun, Frederick brought a message from the Admiralty addressed to Hamilton. It stated that Hamilton, Rockwood and Dellow would be picked up from Le Questel (S 1129) that night, when one ton of ammunition for operations would be landed, the recipient of which was to be Frederick. This message had to be confirmed. Due to the delay in receiving and answering the message – it had been brought and sent to Guingamp by runner – the fact that Hamilton did not know what arrangements Frederick could make to have the ammunition taken away from the beach, and the fact that he did not know the layout of the minefield that had to be crossed, it was decided that the operation could not take place that night.

In the afternoon, Hamilton met an agent from the beach at St Brieuc and they decided to use the same beach that Hamilton and his crew had landed on and organise their own operation. The agent had spoken to the chief of the organisation that day, and the job was laid on for 27 Jun.

On 26 Jun we were moved to M Roper's house, Camblach, Plouha, which was closer to the beach. For three successive nights the operation was postponed because of bad weather and on 30 Jun, it was postponed until the following moon period. Had it taken place, F/O Brennan, F/O Houston, Sgt Trottier, Sgt Dickson and Sgt Elder, who had arrived in the district, would [not] have returned to the UK with us.

The operation, which had now been laid on for 11 Jul, gave the chief, a French-Canadian operating under the name of Leon, about a fortnight to collect as many evaders as possible to go with us. We also met Leon's wireless operator, who works under the name of Claude. During this period, Leon brought in four members of the USAAF (names unknown), a French parachutist, and two members of the RAF. On 11 Jul the operation was again postponed for a day because of bad weather. Until this time the new members of the party had been billeted at different addresses. On 12 Jul we all congregated at a farmhouse and received final instructions for the journey. The remainder of our story is as related in Appendix C to F/O Brennan's report.

During the time we were in the area of Plouha we received help from many of the inhabitants. The local gendarmes were "in the know" and did all they could to help us. Albert Le Marchand, who lives just outside Plouha, gave us assistance in many small ways and arranged with six neighbouring farmers to help feed us. Most of the feeding arrangements for our party were fixed by Pierre Huet. Job Mainguy works on the beaches and showed Hamilton the layout of the mine-field, details of which he has been instructed to report to an Admiralty section. Mainguy also helped to provide food for us." (WO208/5583-2022-2024)

Albert Edouard Marie Le Marchand (born July 1918 in Pléguien) was a policeman (Gardien de la Paix), and one of the local resistance chiefs. He became involved with evasion activities in the summer of 1943, and according to his IS9 recommendation for a KMS, sheltered some twelve Allied service personnel, including two agents (assume Dumais and Labrosse) who stayed with him for nearly a month.

F/O Harold J Brennan (2025), **P/O Alfred J Houston** (2026), **Sgt Ernest J Trottier** (2027), **Sgt Roger J Dickson** (2028) and **Sgt Andrew Elder** (2029) were the Canadian pilot, navigator, bomb-aimer, mid-upper gunner and tail-gunner of 28 OTU Wellington LN896, with 20-year-old radio operator Sgt John Kempson RAFVR from Surbiton in Surrey. They were on a Nickel raid to Blois (Loir-et-Cher) on the evening of 20 April 1944, and had successfully dropped their leaflets on target but then managed to get lost on the way home. By the time Houston had fixed their position as being over northern France, Brennan found they didn't have enough fuel to make it back to the UK, and at about four o'clock in the morning, and at about 6,000 feet, he ordered his crew to bale out.

"On 20 April 1944, the six man crew of 28 OTU Wellington LN896 went out on their first mission, a Nickel operation dropping leaflets over Tours and Orleans. They got lost on the way back, ran out of fuel and abandoned their aircraft over Saint-Norgant, Bourbriac. Five men landed safely near Kerbalen (Maël-Pestivien) but fate was particularly cruel to Sgt John Kempson, the only Englishman in an otherwise Canadian crew. He landed on top of an enormous rock, the only one of the area, fell and smashed his head. Victor Le Coq of Bourbriac collected and hid the airmen, including the critically injured Sgt Kempson, and contacted Georges Le Cun. Le Cun asked Doctor Rivoalen of Guingamp to come immediately to Coat-Maël (Maël-Pestivien) near Peumerit-Quintin. In a cattle shed, under torch-light, the surgeon performed a lumbar puncture and noted the presence of blood in the body fluid, sure sign of a fractured skull. M Lebreton of Bourbriac took

over caring for Sgt Kempson but he only survived for two or three days. The F.T.P. transported his body to their maquis at Toul Goulic, west of Saint-Nicolas-du-Pélem, where they buried him with a salute fired by the men of the maquis. Meanwhile, Georges Le Cun went to Paris to try and contact Lucien Dumais.

As the [Bonaparte] landings had been stopped following the three operations in March, Georges Le Cun needed to see Lucien Dumais so they could decide what to do next. Although he didn't have a contact address in Paris for Dumais, he did know that one of his 'boîtes aux lettres' was the Duphot Bar in rue Duphot and that he should address any letter to Mlle Yvette Latour. Le Cun wrote a love letter to the young lady in question in which he said he wanted to send her five new food parcels, and also expressing his impatience to see her. A few days later Dumais sent his courier Odette (sic) Laure to see Le Cun. Le Cun explained that he needed a written authorisation from Dumais so the five airmen in Brittany would accept his orders while Dumais was away.

Georges Le Cun met Dumais at the rue Duphot exit of La Madeleine Metro station. Dumais told him that he could not consider another operation for the moment and that he would have to be patient and keep the airmen where they were. Le Cun got his letter of authorisation and returned to Guingamp.

Having made five sets of identity cards and ausweis for the Wellington crew, Le Cun went straight to Coat-Maël, but when he arrived, the airmen were gone. He was told they were at Saint-Nicolas-du-Pélem, sheltered by a woman (Mme Thevis – query), who had married an American before war. This would have been alright if they hadn't been displayed at a May Day parade for the local Resistance. By the time Le Cun arrived at Saint-Nicolas-du-Pélem, the presence of the airmen was an open secret. When Le Cun went to see the woman in question, she passed him on to Doctor Yves Le Bonniec but it wasn't until Le Cun produced the airmen's new identity cards that he responded. The doctor asked his visitor to come back an hour later. When Le Cun left the office, he was followed by two men who joined him at his hotel and questioned him. Finally he was taken to the airmen, and after having read the letter from Dumais, they agreed to go with him.

The following day, he and François Kerambrun organised their supposed departure for the English coast, but actually to a flour mill about twenty kilometres away. This proved to be a wise precaution as the German police learned that the airmen had stayed in Coat-Maël and made some arrests. They burned the place where the airmen had been sheltered and the hotel where Georges Le Cun had met them. They arrested the landlord (Armand Grenel) but could not discover where the evaders had gone. Le Cun and Kerambrun had taken the airmen to Joseph Gautier, a miller at the Moulin-du-Bois in Senven-Léhart (about 16 kms south of Guingamp) where they stayed for six weeks in the care of Mr Gautier's daughter. At the nearby Château de Goas-Hamon there was an FTP group of young STO réfractaires commanded by Savary (alias Dartagnan). Georges Le Cun told them about the airmen and asked if they would help protect them if necessary. On 12 June, a German unit came from Guingamp, attacked the Château and destroyed the poorly armed maquis group. The same day, fearing that other police operations would follow, or that one of young prisoners might speak under torture, the airmen were moved from the Moulin-du-Bois to the Plésidy maquis at Coat-Mallouen, before sending them on to Plouha.

Seven maquis were killed during the short engagement or were massacred on the spot, and the eleven survivors captured, taken to Guingamp then to Servel, near Lannion, where they were shot." (taken from my translation of Huguen (1976) with some extra details added)

Harold Brennan followed his crew out of their doomed aircraft, seeing the bomber crash and explode on a hill just outside the village of Bourbriac, about 10 kms south of Guingamp.

"The farmer whom I met in Bulat-Pestivien on 21 April was a member of the resistance movement. After he had given me a meal, he took me up into the hills where I lived in a cave with him and some more patriots for the next two days. In the evening, Sgt Dickson (2028), my mid-upper gunner, was brought.

On 22 April, Dickson and I were taken by car to Coateen (sic), a small village of about five houses. Before leaving, I was given a suit of civilian clothes. There my injured rear gunner, Sgt Elder (2029) and my wireless operator Sgt Kempson, who was also injured, were brought in. While we were here I was given an identity card for which one of my RAF issue photographs was used.

That evening, we were taken to a camp run by patriots somewhere between Peumerit-Quintin and Trémargat. Here we lived in a tent for five days, and during this time my wireless operator died. He was buried near the camp. I filled in his death certificate, and it was given to a Frenchman (name unknown) who was alleged to work for the British agent in that area. I believe the news reached the UK." (Brennan WO208/5583-2025)

Roger Dickson, the 19-year-old mid-upper gunner, landed a few miles east of Pont Melvez. After hiding his parachute, harness and Mae West, Dickson set off walking south-east across the fields. At about 0700 hrs he hid himself in a large bush, where he stayed for the rest of the day until 2230 hrs when he set off walking once more. At about seven o'clock next morning, he went to a farm and asked for help. He was given some food before being taken to another farm about three miles away where he was given a civilian overcoat, and his journey arranged.

"Two boys escorted me from the farm to a wood near Pont-Melvez where I met a patriot who was the owner of a café in Pont-Melvez. He took me to the café and gave me civilian clothes and food. During the day I was shown a photograph of F/O Brennan and was told he was safe with the patriots in the district. I was also told that another member of my crew was safe. I was asked for one of my photographs which was to be taken to F/O Brennan. I was informed that this group of patriots recently had helped F/O Samuel Blackwell (1727).

I remained in this café until 2300 hrs when I was taken to the patriot's headquarters in Bulat where I met F/O Brennan." (Dickson WO/5583-2028)

Alfred Houston landed in a ploughed field near Bulat-Pestivien. After burying his parachute, Mae West and harness, the 30-year-old navigator set off walking. At about nine that morning, he settled down in a field where he slept for two hours before approaching two elderly women outside a farmhouse. He was able to buy some wine, and the ladies directed him towards Callac. Houston says he covered about 10 kilometres before meeting two more women who warned him against going to Callac as it was full of Germans. Houston made his way back to Bulat-Pestivien before setting off once more, this time heading for Saint-Servais. At some point along the way, Houston approached a man in a woodshed who promptly hid him overnight. At about five in the afternoon of the following day (22 April), two patriots took Houston by car to Mael-Pestivien where he found his badly injured wireless-operator, John Kempson, and the two airmen were then driven to another small village nearby (Coat-Maël) where Sgt Kempson died three days later. Houston was joined by Elder, and later Trottier, in this same village.

Ernest Trottier (who Marie-Thérèse Le Calvez says spoke very good, if accented, French), landed a few kilometres from Bourbriac. After burying his parachute, harness and Mae West in bracken, the 21-year-old bomb-aimer walked south-east until about six that morning when he hid himself in a field. That evening, he approached a farmhouse where he was given a meal before setting off once more. The following morning, he met a man who gave him breakfast before hiding him in a field and at about noon, two men arrived to take him by bicycle to Mael-Pestiven and nearby Quodmail (Coat-Maël) where he found Houston, Elder and the badly wounded Sgt Kempson. Later that day, the airmen were taken to a patriot's camp between somewhere Peumerit and Tremarfat, and on the night of 23 April, they were joined by Brennan and Dickson.

Andrew Elder, the 21-year-old rear gunner, landed in a field a few miles south of Kerbolain, spraining his ankle. He managed to hide his parachute, harness and Mae West before walking until daylight, when he hid in some bushes. At about ten o'clock, he approached a farm where he was taken in and given some food. At about noon, a doctor arrived to attend to his ankle, and then after spending the rest of the day in a field, Elder was taken on horseback to another farm (at Coat-Maël) where he joined his navigator Houston and the badly injured Sgt Kempson. Houston left the house that evening while Elder stayed with Kempson until 24 April when he was taken to the patriot camp where he joined Brennan, Dickson and Trottier. Note that these reports do not quite agree with one another.

"In the morning of 27 April we (Brennan, Houston, Trottier, Dickson and Elder) went to a small village, and in the afternoon we were taken to Saint-Nicolas-du-Pélem. Here we stayed with the local doctor (Yves Le Bonniec), for three days and at the end of that time, we returned to the camp near Peumerit-Quintin.

At the end of about a week, a French intelligence agent took us to a small village just outside Saint-Fiacre. There we were taken over by a member of the resistance organisation but before leaving us, the intelligence agent made me out another identity card.

The patriot took us to stay with his uncle (Joseph) Gautier, who was the mayor of Senven-Léhart. We stayed with M Gautier (at Moulin du Bois) for about six weeks, living six to a room. During this time we never left the room. At the end of this time – probably about the middle of June – the Germans came to Saint-Fiacre and wiped out the patriots. We hid in the fields for two days and M Gautier and his nephew took us to Plésidy. Here we were handed over to some more patriots and taken to their camp. We were split up and Sgt Elder and I stayed with M Guillaume (Theophile Guillaume of Toul a Ninette, Plésidy). During the time we were here, Mons Guillaume sheltered two French parachutists for two days. At the end of two weeks we were taken back to Plésidy and told that we would be leaving immediately. The day after we arrived at Plésidy we met P/O Houston (2026), Sgt Trottier (2027) and Sgt Dickson (2028). There we (also) met the chief of the resistance (Mathurin Branchoux) and a French intelligence agent who, we were told, was working for a British intelligence agent in Plouha. The chief of the resistance, who I was told was one of the chiefs for the resistance movement in the whole of France, was a tall man of about 45 years years old. He had a black goatee and a black moustache and spoke only French.

That afternoon we went on foot to Plouha. On the way we stopped at Plouagat and there our guide took us to a house where a White Russian who had deserted from the German army was being sheltered. We left about two hours later. When we were in the centre of the town, we got into a truck that the patriots had captured from the Germans and travelled to Plouha. On the way we passed two carloads of Germans but we were not stopped.

In Plouha we met François (Le Cornec), the chief of the resistance for that area. We were taken to meet a Canadian captain who works under the name of Leon, and his second-in-command, Claude. They put us in the hands of Marie Therese Calvez who took us to a house near the shore in a neighbouring village. We stayed in a barn belonging to a man named Jean (Gicquel) for three days, and during this time we met Sub-Lt Hamilton (2022), Leading Seaman Dellow (2023) and Ordinary Seaman Rockwood (2024). While we were here we were told that we had come into the moon period and that we would have to wait another ten days. We therefore went to stay with Marie Therese Calvez and remained with her until we left. While we were here, Lt

Joe Lilly (#833) and Lt Bill [Hawkins] (#832) both USAAF came for one day. They were then taken off to different addresses. At about 22 hrs (12 Jul) Marie Therese took us back to Jean's house where we met the whole party, which numbered 15. We were searched and handed over all our French money. We were then given instructions for the journey. We left the house in singe file at about 2330 hrs. We were accompanied by about 13 armed Frenchmen. We walked across the fields, and when we came to a mine-field, in which the mines had been previously marked with white cloths, we all joined hands, still continuing in single file. We walked down the cliff and waited in a cove. It was high tide, and after about an hour and a half, two rowing boats came in onto the shore. Some of the armed Frenchmen has stayed outside on the cliffs and were signalling to the boats as they came in. We boarded these boats and were later transferred to a gunboat. We arrived at Dartmouth about 0800 hrs (13 Jul)." (Brennan WO208/5583-2025 – with a few extra details added)

F/Lt Lawrence W F Stark (2046) was the 23-year-old pilot of 263 Sqn Typhoon MN527 on a Ramrod sortie to the Mur de Bretagne area (central Côtes-du-Nord) on 3 July 1944 when his aircraft was hit by flak. Stark was only able to keep his aircraft in the air for a few more minutes before baling out at about 1440 hrs.

Stark landed in a field about mile south of the Bois de Coat-Mallouen (south of Guingamp) where two farmers promptly helped him, taking his parachute, Mae West and flying gear, and directing Stark north towards a wood where they said he would find some patriots (sic). On the way to the wood, he came to a large farm, and after waiting until early evening, he declared himself to the owners and was taken in.

After being given a meal at the farmhouse (and a pair of clogs to replace the shoe he lost during his descent), a girl who was visiting offered to take Stark to the patriots in the woods. They set off at about nine-thirty that evening but then met the girl's brother, who had been watching Stark since he landed, and they took him to an outhouse near a chateau instead. Stark stayed in the outhouse until about five o'clock in the morning when the boy returned with civilian clothes and a pair of German army boots. The boy then led Stark into the wood and a small-arms cache which was being guarded by an escaper from a work camp in Germany. Stark stayed there, spelling the other man while he went to get them both food, and being supplied with more food by the boy, his sister and their two cousins, until ten-thirty that night when a French paratroop lieutenant and about twenty other men arrived. They pitched tents and Stark spent the rest of the night sharing with the lieutenant in one of them.

The following day, small groups of men arrived so that by evening, there were about eighty men in the camp, and that night, Stark joined a group of them to walk to a nearby meadow where they expected a supply drop. They waited until three-thirty but no aircraft appeared and they returned to their camp. Later that day, Stark helped to service a pair of radio sets and then spent much of the following day (7 July) listening to the BBC, hoping for a particular message. Next day, they received a message telling them to expect a parachute drop that night and they returned to the moor. Stark reports that five aircraft arrived at just past midnight, and an estimated twenty-five containers were dropped, the contents being ferried back to the woods.

Next morning, a guide arrived to take Stark on foot to a house near Saint-Fiacre. On arrival there (at about noon) Stark met a French paratroop captain in civilian clothes who claimed to be the CO of all the paratroops in that area, and that evening, Stark and the captain were taken into Saint-Fiacre where they had a meal before being guided to a house near La Villeneuve (about a kilometre SE of Saint-Fiacre). Stark and the captain stayed at La Villeneuve until 0400 on 10 July when their guide led them around the village of Plélo to a farm about a mile NW of La Frênerie (which is just outside the village of La Corderie, and on the edge of the Bois de Beauchamp), where they spent the night. At noon the following day (11 July) a farmer (assume Jean François Gouarin) took them in a cart, with a guide on a bicycle, through Tréguidel to a farm near Pléguien. This was headquarters of the organisation, and they met the local chiefs, two French-Canadians.[60]

They stayed at the house until the evening of 12 July when the French captain went by cart, and Stark walked with the farmer's son (either Marcel or Henri Gouarin), to a farmhouse about a mile from the beach. They met the thirteen others who were to be included in their party to the UK, and at 2300 hrs that evening, were taken to the beach "and brought to the UK by boat".[61]

60 Dumais and Labrosse had only just arrived from Paris after a four-day bicycle ride – Dumais was staying at Garzambic, and Labrosse at le Guern, two houses owned by Jean François Gourin, maire of Pléguien (information from André Fichant of Pludual via Daniel Droniou).

61 Stark says the captain returned to the UK with him and although I've not found any evidence to support this, Guy Hamilton (see earlier) also mentions a French parachutist as coming back with them.

W/O Robert Ossendorf (2031) was the 27-year-old Czech pilot of 312 Sqn Spitfire MJ907 attacking "rail and road transport" in Normandy on 21 May 1944, when he was hit by flak over Caen. He managed to keep his aircraft in the air for a while before being hit again, and crash-landing in a field. Having destroyed his radio and buried his parachute and flying gear, Ossendorf set off walking. He headed generally south-west, acquiring some workman's clothes from a farmer on the first day, and food and assistance along the way until about 26 May when he found overnight shelter on a farm. Next day he was lent a bicycle and a young boy took Ossendorf across the river Sée somewhere east of Avranches and on to a farm somewhere north-east of Ducey (Manche) where he left Ossendorf to continue walking. Two days later, Ossendorf reached a farm near Collinée, (Côtes-du-Nord), from where he was helped by an organisation.

Two men came to the farm to question Ossendorf before taking him by bicycle to Moncontour. He met a French parachutist who told him there was an English Intelligence Officer somewhere near Lamballe (about 20 SE of Saint-Brieuc), and a woman collaborator (name not known) was "compelled" to hand over her car so they could drive there. On arrival however, they found the organisation at Lamballe had been dispersed by the Germans. The French parachutist stayed to link up with others and Ossendorf returned to Moncontour.

While he was with the group at Moncontour, Ossendorf says that they cared for him so well that he felt he should do something to justify himself, and on the evening of 24 June, set off with a man called Jean on an unspecified sabotage mission. Ossendorf was armed with a pistol and two hand-grenades, and Jean with a Sten gun that he carried under his overcoat. Unfortunately, they were soon challenged by a small group of German soldiers, and in the ensuing mêlée, Ossendorf says he shot at least two Germans and probably wounded another, but while making his escape, took a bullet to the leg himself. He met Jean a few minutes later, and after waiting for nightfall, Jean helped him to a nearby farmhouse to rest before taking Ossendorf back to Moncontour where he was nursed by the people of the village.

> *"On about 27 June I was taken to a chateau near Pommeret [west of Lamballe] where I met two American airmen (names not known). I was operated on here by a French doctor and had a bullet taken out of my leg on 1 July." (Ossendorf WO208/5583-2031)*

1/Lt Richard J Gordon (#830) and **1/Lt Frank L Lee Jnr** (#831) were the pilots of 362FG/379FS P-47 Thunderbolts 42-26111 and 42-25404 respectively on an early morning sortie from their base at Lashenden in Kent on 17 June 1944.

> *"We had been on a strafing mission and had stayed out rather longer than we should. We found that we had been blown westwards and were over the Brest peninsula. We were then out of gas, and both of us bailed out at the same time."*

That's what it says on the first page of their joint MIS-X report, and when I first read that opening paragraph, I thought that perhaps they were simply two young pilots who had been carried away with the excitement, but then I realised they were in fact both very experienced pilots, with a total of 101 missions between them. Something didn't sound quite right so I started looking at the incident in more detail.

Although the typed version of their report implies there were just the two of them on the 17 June mission, they later mention being told that Lt Fredenberg "from their flight" had been captured. A hand-written version of their report says they were leading a group of three aircraft and that the third pilot, Lt Fredenberg, had run out of gas and bailed out before them.

A few minutes research suggested there were actually four aircraft in the flight, led by 1/Lt Carroll A Peterson, who returned safely to England that day, and that 2/Lt William R Fredenberg (#2078) in P-47 42-75593, rather than running out of fuel, was shot down by flak. 21-year-old Fredenberg crash-landed near Lamballe and was captured that afternoon but on 22 July 1944, he was among a group of Allied POWs who escaped from a train near Bléré (Indre-et-Loire). Fredenberg remained in and around the Amboise area until liberated by advancing Allied troops in September.

> *ABSA (Association Bretonne du Souvenir Aérien) 39-45 suggest that rather than Gordon and Lee simultaneously running out of fuel due to staying out too long, it was Lee whose engine failed, probably as a result of flak damage from Lamballe, shortly before the two aircraft collided in the clouds above the village of Maroué. My thanks to Daniel Dahiot and Jean Michel Martin of ABSA, and all those who contributed to their web-page article about the events of 17 June, from which I have taken (with permission) so many of the finer details.*

While there may be some question as to why the two pilots bailed out together, there is little doubt that Gordon and Lee landed close to one another just south of Maroué, a small commune about 4 kms south of Lamballe.

After three days of hiding and walking (as per their E&E lectures) the two American pilots were found (not far away) near Plestan by a man connected to a resistance group. Apparently, the man (about 50 years old with grey hair, dressed in worker's clothes) had been looking for them – he was whistling "Tipperary" and calling out "camarade" to try and get their attention – and after bringing them some food and civilian clothing, took them to a shop in Plestan where a dozen French men and women were gathered. From there, the "chief of the local maquis" and two other men, took Gordon and Lee on bicycles to a farm about 5 kms away. They spent the night and next day at the farm with a group known as the "21eme Groupe de Resistance", which included Adrien Pitart, Pierre Olliver and David Marcel, and were told that Lt Fredenburg from their flight had been captured by the Germans.

That night, two men took Gordon and Lee by motorcycle to le manoir de Bréfeillac near Pommeret (which is about half-way between Lamballe and Saint-Brieuc) where they were sheltered by Mme Vve Lucienne Froger Péan de Ponfilly and her two young sons – her husband had been killed earlier in the war. Also staying there was a cousin named Marguerite Pinault whose home was in Dinan but who worked at the American hospital in Paris, and spoke good English having spent 18 years in England.[62]

On 22 June, Gordon and Lee met a man called Jean (about 23 years old, married and with a home in Saint-Brieuc) who had come from Callac where he had been in contact with an Allied parachute unit. Jean took a message from the two Americans to a British major at Callac who replied that he had sent a radio message to London about them. They also met Jean's chief, head of the resistance at Saint-Brieuc (about 50 years old, 5 feet 7 inches tall, very swarthy), and the head of the resistance at Lamballe who suggested he could get them out by aircraft via a French captain who had a chateau from where another evader had (allegedly) left by air for the UK. During their time at the chateau (21 June to 7 July) they also report being joined by a Czech pilot in the RAF (Ossendorf) who had been shot

62 According to Mathurin Branchoux (in Remy), Dumais had planned to send the one hundred plus airmen he claimed to have in Paris to Mme de Ponfilly at the manoir de Bréfeillac to form a maquis but the Allied landings of 6 June made that plan redundant.

down, joined a group of parachutists at Moncontour, and been wounded in a skirmish with the Germans.

On 3 July, they met Mathurin Branchoux (about 55 years old with greying hair, moustache and goatee), chief of resistance for the whole area who had already helped 111 (sic) airmen out of France. He told them that he would put them into the hands of two Canadians at Plouha who went by the names of Leon (a Canadian captain who had been at Dieppe and been moving men out of France ever since) and Ray (about 23 years old with brown hair and sharp features, who was constantly smoking a pipe).

On 7 July, four men from Saint-Brieuc came to the chateau in a German truck. They took Gordon, Lee, Ossendorf and Mme de Ponfilly to Plouha, where they picked up Leon and Ray. They drove on to a side-road from where Ray led the three airmen to a farmhouse where they stayed for the next two days, during which time they were visited by a pharmacist from Saint-Brieuc (assume Françoise Josse of rue Pierre Loti in Plouha) who came to dress Ossendorf's wound. On 9 July, word came that the Germans were aware of the evaders' presence and they were moved out into a field where, on 11 July, they were joined by fellow fighter pilots, William Hawkins (#832) and Joseph Lilly (#833).

On the night of 12 July, they were taken back to the farmhouse where Leon appeared with five Canadians (Brennan, Houston, Trottier, Dickson and Elder), an Englishman (Stark) and three sailors who had been left behind by the last boating party (Hamilton, Dellow and Rockwood). At midnight, the wife of the farmer, the wife of the pharmacist and a woman named Marie (Marie-Thérèse Le Calvez), along with some men from the organisation, led them through the minefields down to the beach.

Ossendorf's version is slightly different – he says that on 7 July, it was the woman who owned the chateau (Lucienne de Ponfilly) that took him and the two Americans by car to a small house past Plouha (the Maison d'Alphonse) – he makes no reference to Canadian agents. Two days later, there was an alarm and they spent the next three days hiding in a field, only returning to the house to sleep overnight. On 12 July, they were told they were leaving for England, and when they returned to the house at about ten o'clock that evening, they found the rest of the party, including Sub-Lt Hamilton (2022), who crossed the Channel with them.[63]

63 Mathurin Branchoux says that he sent the three airman from the chateau to Plouha in a postal car driven by M. Le Bourdonnec, the Saint-Brieuc postal inspector.

"Two American fighter pilots were collected by the Saint-Georges maquis. William Hawkins, shot down near Bourg-Blanc (Nord-Finistere) [about 10 kms north of Brest] was with Docteur de La Marnièrre in Brest. Joseph Lilly was with group Vengeance of 1er Battalion de Concarneau, under Commandant Jean Le Bourhis. The two airmen shared the life of the maquis for two months before being passed on to José Le Goff and Pierre Le Ster of the group Vengeance under Commandant Pierre Dréau of Lesconil, who was in contact with the Shelburne group. According to Lucien Dumais, it was Paul Campinchi who recommended Dréau to him as 'un grand résistant' and because he knew the west of Brittany so well. Pierre Dréau remained in contact with the escape line and sent several airmen to Plouha, including Hawkins and Lilly." (my translation of Huguen 1976)

2/Lt William C Hawkins (#832) was the 21-year-old pilot of 4FG/335FS P-51 43-6316, returning from only his second mission, a fighter sweep to Bordeaux on 20 March 1944, when he realised he didn't have enough fuel left to cross the Channel. Hawkins was somewhere near Brest and down to about 1,000 feet when his engine began to falter and he bailed out.

Hawkins landed in a tree, gashing his leg, and while he trying to pull his parachute down, a group of men ran up to help him. They told Hawkins where he was and he set off inland. Stopping at farms along the way, Hawkins says he was given food gladly enough but with so many Germans in the area, no-one was prepared to shelter him. That evening however, he met two young brothers who gave him blankets and arranged for him to spend the night in a field, and next morning, he was taken to a place from where his journey was arranged.

I am very reluctant to rely on another author's work in order to present a story-line but in the case of Hawkins (and Lilly), it was the newly promoted Captain Emerson who was their interviewing officer – so I have used Don Lasseter's chapter "We didn't start singing until the sun came up" from his excellent 2002 book "Their Deeds of Valor" (published by the Xlibris Corporation) as a framework for what I have managed to decipher from Donald Emerson's notes.

The group helping Hawkins were members of the local resistance, and once

Hawkins had changed into the civilian clothing they brought, he was driven to Brest (on about 22 March) and an apartment at 17 rue Voltaire where he was introduced to Dr Roger de la Marnierre, his wife Yvonne and their four daughters – all of whom spoke passable English except the doctor.[64] He was interrogated at length by Mme de la Marnierre, an experience not helped by Hawkins having left his dog-tags behind, before finally satisfying them that he was a genuine American flyer – confirmation being received two weeks later in a radio message from London saying that a US fighter pilot with his name was indeed MIA. He was also questioned by Paul Le Baron.

While Hawkins was being sheltered in Brest with the de la Marnierre family, he was visited by Colonel Scheidhauer and his wife Jeanne, Jean-Loup Niox (their daughter Ghislaine's son), and their niece Françoise (query). He also met François (aged about 20, with a large nose) and his friend Christian (mentioned by Hugonnet earlier, Hawkins describes him as being tall, slender, well-dressed, with brown wavy hair – active in resistance and made out papers) – and Mme Jeanne Callarec, who he thought might have been head of the local evasion network. He also mentions a middle-aged school teacher, referred to as Cactus, an old maid (sic) who stayed with Mme Callarec for two days.

It's not clear exactly how long Hawkins was sheltered with the de la Marnierres, but in early May, he was joined by fellow Mustang pilot Joe Lilly (see below). Shortly after that, an anonymous note referring to the Americans meant they had to leave Brest and (according to Lasseter), it was Georges Martin (described by Hawkins as being about 39 years old, 5 ft 9 inches tall, with black hair, he was well built and strong as an ox) who contacted Commander Jean Le Bourhis who arranged for the two Americans to be sheltered in the Tiégunc area (near Concarneau). Their journey (probably c.20 May) with Martin, was interrupted when their train was attacked by RAF Spitfires somewhere near Rosporden and they spent the night just outside Quimper with friends of Georges Martin. Next morning, they cycled to Melgven and a farm at Keramborgne where Jules Gerard lived with his wife and three daughters (Yvonne, Lisette and Simone) – who, along with Georges Martin, had helped Lilly when he first landed. Having retrieved Martin's tent from Concarneau, Hawkins and Lilly then spent the next three weeks camping in the local woods, their food supplied by the Gerard family.

64 This is after the de la Marniere home on rue Traverse was destroyed by a bomb.

2/Lt Joseph A Lilly (#833) was the 22-year-old pilot of 354FG/355FS P-51 43-6441, flying as wingman to 1/Lt Franklyn E Hendrikson (#925) on a bomber escort mission to Berlin on 26 April 1944. Hendrickson says they were "separated from the other squadron by heavy flak over Hanover and got lost over Brittany". Thinking they were over England, they attempted to land on a German airfield, and only realised their error when both aircraft were hit by flak. Hendrikson reports staying with Lilly until he bailed out near Nantes – Lilly says he was shot down by flak from Lorient.[65]

Lilly landed near Melgven (which is about 5 miles NE of Concarneau), spraining his ankle, and says that a large group of local people rushed to meet him. When he found they were unable to understand his attempts at speaking French, he ran off but with his damaged ankle, wasn't able to get very far and so started to hide himself in some bushes. A Frenchman ran up and gave him his coat and beret, and explained (mainly by sign-language) that he would come back later with food. The man duly returned at nine that evening with both food and more civilian clothes before taking Lilly (who could hardly walk by this time) on a bicycle to a barn not far from his crashed aircraft. After a night in the barn, Lilly was taken into the farmhouse but knowing the Germans would soon search there, was moved to another house. From there he was taken by bicycle "through a couple of towns" to a place from where his journey was arranged.

Lilly says it was Georges Martin and a man called Albert (assume Albert Gloaguen) who took him by bicycle (he could pedal but not walk) to Concarneau where he stayed with various people (including M. Le Floch (mentioned earlier), and Edouard Priol and his family), for about two weeks until Georges Martin took him by train to Brest on about 3 May. He was sheltered with the de la Marnierre family (where he joined Hawkins), while Martin stayed with Mme Callarec for a week. During his time in Brest, Lilly says he met Colonel Scheidhauer and his wife Jeanne, Paul Le Baron (who took casualty data) and Mlle Genevieve Le Bourhis, whose father was a resistance leader.

On about 20 May, Georges Martin took Lilly and Hawkins by train to Quimper and Rosporden, being strafed by Spitfires on the way, before leaving them camping out close to the Gerard farm at Keramborgne, near Melgven, where they stayed until 20 June.

65 Hendrikson later ran out of fuel and bailed out near Plesder, about 10 kms SE of Dinan. He was helped by local people and sheltered until 4 August when advancing US forces reached the area.

"I was at a small resistance camp when news of the Normandy landings came. Resistance men from all over the section assembled in the groups in the woods. The one with which I was was badly armed, with something like 12 pistols amongst 100 men. We went out with them a couple of times, wearing their combat brassards, while they were cutting communication cables. The effectiveness of these groups in cutting communications was so great that the Germans finally posted Frenchmen about every 100 feet along the cables and said that they would shoot Frenchmen every time the cable was cut." (Lilly MIS-X #833)

Both reports mention an attack that the airmen witnessed at Concarneau harbour when RAF light bombers attacked some German ships that had just arrived from the Normandy beach-heads – and Lasseter says that Hawkins was staying in Concarneau with chemist Pierre Grall and family at the time.

"On 30 June, informant (Lilly) saw Mosquitos and Beaufighters attack ships in Concarneau harbour. The ships had arrived just a couple of hours before the attack. One ship was sunk, another laid on its side, and a third was damaged. On the ship that was sunk 150 Germans and two French whores were killed. Altogether 189 Germans were killed. Four truck-loads of German wounded were taken away." (MIS-X #833 Lilly Appendix B)

Hawkins reports that on Sunday 2 July, a Frenchwoman rushed up their camp screaming that "the Boches, the Gestapo, were coming", and as they tried to get away, the Germans opened up with machine guns from about 300 yards. I haven't managed to decipher much in the way of additional detail from Captain Emerson's notes but I think he says that Hawkins had being sharing a tent with Jacques and Georges Borgeon (query writing), who was later shot, and Lilly reports that two men were captured and "literally kicked to death" before being shot in the head. The others escaped to hide in some fields, and later in a barn, before leaving the area – Paul Le Baron taking Hawkins to be sheltered by Mme Trehin at Tregunc while Lilly was taken to Concarneau where he stayed with Mme Gloaguen (assume wife of Albert, at 10 avenue Pierre Gueguen). Hawkins also mentions Mme Yan (nf), a midwife whose husband was a prisoner in Rennes, and Mme Genevieve Le Bourhis, who Le Baron confirms helped both Americans.

Lasseter says (the Americans' reports are almost illegible at this point) that it was early July when Pierre Dréau arrived to tell Hawkins that he would be going to Plouha. After farewells to the Grall family (and members of Georges Martin's resistance group), Dréau took Hawkins and Lilly by bicycle on the 100 mile ride to Plouha, arriving there on 11 July to spend the night in a barn next to a pharmacist's home (assume Françoise Josse of rue Pierre Loti). Hawkins report says they went to another house during the day where they met five Canadians (Brennan and his crew, who were being sheltered by Léonie Le Calvez at Kerlérot) before returning to the pharmacist. Early next morning, Dréau took them to the Maison d'Alphonse where they joined the other twelve evaders to be evacuated that night.

SIS/MI9 Operation Crozier II (23-24 July 1944)
MGB 502 (Peter Williams)

Ten nights later there was a second Crozier operation, this one to collect an SAS team that had been sent into Brittany the previous month.

> *"The Plouha group were now determined to form their own maquis under François Le Cornec, advised by Lucien Dumais, and based at the Bois de la Salle. The headquarters was transferred from Gilles Lemarchand's farm to his neighbour, François Goarin, mayor of Pludual (sic). In the attic of a vast barn on the Goarin farm, Dumais, assisted by Francis Baudet and François Le Cornec, taught weapons handling to the young recruits.*
>
> *Section heads for the new maquis were appointed: Louis Le Bail of Pléguien, Louis Le Breton of Plourhan, Eugene Courson, Hamon, Jean Auffret, Carbonnier, François Le Cavorzin, Pierre Huet and Guy Mainguy. They also recruited others until the company had about a hundred and sixty men. At first, they couldn't all stay together as a group but by about 20 July they had tents and a kitchen, with regular supplies, and the maquis took on a permanent character. Raymond Labrosse's radio was set up and monitored by Dumais, or Le Cornec as the maquis commander.*
>
> *Having suddenly left the maquis to go secretly to Coat-Mallouen, Dumais and Le Cornec returned to Plouha on Saturday 22 July accompanied by five Anglo-American soldiers, including two officers. They arrived at the Maison d'Alphonse that evening and Dumais gave Jean Gicquel the responsibility*

of lodging and feeding their new guests who he intended to evacuate on the next operation, planned for the following night. London seemed impatient to recover the members from an apparently very important mission." (taken from my translation of Huguen 1976)

The Evaders

Major Oswald A J Cary-Elwes had led a seven-man SAS team which was parachuted into Brittany on the night of 22-23 June 1944 to find out what had happened to the French (4 Regiment) SAS. They had been dropped on the night of 5-6 June, and their commander, 36-year-old Colonel Pierre Bourgoin, had joined them at the Dingson drop-zone near Saint-Marcel (Morbihan) on the night of 10-11 June but a few days later, radio communications with London ceased.

There are no MI9 reports for Cary-Elwes or any of his team but King's College London have a file in their archives with reports by both Cary-Elwes and his batman, Cpl Eric Mills. I don't know if Mills account was ever published but Cary-Elwes (in whose report the names have been changed) was writing for the 1947 Military Intelligence Review, and the following section has been compiled using both (sometimes contradictory) reports, and other sources.

Part of the Allied Invasion Plan of 1944 called for parties of the French SAS Battalion to be parachuted into Brittany to work with the local maquis and cut German lines of communication. They were then to arm and train the Breton maquis in order to help the Allied occupation of the area. However, such was the enthusiasm of the local groups that large numbers of untrained local men were gathered around Saint-Marcel (just SW of Malestroit), and on 18 June, they were attacked by German forces. The last news that British Intelligence had from the head of the French SAS, Colonel Bourgoin, was that his camp was surrounded and he would be closing down his radio to avoid being pin-pointed by German detection apparatus. Other SAS parties in Brittany were in similar positions, and 31-year-old Major Oswald Cary-Elwes was sent to try and re-establish contact with them, an operation known as "Lost".

Cary-Elwes, Cpl Mills, a French officer (Lt Fleuriot) and his batman, and a three-man French radio team, were dropped blind (with no landing party) at about three o'clock on the morning of Friday 23 June 1944. After landing safely, apart from one of the radio team spraining his ankle, the group moved away from their landing site and then settled down for the rest of the night. They set off at first light to try and make contact with anyone who might know the whereabouts of the local maquis, their efforts hampered by rumours of the Germans impersonating Allied parachutists to try and find the SAS men themselves. They finally found a farmer who seemed as though he might be able to help, and they gave him Cary-Elwes and Fleuriot's identity cards to see if any of his contacts could recognise their pictures and so confirm their story. Two days later, a guide collected Cary-Elwes and took him to Colonel Bourgoin's headquarters – which I think was near Plumelec (Morbihan), on the farm of a M. Josse.

After some discussion, it was decided that Cary-Elwes would take his party to one of the SAS company commanders, Capitaine Pierre Marienne (C-E calls him Maurice), at his base near Trédion. The task was to train and arm local maquis groups, then arrange a parachute drop of arms and equipment, but not allow them to congregate in large numbers. Communication with London was by radio, and between the groups by young female runners. After about a week at Trédion, London ordered Cary-Elwes to move to a second SAS group near Guern, about 40 kilometres away. Cary-Elwes and Mills spent a week with Capitaine Henri Deplante (C-E says David) before receiving a message from London, ordering them back to England with the SAS plans for future operations. They were to contact someone called Frederick (C-E says Robert) at a given map reference, somewhere near Guingamp (some 70 kilometres away) where Frederick would pass them to an MI9 escape organisation. Before they left, Cary-Elwes was also given details of the port defences at Morlaix, Vannes and Lorient to take back with him.

Mills (who was carrying a wireless receiver) says that they walked for several days (helped by a series of local maquis guides), covering some 60 kms, picking up an American pilot (William Jones) along the way (no details of their meeting are given but Mills says that Jones was excellent company), before crossing a river, which C-E says was the river Blavet, and finding that Jones was the only one who knew how to row a boat. They were sheltering in a maquis camp when the offer was made to take them to another camp by car, and they were delivered to a farm where they found two men from the 4th French Parachute Battalion with about 25 young local men, all well armed and seemingly well trained. Cary-Elwes, Mills and Jones stayed at the farm until Friday evening (14 July) when they were again offered motorised transport but this time, through the night. The driver left them on a road near the given co-ordinates, and as it was still quite dark, they spent the rest of the night in the outhouse of a deserted farm. Setting off again at dawn, they were fortunate to be given coffee at the first farmhouse they tried but the only Frederick the family knew turned out to be an elderly local man. However, word was spread through the local resistance and news soon came through that Frederick's camp had been attacked two days earlier, and no-one seemed to know where he and his men had gone.

On Sunday 16 July, Cary-Elwes set off alone, leaving instructions for Mills that if he failed to return then Mills was to hide the plans, and he and Jones were to try and make their own way to Allied lines. Fortunately this did not become necessary as at about five o'clock that afternoon, two guides arrived with a note from Cary-Elwes telling Mills to be ready to move in 45 minutes. The two Frenchmen took Mills and Jones on foot for what Mills says was about 20 nerve-wracking kilometres, and it was getting dark when they approached a village with a large lake (l'Etang Neuf – query), overlooked by a forest. They crossed a small bridge, which was guarded by sentries, to Frederick's camp in the forest where they found numerous young Frenchmen, all armed with British weapons, and eager to meet their first British Tommy. Cary-Elwes says that Robert (sic) was only a young sergeant in the French SAS but he commanded a number of French army reserve officers who willingly accepted him as their Commanding Officer. [66]

On the morning of Wednesday 19 July, a man arrived with his horse and cart, along with civilian clothes and French ID cards, and Mills was grieved to learn that he had to leave his rifle behind. Mills says they had been joined by an RAF pilot (Philip Fargher) by this time, and apart from an unwise stop at a café (where Mills and Jones sampled Calvados for first time) their journey by cart to yet another farm was uneventful.

The farmer told them that the man responsible for their evacuation would arrive shortly and when he did, he (Dumais) told them they might leave the following evening (Thursday) but they actually spent three days at the farm, being joined there by SAS liaison officer, Sq/Ldr Patrick Smith, before finally setting off once more.

66 The true identity of "Frederick" is a mystery to me – see also Guy Hamilton et al earlier.

For the last part of their journey the party were divided – Mills, Smith and Fargher going by horse and cart while the others went by bicycle to a pre-arranged spot from where they walked in single file to a house near the coast, arriving at the Maison d'Alphonse late in the evening of Saturday 22 July.

Major William A Jones (#834) was the pilot of 367FG/393FS P-38 42-104277 Laura Lee attacking Plaines Villes aerodrome at Ploufragan, just SW of Saint-Brieuc, on 24 May 1944 when he was hit by light flak which stopped his left engine and set the aircraft on fire. Jones bailed at very low altitude, hitting the ground almost immediately after his parachute opened, banging his knees and bruising both eyes. He also came under automatic weapons fire as he ran with his parachute to take cover in an anti-tank ditch. He was able to follow the ditch north to a road, which he crossed before being helped by some local people who led him to a cow-shed where he was given soup and a civilian coat. That evening, Jones was sent on his way but having been told in England not to travel after dark, he only went about half a mile before bedding down for the night in a field.

The following morning, Jones set off south, using his escape-kit compass and generally heading towards Spain. He says that his bruised appearance frightened everyone who saw him, although they must have realised what he was from his GI shoes and uniform shirt and trousers, and after being seen managing to avoid a German soldier on a bicycle, three people decided help him. Jones was passed on to a woman who in turn passed him to a man but his help didn't extend beyond directing Jones towards a church.

That evening, Jones approached a woman for a drink and he was allowed to spend the night in the loft of her house. Next morning, a red-headed man arrived on a motorcycle to present Jones with trousers, dark glasses and a fishing pole before taking him on his bike to the home of a very small woman who lived on the north side of Saint-Brieuc, from where his journey was arranged.

Unfortunately, the Appendix C of Jones' report is a real challenge to decipher – but Huguen provides a few clues in a footnote on pages 377-8 of his book "Par les nuits les plus longues".

According to Huguen, Jones landed somewhere near Plélo, where he was helped by a farmer who passed him on to members of the local MLN network (*Mouvement de la Libération Nationale*), and it was Alfred Millet (aka

Erlini) who asked Mlle Julie Meheust to find a place to shelter him. Huguen says that it was a few days before Whitsun when Millet and Mlle Meheust took Jones by bicycle to Saint-Brieuc and the rue du Port although I think this date is wrong. Jones was hidden on the second floor of an unoccupied house belonging to a cousin of Mlle Meheust, where his injured knee was treated by MLN member, Doctor Despas (nf), with food was supplied by Jean Metaire (of 5 rue Docteur Rochard) and the abbé Fleury (nf), and clothes from M. Morin (nf), a tailor living in the rue de Gouédic. It is not clear how long Jones stayed in the apartment before he was moved to 102 rue du Légué, where he was sheltered by Pierre Cahn, nor when Jean Metaire's son (also called Jean) took Jones from Saint-Brieuc to the maquis at Coat-Mallouen.

"A number of days after the Normandy landings, I was put in the hands of resistance groups. In civilian clothes, I was walked through the town in which I was staying, passing right by Gestapo headquarters with its German guard and his machine-gun, and was taken to meet the resistance men. A Citroen full of young fellows armed with machine-guns pulled up in best gangster style. I was given a Spanish automatic and taken to a farm which served as the headquarters for this group. The Cross of Lorraine was flying and guards posted.

From this place I was taken to another group, the main concentration of which had just been attacked by the Germans and forced to disperse. The resistance chief here asked whether I wanted to join his group. I explained that I was trying to get back to England. When he said that he had no way for me to return, I said that I might as well join his group. I was put with one section and moved with them to a number of places over the next couple of days. We were continually meeting other French resistance men or Frenchmen of the FFI who had been sent over to organise further resistance activities. I was given a French parachute battle jacket.

We tried to get in touch with another large resistance group, only to discover that it had also been attacked and forced to disperse. Once again some 200 or more French resistance men and parachutists assembled when word came that the Germans were close, and we moved to another place. On this dispersal, I carried a bazooka.

At another camp, I learned once again that there was no possibility of getting away, so I put on battle dress and carried a .45, trying to do my best as a member of a resistance section. I made a number of moves with these resistance people and finally, pretty much by chance, ran into some men who had contacts for evacuation and was taken to some people by whom the rest of my journey was arranged .." (Jones MIS-X #834)

Jones seems to mention Moncontour (which is about 15 kms south of Saint-Brieuc) a couple of times (see also Ossendorf earlier), and then pitching tents somewhere east of Callac (which is about 25 kms SW of Guingamp) just before meeting the men in the Citroën. Then to a big chateau where a lady, aged about 40, spoke English, and being driven to Callac. He mentions Lt Robert, a parachutist, and being taken by horse and cart to Plélo, and a farmhouse with good food. Major Smith (sic) gets a few mentions, and walking about 17 kilometres north with Mills to contact someone called Frederick at certain grid coordinates, he thought near Saint Nicholas (query).

"At one farmhouse where we were staying (the Maison d'Alphonse), a German patrol came. We heard the scrape of their shoes and ducked upstairs. A few minutes later, the woman of the house screamed and the Germans started firing wildly. Shots came through the floor and some through the roof. The Germans failed to come upstairs or we would have been gone for sure, for we had practically no arms. After more wild shooting, the Germans left. In the confusion they had shot one of their own men and wounded another. The man of the house took us to the woods." (Jones MIS-X #834)

F/Sgt Thomas P Fargher (2057) was the 22-year-old pilot of 234 Sqn Spitfire AA973 on a Rhubarb operation – a freelance sortie against ground targets of opportunity – to Brittany on 11 July 44. He had just crossed the coast at low level near Plouescat (about 15 kms west of Roscoff) when his aircraft was hit by light flak. He continued on a roughly easterly course for some time before his engine failed and he baled out, landing in a field near Saint-Bihy, which is about 20 kms south-west of Saint-Brieuc.

Fargher was helped almost immediately after landing, and a girl (Huguen says this was Josephine Le Lay, and IS9 has Marie-Jose Lelay of Guercle, Saint-Gildas) from a nearby farmhouse took him into a field where he met a local maquis man. The man led Fargher to a wood, treated the cuts that Fargher had received on baling out, gave him some food, and asked him a series of personal questions, saying that a message would be sent to London about him. That evening, Fargher was taken into Saint-Bihy where he stayed overnight at the home of a priest (assume Abbe Jean-Baptiste Robin) and the following day, L/Cpl La Floch, a French parachutist, arrived to tell him that British Intelligence knew about him and that he was to follow orders from a British army major who was in the area. That afternoon, La Floch took Fargher to a farm near La Croix (about 6 kms south-west of Saint-Bihy) where he met two more French parachutists, Sgt Louis and L/Cpl Darraud.

Next day (13 July) a French paratroop lieutenant came to the house. He insisted that Fargher change into civilian clothes – which Fargher was reluctant to do – and gave him a French identity card in the name of Paul Merot. He then told Fargher that the headquarters of the paratroop detachment had been raided the previous evening and their plans and radio transmitter found. That evening, Fargher went with the three paratroopers, and a young French boy and girl, to another farm, this one about 5 kms north-east of La Croix (which if correct would put him back near Saint-Bihy). Fargher stayed on the farm until the morning of 17 July when the whole party moved to yet another farm, this one about 3 kms north of La Croix. The following evening, a radio message came to tell them to expect a parachute delivery, and in the early hours of the following morning, an aircraft dropped 24 canisters of supplies.

Fargher met a Captain Dimoudi at the drop site who told him that he was the officer in command of the area and that as Fargher now had civilian clothes, it would be possible to send him to England at once. Dimoudi introduced Fargher to a Lt Robert (Huguen says this was Lt Jean Robert SAS) and the two men were driven that night by car to a maquis camp (position unknown) where in the morning, Fargher met Major Oswald Cary-Elwes (SAS) and liaison officer, Sqn/Ldr Patrick Smith.

Half an hour later, a guide took Fargher, Cary-Elwes, his batman Cpl Eric Mills, and Major William Jones USAAF by horse-drawn wagon to a farm near Plélo (about 3 kms north-east of Châtelaudren). Sqn/Ldr Smith joined them later and Fargher met Captain Harrison (Dumais) there. According to Huguen, it was Albert Le Marchand of Pléguien who took them by horse and cart to a house near the coast, arriving just after midnight, and Fargher reports a German (sic) patrol calling at the house about an hour later. Their visit caused the men to dash upstairs but apparently, the patrol had only been attracted by faulty black-out curtains. Unfortunately the soldiers were drunk and shots were fired, injuring one of the Germans.

Jean Gicquel had not been warned in advance and so was unprepared when Dumais and François Le Cornec delivered the five men to his little house. According to Mills, he lit an oil lamp but omitted to set the blackout curtains, and it was the light from his window that attracted the attention of group of Russian soldiers. Dumais and Le Cornec had only been gone a few minutes when there was the sound of men outside, and shots were fired. Patrick Smith promptly extinguished the lamp and the five evaders rushed to hide in the loft while Jean guarded the door and his wife Marie (and their new baby) screamed and generally added to the confusion.

These were Vlasov Russian troops (named for the Russian General Andrei Vlasov who defected to the Germans after being captured at Leningrad) of the Russian Liberation Army. Composed of mainly Soviet ex-POWs, many battalions had been integrated into German forces in western France. They wore grey German uniforms (but with fur caps and a different style of boot) but were famously undisciplined and never really trusted. One of the mistakes the Allies made in their propaganda was to promise the Vlasovs repatriation to Russia if they surrendered – the very last thing they wanted.

The evaders were in a difficult position as there was no other exit from the loft, and any armed resistance would almost certainly have harmed the Gicquels. Then another shot was fired, followed by screams – one of the Russians (most of whom were drunk) had wounded one of his comrades. In the almost total chaos, Jean produced a bottle of cognac before running to a neighbour's house to borrow a horse and cart for the Russians to take their wounded comrade for treatment. As soon as they left, the evaders were promptly rushed out of the house to spend the rest of the night in a nearby field.

At first light, Dumais and Jean Gicquel moved the five evaders to a safer location some miles away, where they spent an uncomfortable day and evening hiding in a large patch of gorse until being collected and led down to the beach at l'Anse-Cochat.

Jean Gicquel was also taken on board MGB 502 that night, while Marie and the infant Marie Thérèse were sheltered with relatives. Their house, the Maison d'Alphonse, had been blown up earlier in the day and destroyed by Russian soldiers – it was never rebuilt.

Technically there was a third Crozier operation when MTB 718 (Seddon) revisited the beach at l'Anse-Cochat in the early hours of 10 August 1944. With the shorter nights (and the gun positions on Pointe de la Tour by then abandoned following the liberation of Plouha four days earlier), the actual embarkation took place in daylight, its only objective being to pick up Shelburn members Mathurin Branchoux and Fernand Trochel, and radio operator Ray Labrosse.

Labrosse had stayed on in the area after the second Crozier operation and Pierre Huet describes how, when tasked on 4 August with taking a group of men by truck from the Bois de la Salle near Pléguien to occupy the public school in Plouha, it was Fernand Trochel and Ray Labrosse who led the way on a motorcycle.

Appendix A

Val Williams (born Vladimir Bouryschkine on 30 August 1911 in Moscow) emigrated from Russia with his parents, first to France and then to the United States. He says in his report that he was in the United States when Germany invaded Poland and promptly took a ship to France where he volunteered for the French army. He was due to join the army in June 1940 but events overtook him and he became involved with sending food supplies to French POWs.

In 1942, Williams was working in Monte Carlo as a basket-ball coach when he came into contact with the Allied detainees of "Detachement W" held at Fort de la Rivere in the hills above Monaco. He also came into contact with local police inspector, Australian-born Anthony Friend, when they both helped the Pat O'Leary organisation with the mass escape from Fort de la Rivere on 5 September 1942. Williams was evacuated with many of the escapers from the beach at Canet Plage the night of 21-22 September by the felucca Seawolf on Operation Titania, and taken to Gibraltar.

On his arrival in London, and after extensive interrogation at the Victoria Patriotic School, Williams was recruited into MI9 by Airey Neave to be sent back to France to establish the Oaktree escape line.

Williams says that he trained with a man called George Goodwin who was being sent as a radio operator for Pat O'Leary – this was Australian Tom Groome who was landed at Port Miou near Marseille by the felucca Seadog on the night of 3-4 November 1942. Williams was scheduled to be delivered by Lysander the following month but both attempted operations were aborted, and before the next moon period came around, Groome was captured in Montauban on 11 January 1943. It was decided that Williams should wait for a radio operator of his own, and at the end of February, a young Canadian army signalman named Raymond Labrosse was selected to join him. On 20 March 1943, Williams and Labrosse were parachuted into France where, after some delay, they contacted Paul Campinchi in Paris.

The only contacts that Williams was given in Paris were Pat Line logeur Armand Leveque, and Paul Campinchi, whose name was known in London after he helped Sgt Reginald Smith to return to England in

February 1943. The Leveque apartment at 19 avenue d'Orleans was sealed (following a raid on 4 March 1943) and so Williams went to find a pre-war friend, Mme Leotitia Beatrice Bréauté (born Oct 1890), at her shop at 26 rue Paradis. Through her and other friends, Williams was put in touch with Elisabeth Barbier at 72 rue Vaneau, and it was her group of contacts that sheltered subsequent Oaktree evaders in Paris. Having left Ray Labrosse and his radio with Paul Campinchi, Williams went to Brittany to build on contacts made by Louis Nouveau of the Pat Line, where he says he appointed Georges Jouanjean (of Carhaix) as head of his Brittany sector.

On 7 May 1943, the radio message "Denise, ta soeur est morte" was received from London, meaning that operations by MGB were postponed indefinitely, and so the many evaders gathered in Brittany by Oaktree would have to be sent out via the Pyrenees.[67] Two parties of evaders were passed successfully into Spain but when Williams went himself, taking an American he names as Buckley, and two Polish airmen (Sgts Leszek Zaborowski and Rech Urbanski from 138 SD Sqn Halifax BB340, who had been collected from Saint-Quay-Portrieux by Genevieve de Poulpiquet), they were captured on a train near Dax on 4 June. The remaining Oaktree evaders were passed to the Bourgogne organisation and they (and Ray Labrosse) were taken to Spain over the following weeks.

Lucien Dumais, who didn't actually meet Williams until he turned up at Plouha in January 1944, is particularly scathing about him, repeatedly commenting in his book on Williams amateur status and lack of security but it should be noted that following Williams capture during a routine ticket-check – something which could have happened to anyone – there were no subsequent arrests. The Germans apparently had a file on Williams from his earlier days but Neave says they were unable to break his unlikely cover story of joining the RAF in England and then being shot down whilst travelling as a passenger.[68]

Williams was held at the Jacques Cartier prison at Rennes and on 20 December 1943, he escaped, along with a Russian named as Ivan Bougaiev (Neave) or Bogolomov (Loiseau). Williams managed to break one of his ankles during the escape but nonetheless, he and Ivan made their way south to a farm in Poligné (about 5 kms north of Bain-de-Bretagne) where Ivan had once worked for Mme Vve Marie Dubois at Le Petit Feuil. Williams

67 I am not certain of the actual wording – Neave says the radio message was "Denise est morte" – which seems a little harsh – and that it was sent on 29 May but that date has to be wrong.

68 See Airey Neave (1969) "Saturday at MI9" Hodder and Stoughton.

tried to contact Paul Campinchi but he had moved from his apartment at 19 rue des Ursins following a visit by German police and so Williams called another contact, Paul Barrelet de Ricou. The professional tennis player lived at 10 Villa Spontini, Paris XVI – born July 1910, he is listed by Marcel Cola as a member of equipe Jacques – was married to American Margaret Louise Miller, and spoke good English. Barrelet de Ricou then asked (amateur) tennis player Jacky du Pac, who was lodging with the Loiseau family, to collect the two men from Poligné, and René Loiseau went with him to Brittany. When they arrived back at Montparnasse station, two gendarmes were waiting for them. The gendarmes had been sent by René Loiseau's mother Suzanne, and they escorted Williams and Ivan to the north-western suburb of Levallois-Perret where they were sheltered across the road from the Loiseau home with Marguerite Di Giacomo at 5 rue Baudin.

The fact that Williams escaped from the notorious Jacques Cartier prison, along with one of the Russian warders, despite having broken his ankle (or at least his foot) during the escape, suggests that he was a man of some determination, and IS9 recommended that he be awarded the BEM.

My thanks to Michael Moores LeBlanc, Dominique Lecomte and Daniel Droniou for providing some of the finer details included in this piece about Val Williams.

Appendix B

Robert Vanier (885) was a private in Les Fusiliers Mont-Royal when he was (like Dumais) captured at Dieppe on 19 August 1942. Having been wounded, he was transferred to Sacre Coeur Hospital at Rouen, along with Pte Conrad Lafleur (884), who was also wounded, and Pte Guy Joly (886), who was only pretending, before all three escaped together on 24 August from a hospital train taking them to Germany. They made their way via Paris and the American consulate in Lyon to Marseille where they were sheltered by Louis Nouveau and later evacuated from the beach at Canet Plage on board the felucca Seawolf (Operation Titania) the night of 21-22 September 1942.[69]

On the night of 14-15 June 1943, when Yves Le Hénaff (Fanfan) was parachuted into France to set up the Dahlia escape line, Robert Vanier jumped with him as his radio operator.

Dumais says in his book that he found Vanier at a house in Guingamp where he was being sheltered by Mathurin Branchoux, recognising him at once as a soldier from his own battalion. Branchoux (who makes no mention of Vanier in his own report) had apparently promised to get the stranded radio operator back to England – and Dumais told him he would be leaving that very night.

Roger Huguen says that Vanier was with Yves Le Hénaff on board the Jouet des Flots when they were ship-wrecked near Plogoff in early February but I don't know what happened to him after that, or which operation may have brought him back to England.

69 As mentioned earlier, Conrad Lafleur also returned to France – he was radio operator to Possum organiser Edgard Potier. Following Potier's arrest in December 1943, Lafleur made his way to Paris and joined a group of Comète line agents, crossing the Pyrenees to Spain in February 1944.

Bibliography

Bott, Lloyd (1997) "The Secret War from the River Dart" Dartmouth History Research Group

Chorley, W R (1997) "RAF Bomber Command Losses – Volume 5" Midland Publishing

Cherillon, Claire (1995) "Code Name Christianne Clouet" Texas A&M University Press

Dumais, Lucien (1975) "The Man Who Went Back" Leo Cooper

Hentic, Pierre (2006) "Tant qu'il y aura des étoiles" Maho

Higgins, Tony (1994) "The Free French in Kingswear" Dartmouth History Research Group

Huguen, Roger (1976) "Par les nuits les plus longues" Les Presses Bretonne

Huguen, Roger (2003) "La Bretagne dans la Bataille de l'Atlantique" Coop Breizh

Janes, Keith (2017) "They came from Burgundy" Matador

Lasseter, Don (2002) "Their Deeds of Valor" Xlibris

Lavender and Sheffe (1992) "The Evaders" McGraw-Hill

Lecomte, Dominique (2006) "Tail End Charlie" Cercle Maurice-Blanchard

Le Trividic, Dominique-Martin (2002) "Une héroïne de la Resistance" Ouest-France

Massieu, Benjamin (2017) "Les Gendarmes dans la bataille de Normandie"

Milner, Hamilton & Seddon (2014) "HM MTB 718 Something Special" York Publishing

Neave, Airey (1969) "Saturday at MI9" Hodder and Stoughton

O'Neill, Brian D (1998) "Half a Wing, Three Engines and a Prayer" McGraw-Hill

Remy, Colonel (1968) "La Maison d'Alphonse" Librarie Académique Perrin

Richards, Brooks (1996) "Secret Flotillas" HMSO

Verity, Hugh (1998) "We Landed by Moonlight" Crecy

Williams, David (2011) "Kingswear at War" Kingswear Historians

Index

(numbers in brackets for military personnel are MI9, IS9, Liberation or MIS-X reports)